WIN

GW00362113

BUYER'S
GUIDE
1999

DORLING KINDERSLEY
London•New York•Sydney•Moscow

A DORLING KINDERSLEY BOOK

First published in Great Britain in 1998
by Dorling Kindersley Limited,
9 Henrietta Street,
London WC2E 8PS
Visit us on the World Wide Web at
http://www.dk.com
Copyright © 1998
Dorling Kindersley Ltd, London
Text and illustration copyright ©
1998, WINE Magazine.

All rights reserved. No part of this
publication may be reproduced,
stored in a retrieval system, or trans-
mitted in any form or by any means,
electronic, mechanical, photo-copy-
ing, recording or otherwise, without
prior written permission of the
copyright owner.

A CIP catalogue second for this
book is available
from the British Library.

ISBN 0 7513 06150

CONTENTS

INTRODUCTION

Buying wine today can be a terrifyingly confusing experience. Britain's biggest supermarkets, for example, each offer around 100 different wines made solely or partly from Chardonnay. Some come from reassuringly well-known regions or producers; others, however, may fail to ring even the faintest bell of recognition. Besides, as most of us have discovered to our dismay, when their corks are pulled many of those well-known wines prove to be quite unworthy of their reputation and often their price.

So, what's the answer? How can one improve the odds of getting a wine that tastes good and interesting and warrants its price tag? One solution would be to convene a group of experienced palates and get them to taste their way "blind" through the wines that are on offer. Why not, however, allow someone else to hold that tasting for you - in the shape of the annual International Wine Challenge.

REAPING THE REWARDS

Since its launch in 1983, WINE magazine's International WINE Challenge has become the world's leading, and most influential, wine competition. This year it brought together some 7,500 wines and over 350 finely-tuned palates. The results of those tasters' efforts appear on the following pages in the form of the 2,100 winners, descriptions of how they taste, where to buy them and how much they should cost. All of which should help you to find your way around all those Chardonnays - and every other variety you care to mention.

THE CHALLENGE

The International WINE Challenge was created in 1983 by Robert Joseph, WINE's publishing editor, and Charles Metcalfe, associate editor, as the basis of an article which examined how English wine makers were doing compared to their counterparts in other countries. Neither had any idea at that stage that the Challenge would transform itself into the world's most international,

Oz contemplates yet another wine

most comprehensive and, increasingly, most respected wine competition. During the past 15 years, the number of wines entered into the Challenge has grown from 38 to 7,500. The number of professional judges has risen from 20 to 350.

WITH A LITTLE HELP FROM OUR FRIENDS

Broken down to a basic level, the Challenge's success lies in two essential factors. The first is the support it receives from both the wine trade in this country and the wine producers elsewhere in the world; the second is the ruthless impartiality and organisation with which it is run.

During the past fifteen years, wines appearing in the United Kingdom have become increasingly diverse. Wines from the former Soviet republic of Moldova now sit alongside Australian Chardonnay and German Gewürztraminer on the shelves, and each one tries to force its way into your field of vision and screaming "Try me!".

WE CAN WORK IT OUT

The difficulty for retailers, however, is that diversity is not enough; quality and value for money are the real selling points, especially to discerning British consumers. The same is true within the wine trade itself, where restaurateurs buying from importers are justly looking to make money from the wines they put on their lists. Consequently, both retail and wholesale merchants quickly recognised the need for a fair method of evaluating the wines on the market and, more importantly, for an effective mechanism of putting the results across to the wine drinker.

CREATING AN INTERNATIONAL BENCHMARK

It is this simple method of guiding people through the minefield of wine buying that has gained the International WINE Challenge its support from the trade. Companies ranging from retail giants such as Tesco, chains such as Unwins, to specialist merchants such as Justerini & Brooks all enter wines.

Wines from around the world jostled for position

Equally important is the support of such companies in the evaluation of Challenge wines, for it is their representatives who judge each and every wine. Buyers from these companies, renowned for their experience and accuracy, together with winemakers from all over the world and Britain's most respected wine writers make up the tasting team which works so hard for the two weeks of the Challenge. It is their involvement that generates the unique trust in the results, and reinforces the care with which every entrant to the Challenge is examined.

UNDER STARTER'S ORDERS
The process begins in January, when entry kits are distributed to thousands of companies worldwide, inviting them to submit their wines. Within a few weeks, the replies start pouring in, detailing information on every wine to be tasted, such as the principle grape varieties used and the regions in which the grapes were grown.

Once this information is logged in, the entire Challenge team descends to the venue to begin receiving the wines themselves. Some delivered by local companies; others are samples brought in specially by courier.

Tasting progressed at a furious pace involving 350 expert tasters over the two weeks

GET READY

Next comes the 'flight-
ing': placing entries into
groups of 12-18 wines. All
wines within a group are
similar in origin, variety
and retail price so that
they can be evaluated
fairly among equals. This

Nearing the finishing post

process normally takes the team of 24 Challenge
helpers several days. Bottles are then inserted into
special 'co-extruded' wine bags, tagged with tamper-
proof seals, and boxed, ready for tasting. Sparkling
wines are chilled, vintage ports decanted and wines
with distinctive bottles transferred.

THEY'RE OFF

It is now that the tasters arrive in droves, only to be split
into tasting teams of five or six to tackle the wines.
Flights are tasted, removed and recorded. Corked bottles
are replaced within four minutes, and corks pulled at an
alarming rate. Over 1,500 wines are tasted each day.

Attention to detail is meticulous: even the chlorine
was removed from a nearby fountain to reduce the risk
of contaminating smells! Lurking beneath is the less
glamorous process of control. All results are double-
checked; discarded wines are tasted once again by a
'Super Juror', an experienced and respected trade
member or Master of Wine whose task it is to ensure no
worthy wine slips the net.

Tasting sheets proceed to the computer, the 'nerve-
centre', where every result is recorded by helpers
working in pairs, one reading, one inputting. The results
are checked and double-checked by another pair to
ensure that no errors are made. The second-round
flights are born, wines are re-flighted, re-bagged, re-
tagged and re-tasted by new judges.

WINES OF THE YEAR

One of the main roles of the International WINE Challenge is to introduce the consumer to readily available, great value wines. The Wines of the Year are the best Gold, Silver, and in the case of sparkling wines, Bronze, medal winners which fit two crucial criteria: widespread availability and reasonable price (under £8 for table wines and under £12.50 for sparkling). Wines were shortlisted by these criteria and then tasted by the trophy panel, who chose their favourite wines in each category.

THE WHITE WINES

An eclectic mix of countries and grape varieties rose to the top this year. From France the attractive **Chablis Cuvée La Chablisienne 1996** from the largest co-operative in the area. New Zealand is represented by another Chardonnay, the ripe and tropical fruit **Stoneleigh Marlborough Chardonnay 1996** made by Corbans on the South Island. Staying with the New World, Chile is the source of our third white wine, the gooseberry-laden **Antu Mapu Sauvignon Blanc Reserva 1997**. Hungary produced our final white wine the apocryphally named **Woodcutter's White 1997** from Safeway. This wine is made from an almost unpronounceable, indigenous variety, the Czerzegi Fuszeres.

THE RED WINES

Again we have a broad mix of styles and grape varieties but South Australia leads the way in this section with two out of the three winners. Firstly, **Norman's White Label Cabernet Sauvignon L106 1996** made by Roger Harbord and Peter Fraser in the Adelaide hills. Secondly the stunningly consistent **Maglieri Mclaren Vale Shiraz 1996** by Steve Maglieri, a regular gold medal winner and, for the past five years, a Red Wine of the Year winner and as if that was not enough, it also took the Rhone & Shiraz/Grenache Trophy in 1997. France is, however, still showing its colours with a Minervois made from a Syrah and Grenache based blend, the smokily-spicy **Seigneur de Siran Minervois 1996** from the S.C.V de Siranaise.

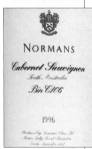

THE FIZZ

Another former Wine of the Year makes a welcome reappearance in this section. The yeastily attractive **Seaview Pinot Noir Chardonnay Brut 1995** from Southcorp Wines is joined by one of Australia's more unique gifts to the wine world - the unusual sparkling red **Yalumba Cuvée Two Prestige Cabernet Sauvignon NV**. This surprisingly soft and spicy red fizz impressed all who tasted it. New Zealand continued to prove that it can make great sparkling wines with the **Deutz Marlborough Cuvée NV**. Finally, the home of great fizz, Champagne has a fine ambassador for our last Wine of the Year, the **Champagne Le Brun de Neuville Cuvée Chardonnay Blanc de Blancs NV**. A crisp, lemony, attractive Champagne that delivers all it promises and much more. We hope that you will enjoy trying these wines and discover for yourself the qualities recognised by our judges.

THE TROPHIES

Once all the wines have been tasted and the results analysed and checked all the Gold medal winners fight it out for the ultimate acolades, the final Trophy Awards. The judges in this year's trophy tasting were: Paul Bastard, Hew Blair, Julian Brind MW, Dr Caroline Gilby MW, Keith Isaac MW, Peter McCombie MW, Maggie McNie MW, Jeremy Randall, Antony Rose, Derek Smedley MW and Simon Woods.

Being the supreme awards the judges were under no restrictions with regard to price. Trophies are only awarded to wines deemed to be the best in their respective category. If, in any section, there was no wine of a high enough standard then no Trophy was given

The first Trophy awarded in the white wine section was for a CHARDONNAY. From France, the **Château de Meursault 1993** from Burgundy exhibits creamy oak, tropical fruit and a slight vegetal character showing attributes more akin to the New World than more tradi-

tional wine growing areas.

The New Zealanders, however, fought back by taking the award for this year's SAUVIGNON BLANC TROPHY which was presented to the **Palliser Estate Marlborough Sauvignon Blanc 1997** which exhibited intense, grassy fruit and delicate acidity on the palate. THE AROMATIC WHITE WINE TROPHY was taken by the French, for the **Domaine Zind-Humbrecht Gewurztraminer Heimbourg Vendanges Tardive 1996**, still in its infancy with its overtly honeyed palate and rich flavours of lychee and honeysuckle.

Yet again the French hit the mark when the judges awarded **Les Marionnettes Marsanne 1997**, with its subtle floral dry palate the new MIDI & SOUTH WEST FRANCE WHITE WINE TROPHY for outstanding effort.

The Hungarians, not suprisingly, walked off with the DESSERT WINE TROPHY for the superb **Chateau Messzelato Tokaji Aszú 5 Puttonyos 1988** with its age and fantastic flavours, aromas of sweet orange, marmalade and a barley sugar finish.

For the reds, less Trophies were awarded than last year but the competition proved much tougher. First off was the prize for the BORDEAUX & CABERNET /MERLOT TROPHY where the USA triumphed with the full and ripe **Vichon Napa Valley Cabernet Sauvignon 1990** with its lovely mint, tobacco cassis fruit and mature tannins.

The Australians took the laurels for the RHONE & SHIRAZ/GRENACHE TROPHY with the fantastic **Tatachilla Foundation Shiraz 1996**, with its glorious smoky, spiced fruit, juicy brooding flavours and drying tannins.

For Italy a double victory was awarded by the panel, unable to separate the **Beradenga Vigneto Rancia Chianti Classico Riserva 1994** and the **La Poja Allegrini 1993** Tasters were impressed by the almond cedar flavours of these wines and gave a joint ITALIAN RED TROPHY to both.

The return of the SPANISH RED TROPHY, missing in 1997, saw the mature **Viña Ardanza Rioja Reserva 1990** with its lovely vanilla fruit and full berry palateforced the panel to reinstate this award

For the CHAMPAGNE & SPARKLING WHITE WINE TROPHY, the outright winner was **Champagne Charles Heidsieck Brut Réserve "Mis en Caves 1993" NV,** a new wine dated from the year it was laid down showing lovely bready, lemon flavours, enough quality in fact to secure the overall SPARKLING WINE TROPHY OF THE YEAR

The fortified section as usual provided some excellent wines with the **Henriques & Henriques 10 Yr Old Bual**, with its rich figgy, fruit and strong, layered finish taking not only the MADEIRA TROPHY but also the overall FORTIFIED WINE TROPHY

There were two other TROPHIES OF THE YEAR given. For the reds, the wine that shone through was the **Vichon Napa Valley Cabernet Sauvignon 1990** while in the white category the award went to the **Château de Meursault 1993.**

The final Trophy given was to the creamy **Hunter's Miru Miru Marlborough Brut 1995,** which pulled through to win the JAMES ROGERS TROPHY, awarded to the most outstanding wine in its first year of production.

WINES OF THE YEAR AND TROPHY WINES

You will find a complete list of the 1998 International WINE Challenge **Wines of the Year** and **Trophy Wines** on this and the following page. We have also included a page reference so that you can turn to the appropriate section of the book to find out more about the wines, including where to buy them!

SPARKLING WINES OF THE YEAR

Champagne Le Brun de Neuville Cuvée
  Blanc de Blancs Brut NV *(£12.80)*   *p119*

Deutz Marlborough Cuvée Brut NV *(£11.00)*   *p207*

Seaview Pinot Noir Chardonnay Brut 1995 *(£8.50)*   *p79*

Yalumba Cuvée Two Prestige
  Cabernet Sauvignon NV *(£9.40)*   *p79*

WHITE WINES OF THE YEAR

Antu Mapu Sauvignon Blanc Reserva 1997, *(£4.00) p279*

Chablis Cuvée La Chablisienne 1996, *(£9.00)*   *p114*

Safeway's Woodcutter's White 1997, *(£3.00)*   *p89*

Stoneleigh Chardonnay 1996, *(£7.00)*   *p189*

RED WINES OF THE YEAR

Maglieri McLaren Vale Shiraz 1996, *(£8.00)*   *p41*

Norman's White Label Cabernet
  Sauvignon L106 1996, *(£6.00)*   *p21*

Seigneur de Siran Minervois 1996, *(£6.60)*   *p135*

TROPHY WINNERS

SPARKLING WINE TROPHY WINNERS

CHAMPAGNE AND SPARKLING WINE TROPHY
Champagne Charles Heidsieck Brut Réserve
"Mis en Cave 1993" NV *(£22.50)*   *p124*

WHITE WINE TROPHY WINNERS

AROMATIC TROPHY
Gewürztraminer Heimbourg Vendanges
Tardive 1996 *(£24.40)*   *p96*

CHARDONNAY TROPHY
Meursault 1993, Château de Meursault *(£23.20)*   *p118*

SAUVIGNON BLANC TROPHY
Palliser Estate Sauvignon Blanc 1997 *(£9.00)*   *p203*

MIDI & SOUTH WEST FRANCE WHITE TROPHY
Les Marionettes Marsanne VDP d'Oc 1997 *(£4.00)*   *p136*

RED WINE TROPHY WINNERS

BORDEAUX & CABERNET MERLOT TROPHY
Vichon Napa Valley Cabernet Sauvignon 1990 *(£13.80)* *p211*

ITALIAN RED TROPHIES
La Poja 1993 *(£25.30)*   *p176*
Chianti Classico Riserva Vigneto
Rancia 1994 *(£13.30)*   *p164*

RHÔNE & SYRAH GRENACHE TROPHY
Tatachilla Foundation Shiraz 1996 *(£11.10)*   *p46*

SPANISH RED TROPHY
Viña Ardanza Reserva 1990 *(£11.70)*   *p298*

DESSERT & FORTIFIED WINE TROPHY WINNERS

DESSERT WINE TROPHY
Château Messzelato Tokaji Aszù
5 Puttonyos 1988 *(£8.00)*   *p90*

FORTIFIED WINE TROPHY
Henriques & Henriques 10 Year Old
Bual Madeira *(£16.40)*   *p240*

THE
WINES

HOW TO USE THIS BOOK

Every wine in this guide has been awarded a medal at the **1998 International WINE Challenge**. The wines are listed by country and region, with up to seven wine headings in the following order: red, white, sweet white, rosé, sparkling, sparkling rosé and fortified.

Under each heading the wines are listed in price order, from the least to the most expensive. Wines of the same price are listed in medal order: Gold, Silver and Bronze. Each wine carries the same range of information: its name (and vintage where applicable), a tasting note, average retail price, three-letter stockist's code (*see page 322*), and the medal it was awarded. Below is an explanation of how wines are listed, using the Red Wine of the Year on the opposite page as an example.

The wine name, vintage, producer and region		*The average retail price*		*The Medal: G Gold, S Silver, or B Bronze*
NORMAN'S WHITE LABEL CABERNET SAUVIGNON L106 1996, NORMAN'S CLARENDON WINERY South Australia	*Smoky, tobacco and cigar box notes on the ripe plum nose with flavours of blackcurrant, vanilla, mint and spice.*	£6.00	ODD TBC	**G**

A tasting note provided by Challenge tasters

Codes for stockists (see page 322)

WINE OF THE YEAR

Gold medal winning wines are shaded gold

These symbols indicate a Wine of the Year or Trophy Wine

Silver medal winning wines are shaded silver

Wines of the Year and Trophy Wines that don't have a Gold or Silver medal are shaded this colour

TROPHY WINE

AUSTRALIA

A s predicted last year, Australia has virtually cleaned up, sweeping through all categories picking up a bonzer load of medals along the way. The following pages are probably the most colourful in this year's Pocket Guide. From Cabernet Sauvignon to Shiraz and fabulous blends of the two, Riesling and the more toned down, subtle styles of the ubiquitous Chardonnay. As a country Australia is once again leading the charge for medals, this can only be healthy for the vinous world. Ripper!

AUSTRALIA • CABERNET SAUVIGNON

SAFEWAY'S AUSTRALIAN OAKED CABERNET SAUVIGNON 1997, BRL HARDY WINE COMPANY South Eastern Australia	*Tasters enjoyed flavours of blackberry and spice on the rounded palate of this easy wine.*	**£5.00**	SAF	**B**
ANGOVE'S CLASSIC RESERVE CABERNET SAUVIGNON 1996, ANGOVE'S PTY LTD South Australia	*New oak aromas lead to a lingering palate of eucalyptus, vanilla and fruits of the forest.*	**£5.40**	COK HOU D&D NEI ODD MWW	**S**
LINDEMANS BIN 45 CABERNET SAUVIGNON 1996, SOUTHCORP WINES South Australia	*Ripe black fruit aromas with hints of liquorice and mint before a ripe red fruit palate.*	**£5.90**	Widely Available	**B**
NORMAN'S WHITE LABEL CABERNET SAUVIGNON L106 1996, NORMAN'S CLARENDON WINERY South Australia	*Smoky, tobacco and cigar box notes on the ripe plum nose with flavours of blackcurrant, vanilla, mint and spice.*	**£6.00**	ODD TBC	**G** WINE OF THE YEAR
FOX RIVER CLASSIC RED CABERNET SAUVIGNON SHIRAZ 1996, FOX RIVER ESTATE Western Australia	*Mint and spice with sweet fruit. The palate is oak dominant although plums overpower the strident tannins.*	**£6.00**	ORB	**S**

AUSTRALIA • RED • CABERNET SAUVIGNON

YALDARA CABERNET SAUVIGNON MERLOT 1996, YALDARA WINES South Australia	*Aromas of lanolin and cedar followed by concentrated black fruit flavours on a full palate.*	**£6.00**	Widely Available	(S)
MILDARA CABERNET SAUVIGNON 1995, MILDARA BLASS South Australia	*Crisp aromas of slightly under ripe berries with hints of eucalypt carry over onto the balanced palate.*	**£6.00**	WFB PHI	(B)
PIRRAMIMMA CABERNET SAUVIGNON 1996, PIRRAMIMMA WINERY South Australia	*Plummy nose and full blown New World oak aromas. Blackcurrant and mint flavours on a long, lingering palate.*	**£6.10**	GRA	(G)
KINGSTON ESTATE CABERNET SAUVIGNON 1996, KINGSTON ESTATE WINERY South Australia	*A nose of warm berry fruit a mouthful of damsons and plums with fine tannins.*	**£6.40**	WES BNK HAS WWI VNO VIC GNW	(B)
HASELGROVE MCLAREN VALE CABERNET SAUVIGNON 1994, HASELGROVE WINES South Australia	*Rich, creamy cassis nose leads to a palate of raspberry and mint with elegant tannins and vanilla to boot.*	**£6.50**	BEN NYW	(S)
SEPPELT TERRAIN SERIES CABERNET SAUVIGNON 1995, SOUTHCORP WINES South Australia	*Loganberries and sweet tannins on the nose, followed by lightish, pleasing fruit on the palate.*	**£6.50**	WCS ODD	(B)
THE PAXTON OAK MATURED CABERNET SAUVIGNON 1997, WINGARA WINE GROUP South Australia	*Vanilla and creamy oak on a textured palate of plums and juicy red berry fruits.*	**£6.70**	BDR	(S)

Pinpoint who sells the wine you wish to buy by turning to the stockist codes. If you know the name of the wine you want to buy, use the alphabetical index. If the price is your motivation, refer to the invaluable price guide index; red and white wines under £5, sparkling wines under £12 and Champagne under £16. Happy hunting!

CABERNET SAUVIGNON • RED • AUSTRALIA

SHAREFARMERS RED 1995, PETALUMA WINERY South Australia	*Simple bitter cherry aromas and flavours with nuances of eucalypt and herb and a creamy sweet finish.*	£6.70	WCS MGN CPW WCR	(B)
BALLANDEAN CABERNET SAUVIGNON MALBEC MERLOT 1995, ANGELO PUGLISI Queensland	*Slightly savoury fruity nose with complex, intense flavours of soft black fruits on the palate.*	£6.80	DNL GNW	(B)
WYNDHAM ESTATE BIN 444 HUNTER VALLEY CABERNET SAUVIGNON 1996, ORLANDO WINES New South Wales	*Lean smoky bacon on the nose, then onto a palate of woody tannins and a rich rewarding finish.*	£6.80	MTL MRN HOU A&A WIN MWW DBY PEA	(B)
McGUIGAN BROTHERS SHAREHOLDERS CABERNET SAUVIGNON MERLOT 1996, McGUIGAN BROS South Eastern Australia	*Minty toffee aromas followed by rich flavours of stewed plums and menthol on the smooth, soft palate.*	£6.90	DBY VNO	(S)
TYRRELL'S OLD WINERY CABERNET SAUVIGNON MERLOT 1997, TYRRELL'S WINES New South Wales	*Medicinal and cedary oak notes on a blackberry nose with plum and wild cherry fruit flavours*	£6.90	Widely Available	(B)
ROSEMOUNT ESTATE TRADITIONAL BLEND 1995, ROSEMOUNT ESTATE South Australia	*Pungent aromas of eucalypt, spice and cedar develop into rich flavours of concentrated blackcurrant fruit.*	£7.00	HOU BWC	(S)
MONTROSE MUDGEE CABERNET SAUVIGNON 1995, ORLANDO WINES New South Wales	*Mint and cassis on the nose backed by a palate of blackcurrants and ripe berry fruit.*	£7.00	DBY PEA SEL	(B)
RIDDOCH CABERNET SAUVIGNON SHIRAZ 1996, WINGARA WINE GROUP South Australia	*A lovely eucalypt, spice nose leads to a palate of tar and liquorice with red fruit overtones and fine tannins.*	£7.00	DIR THS GGW ODD BTH BWL SAF	(B)

AUSTRALIA • RED • CABERNET SAUVIGNON

TESCO COONAWARRA CABERNET SAUVIGNON 1996, RYMILL WINERY South Australia	*Worth hunting out for its warm cassis fruit and generous oaky character with excellent tannins.*	**£7.00**	TOS	Ⓑ
MAMRE BROOK CABERNET SAUVIGNON SHIRAZ 1995, SALTRAM WINES South Australia	*Blackcurrants and tarry spice notes with a delightful mouth feel and a clean finish.*	**£7.20**	Widely Available	Ⓢ
D'ARENBERG THE HIGH TRELLIS CABERNET SAUVIGNON 1996, D'ARENBERG WINES South Australia	*Juicy blackberry and damson fruit with rich grippy tannins and an enticing mint finish.*	**£7.20**	VDV WES ODD DBY BWL	Ⓑ
ROSEMOUNT ESTATE CABERNET SAUVIGNON 1996, ROSEMOUNT ESTATE New South Wales	*A tight, minty Cabernet nose of blackcurrants, cedar and vanilla carries over onto a slightly dry palate.*	**£7.40**	Widely Available	Ⓑ
WOLF BLASS YELLOW LABEL CABERNET SAUVIGNON 1996, MILDARA BLASS South Australia	*Lean and dusty on the nose but the palate exudes charming, rich if tarry black fruits.*	**£7.40**	Widely Available	Ⓑ
GEOFF MERRILL RESERVE CABERNET SAUVIGNON 1994, GEOFF MERRILL WINES South Australia	*Strong vanilla oak notes with brambly cassis running through its fine tannin backbone.*	**£7.50**	DIR PLE SAF	Ⓢ
MARIENBERG RESERVE CABERNET SAUVIGNON 1994, MARIENBERG WINES South Australia	*Splendid oaky vanilla notes lead to a palate of brambly damsons with soft acidity.*	**£7.70**	CPW LAY	Ⓢ
MOCULTA CABERNET SAUVIGNON MERLOT 1996, BRL HARDY WINE COMPANY South Australia	*Fresh, rich vegetal nose with coffee and tar elements, not to mention rich cherry fruits.*	**£7.80**	MTL HBR VLW	Ⓑ

JAMIESON'S RUN RESERVE 1996, MILDARA BLASS South Australia	*Tobacco notes on a quite lean nose which develops into cedary fruit with hints of plum pudding.*	£8.00	WCR PHI	G
MAGLIERI MCLAREN VALE CABERNET SAUVIGNON 1996, MAGLIERI WINES South Australia	*A nose of sinewy fruit leads to a palate of dried prunes and warm vanillan oak notes.*	£8.00	TOS	S
PEWSEY VALE CABERNET SAUVIGNON 1996, S SMITH & SON South Australia	*Classic cedar, currant bouquet leads to a mellow soft yet concentrated blackcurrant palate with spice.*	£8.00	JSM MCW GRA	S
ANNIE'S LANE CABERNET SAUVIGNON MERLOT 1996, MILDARA BLASS South Australia	*Ripe, complex aromas of eucalyptus and mint with soft tannins on the rich rounded palate.*	£8.00	WFB ODD	B
BENDIGO WATER WHEEL CABERNET SAUVIGNON 1996, WATER WHEEL VINEYARDS Victoria	*Eucalyptus and pine on the nose of this wine with big chewy fruits on the palate.*	£8.00	AUC	B
ELDERTON CABERNET SAUVIGNON SHIRAZ MERLOT 1995, ELDERTON WINES South Australia	*Big hot fruits with lots of spice and firm tannins, creamy light oak to finish.*	£8.00	DBY	B
HANGING ROCK CABERNET SAUVIGNON MERLOT 1996, HANGING ROCK Victoria	*Spicy nose with cassis, mint and eucalypt leads to soft rounded flavours on the palate.*	£8.00	SEL	B
NINE PINES CABERNET SAUVIGNON 1997, CRANSWICK ESTATE New South Wales	*Leafy and herbaceous on the nose with elements of capsicum on the forest fruit palate.*	£8.00	ODD	B

ST. HALLETT CABERNET SAUVIGNON MERLOT 1996, ST. HALLETT WINES South Australia	*Lean smooth tannins on the nose are proven by a rich mint palate with juicy oak.*	**£8.10**	ADN RDS HVW	**B**
PETER LEHMANN CABERNET SAUVIGNON 1996, PETER LEHMANN WINES South Australia	*Aromas of bramble jelly with complex nuances of chocolate, oak and mint. An elegant and balanced palate.*	**£8.20**	Widely Available	**G**
JAMIESON'S RUN RED 1995, MILDARA BLASS South Australia	*Herbaceous nose with hints of green bell pepper carrying onto a soft, black fruit palate.*	**£8.20**	WCR CVR GDS ODD MRN SMF	**S**
MIRANDA HIGH COUNTRY CABERNET SAUVIGNON 1996, MIRANDA WINES Victoria	*Aromas of blackcurrant purée and creamy oak with a crème de cassis and sweet oak palate.*	**£8.30**	DIR HOH WCS VIL AVB NYW	**S**
PETER LEHMANN CLANCY'S 1996, PETER LEHMANN WINES South Australia	*Nose has ripe berries and creamy oak aromas that continue onto the palate of delicious oak with raspberries and cherries.*	**£8.30**	Widely Available	**S**
TIM KNAPPSTEIN CABERNET SAUVIGNON MERLOT 1996, TIM KNAPPSTEIN WINES South Australia	*Elegant well made with mint and bramble flavours backed by red currant tannins.*	**£8.30**	VDV BBR WCS MGN ODD VIL SAF HAR	**B**
WINDY PEAK CABERNET SAUVIGNON SHIRAZ MERLOT 1995, DE BORTOLI WINES Victoria	*Triumphant blend of three flavours: blackberries, liquorice and morello cherries. No wonder tasters wanted more.*	**£8.30**	VDV NEI GGW	**B**

Pinpoint who sells the wine you wish to buy by turning to the stockist codes. If you know the name of the wine you want to buy, use the alphabetical index. If the price is your motivation, refer to the invaluable price guide index; red and white wines under £5, sparkling wines under £12 and Champagne under £16. Happy hunting!

RYMILL COONAWARRA MERLOT CABERNET 1995, RYMILL WINERY South Australia	*Aromas of concentrated berries with elements of eucalyptus and vanilla precede a fruitcake and cedar palate.*	**£8.50**	VDV PKR	(S)
TATACHILLA CABERNET SAUVIGNON 1996, TATACHILLA WINERY South Australia	*Mellow sultana fruit with cherry and blackcurrant on a rich damson palate of fine elegant tannins.*	**£8.50**	NIC D&D ODD WTS	(B)
RYMILL CABERNET SAUVIGNON 1995, RYMILL WINERY South Australia	*Tobacco and cedar notes on both the nose and palate of this very forward wine.*	**£8.70**	VDV HOT MWW HVW WCR PKR	(S)
BEST'S VICTORIAN CABERNET 1995, BEST'S GREAT WESTERN Victoria	*Fresher, fruitier and silkier than some, this wine was liked for its generous fruit and fine texture.*	**£8.70**	Widely Available	(B)
GEOFF MERRILL CABERNET SAUVIGNON MERLOT 1995, GEOFF MERRILL WINES South Australia	*Cedary blackcurrant on the nose leading to succulent warm fruit on the palate of blueberries.*	**£8.80**	DIR PLE VIL HVW ENO NYW ASD	(B)
YALUMBA CABERNET SAUVIGNON MERLOT 1996, YALUMBA WINERY South Australia	*Medicinal, eucalyptus qualities on the nose carry over into the stewed plum flavours of the palate.*	**£8.90**	WCR WIN ODD MWW	(B)
BROWNS MYRA FAMILY RESERVE CABERNET SAUVIGNON 1995, BROWNS OF PADTHAWAY South Australia	*Subtle and fragrant on the nose of raspberries and juicy fruits, matched by its warm palate.*	**£9.00**	D&D WTS	(S)
PENDARVES CABERNET SAUVIGNON MERLOT MALBEC 1995, PENDARVES ESTATE New South Wales	*Hunter Valley wines tend to be more earthby and drier than some, tasters enjoyed warm tannins and full fruit.*	**£9.00**	HOU	(S)

AUSTRALIA • RED • CABERNET SAUVIGNON

SEPPELT HARPER'S RANGE CABERNET SAUVIGNON 1993, SOUTHCORP WINES Victoria	*Sweet red berry fruit on a forward nose which follows onto a broad palate of crème de cassis.*	£9.00	COK WCS CTH COC	(B)
YALUMBA THE MENZIES COONAWARRA CABERNET SAUVIGNON 1994, YALUMBA WINERY South Australia	*Cool climate fruit with blackcurrant and tobacco flavours on a bed of vanilla oak.*	£9.00	VDV DBY JNW QWW MWW ODD	(B)
VASSE FELIX CABERNET SAUVIGNON MERLOT 1996, VASSE FELIX Western Australia	*Fruit cake and oak aromas with hints of plum and damson complement concentrated blackcurrant flavours.*	£9.10	Widely Available	(S)
GOUNDREY CABERNET SAUVIGNON MERLOT 1995, GOUNDREY WINES Western Australia	*A classic nose of blackcurrants and cedar then a sweet, jammy, blackberry flavour in the mouth.*	£9.10	HOU WIN GRT CRS VIL TPE SWS WON	(B)
GRANT BURGE CABERNET SAUVIGNON 1996, GRANT BURGE South Australia	*Pencil shavings and wood notes are matched by dark brooding fruit on a layered palate.*	£9.30	Widely Available	(S)
MORRIS RUTHERGLEN CABERNET SAUVIGNON 1995, MICK MORRIS Victoria	*Attractive cedary elements to the cassis nose and a clean finish to the balanced palate.*	£9.30	VDV CAP PEA	(B)
JIM BARRY CLARE CABERNET SAUVIGNON 1996, JIM BARRY WINES South Australia	*Spicy eucalypt and new oak notes to the nose and palate of this well-structured wine.*	£9.40	BEN VDV ADN CPW	(S)
BRAND'S LAIRA CABERNET SAUVIGNON 1994, MCWILLIAM'S WINES South Australia	*Lifted tobacco and cedar notes on a condensed rich palate on this maturing wine.*	£9.50	CDT	(S)

CABERNET SAUVIGNON • RED • AUSTRALIA

FRANK POTTS CABERNET SAUVIGNON MERLOT MALBEC 1995, BLEASDALE South Australia	*Oak and dried fruit aromas lead to a balanced palate of red cherries and succulent fruits.*	£9.50	TOS	**(S)**
LECONFIELD CABERNET SAUVIGNON 1996, LECONFIELD WINERY South Australia	*Herbaceous ripe fruit aromas develop intense flavours of mellow ripe blackcurrants on a softly finishing palate.*	£9.50	VDV POR J&B	**(S)**
COLDSTREAM HILLS BRIASTON 1996, COLDSTREAM HILLS Victoria	*Youthful but complex aromas of drying fruit, capsicum and cedar-wood. Rich palate of minty crème de mûre.*	£9.70	BWC	**(B)**
TISDALL MOUNT HELEN CABERNET SAUVIGNON MERLOT 1996, TISDALL WINES Victoria	*A rich cassis nose is followed by a balanced palate full of spicy dark fruits.*	£9.70	HWL WFB ODD	**(B)**
LEASINGHAM CABERNET SAUVIGNON MALBEC 1996, BRL HARDY WINE COMPANY South Australia	*Really impressive silky wine, finely tuned, with rich opulent fruit and a lovely silky finish.*	£9.80	Widely Available	**(S)**
ROUGE HOMME CABERNET SAUVIGNON 1994, SOUTHCORP WINES South Australia	*Rich, plummy concentrated Dundee cake aromas with stunning ripe fruit, figgy character and toasty oak.*	£9.90	VDV WTS NYW FUL AMW	**(G)**
WYNNS COONAWARRA ESTATE CABERNET SAUVIGNON 1995, SOUTHCORP WINES South Australia	*Cedary, menthol aromas on the nose of this richly flavoured wine with elegant ripe blackcurrant flavours.*	£9.90	Widely Available	**(S)**

Pinpoint who sells the wine you wish to buy by turning to the stockist codes. If you know the name of the wine you want to buy, use the alphabetical index. If the price is your motivation, refer to the invaluable price guide index; red and white wines under £5, sparkling wines under £10 and champagne under £15. Happy hunting!

AUSTRALIA • RED • CABERNET SAUVIGNON

HOLLICK'S COONAWARRA CABERNET SAUVIGNON MERLOT 1994, HOLLICK WINES South Australia	*Really rich and full. An elegant nose precedes a warm generous palate of red fruits and mint.*	£10.00	VDV L&W DBY NYW	(S)
ROBERTSON'S WELL CABERNET SAUVIGNON 1996, MILDARA BLASS South Australia	*Cedary nose followed by a ripe palate of blackcurrants with elements of vanilla, menthol and chocolate.*	£10.00	WFB ODD FUL	(S)
McGUIGAN BROTHERS HERITAGE ROAD CABERNET SAUVIGNON 1996, McGUIGAN BROS South Eastern Australia	*Rich cassis aromas with notes of cedar wood lead to a plummy palate with good tannins.*	£10.00	JAS	(B)
TISDALL MOUNT HELEN CABERNET SAUVIGNON MERLOT 1994, TISDALL WINES Victoria	*Gorgeous nose with lots of fruit and cedar leads to ripe structured black fruit palate.*	£10.00	HWL WFB ODD	(B)
YALUMBA THE SIGNATURE CABERNET SAUVIGNON SHIRAZ 1994, YALUMBA WINERY South Australia	*Integrated oak, mint and sweet berry fruit bouquet leads to a big palate full of ripe blackcurrants.*	£10.00	VDV JNW DBY ODD MCW	(B)
INGLEWOOD SHOW RESERVE CABERNET SAUVIGNON 1995, INGLEWOOD WINES New South Wales	*Dense rich coffee flavours on the cassis palate are preceded by smoky, minty elements on the nose.*	£10.20	HWL SVT QWW	(B)
LEASINGHAM CABERNET SAUVIGNON MALBEC 1995, BRL HARDY WINE COMPANY South Australia	*Mint and blackcurrants on the nose are followed by rich full raspberry jam flavours.*	£10.20	WCR VDV HBR DBY JSM TOS VLW	(B)
RICHARD HAMILTON HUT BLOCK CABERNET SAUVIGNON 1996, RICHARD HAMILTON South Australia	*Complex aromas of liquorice, spice and tar. Intense palate of black fruits and creamy mint.*	£10.40	DIR DBY ENO	(S)

HASELGROVE MCLAREN VALE CAB. SAUVIGNON MERLOT SHIRAZ 1996, HASELGROVE WINES South Australia	*Concentrated nose of mint and plums with cedar characters on its warm and full finishing palate.*	£10.50	NYW	(B)
GOUNDREY CABERNET SAUVIGNON RESERVE 1995, GOUNDREY WINES Western Australia	*Quite tannic but with strong fruit notes of spice and woody blackcurrant leads into a lingering finish.*	£10.90	COK HOU GRT VIL PLA WOC	(S)
CHAPEL HILL CABERNET SAUVIGNON 1996, CHAPEL HILL WINES South Australia	*A nose of rich oaky berry fruit, a palate showing vanillan character and drying tannins.*	£11.00	NRW TOS	(G)
BROKENWOOD CABERNET SAUVIGNON 1996, BROKENWOOD South Eastern Australia	*Ripe cassis aromas with spicy oak notes. Lengthy balanced palate with soft tannins.*	£11.00	MIS NYW	(S)
CHATEAU REYNELLA BASKET PRESSED CAB. SAUVIGNON MERLOT 1995, BRL HARDY WINE CO. South Australia	*Rich berry aromas lead onto a minty herbaceous palate packed full of juicy blackcurrants.*	£11.00	Widely Available	(S)
KATNOOK ESTATE CAB. SAUVIGNON 1995, WINGARA WINE GROUP South Australia	*Black fruit, olives and liquorice dominate the nose of this elegant cool climate wine.*	£11.00	DIR BWL VLW	(S)
MITCHELTON VICTORIA CAB. SAUVIGNON 1996, MITCHELTON WINERY Victoria	*Peppery, spicy notes and soft fruit aromas on this richly flavoured blackberry and eucalyptus palate.*	£11.10	JEF WCS VIL COT HOF MFS	(S)
SIMON HACKETT FOGGO ROAD CABERNET SAUVIGNON 1995, SIMON HACKETT South Australia	*A superb example. Rich, silky berry fruit, smooth and voluptuous on its long lasting low tannin palate.*	£11.20	HOU CNL NYW GNW	(S)

WOLF BLASS PRESIDENT'S SELECTION CABERNET SAUVIGNON 1995, MILDARA BLASS South Australia	*Minerals, berries and wood shavings on a nose and palate of dense purple fruits.*	£11.20	Widely Available	(B)
HARDY'S COONAWARRA CABERNET SAUVIGNON 1995, BRL HARDY WINE COMPANY South Australia	*Nose of ripe cassis fruit with tobacco, new oak, mint and eucalyptus hints on the palate.*	£11.60	VDV VLW HOU HBR CWS DBY SAF WCR	(G)
PLANTAGENET MOUNT BARKER CABERNET SAUVIGNON 1995, PLANTAGENET WINES Western Australia	*Creamy cassis fruit with hints of oak and eucalypt carry over onto the rich palate.*	£11.60	HOU DBY SGL NAD BBR	(B)
YARRAMAN ROAD CABERNET SAUVIGNON SHIRAZ 1995, BARRINGTON ESTATE New South Wales	*Sweet ripe luscious raspberries with lots of spicy oaky complexity and creamy vanilla on the finish.*	£11.80	ENO	(B)
PENFOLDS BIN 389 CABERNET SAUVIGNON SHIRAZ 1994, SOUTHCORP WINES South Australia	*Always reliable, comes up trumps; quite dry but underpinned by rich woody spice and cassis.*	£11.90	Widely Available	(B)
STONIER'S RESERVE CABERNET SAUVIGNON 1993, STONIER'S WINERY Victoria	*Slightly closed nose of ripe berries leads to a rich minty palate with cooked blackcurrant flavours.*	£12.00	WAW QWW DIR	(B)
DE BORTOLI YARRA VALLEY CABERNET SAUVIGNON 1994, DE BORTOLI WINES Victoria	*Berries and oak on a complex nose with medicinal highlights leading onto a palate of stewed fruit.*	£12.40	BOR VDV GGW DBY	(S)

Pinpoint who sells the wine you wish to buy by turning to the stockist codes. If you know the name of the wine you want to buy, use the alphabetical index. If the price is your motivation, refer to the invaluable price guide index; red and white wines under £5, sparkling wines under £10 and champagne under £15. Happy hunting!

CABERNET SAUVIGNON • RED • AUSTRALIA

WIRRA WIRRA THE ANGELUS CABERNET SAUVIGNON 1996, WIRRA WIRRA South Australia	*Aromas and flavours of leafy, peppered raspberries with a toffeed oak and spicy finish to the palate.*	£12.50	MFS VDV ODF FUL	**S**
EBENEZER CABERNET SAUVIGNON 1996, BRL HARDY WINE COMPANY South Australia	*Tobacco notes and intense woody aromas lead to a palate of ripe mint and cedar.*	£12.50	NEI HBR DBY VLW	**B**
FRANKLAND ESTATE OLMO'S REWARD 1994, FRANKLAND ESTATE Western Australia	*Cedary, cigar hints to a ripe black cherry aroma developing into herbaceous cassis flavours.*	£12.60	MIS NYW	**S**
PENFOLDS BIN 389 CABERNET SAUVIGNON SHIRAZ 1995, SOUTHCORP WINES South Australia	*Rich dark bramble fruit laced with black spice and big oak overtones with a finish to savour.*	£12.80	Widely Available	**S**
LINDEMANS ST GEORGE VINEYARD CABERNET SAUVIGNON 1994, SOUTHCORP WINES South Australia	*Earthy, rich blackcurrant fruit with dusty tannins, almond oak character and a finish to die for.*	£12.90	Widely Available	**B**
DEVIL'S LAIR MARGARET RIVER RED 1995, DEVIL'S LAIR WINES Western Australia	*Curranty, eucalypt and spicy oak aromas lead onto an intense palate of rich fruit cake and mint.*	£13.10	JNW HOU WIN NYW GNW	**S**
VOYAGER ESTATE CABERNET SAUVIGNON MERLOT 1994, VOYAGER ESTATE Western Australia	*A combination of blackberries, cherries and smoky oak blend to a lovely finish of damson notes.*	£13.20	VDV J&B NYW	**B**
SKILLOGALEE THE CABERNETS 1996, SKILLOGALEE WINES South Australia	*Quite austere fruit for this youngster showing youthful hints of cedary blackcurrant and mint.*	£13.50	DIR DBY ENO NYW	**B**

AUSTRALIA • RED • CABERNET SAUVIGNON

VASSE FELIX CABERNET SAUVIGNON 1996, VASSE FELIX Margaret River	*A lovely nose of violets leads onto a lifted herbaceous palate of damson and fruit cake.*	£14.00	Widely Available	(S)
LINDEMANS PYRUS 1994, SOUTHCORP WINES South Australia	*Traditional Bordelais blend, here quite dry and lean but still with good juicy fruit and tannin.*	£14.00	Widely Available	(B)
McGUIGAN BROTHERS PERSONAL RESERVE CABERNET SAUVIGNON 1996, McGUIGAN BROS South Eastern Australia	*Attractive leathery notes to the nose and palate of this wine with sweet almost stewed plum flavours.*	£14.00	NRW LVC CER VNO	(B)
JIM BARRY McCRAE WOOD CABERNET SAUVIGNON MALBEC 1995, JIM BARRY WINES South Australia	*Complex aromas of tar, cigar box and cassis dominate the nose with intense flavours of sweet blackcurrant.*	£14.20	VDV QWW ODF NYW	(S)
D'ARENBERG THE COPPERMINE ROAD CAB. SAUVIGNON 1996, D'ARENBERG WINES South Australia	*Cool McLaren Vale fruit makes for a rich earthy wine with prune and blackberry nuances.*	£14.50	ODD DBY BWL	(S)
ORLANDO ST. HUGO COONAWARRA CABERNET SAUVIGNON 1994, ORLANDO WINES South Australia	*Damson aromas with oak and pencil shavings and hints of mocha and vanilla on the rich palate.*	£14.80	NRW VDV SMF WIN DBY UNS PEA CAP	(G)
COLDSTREAM HILLS RESERVE CABERNET SAUVIGNON 1995, SOUTHCORP WINES Victoria	*Intense aromas and flavours of spicy oak, white chocolate and ripe blackcurrants with a lingering super finish.*	£15.00	VDV ODD BWC	(S)
ROSEMOUNT SHOW RESERVE COONAWARRA CAB. SAUVIGNON 1995, ROSEMOUNT ESTATE South Australia	*Deep spicy aromas of soft black fruits lead onto a softly welcoming palate of herbaceously spicy cassis.*	£15.00	TOS	(S)

CABERNET SAUVIGNON • RED • AUSTRALIA

NEPENTHE MERLOT CABERNET SAUVIGNON 1997, NEPENTHE WINES South Australia	*Blackcurrants on the nose with hints of chocolate lead to a minty, blackberry driven palate.*	£15.00	ODD SWS	B
ROSEMOUNT ROSE LABEL ORANGE CABERNET SAUVIGNON 1994, ROSEMOUNT ESTATE New South Wales	*Minerally fruit character on a nose of red berries and earthiness. The palate follows with mocha and cassis.*	£15.00	HOU BWC	B
CULLEN CABERNET SAUVIGNON MERLOT 1996, CULLEN WINES Western Australia	*Menthol, eucalypt, blackcurrant and cherry aromas combine to produce an exquisitely balanced palate.*	£15.50	WCR HAS NYW ADN DIR DBY PFT HVN SHB	G
YALDARA THE FARMS MERLOT CABERNET SAUVIGNON 1996, YALDARA WINES South Australia	*Rich black fruits with elements of mint leaves, chocolate and oak dominate the nose and palate.*	£15.70	VDV VIL TPE SWS BDR	S
PENLEY ESTATE CABERNET SAUVIGNON 1994, PENLEY ESTATE South Australia	*Tasters were impreesed by the lean smoky nose and palate of dried fruits and vanillan oak.*	£15.90	MFS VDV VLW NYW	S
CHATEAU XANADU CABERNET SAUVIGNON 1996, CHATEAU XANADU Western Australia	*Spicy, herbaceous and chocolate aromas with smokey wood notes on a densely formed palate.*	£16.00	DIR MWW	S
YALDARA THE FARMS MERLOT CABERNET SAUVIGNON 1995, YALDARA WINES South Australia	*Ripe, leathery nose of jammy cassis with hints of spice. Sweet ripe black fruits on the palate.*	£16.10	VIL SWS BDR	S
PENLEY ESTATE CABERNET SAUVIGNON 1995, PENLEY ESTATE South Australia	*Nose of cedarwood and black fruits flows onto intensely flavoured palate of forest fruits and new oak.*	£16.20	MFS VDV VLW	S

LEASINGHAM CLASSIC CLARE CABERNET SAUVIGNON 1994, BRL HARDY WINE CO South Australia	*Huge aromas of minty cassis with elements of spice and smoke. Complex blackcurrant dominated palate.*	**£17.90**	Widely Available	**G**
DALWHINNIE CABERNET SAUVIGNON 1996, DALWHINNIE Victoria	*Herbal, minty notes to the cassis bouquet with a palate full of ripe blackberry flavours.*	**£17.90**	VDV GON J&B NYW	**B**
LEASINGHAM CLASSIC CLARE CABERNET SAUVIGNON 1995, BRL HARDY WINE CO South Australia	*Full of thick tar and tobacco aromas with concentrated flavours of ripe cassis and creamy new oak.*	**£18.50**	Widely Available	**G**
ORLANDO JACARANDA RIDGE CABERNET SAUVIGNON 1994, ORLANDO WINES South Australia	*Upfront aromas of currany fruit with hints of chocolate, mint and eucalypt on a ripe berry palate.*	**£19.30**	NRW VDV BNK DBY SEL ODF UNS	**S**
GRANT BURGE SHADRACH CABERNET SAUVIGNON 1994, GRANT BURGE South Australia	*Juicy aromas of fresh blackcurrants lead to a massive palate of cassis, mint and spicy eucalypt.*	**£22.80**	COK BLS HOU FUL GGW CTC ASH GNW	**B**
HOWARD PARK CABERNET SAUVIGNON MERLOT 1995, HOWARD PARK WINES Western Australia	*Rich aromas of ripe currants, tobacco and cedar wood carry onto the intense blackcurrant and oak palate.*	**£23.30**	MFS VDV JNW SEL WIN NYW	**B**
VASSE FELIX HEYTESBURY 1996, VASSE FELIX Western Australia	*Oak and cigar notes to the dried fruit aromas. Lingering palate dominated by ripe red cherry flavours.*	**£23.70**	BEN VDV BWC NYW	**S**
WOLF BLASS SHOW RESERVE CABERNET SAUVIGNON 1993, MILDARA BLASS South Australia	*Creamy vanilla and cassis flavours develop from a similar nose on this approachable easy drinking wine.*	**£24.00**	WFB BDR VLW	**B**

CABERNET SAUVIGNON – SHIRAZ • RED • AUSTRALIA

THOMAS HARDY CABERNET SAUVIGNON 1994, BRL HARDY WINE COMPANY South Australia	*Hints of mint, rubber and raspberry jam on the nose and palate of this soft easy wine.*	£24.20	VDV MTL HBR DBY EDC JHL JSS VLW	B
CHATEAU XANADU CABERNET SAUVIGNON RESERVE 1995, CHATEAU XANADU Western Australia	*Tobacco and oak dominate the nose. Palate of ripe damsons with nuances of bitter chocolate.*	£25.00	DIR	S
WYNNS COONAWARRA ESTATE JOHN RIDDOCH CABERNET SAUVIGNON 1994, SOUTHCORP WINES South Australia	*Complex nose of minty, smoky blackcurrants with a tightly dense palate of minty cassis and plum fruit.*	£33.60	Widely Available	G

AUSTRALIA • SHIRAZ

SAFEWAY'S AUSTRALIAN SHIRAZ RUBY CABERNET 1997, BRL HARDY WINE COMPANY South Eastern Australia	*Intensely fruity soft wine sporting spice and blackcurrant flavours on a pleasing palate with little tannin.*	£4.00	SAF	B
CO-OP JACARANDA HILL SHIRAZ 1997, ANGOVE'S South Eastern Australia	*Lighter ruby red in colour with a soft bramble fruit nose, simple, straight-forward and enjoyable.*	£4.20	D&D CWS	B
ANGOVE'S STONERIDGE SHIRAZ 1996, ANGOVE'S South Australia	*Nice ripe fruit characters, rich and deep. Feels good in the mouth and has good length.*	£5.00	NEI WRT WR	S
DEAKIN ESTATE SHIRAZ 1997, WINGARA WINE GROUP Victoria	*Vibrant ruby colour with sappy pepper, good quality fruit and soft oak. Well-made with a firm finish.*	£5.10	MTL NEI GGW ODD BWL NYW	G

37

AUSTRALIA • RED • SHIRAZ

ANGOVE'S CLASSIC SHIRAZ 1996, ANGOVE'S PTY LTD South Eastern Australia	*Clean and oaky with intense fruity flavours, a rounded spicy wine with smooth, soft tannins.*	£5.80	HOU D&D NEI ODD MWW	(B)
SALTRAM SHIRAZ 1996, SALTRAM WINES South Australia	*A deeply coloured, oaky wine pleasing to the eye. Warm and rich with good fruit and tannins.*	£5.90	NRW WFB COK NEI VWE DBY JSM	(S)
KINGSTON ESTATE RESERVE SHIRAZ 1997, KINGSTON ESTATE WINERY South Australia	*Smoky black fruits on a strong spicy palate with rich tannins and a finish that lasts.*	£6.00	VNO TOS	(S)
PENFOLDS BIN 2 SHIRAZ MOURVÈDRE 1996, SOUTHCORP WINES South Australia	*Tasters were inspired by a combination of sweet blackcurrant fruit with tarry spice in a juicy finish.*	£6.00	Widely Available	(B)
PRIORY HILL SHIRAZ 1997, COOPER COUNTY WINES South Australia	*Elegant fruit strong flavours of cinnamon, damsons and woody vanilla notes precede its ripe finish.*	£6.00	BDR	(B)
ROSEMOUNT PYRAMID SHIRAZ CABERNET SAUVIGNON 1997, ROSEMOUNT ESTATE South Eastern Australia	*A sweet tinned fruit aroma with dark cherries on the palate and a jammy finish.*	£6.00	HOU BWC	(B)
KINGSTON ESTATE SHIRAZ 1996, KINGSTON ESTATE WINERY South Australia	*Garnet red colour with strong oak astringent character, spicy, light fruit and firm tannin finish.*	£6.20	WES BNK HAS GLY VNO TOS	(B)
McGUIGAN BROTHERS BIN 2000 MILLENIUM SHIRAZ 1997, McGUIGAN BROTHERS South Eastern Australia	*Rich ruby red with a raspberry nose, super ripe fruit and a soft tannin finish.*	£6.20	Widely Available	(B)

HOUGHTON WILDFLOWER RIDGE SHIRAZ 1996, HOUGHTON WINERIES Western Australia	*Fresh and vibrant showing soft fruits and good use of wood, making for an easy-drinking red.*	£6.30	MTL COK WCS POR CNL VIL LLV	B
ELLISTON ESTATE OAK AGED SHIRAZ CABERNET SAUVIGNON 1997, WINGARA WINES South Australia	*Sweet juicy nose precedes a rich palate of blackcurrant and spicy cinnamon softened by judicious use of oak.*	£6.50	BDR	B
MIRANDA OAK AGED SHIRAZ CABERNET SAUVIGNON 1994, MIRANDA WINES South Australia	*The use of oak gives this more body and adds creamy flavours to the tarry black fruit.*	£6.70	HOH WCS VIL BDR	B
TYRRELL'S OLD WINERY SHIRAZ 1996, TYRRELL'S WINES New South Wales	*Minty with a rich fruity palate, a spicy balanced wine with a good texture.*	£6.80	Widely Available	B
PETER LEHMANN SHIRAZ 1996, PETER LEHMANN WINES South Australia	*Sweet restrained oak with rich damson and blackcurrant pastilles aromas, spicy flavours and reasonable length.*	£6.90	Widely Available	B
PENFOLDS KOONUNGA HILL SHIRAZ CABERNET SAUVIGNON 1996, SOUTHCORP WINES South Australia	*Vibrant red colours, quite strong tannins and good structure. Hints of spice married with dark fruit flavours.*	£7.00	Widely Available	S
ROTHBURY ESTATE BROKENBACK SHIRAZ 1995, MILDARA BLASS New South Wales	*Lovely rich plum, lots of fruit, jam and spice aromas and tarry chocolate notes.*	£7.00	WFB DIR ODD	B
ROUGE HOMME SHIRAZ CABERNET SAUVIGNON 1994, SOUTHCORP WINES South Australia	*Full sweet dried fruit flavours with concentrated tight tannins, high alcohol and outstanding length and finish.*	£7.00	Widely Available	S

AUSTRALIA • RED • SHIRAZ

SEPPELT TERRAIN SERIES SHIRAZ 1996, SOUTHCORP WINES South Australia	*A well-balanced, minty soft wine with very big fruit flavours, ripe tannins and an inky finish.*	£7.00	NEI ODD NYS	(S)
TESCO MCLAREN VALE SHIRAZ 1995, MAGLIERI WINES South Australia	*Deep inky red with intense spicy leather and soft ripe fruit nose. Firm tannins and bramble fruit finish.*	£7.00	TOS	(S)
TESCO MCLAREN VALE SHIRAZ 1996, MAGLIERI WINES South Australia	*Cigar box nose with sweet bramble fruit, some plum and spice on the palate. Soft tannins and a lengthy finish.*	£7.00	TOS	(S)
WYNNS COONAWARRA ESTATE SHIRAZ 1996, SOUTHCORP WINES South Australia	*Supremely smooth with spice and cinnamon on its generous palate with grippy tannins and good finish.*	£7.10	Widely Available	(B)
D'ARENBERG THE FOOTBOLT OLD VINE SHIRAZ 1996, D'ARENBERG WINES South Australia	*Light spice aroma with varietal character on the palate gives way to an elegant fruit finish.*	£7.20	ODD DBY BWL NYW	(S)
D'ARENBERG D'ARRYS ORIGINAL 1996, D'ARENBERG WINES South Australia	*This wine is warm and long with good fruit, excellent structure and good use of oak.*	£7.20	NRW VDV WES ODD DBY NYW	(S)
ROSEMOUNT ESTATE SHIRAZ 1996, ROSEMOUNT ESTATE South Eastern Australia	*Spicy cherry aromas with jammy fruit. Sweet oak mingles with red fruit in a lovely well-balanced wine.*	£7.20	Widely Available	(S)
WILDERNESS ESTATE SHIRAZ RESERVE 1996, WILDERNESS ESTATE New South Wales	*Subtle and interesting nose of wood shavings and seaweed. Has loads of intense sweet fruit.*	£7.30	WOW	(B)

SHIRAZ • RED • AUSTRALIA

ROSEMOUNT ESTATE SHIRAZ 1997, ROSEMOUNT ESTATE South Eastern Australia	*This is a well made, well-integrated minty wine with a dark intense colour. Has a lingering if simple finish.*	£7.40	Widely Available	B
PIRRAMIMMA SHIRAZ 1996, PIRRAMIMMA WINERY South Australia	*Light vegetal, pepper and astringency on the nose. A huge tannic finish with some vanilla.*	£7.50	GRA	S
YALUMBA BAROSSA SHIRAZ 1995, YALUMBA WINERY South Australia	*A herby, farmyard nose and decent finish surround an introverted ripe berry fruit palate.*	£7.50	VDV JNW MWW	B
PENFOLDS CLARE VALLEY ORGANIC SHIRAZ CABERNET SAUVIGNON 1996, SOUTHCORP WINES South Australia	*Cool climate fruit and organically grown grapes produce a lovely rich blend of black spice.*	£7.80	Widely Available	S
MAGLIERI MCLAREN VALE SHIRAZ 1996, MAGLIERI WINES South Australia	*A rich compote of black spiced fruits with hints of leather and tobacco, strong in the finish.*	£8.00	DBY TOS UNS PXR	G
				WINE OF THE YEAR
ANNIE'S LANE SHIRAZ RESERVE 1995, MILDARA BLASS South Australia	*Well-balanced acidity, fruit and tannins. Good on the finish with intense juicy sweet oak characters.*	£8.00	DIR PHI	S
BREMNER VIEW SHIRAZ 1996, BLEASDALE VINEYARDS South Australia	*Nicely crafted New World style with spicy fruit aroma. Blackcurrant pastille flavour with a long silky finish.*	£8.00	TOS	S
BROWN BROTHERS KING VALLEY SHIRAZ 1995, BROWN BROTHERS Victoria	*Easy smooth and very pleasant. A well-balanced wine with good fruit and spice flavours.*	£8.00	Widely Available	B

41

AUSTRALIA • RED • SHIRAZ

MIRANDA ROVALLEY RIDGE SHIRAZ 1994, MIRANDA WINES South Australia	*Polished wood and pastille sweet nose. Juicy fruit on the palate and sympathetic wood treatment.*	£8.00	WCR DIR HOH VIL AVB BDR	**B**
MITCHELTON GOULBURN VALLEY SHIRAZ 1996, MITCHELTON WINERY Victoria	*A chewy elegant wine that develops in the mouth. Quite dominant oak and menthol flavours.*	£8.20	COK DBY HOU JEF POR VIL AMW RAM	**B**
LINDEMANS PADTHAWAY SHIRAZ 1996, SOUTHCORP WINES South Australia	*An uncomplicated enjoyable wine with smoky pepper and dense blackcurrant nose, plenty of spicy vanilla.*	£8.30	VDV HOU GGW ODD DBY TOS	**B**
MIRANDA HIGH COUNTRY SHIRAZ 1996, MIRANDA WINES Victoria	*A gamey, woody nose, overtones of leather and spice with ripe damson fruits and a long finish.*	£8.30	HOH VIL AVB NYW	**B**
BASEDOW SHIRAZ 1996, O BASEDOW WINES South Australia	*A rich and spicy nose of damson and redcurrant fruit. Pleasing oak structure with balanced tannins.*	£8.40	Widely Available	**S**
RYMILL SHIRAZ 1995, RYMILL WINERY South Australia	*Massive, young with baked fruit with great balance. Huge length in each fragrant and delicious mouthful.*	£8.70	VDV HOT SHJ MWW WCR PKR	**G**
CAPEL VALE SHIRAZ 1996, CAPEL VALE Western Australia	*A gamey nose leads to brambly, spice flavours on the palate with a long sweetish finish.*	£8.70	HOT NYW	**S**
CHAPEL HILL SHIRAZ 1996, CHAPEL HILL WINES South Australia	*A good concentration of ripe red fruit on the palate, finishing smoky and sweet.*	£8.70	CVR TOW	**S**

PENFOLDS BIN 128 COONAWARRA SHIRAZ 1995, SOUTHCORP WINES South Australia	*A garnet coloured rim confirms some mature characteristics, with ripe rounded fruit, and sweet lingering tannins.*	**£8.80**	Widely Available	**B**
YALUMBA BAROSSA SHIRAZ 1996, YALUMBA WINERY South Australia	*A well-made uncomplicated wine where ripe, jammy fruit flavours dominate to a decent finish.*	**£8.80**	VDV ODD MWW	**B**
MORRIS RUTHERGLEN SHIRAZ 1995, MORRIS WINES Victoria	*A round, rich and ripe wine. It is big but supple with a long juicy finish.*	**£8.90**	VDV JEF DBY CAP PEA	**S**
PENFOLDS BIN 28 KALIMNA SHIRAZ 1994, SOUTHCORP WINES South Australia	*Packed with powerful fruit flavours dry tannins with a dusty drying palate and strong lingering tannins.*	**£8.90**	Widely Available	**B**
ST. HALLETT FAITH SHIRAZ 1996, ST. HALLETT WINES South Australia	*Showing an earthy rubbery nose with black fruit and pepper emerging on the mid palate.*	**£9.00**	TOS	**B**
TIM ADAMS SHIRAZ 1996, TIM ADAMS WINES South Australia	*Concentrated mint berry and cedar with enjoyable complex aromas of peppermint and black forest fruit.*	**£9.00**	AUC	**B**
GEOFF MERRILL SHIRAZ 1995, GEOFF MERRILL WINES South Australia	*Good balance, intense full fruit and structure in the mouth with blackcurrant and liquorice flavours.*	**£9.10**	DIR PLE VIL HVW NYW	**B**
SEPPELT CHALAMBAR SHIRAZ 1993, SOUTHCORP WINES Victoria	*A firm fruity wine with a delicious dusty nose. Robustly structured with meaty, cooked fruit characters.*	**£9.20**	VDV NEI POR ODD WIL CCL NYW	**S**

GEOFF MERRILL SHIRAZ 1994, GEOFF MERRILL WINES South Australia	*Rich fruitcake aromas, sweet and nicely structured. Pungent fresh fruit notes, very tasty and attractive depth.*	£9.20	DIR PLE VIL NYW	**B**
CAMPBELL'S BOBBIE BURNS RUTHERGLEN SHIRAZ 1996, CAMPBELL'S WINES Victoria	*Concentrated hot alcohol, eucalyptus and oak characteristics make this powerful wine highly attractive to tasters.*	£9.30	VDV COK WCS CPW ODD BOO NYW	**B**
LEASINGHAM SHIRAZ 1995, BRL HARDY WINE COMPANY South Australia	*Inky black wine, pungent aroma has layers of damson, black fruit and silky texture with approachable tannins.*	£9.40	Widely Available	**S**
INGLEWOOD SHOW RESERVE SHIRAZ 1994, INGLEWOOD New South Wales	*A serious tarry nose with a deep colour. Very concentrated spicy palate, balanced and long.*	£9.50	HWL SVT HVW	**B**
MARIENBERG RESERVE SHIRAZ 1995, MARIENBERG WINES South Australia	*Big on blackcurrant and green pepper with fruit and mint undertones emerging on the palate.*	£9.50	CPW	**B**
BAILEY'S 1920s BLOCK SHIRAZ 1996, BAILEY'S OF GLENROWAN Victoria	*This is a big, rich, ripe and opulent with an oaky rich and lasting finish.*	£9.80	Widely Available	**B**
TISDALL MOUNT IDA SHIRAZ 1996, TISDALL Victoria	*Deeply coloured with dark fruit, leather and tar flavours. A ripe and peppery wine with many dimensions.*	£9.90	HWL BNK ODD NYW	**S**
BILLI BILLI CREEK SHIRAZ CABERNET SAUVIGNON 1996, MOUNT LANGI GHIRAN VINEYARDS Victoria	*Ripe spicy and soft yet slightly woody flavours lead onto a supple and juicy finish.*	£10.00	JNW UNS GGW DBY NYW VLW CWI	**B**

TIM ADAMS THE ABERFELDY 1996, TIM ADAMS WINES South Australia	*The balance between the fruit tannins, woody notes and acid is close to perfection. A massive wine.*	£10.00	JNW AUC	(G)
NORMANS CHAIS CLARENDON SHIRAZ 1995, NORMANS CLARENDON WINERY South Australia	*Up front spicy fruit and rubber with juicy summer fruits on a full rich palate.*	£10.00	ODD	(B)
PENLEY ESTATE HYLAND SHIRAZ 1996, PENLEY ESTATE South Australia	*This is a big wine, very well-balanced and deep with great fruit flavours.*	£10.00	L&W VLW	(B)
WILLOWS VINEYARD SHIRAZ 1995, WILLOWS VINEYARD South Australia	*Commercial style but with a concentrated fruit character. Clean strong pepper and blackberry fruit flavours.*	£10.00	AUC	(B)
GRANT BURGE SHIRAZ 1996, GRANT BURGE South Australia	*A very obvious berry fruit and cassis nose. Loads of fruit and really easy drinking.*	£10.10	Widely Available	(B)
BEST'S GREAT WESTERN SHIRAZ 1995, BEST'S GREAT WESTERN Victoria	*A huge smoky affair with well-integrated fruit, a toasty palate and reasonable length.*	£10.50	Widely Available	(B)
BROKENWOOD SHIRAZ 1996, BROKENWOOD South Eastern Australia	*Medium acidity and blackcurrant fruit character. Balanced structure, firm tannin, clean finish and length.*	£10.60	MIS NYW	(B)
WOLF BLASS PRESIDENT'S SELECTION SHIRAZ 1995, MILDARA BLASS South Australia	*Broad and sweet fruit upfront, on a well-rounded palate in a smooth restrained style.*	£10.90	Widely available	(B)

BOWEN ESTATE SHIRAZ 1996, BOWEN ESTATE South Australia	*Dense, big and minty, this wine is well-balanced and should develop further in bottle.*	£11.00	AUC	(S)
WATER WHEEL BENDIGO SHIRAZ 1996, WATER WHEEL VINEYARDS Victoria	*With menthol and oak notes on the nose, this is a juicy, ripe wine with good acidity.*	£11.00	DBY	(S)
TATACHILLA FOUNDATION SHIRAZ 1996, TATACHILLA WINERY South Australia	*With tremendous character, soft but firm and immensely complex, this wine is perfect in nearly every way.*	£11.10	QWW NIC D&D ODD BDR	(G) TROPHY WINE
BROKENWOOD SHIRAZ 1996, BROKENWOOD South Australia	*Deep plum colour with warm Shiraz fruit and spicy, hot, vanillan character leading to a long finish.*	£11.30	VDV MIS NYW	(G)
CHATEAU REYNELLA BASKET-PRESSED SHIRAZ 1994, BRL HARDY WINE COMPANY South Australia	*Rich and opulent with warm fruit on a palate of Victoria plum and spice notes.*	£11.40	WCR NRW VDV NEI HBR VLW	(B)
YALUMBA CLARE SHIRAZ 1995, YALUMBA WINERY South Australia	*This Shiraz from the Clare Valley is big, rich and minty with intense fruit flavours.*	£11.50	JNW ODD	(S)
CHATEAU REYNELLA BASKET-PRESSED SHIRAZ 1995, BRL HARDY WINE COMPANY South Australia	*Dense and extracted, earthiness and pepper on the nose, lots of fruit in the mouth.*	£11.90	Widely Available	(B)
PENLEY ESTATE SHIRAZ CABERNET SAUVIGNON 1994, PENLEY ESTATE South Australia	*Deep colour with woody aromas. Palate develops into wild raspberry with bags of opulent sweet ripe fruit flavours.*	£12.00	VLW	(S)

SHIRAZ • RED • AUSTRALIA

PLANTAGENET MOUNT BARKER OMRAH SHIRAZ 1996, PLANTAGENET WINES Western Australia	*This deep, youthful wine has berry fruit flavours, good acidity and tannins with a long finish.*	**£12.10**	HOU SHJ DBY SGL NAD BBR	**B**
EBENEZER SHIRAZ 1995, BRL HARDY WINE COMPANY South Australia	*A huge nose leads to a mulberry, white pepper and sweet vanilla palate with integrated oak and tannins.*	**£12.30**	WCR HOU PON HBR DBY VLW	**G**
WIRRA WIRRA "RSW" SHIRAZ 1996, WIRRA WIRRA South Australia	*Vanilla, sweet fruit aromas on the nose with smooth tannins. Well-balanced for easy drinking.*	**£12.30**	BEN VDV ODF	**B**
MIRANDA FAMILY RESERVE SHIRAZ 1994, MIRANDA WINES South Australia	*Red and black fruits, liquorice and spice mingle on a creamy oak palate of good length.*	**£12.40**	DIR HOH WCS VIL AVB BDR NYW	**S**
DE BORTOLI YARRA VALLEY SHIRAZ 1994, DE BORTOLI WINES Victoria	*Rich and ripe with a touch of tar, this complex wine is clean and well made.*	**£12.80**	BOR FSW VDV QWW MIS GGW	**B**
SKILLOGALEE SHIRAZ 1996, SKILLOGALEE WINES South Australia	*Very soft on the palate with mint, liquorice and excellent raspberries. Big smoky vanilla finish.*	**£12.90**	HOU VIL DBY ENO NYW	**B**
MCGUIGAN BROTHERS PERSONAL RESERVE SHIRAZ 1996, MCGUIGAN BROTHERS South Eastern Australia	*Very seductive, deep and dark, this wine has delicious concentrated fruit and oak flavours on a long finish.*	**£13.00**	NRW DBY LVC VNO	**S**
ROBERTSON'S WELL RESERVE SHIRAZ 1996, MILDARA BLASS South Australia	*This full-flavoured wine is rich and deeply coloured with a good full and long finish.*	**£13.00**	WFB PHI	**S**

AUSTRALIA • RED • SHIRAZ

MOUNT LANGI GHIRAN SHIRAZ 1996, MOUNT LANGI GHIRAN VINEYARDS Victoria	*Vanilla oak and blackberry fruit on the nose precede a juicy mouthful of fruit, tannins and acidity.*	£13.30	Widely Available	**S**
LINDEMANS LIMESTONE RIDGE VINEYARD SHIRAZ CABERNET SAUVIGNON 1994, SOUTHCORP WINES South Australia	*This Shiraz Cabernet blend has plummy fruit, good acidity and some complexity. A powerful, elegant wine.*	£13.90	Widely Available	**S**
ST. HALLETT OLD BLOCK SHIRAZ 1994, ST. HALLETT WINES South Australia	*This oaky Barossa Shiraz is well-rounded with a full nose and minty fruit characters.*	£14.10	NRW ADN RDS POR DBY HVW AUC TOS	**B**
JIM BARRY MCCRAE WOOD SHIRAZ 1995, JIM BARRY WINES South Australia	*An uncomplicated sweet, ripe, fruit driven wine that is well-balanced and rich in its elegant finish.*	£14.50	Widely Available	**B**
VASSE FELIX SHIRAZ 1996, VASSE FELIX Western Australia	*A fat, rich wine with lots of fruit, smooth tannins, lovely pepper flavour and a smoky finish.*	£15.00	BEN CPW BWC RBS TAN NYW	**S**
PENFOLDS ST HENRI SHIRAZ CABERNET SAUVIGNON 1994, SOUTHCORP WINES South Australia	*A subdued nose, but decent palate with subtle berry fruit flavours dominant. A medium finish.*	£15.00	DIR ODD	**B**
D'ARENBERG THE DEAD ARM SHIRAZ 1996, D'ARENBERG WINES South Australia	*Rich and warm with drying tannins, heaps of black fruit with earthy flavours and sweet oak.*	£15.50	VDV ODD DBY BWL NYW	**S**
YALDARA JULIAN'S SHIRAZ 1996, YALDARA WINES South Australia	*A herbal nose carries through to the palate and meets peppery and violet tones and light oak.*	£16.00	SWS BDR	**S**

YALDARA JULIAN'S SHIRAZ 1997, YALDARA WINES South Australia	*A perfumed nose leads to sweet fruit with jammy, liquorice tones upfront. Nicely balanced with a long finish.*	£16.00	SWS BDR	S
STEVE MAGLIERI SHIRAZ 1995, MAGLIERI WINES South Australia	*Vanilla, plum jam and white pepper notes. A lovely mouthful of fruit with a firm tannic finish*	£16.00	EPO TOS UNS	B
TYRRELL'S PRIVATE BIN VAT 9 SHIRAZ 1993, TYRRELL'S WINES New South Wales	*Mid brick showing some mature character, tarry, jammy and smoky with a very good structure.*	£16.20	Widely Available	B
ORLANDO LAWSON'S PADTHAWAY SHIRAZ 1993, ORLANDO WINES South Australia	*Very big with intense liquorice and eucalyptus aromas, boasting excellent concentration and appealing warmth.*	£16.90	NRW VDV BNK DBY SEL ODF CAP	S
PETER LEHMANN STONEWELL SHIRAZ 1992, PETER LEHMANN WINES South Australia	*This complex, deep and fruity wine is soft, long and rounded with a good finish.*	£16.90	VDV G&M ODD BDR BOO	S
HASELGROVE MCLAREN VALE RESERVE SHIRAZ 1996, HASELGROVE WINES South Australia	*Complex, toasty, tarry aroma, juicy fruit, pepper, liquorice notes and a balanced, long grippy finish.*	£17.60	LIB NYW WTS	S
ROSEMOUNT SHOW RESERVE SHIRAZ 1995, ROSEMOUNT ESTATES New South Wales	*Very forward with rich fruit cake spice, big earthy tannins and lean acidity wrapped up in vanillan wood notes.*	£18.00	HOU	B
LEASINGHAM CLASSIC CLARE SHIRAZ 1995, BRL HARDY WINE COMPANY South Australia	*Intense alcoholic nose with dusty violets to the fore. Ripe concentrated fruits dominate a vibrant palate.*	£18.60	Widely Available	S

DALWHINNIE SHIRAZ 1996, DALWHINNIE Victoria	*Perfectly balanced tannins and acidity are supported by lively spicy fruit leading to a long finish.*	£19.60	VDV J&B NYW	S
MITCHELTON PRINT LABEL SHIRAZ 1995, MITCHELTON WINERY Victoria	*This youthful wine has spicy fruits supported by firm tannins with a very long sweet finish.*	£20.70	MFS VDV JEF VIL DBY COK AMW	B
PENFOLDS MAGILL ESTATE SHIRAZ 1995, SOUTHCORP WINES South Australia	*Well made, dark in colour and rounded in the mouth showing nicely integrated oak and fruit characters.*	£20.90	MGN MWW ODD	S
CLARENDON HILLS SHIRAZ 1996, CLARENDON HILLS ESTATE South Australia	*A well-structured wine of medium weight, deeply coloured with good fruit and tannins.*	£22.50	VDV J&B NYW	B
EILEEN HARDY SHIRAZ 1995, BRL HARDY WINE COMPANY South Australia	*A beady nose and rich palate dominated by mulberry fruit and spice. Finishes with gorgeous sweet tannins.*	£24.50	VDV VLW HOU HBR DBY WCR ROD	G
HENSCKE'S MOUNT EDELSTONE SHIRAZ 1995, HENSCKE WINES South Australia	*A spicy baby wine with an intense berry fruit nose and a dark, inky rich colour.*	£25.00	VDV JNW COK SHJ HOT L&W HVW	B
E & E BLACK PEPPER SHIRAZ 1994, BRL HARDY WINE COMPANY South Australia	*Deep, dark colour and attractive nose give way to excellent fruit with redcurrants and blackberries to the fore.*	£25.20	MFS VDV HOU UNS HBR CWS DBY VLW	S

Pinpoint who sells the wine you wish to buy by turning to the stockist codes. If you know the name of the wine you want to buy, use the alphabetical index. If the price is your motivation, refer to the invaluable price guide index; red and white wines under £5, sparkling wines under £12 and Champagne under £16. Happy hunting!

SHIRAZ – OTHER • RED • AUSTRALIA

YALUMBA THE OCTAVIUS 1994, YALUMBA WINERY South Australia	*Beautifully integrated ripe fruit flavours. Velvety oak and spice usher in a fruit laden finish.*	**£26.20**	VDV DBY QWW ODD MWW MCW	(G)
ELDERTON COMMAND SHIRAZ 1994, ELDERTON WINES South Australia	*Sweet ripe fruit flavours dominate. Spice and tar tones combine on the palate leading to a long drying finish.*	**£27.50**	QWW DBY	(S)
GRANT BURGE MESHACH SHIRAZ 1994, GRANT BURGE South Australia	*A big, sleeping monster, dark inky in colour with heavy tannins and deep black fruits.*	**£31.50**	LEA HOU GGW CNL DBY WIM VLW	(S)
WYNNS COONAWARRA ESTATE MICHAEL SHIRAZ 1994, SOUTHCORP WINES South Australia	*While still in its infancy this wine shows forthright fruit with layered tannins and prudent use of oak.*	**£33.80**	Widely Available	(G)
ROSEMOUNT BALMORAL SHIRAZ 1995, ROSEMOUNT South Australia	*A rich spicy nose, big palate, burnt characteristics of spice and leather and a silky finish.*	**£35.00**	UNS TOS	(S)
ASTRALIS SHIRAZ 1996, CLARENDON HILLS ESTATE South Australia	*A big very deeply-coloured wine showing plenty of sweet oak and youthful eucalypt character, one to keep.*	**£74.00**	VDV J&B NYW	(B)

AUSTRALIA • OTHER RED

JACOB'S CREEK ROWLAND FLAT GRENACHE SHIRAZ 1997, ORLANDO WINES South Australia	*Pale brick red, light spice with perhaps a confected aroma, reasonable but simple commercial style.*	**£3.90**	BNK DBY WRC BUP JSM	(B)

AUSTRALIA • RED • OTHER

JARRAH RIDGE SOFT RED 1996, KINGSTON ESTATE WINERY South Australia	*Soft fruit and spice preclude a well formed palate with an attractive finish lighter in tannin than some.*	£3.90	NRW WES HAS WWT SCA BKT	B
MCGUIGAN BROTHERS THE BLACK LABEL 1997, MCGUIGAN BROTHERS South Eastern Australia	*This is a very approachable well-structured soft red with gentle tannins firming to an enticing finish.*	£5.20	Widely Available	B
LARAGHY'S GRENACHE SHIRAZ 1997, AUSTRALIAN WINE AGENCIES South Australia	*This has splendid white pepper notes leading to spicy black fruits with tarry tannins and a long finish.*	£6.00	TOS	S
TATACHILLA GRENACHE SHIRAZ 1997, TATACHILLA WINERY South Australia	*Raspberry fruit and oak aromas lead to a palate of black berry fruit and boiled sweets.*	£6.00	D&D THS	B
BLEASDALE MALBEC 1997, BLEASDALE WINES South Australia	*Big creamy black fruits on the nose and palate. A velvet feel and an enormous chewy finish.*	£6.50	TOS	S
SAMUELS BAY MALBEC 1995, ADAM WYNN South Australia	*Minty, ripe fruit aromas lead to a palate reminiscent of blackcurrant jelly and silky fruits.*	£6.50	BUP THS	B
FOX RIVER WESTERN AUSTRALIAN PINOT NOIR 1997, FOX RIVER ESTATE Western Australia	*Rich fruit and violets on the nose, simple palate with soft fruit and firm tannins.*	£7.00	ORB	B
BASEDOW BUSH VINE GRENACHE 1996, O. BASEDOW WINES South Australia	*Lightish in colour, this is a straight-forward wine with a fruity, sweet and juicy palate.*	£7.20	GGW BWL VWE SAF	B

GEOFF MERRILL BUSH VINE GRENACHE 1996, GEOFF MERRILL WINES South Australia	*Deep colour with fresh plums. Very forward palate showing impressive depth of character and length.*	£7.20	DIR PLE ODD VIL ENO NYW	B
D'ARENBERG THE TWENTYEIGHT ROAD MOURVÈDRE 1996, D'ARENBERG WINES South Australia	*An elegantly structured wine with a peppery nose and good ripe concentrated black earthy fruit.*	£7.40	VDV DBY BWL ODD MHV	B
TATACHILLA KEYSTONE GRENACHE SHIRAZ 1997, TATACHILLA WINERY South Australia	*This Rhône blend wine is elegant and charming, expertly put together, powerful and rich.*	£7.50	D&D BDR THS	G
MITCHELTON GRENACHE MOURVÈDRE SHIRAZ 1995, MITCHELTON WINERY Victoria	*A well-balanced wine with dry berry fruits and decent tannins, this has some definite ageing potential.*	£7.70	VIL DBY COK	B
ROSEMOUNT ESTATE MERLOT 1996, ROSEMOUNT ESTATE South Eastern Australia	*Soft and spicy on the nose. Cherries and plums coming through on a palate of well intergrated oak.*	£7.70	HOU ODD DBY TOS THS BUP	B
TATACHILLA MERLOT 1996, TATACHILLA WINERY South Australia	*Brambley, black fruit aromas with hints of liquorice and a well-structured palate of plums and chocolate.*	£8.00	NIC D&D WTS	S
D'ARENBERG THE CUSTODIAN GRENACHE 1996, D'ARENBERG WINES South Australia	*White pepper on the nose backed by hot fruit flavours on a spicy lingering palate.*	£8.50	VDV ODD DBY BWL	S
LINDEMANS PADTHAWAY PINOT NOIR 1997, SOUTHCORP WINES South Australia	*Concentrated strawberry aromas, reflected on a well-structured palate of soft fruits and woody overtones.*	£8.50	JSM	B

53

YALUMBA BUSH VINE GRENACHE 1996, YALUMBA WINERY South Australia	*Big and bold, appearing to be quite alcobolic this wine has good weight and length.*	£8.50	JNW ODD MWW THS TOS	B
MORRIS OF RUTHERGLEN DURIF 1995, MORRIS WINES Victoria	*Garnet with purple hues. Ripe fruit with boiled sweets, plum flavours, tight tannins and lingering finish.*	£8.60	SEL CVR DBY CEN HOU TOS	S
WIRRA WIRRA ORIGINAL BLEND GRENACHE SHIRAZ 1997, WIRRA WIRRA South Australia	*Warm, succulent and light in colour with hints of white pepper backed by ginger spice.*	£8.70	VDV ODD FUL	B
HIGHLAND HERITAGE PINOT NOIR 1995, REX D'AQUINO New South Wales	*Earthy tones and oak on the nose, strawberry fruit palate, meaty complex characters and firm tannins.*	£9.00	GNW	S
GRAMP GRENACHE 1997, TIM GRAMP South Australia	*A good ripe, spicy wine with impressive depth of rich fruit and grippy tannins.*	£9.00	JNW ADN HAS DBY NYW	B
TIM ADAMS THE FERGUS 1996, TIM ADAMS WINES South Australia	*With its ripe fruit dominated nose this Grenache shows great concentration and spicy characters.*	£9.00	BUP	B
CAPEL VALE MERLOT 1996, CAPEL VALE Western Australia	*Ripe berries and oak on the nose with creamy, blackcurrant flavours on a lingering palate.*	£9.10	BNK CVR HOT NYW	B
LONG GULLY RESERVE PINOT NOIR 1995, LONG GULLY WINES Victoria	*Fragrant fruit with earthy tones on the nose, rich ripe fruit and firm tannin structure.*	£9.20	DBY ARM LUC AMW	B

TEMPLE BRUER MERLOT RESERVE 1996, TEMPLE BRUER South Australia	*Dark fruit aromas with complex nuances of cedar, mint, eucalypt, new vanilla oak and ripe fruit palate.*	£10.00	TOS	**G**
GOUNDREY MERLOT RESERVE 1995, GOUNDREY WINES Western Australia	*Blackcurrant fruit nose with minty highlights a rich eucalypt and berryfruit palate that lasts.*	£10.00	SWS	**B**
SCOTCHMANS HILL PINOT NOIR 1996, SCOTCHMANS HILL Victoria	*Spicy fruit with hints of vegetal characters on the nose, medium body with balanced tannins.*	£10.40	VDV POR J&B FUL	**B**
D'ARENBERG THE IRONSTONE PRESSINGS 1996, D'ARENBERG WINES South Australia	*This wine has a terrific mineral character with grip and tannin on its tarry fruit palate.*	£10.50	VDV ODD DBY BWL	**B**
KATNOOK ESTATE MERLOT 1995, WINGARA WINE GROUP South Australia	*Cassis fruit and subtle oak aromas, crushed blackcurrant leaves with an integrated palate, showing subtle oak.*	£10.90	DIR DBY BWL VLW	**G**
PENFOLDS BAROSSA VALLEY OLD VINE RED 1995, SOUTHCORP WINES South Australia	*Good colour with a berry fruit nose. Warm jammy palate and an excellent tannic structure.*	£11.20	Widely Available	**S**
HEGGIES MERLOT 1994, YALUMBA WINERY South Australia	*Cedar and vanilla dominate the nose before spicy fruits appear in the soft, delicate mouth.*	£11.80	BEN VDV CPW ADN EPO HER NYW	**B**
TYRRELL'S ECLIPSE PINOT NOIR 1996, TYRRELL'S WINES New South Wales	*Warm toasty oak and meaty characters on the nose, spicy peppery fruit with good structure.*	£12.00	PRG	**B**

TarraWarra Pinot Noir 1996, TarraWarra Vineyards Victoria	*Strawberries with charred oak characters on the nose with a palate of loganberries and firm tannins.*	£13.60	MFS COK GRT ODF DBY PHI HVN	B
Henscke's Keyneton Estate 1995, Henscke Wines South Australia	*Well-balanced. High levels of acid and tannin give it tremendous age-ing potential. Complex with a long finish.*	£14.90	JNW COK HOT SHJ L&W DBY NYW	S
Coldstream Hills Reserve Pinot Noir 1997, Southcorp Wines Victoria	*Raspberry and cherries with heavy oak aromas. Big fruit supported by toasty oak on the palate.*	£15.00	BWC MFS VDV ODD	B
Rosemount Grenache Shiraz Mourvèdre 1995, Rosemount Estate South Australia	*A full, spicy, alcoholic wine with good oak complexity and a sweet fruit finish.*	£15.00	BWC THS	B
Lenswood Pinot Noir 1996, Lenswood Knappstein Vineyards South Australia	*Cooked strawberry fruit on the nose followed by a palate of warm berries and soft tannins.*	£15.30	BWC LNR PAG	B
Best's Great Western Pinot Meunier 1994, Best's Great Western Victoria	*Garnet coloured. Spicy, smoky berry fruit in a big, opulent fruity style, good woody finish.*	£15.80	Widely Available	B
Clarendon Hills Merlot 1996, Clarendon Hills Estate South Australia	*Immense power and length, this wine has gobs of dark berries that will mature into a monster wine.*	£25.60	VDV J&B NYW	G

Pinpoint who sells the wine you wish to buy by turning to the stockist codes. If you know the name of the wine you want to buy, use the alphabetical index. If the price is your motivation, refer to the invaluable price guide index; red and white wines under £5, sparkling wines under £12 and champagne under £16. Happy hunting!

JACK MANN 1995, HOUGHTON WINERIES Western Australia	*Big sweet cassis and plum fruit aromas matched with sweet oak and succulent fruits on the palate.*	**£35.00**	PFC	S

AUSTRALIA • CHARDONNAY

LONE GUM CHARDONNAY 1997, NORMANS WINES South Eastern Australia	*Grassy, herbal aromas, clean tropical melon and pineapple flavours with a zesty kiwi fruit finish.*	**£4.50**	ODD	S
DEAKIN ESTATE CHARDONNAY 1997, WINGARA WINE GROUP Victoria	*Full rich mango and tropical fruit aromas with Rubenesque fruit, balanced acidity and integrated oak.*	**£5.10**	DIR MTL GGW ODD BTH BWL	B
SACRED HILL CHARDONNAY 1997, DE BORTOLI WINES South Eastern Australia	*Lime and subtle oak aromas, soft round creamy palate, honey and high acidity, balanced finish.*	**£5.30**	BOR LEA FSW BNK QWW HVW GGW	S
SEPPELT MOYSTON UNOAKED CHARDONNAY 1997, SOUTHCORP WINES South Eastern Australia	*Attractive lime and lemon aromas are followed by flinty notes on a crisp, zesty palate.*	**£5.60**	Widely Available	B
PENFOLDS KOONUNGA HILL CHARDONNAY 1997, SOUTHCORP WINES South Australia	*Rich, creamy aromas and flavours of pineapples, mangos and melons with vanilla and zippy lime.*	**£5.70**	Widely Available	S
TESCO McLAREN VALE CHARDONNAY 1997, MAGLIERI WINES South Australia	*Full fruit aromas, abundant tropical fruits on the palate with backbone acidity and good balance.*	**£6.00**	TOS	S

FOX RIVER WESTERN AUSTRALIAN CHARDONNAY 1997, FOX RIVER ESTATE Western Australia	*Ripe aromas of warm tropical fruits with hints of coconut are reflected on the rich palate.*	**£6.00**	ORB	(B)
TESCO MAGLIERI MCLAREN VALE CHARDONNAY 1997, MAGLIERI WINES South Australia	*Creamy aromas of peaches and oak with sweet, round, fat flavours of mango and pineapple.*	**£6.00**	TOS	(B)
WOOLSHED CHARDONNAY 1996, WINGARA WINE GROUP South Australia	*Soft buttery nose with full savoury almost cheesy palate good fresh acidity and excellent finish.*	**£6.20**	DIR BWL SAF FUL	(B)
WILDFLOWER RIDGE CHARDONNAY 1997, HOUGHTON WINES Western Australia	*Limey, citrus aromas with flavours of ripe melons and zippy sherbet finish to this attractive wine.*	**£6.30**	MTL WCS CWS POR CNL VIL	(B)
JIM BARRY UNWOODED CHARDONNAY 1997, JIM BARRY WINES South Australia	*Gentle, complex aromas and flavours of green apples and peaches tropical fruits and vanilla nuances.*	**£6.40**	BEN VDV QWW SHJ ODD FUL	(S)
HASELGROVE MCLAREN VALE CHARDONNAY 1997, HASELGROVE WINES South Australia	*Tangerine citrus and custard on the nose fresh citrus fruit flavours with grainy oak characters.*	**£6.50**	BEN HOU LIB	(S)
NORMANS CHARDONNAY BIN C207 1997, NORMANS WINES South Australia	*Butterscotch aromas leading to intensely crisp fresh tropical fruits with hints of creamy oak and herbs.*	**£6.50**	VDV ODD	(S)

Pinpoint who sells the wine you wish to buy by turning to the stockist codes. If you know the name of the wine you want to buy, use the alphabetical index. If the price is your motivation, refer to the invaluable price guide index; red and white wines under £5, sparkling wines under £12 and Champagne under £16. Happy hunting!

TATACHILLA CHARDONNAY 1997, TATACHILLA WINERY South Australia	*Tropical fruit with vanilla oak aromas. Rich fruit on palate with a slightly oily texture.*	£6.50	NIC D&D THS	B
WAKEFIELD WHITE CLARE CROUCHEN CHARDONNAY 1995, WAKEFIELD WINES South Australia	*Smoke and gooseberries on the nose with mouthwatering pineapple and grapefruit on the palate.*	£6.60	QWW TPE UNS RAE SWS	B
SHAREFARMERS CHARDONNAY SAUVIGNON BLANC 1997, PETALUMA WINERY South Australia	*Hints of ripe fruit and spice on the nose with lots of ripe tropical, integrated oak.*	£6.70	WCS MGN CPW WCR QWS	B
TYRRELL'S OLD WINERY CHARDONNAY 1997, TYRRELL'S WINES New South Wales	*Delicate style Chardonnay with mild tropical aromas and zesty citrus fruit palate, subtle oak characters.*	£6.70	Widely Available	B
D'ARENBERG THE OLIVE GROVE CHARDONNAY 1997, D'ARENBERG WINES South Australia	*Restrained, elegant nose with resinous oak then ripe stone fruit and bananas with grapefruit hints.*	£6.80	NRW VDV WES NEI ODD DBY NYW	G
HARDY'S BANKSIDE CHARDONNAY 1997, BRL HARDY WINE COMPANY South Australia	*Tropical fruit characters on the nose with full bodied fruit, good acidity and slightly astringent finish.*	£7.00	NEI HBR SAF VLW	B
HUNTER RIDGE CHARDONNAY 1996, BRL HARDY WINE COMPANY South Australia	*Creamy oak with full fruit flavours and fresh cut grass producing a soft smooth palate.*	£7.00	MTL NEI HBR DBY FUL	B
MAGLIERI MCLAREN VALE CHARDONNAY 1997, MAGLIERI WINES South Australia	*Sweet honey and grapefruit aromas with buttery, sun ripened mangos and cantaloupe melon flavours.*	£7.10	DBY	S

INGLEWOOD TWO RIVERS CHARDONNAY 1997, INGLEWOOD VINEYARDS New South Wales	*Good clean tropical pineapple nose with melon fruit flavours on a zesty citrus palate.*	£7.10	HWL SVT HVW HOU	(B)
DEEN DE BORTOLI CHARDONNAY 1997, DE BORTOLI WINES Victoria	*Exotic honey aromas, lime fruit characters. Firm acidity in harmony with balanced oak, wonderful lime finish.*	£7.20	BOR LEA VDV	(S)
MOCULTA CHARDONNAY 1996, BRL HARDY WINE COMPANY South Australia	*Lemon lime and toasty aromas. Lovely citrus fruit with weight and a long finish.*	£7.20	WCR MTL HBR DBY VLW	(B)
MAMRE BROOK CHARDONNAY 1997, SALTRAM WINES South Australia	*Resinous oak on the nose with creamy spiced citrus fruit producing a pleasantly drinkable drop.*	£7.30	Widely Available	(B)
WILDERNESS ESTATE RESERVE CHARDONNAY 1997, WILDERNESS ESTATE South Australia	*Light and clean on the nose with milky soft fruit medium weight and moderate length.*	£7.30	WOW CHF	(B)
WYNNS COONAWARRA ESTATE CHARDONNAY 1997, SOUTHCORP WINES South Australia	*Full bodied Chardonnay with tropical fruit and creamy buttery oak, slightly confected nose and palate.*	£7.30	Widely Available	(B)
PETER LEHMANN CHARDONNAY 1997, PETER LEHMANN WINES South Australia	*Rich fruit and walnut aromas. Soft round peaches and nutty palate, finish is slightly coarse.*	£7.50	VDV G&M PFT WMK	(B)
LEASINGHAM CHARDONNAY 1996, BRL HARDY WINE COMPANY South Australia	*Rich fruit and vanilla oak on nose, lemon and lime flavours, excellent structure and length.*	£7.60	Widely Available	(G)

PENFOLDS THE VALLEYS ORGANIC CHARDONNAY 1997, SOUTHCORP WINES South Australia	*Rich aromas of tropical fruits carry over to a rounded palate of bananas and coconut.*	£7.60	Widely Available	(S)
CHATEAU TAHBILK CHARDONNAY 1996, CHATEAU TAHBILK Victoria	*Ripe pineapple aromas with sweet round fruit on the palate, well-balanced with integrated oak.*	£7.60	VDV G&M ODD	(B)
BASEDOW CHARDONNAY 1997, O. BASEDOW WINES South Australia	*Limes, fig and banana mingle with vanilla oak characters on the nose. Buttery, citrus palate.*	£7.80	Widely Available	(S)
HARDY'S PADTHAWAY CHARDONNAY 1996, BRL HARDY WINE COMPANY South Australia	*Tropical fruit aromas, full bodied, creamy peaches and bananas palate. Elegantly balanced with excellent length.*	£7.90	Widely Available	(G)
PENFOLDS CLARE VALLEY ORGANIC CHARDONNAY SAUVIGNON BLANC 1997, SOUTHCORP WINES South Australia	*Soft, banana and pineapple aromas, clean palate of crunchy tropical lychees and kiwi fruits.*	£7.90	Widely Available	(S)
HILL SMITH ESTATE CHARDONNAY 1997, S SMITH & SON South Australia	*Tropical fruits and nuts stand out on the nose and palate of this easy drinking Chardonnay.*	£8.00	ODD JSM	(B)
BASEDOW CHARDONNAY 1996, O. BASEDOW WINES South Australia	*Smoky oak and hints of tobacco aromas with lime, citrus and succulent apricot fruit characters.*	£8.10	VDV GGW WTS FUL	(B)
NINTH ISLAND CHARDONNAY 1997, PIPERS BROOK Tasmania	*Clean lemon vanilla nose with ripe tropical fruit flavours and herby hints on a zesty finish.*	£8.20	Widely Available	(B)

AUSTRALIA • WHITE • CHARDONNAY

JAMIESON'S RUN CHARDONNAY 1997, MILDARA BLASS South Australia	Delicately aromatic and slightly fragrant with a buttery fruit palate, well-balanced with good length.	£8.30	WCR WFB MTL CVR ODD MRN	B
ORLANDO ST. HILARY CHARDONNAY 1997, ORLANDO WINES South Australia	Ripe tropical aromas with citrus fruit and toasty oak, opulent palate of limes and oak.	£8.70	NRW WIN DBY SMF CAP	G
OMRAH UNOAKED CHARDONNAY 1997, PLANTAGENET Western Australia	Restrained aromas of pears and green apples complement the fresh citrus palate containing mineral highlights.	£8.70	HOU DBY SGL NAD BBR GNW	S
GEOFF MERRILL CHARDONNAY 1996, GEOFF MERRILL WINES South Australia	Tropical fruit driven nose with traces of oak, the palate is full bodied with crisp acidity.	£8.90	DIR PLE ODD DBY ENO ASD NYW	G
ROUGE HOMME CHARDONNAY 1996, SOUTHCORP WINES South Australia	Tropical fruit aromas mingled with toasty oak, balanced palate of opulent fruit and integrated oak.	£9.00	VDV AVB NYW AMW	G
CHITTERING ESTATE CHARDONNAY 1997, CHITTERING ESTATE Western Australia	Nutty oak and delicate fruit with malo creaminess and elegant clean citrus fruit. Delicate finish.	£9.00	PAT	S
GRANT BURGE CHARDONNAY 1997, GRANT BURGE South Australia	Clean aromas of apricot and mango jam with rich fruit flavours and a citric finish.	£9.10	FSW COK HOU GGW DBY CTH GNW	B
GOUNDREY UNWOODED CHARDONNAY 1997, GOUNDREY WINES Western Australia	Fresh aromas of honeysuckle lead to a sweet palate of ripe tropical fruits with a classy citrus finish.	£9.20	COK GRT SHJ VIL TPE UNS SWS BOO	B

CHARDONNAY • WHITE • AUSTRALIA

Wine	Notes	Price	Availability	
CHATEAU REYNELLA CHARDONNAY 1996, BRL HARDY WINE COMPANY South Australia	*Buttery oak and tropical fruit nose, lemon acidity combined with soft creamy flavours, well-balanced.*	£9.30	Widely Available	S
CAPEL VALE UNWOODED CHARDONNAY 1997, CAPEL VALE Western Australia	*Uplifted and tangy, showing cut grass and green apples. Youthful and acidic holding clean crisp fruit.*	£9.50	WCR HOT UNS CPW NYW	S
ROTHBURY ESTATE BROKENBACK CHARDONNAY 1996 1996, MILDARA BLASS New South Wales	*Creamy, buttery nose with rich, ripe pineapple fruit reasonable length and a slightly hot alcoholic finish.*	£9.50	WFB DIR ODD	B
EBENEZER CHARDONNAY 1996, BRL HARDY WINE COMPANY South Australia	*Slightly spicy fruit on the nose, buttery oak and balanced tropical fruit palate. Needs time.*	£9.70	HOU HBR DBY VLW	S
NORMANS CHAIS CLARENDON CHARDONNAY 1996, NORMANS WINES South Eastern Australia	*A ripe melon nose with a rich, concentrated palate of juicy pineapple chunks and pink grapefruit.*	£9.80	VIL TBC	S
ROSEMOUNT SHOW RESERVE CHARDONNAY 1996, ROSEMOUNT ESTATE New South Wales	*Intense new oak and citrus aromas, rich round fruit with slight sweetness and balanced oak.*	£9.90	Widely Available	B
BROWNS MELBA FAMILY RESERVE CHARDONNAY 1997, BROWNS OF PADTHAWAY South Australia	*Lemon curd, tropical fruit and honey, integrated oak and balanced acidity with long toasty finish.*	£10.00	D&D	S
NEPENTHE LENSWOOD UNWOODED CHARDONNAY 1997, NEPENTHE VINEYARDS South Australia	*Warm gooseberry aromas lead onto green nettley flavours and a crisp finsh.*	£10.00	ODD SWS	B

63

AUSTRALIA • WHITE • CHARDONNAY

ROSEMOUNT GIANTS CREEK CHARDONNAY 1995, ROSEMOUNT ESTATE New South Wales	*Earthy green pepper aromas smooth buttery palate with zippy fresh acid and slightly oily texture.*	£10.00	BWC	**B**
PLUNKETT RESERVE CHARDONNAY 1995, PLUNKETT WINES Victoria	*Buttery toasty nose with hints of chestnut, rich tropical fruit with moderate complexity and length.*	£10.00	ALL	**B**
BRIDGEWATER MILL CHARDONNAY 1996, PETALUMA WINERY South Australia	*Fresh lemon on the nose, lime and grapefruit palate weight, crisp acidity and subtle complexity.*	£10.10	WCS ODD WCR	**S**
DOMAINE CHANDON GREEN POINT CHARDONNAY 1996, DOMAINE CHANDON Victoria	*Buttery, well oaked wine with a backbone of acidity that comes through on the finish.*	£10.10	DIR CVR HOU ODD MWW TPE FUL	**S**
KATNOOK ESTATE CHARDONNAY 1995, WINGARA WINE GROUP South Australia	*Tropical fruit and pineapple with buttery oak aromas balanced with slightly warm alcohol, Medium length.*	£10.20	DIR BWL VLW	**B**
WOLF BLASS PRESIDENT'S SELECTION CHARDONNAY 1997, MILDARA BLASS South Australia	*Soft fresh fruit aromas with hints of vanilla oak, powerful fruit on palate. Good length.*	£10.20	WFB MTL ODD VLW	**B**
SCOTCHMANS HILL CHARDONNAY 1996, SCOTCHMANS HILL Victoria	*Melon, capsicum and hazelnut aromas with honeyed tropical fruit palate and subtle integrated oak characters.*	£10.50	POR J&B	**B**
ROSEMOUNT SHOW RESERVE CHARDONNAY 1995, ROSEMOUNT ESTATE New South Wales	*Buttery oak on the nose with loads of tropical fruit, straightforward structure and good finish.*	£10.80	WCR SEL HOU MWW	**B**

CHAPEL HILL RESERVE CHARDONNAY 1996, CHAPEL HILL WINES South Australia	*Sweet citrus and lime on the nose with savoury mineral palate, balanced acidity and good length.*	£10.90	RDS TOS	**B**
BEST'S GREAT WESTERN CHARDONNAY 1997, BEST'S GREAT WESTERN Victoria	*Limey, citrus notes to the nose with fat, creamy tropical fruit flavours on the palate.*	£11.00	JNW UNS GON HOT WIN GRT SWS BOO	**B**
GOUNDREY RESERVE CHARDONNAY 1997, GOUNDREY WINES Western Australia	*Rich creamy aromas of vanilla and tropical fruits assault the palate before a mouthwatering finish.*	£11.10	GRT VIL TPE WOC SWS BOO	**B**
PENLEY ESTATE CHARDONNAY 1996, PENLEY ESTATE South Australia	*Pineapple and lemon aromas with plenty of ripe fruit and slightly drying tannins on finish.*	£11.10	VDV L&W JLW VLW NYW	**B**
DE BORTOLI YARRA VALLEY CHARDONNAY 1996, DE BORTOLI WINES Victoria	*Elegant fruit combined with subtle oak on nose, delicate mango flavours with zappy citrus finish.*	£11.60	LEA FSW VDV BNK MIS DBY CWI	**G**
LENSWOOD CHARDONNAY 1996, LENSWOOD KNAPPSTEIN VINEYARDS South Australia	*This outstanding Chardonnay has melon and pear characters, good complexity and a fine finish.*	£11.80	BWC PAG ROB	**S**
STONIER'S RESERVE CHARDONNAY 1995, STONIER WINERY Victoria	*Lovely nose producing rich tropical fruit, vanilla and toasty characters harmonious palate, slightly bot finish.*	£12.20	WAW QWW DIR ODD	**B**
GEOFF MERRILL RESERVE CHARDONNAY 1996, GEOFF MERRILL WINES South Australia	*Quince combined with complex buttery oak on the nose, upfront fruit and a rich finish.*	£12.50	DIR PLE VIL	**B**

AUSTRALIA • WHITE • CHARDONNAY

BROOKLAND VALLEY VINEYARDS CHARDONNAY 1996, BROOKLAND VALLEY VINEYARDS Western Australia	*This Chardonnay has lemon curd and peach characters with slightly oily texture and almond shavings.*	£12.60	DBY	(B)
MOUNTADAM CHARDONNAY 1996, MOUNTADAM WINES South Australia	*Light fruit with a strong lacing of oak. Wonderful mouthfeel showing refined acid finish.*	£12.90	Widely Available	(B)
COLDSTREAM HILLS RESERVE CHARDONNAY 1997, SOUTHCORP WINES Victoria	*Expressive oak and ripe fruit on the nose with full round melon and balanced acidity.*	£13.00	BWC NEI ODD	(B)
NEPENTHE CHARDONNAY 1997, NEPENTHE VINEYARDS South Australia	*Full oaky vanilla aromas with rich full bodied tropical fruit, lovely lemon acidity on finish.*	£13.00	ODD SWS	(B)
GEOFF MERRILL RESERVE CHARDONNAY 1995, GEOFF MERRILL WINES South Australia	*Ripe tropical fruit with citrus. French oak on the nose, harmonised fruit palate, good length.*	£13.70	DIR ODD DBY SAF NYW	(G)
EILEEN HARDY CHARDONNAY 1996, BRL HARDY WINE COMPANY South Australia	*Tropical fruit aromas with fine grain oak, high acidity and creamy malic characters, long finish.*	£13.80	WCR VLW VDV HOU HBR DBY	(S)
PETALUMA CHARDONNAY 1996, PETALUMA WINERY South Australia	*Lightly stewed apple aromas with fresh plentiful fruit characters well-balanced with subtle integrated oak.*	£13.90	Widely Available	(B)
DEVIL'S LAIR CHARDONNAY 1996, DEVIL'S LAIR WINES Western Australia	*Limes, tropical fruit and vanilla nose, lively citrus fruit on palate with integrated oak.*	£14.20	MFS VDV JNW WIN NYW GNW	(S)

ROSEMOUNT ROSE LABEL ORANGE CHARDONNAY 1996, ROSEMOUNT ESTATE New South Wales	*Light elegant fruit with hints of oak on the nose balanced and integrated vanilla palate.*	**£15.00**	HOU BWC	(B)
HOWARD PARK CHARDONNAY 1996, HOWARD PARK WINES Western Australia	*Buttery fruit and lime on the nose. Mandarin and lime flavours on the oily palate.*	**£15.10**	MFS JNW SEL WIN NYW	(S)
D'ARENBERG THE OTHER SIDE CHARDONNAY 1996, D'ARENBERG WINES South Australia	*Buttery lemon on the nose with ripe fruit some complexity and fantastic lemon, biscuity finish.*	**£15.50**	VDV BWL ODD	(B)
DALWHINNIE CHARDONNAY 1996, DALWHINNIE Victoria	*Peachy hints of vegetal characters, abundant fruit on the palate, complex oak and a long finish.*	**£15.90**	VDV J&B NYW	(S)
VASSE FELIX HEYTESBURY CHARDONNAY 1997, VASSE FELIX Margaret River	*Delicate citrus and spicy fruit, elegant palate with lemon and lime and subtle oak balance.*	**£16.00**	VDV	(S)
TYRRELL'S VAT 47 CHARDONNAY 1996, TYRRELL'S WINES New South Wales	*Melon and buttery oak aromas, summer tropical fruit crisp acidity with moderate amounts of oak.*	**£16.50**	Widely Available	(B)
ROSEMOUNT ROXBURGH CHARDONNAY 1995, ROSEMOUNT ESTATE New South Wales	*Big oaky nose followed by nutty palate of tropical fruit cocktail with weight and length.*	**£30.00**	HOU TOS UNS	(B)

Pinpoint who sells the wine you wish to buy by turning to the stockist codes. If you know the name of the wine you want to buy, use the alphabetical index. If the price is your motivation, refer to the invaluable price guide index; red and white wines under £5, sparkling wines under £12 and Champagne under £16. Happy hunting!

AUSTRALIA • RIESLING

PENFOLDS RAWSONS RETREAT BIN 202 RIESLING 1997, SOUTHCORP WINES South Australia	*Full bodied with a rich palate of sherbet and lime but packed with soft fruit flavours behind.*	£4.40	Widely Available	G
NOTTAGE HILL RIESLING 1997, BRL HARDY WINE COMPANY South Australia	*Fresh lemon and creamy lime notes on a lively fresh palate with soft citric notes.*	£5.00	WCR MTL HBR VWE FUL	B
WYNNS COONAWARRA ESTATE RIESLING 1997, SOUTHCORP WINES South Australia	*A sherbet, gooseberry and cream nose leads on to a fresh zippy grapefruit palate.*	£5.00	Widely Available	B
PETER LEHMANN RIESLING 1997, PETER LEHMANN WINES South Australia	*Light fresh style with soft zingy fruit and lively acidity tripping across the palate.*	£6.00	PLE ODD	B
D'ARENBERG THE DRY DAM RIESLING 1997, D'ARENBERG WINES South Australia	*Soft fruits and citrus lime notes with a palate showing crisp and lively acidity.*	£6.30	WES BWL ODD	B
WAKEFIELD ESTATE RIESLING 1996, WAKEFIELD WINES South Australia	*Uplifting full blown acid on the nose leading to a generous palate of zesty greengage fruit.*	£7.00	VDV SWS ADW BOO	S
TIM KNAPPSTEIN RIESLING 1997, TIM KNAPPSTEIN WINES South Australia	*Pleasant, elegant nose, on to a palate blessed with green fruits and a floral finish.*	£7.10	WCR VDV WCS MGN ODD F&M	S

MITCHELL WATERVALE RIESLING 1996, MITCHELL WINERY South Australia	*Tasters were impressed with the elegant tropical grapefruit flavours in this lively wine.*	£7.20	ADN HOT SHJ L&W POR	**B**
BEST'S GREAT WESTERN RIESLING 1996, BEST'S GREAT WESTERN Victoria	*This well made wine shows textured fruit flavours and creamy richness on its soft palate.*	£8.00	VDV JNW WIN GRT NEI SWS	**S**
ST. HALLETT EDEN VALLEY RIESLING 1997, ST. HALLETT WINES South Australia	*Cool climate soft, citrus fruit with balanced acidity, zippy, kerosene character and full finish.*	£8.00	AUC	**B**
ORLANDO ST. HELGA EDEN VALLEY RIESLING 1997, ORLANDO WINES South Australia	*Rich and full bodied with creamy textures of ripe sweet fruit with fresh lime acidity.*	£8.10	VDV WIN PEA CAP	**B**
TIM ADAMS RIESLING 1997, TIM ADAMS WINES South Australia	*Lively fruit with tingling spangle acidity brilliantly complemented by delicious ripe mouth-filling fruit.*	£8.50	JNW RDS TOS	**S**
GOUNDREY RESERVE RIESLING 1997, GOUNDREY WINES Western Australia	*Spicy floral notes on a palate of clean fruit with hints of boneysuckle.*	£9.30	VDV	**B**
PIPERS BROOK RIESLING 1997, PIPERS BROOK VINEYARDS Tasmania	*Fresh lime green fruit on the nose, with super acidity with sherbet and apple nuances.*	£9.60	COK WCS GRT DBY	**B**
PETALUMA RIESLING 1997, PETALUMA South Australia	*Soft petrol flavours with a crisp lime feel to a weighty palate of citrus.*	£9.80	Widely Available	**B**

AUSTRALIA • WHITE • RIESLING – SEMILLON

HOWARD PARK RIESLING 1996, HOWARD PARK WINES Western Australia	*A lovely well made wine with honey and floral notes on a full palate.*	£10.50	MFS VDV JNW NYW	B
PETER LEHMANN RESERVE RIESLING 1993, PETER LEHMANN WINES South Australia	*Fuller bodied, rich creamed greengages and pink grapefruit with a ripe long finish.*	£11.00	VDV PLE UDV BDR	B

AUSTRALIA • SEMILLON

HAWKES RUN SEMILLON CHARDONNAY NV, McWILLIAM'S WINES South Eastern Australia	*Full bodied wine with tropical fruit and peach on the palate finished with crisp acid.*	£4.30	CDT	B
DE BORTOLI WILLOWGLEN SEMILLON CHARDONNAY 1997, DE BORTOLI WINES New South Wales	*Tropical fruit, nutty complexity and butter. Dry, full-bodied with hazelnuts, excellent structure and complexity.*	£4.50	BOR LCC	S
DE BORTOLI SACRED HILL OAKED SEMILLON CHARDONNAY 1997, DE BORTOLI WINES Victoria	*Golden colour, rounded complex style containing ripe tropical fruit and smoky oak.*	£4.80	Widely Available	S
WYNDHAM ESTATE BIN 777 HUNTER VALLEY SEMILLON CHARDONNAY 1997, ORLANDO WINES New South Wales	*The nose has hints of ginger spice. Melon fruits with good acidity and length.*	£4.80	MTL HOU DBY MWW PEA	B
MIRANDA OAK AGED SEMILLON CHARDONNAY 1997, MIRANDA WINES New South Wales	*Lemons on the nose. Citrus and honey with some sandalwood characters. Length good and persistent.*	£5.30	HOH BDR	B

70

SEMILLON • WHITE • AUSTRALIA

St. Hallett Semillon Select 1997, St. Hallett Wines South Australia	*Vanilla and apple aromas with a touch of perfume. Tight with a combination of oak and fruit.*	£5.50	RDS	(S)
Grafton Reach Oak-Aged Semillon 1997, Miranda Wines South Australia	*A clean, forward bouquet, excellent melon and woody flavours with refreshing acidity on the finish.*	£5.70	BDR	(B)
Tatachilla Keystone Semillon 1997, Tatachilla Winery South Australia	*This fruit packed wine consists of lemon, lime and grapefruit with zippy acidity and depth.*	£6.20	D&D BDR	(B)
Marienberg Reserve Semillon Chardonnay 1996, Marienberg Wines South Australia	*Nutty, biscuity nose with vanilla. Ripe lemon, creamy oak and a well-integrated persistent finish.*	£6.50	LAY	(S)
Kingston Estate Semillon Sauvignon Blanc 1997, Kingston Estate Winery South Australia	*Abundent upfront fruit with a touch of minerals prelude a fresh mouthfeel with notes of citrus.*	£7.00	NRW BNK WES VNO DBY GNW	(G)
Leasingham Semillon 1997, BRL Hardy Wine Company South Australia	*Butter and lemon aromas with floral hints. Citrus fruit with vanilla, minerals and an acidic finish.*	£7.00	HBR ODD VLW	(S)
Geoff Merrill Mount Hurtle McLaren Vale Semillon 1997, Geoff Merrill Wines South Australia	*A youthful, well-textured wine with high acids and good, clean fruit flavours coming through.*	£7.00	PLE	(B)
Rosemount Estate Semillon 1997, Rosemount Estate South Eastern Australia	*Citrus fruit characters which have depth and well-integrated oak showing crisp clean lively acidity.*	£7.00	MTL HOU ODD SMF TOS	(B)

AUSTRALIA • WHITE • SEMILLON

SIMON HACKETT SEMILLON 1997, SIMON HACKETT South Australia	*Pale yellow colour with a fresh, creamy nose. Well integrated acidity and a long finish.*	£7.20	HOU CPW CNL NYW GNW	B
BASEDOW SEMILLON 1997, O. BASEDOW WINES South Australia	*Peachy fruit aromas and good depth on the palate. A dry and slightly metallic finish.*	£7.30	VDV GGW BWL VWE SAF	B
MAGLIERI MCLAREN VALE SCENARIO 1997, MAGLIERI WINES South Australia	*Tight and youthful mandarin and floral tones. Lean minerally fruit and a dry, aromatic finish.*	£7.30	PLB	B
GRANT BURGE OLD VINE SEMILLON 1997, GRANT BURGE South Australia	*A subtle nutty nose with full bodied and lemony flavours. Good acidity and a fresh finish.*	£8.10	Widely Available	B
WILLOWS VINEYARD SEMILLON 1996, WILLOWS VINEYARD South Australia	*Dry and balanced with pronounced toasty oak. Tropical fruits and high alcohol on the finish.*	£8.50	AUC WRC BUP	B
TIM ADAMS SEMILLON 1994, TIM ADAMS WINES South Australia	*Aromas of nuts and honey. Well textured palate, with a long but soft well rounded finish.*	£8.70	JNW RDS AUC	S
CHAIN OF PONDS SEMILLON 1996, CHAIN OF PONDS WINES South Australia	*Toasty nectarine fruit. A dry and delicate palate with balance, acidity and a long finish.*	£9.00	VDV JNW	S
TIM ADAMS SEMILLON 1995, TIM ADAMS WINES South Australia	*Banana and nut aromas. Tropical and floral fruits with creamy oak flavours, showing balance and length.*	£9.00	JNW AUC	S

MOUNT PLEASANT SEMILLON ELIZABETH 1992, McWILLIAMS WINES New South Wales	*Cream soda and ripe fruit on the nose. Lemon fruit and an oaky, minerally finish.*	£9.20	LAW QWW BNK BHW C&H	Ⓑ
VASSE FELIX SEMILLON SAUVIGNON BLANC CHARDONNAY 1996, VASSE FELIX Western Australia	*Uplifted floral nose, showing crisp acidity. Lingering, clean citrus fruit with a long finish.*	£9.20	BWC BEN VDV SHJ CPW RBS TAN NYW	Ⓑ
AMBERLEY MARGARET RIVER SEMILLON 1997, AMBERLEY ESTATE Western Australia	*Sweet oak and melon nose. Peaches and pineapples on a weighty mid-palate. A long finish.*	£9.80	BEN MFS ADN HAS MWW DBY PFT ADN	Ⓑ
VASSE FELIX SEMILLON 1997, VASSE FELIX Western Australia	*Baked bananas and lime aromas, with toasty oak, nutty flavours and pronounced, balanced acidity.*	£10.60	BEN VDV BWC NYW	Ⓑ
HENSCKE'S LOUIS SEMILLON 1996, HENSCKE WINES South Australia	*Golden colour hinting honey. Grapefruit acidity and well-integrated oak exhibiting good length.*	£10.80	VDV ADN HOT L&W NYW	Ⓢ
NEPENTHE SEMILLON 1997, NEPENTHE VINEYARDS South Australia	*Mouth-watering fruit and delicious mineral characteristics. The finish has fresh, dominant acidity and great length.*	£12.00	ODD SWS	Ⓑ
TYRRELL'S LOST BLOCK SEMILLON 1997, TYRRELL'S WINES New South Wales	*Big Australian Semillon. Abundant fruit and smoky integrated oak, balanced with moderate amounts of acid.*	£12.00	WIN VIL HVN HAR FSW	Ⓑ
TYRRELL'S VAT 1 SEMILLON 1993, TYRRELL'S WINES New South Wales	*Warm climate rich complex Hunter Valley Semillon with clean lemon and pineapple fruit, Good length.*	£16.80	WIN VIL HVN HAR FSW	Ⓑ

AUSTRALIA • OTHER WHITE

SOMERFIELD AUSTRALIAN DRY WHITE NV, SOUTHCORP WINES South Eastern Australia	*An intense and aromatic nose with pronounced fruit flavours on the palate. Great finish.*	£3.50	SMF	B
SAFEWAY'S AUSTRALIAN OAKED COLOMBARD 1997, BRL HARDY WINE COMPANY South Eastern Australia	*Vegetal and oak characters on the nose, sweet melon fruit with a long, fresh finish.*	£4.00	SAF	B
OXFORD LANDING SAUVIGNON BLANC 1997, YALUMBA WINERY South Australia	*Restrained aromas of tinned peas. The palate is soft but not flabby. Easy drinking, tasty.*	£5.10	Widely Available	B
ST. HALLETT POACHERS BLEND 1997, ST. HALLETT WINES South Australia	*Aromatic lime and crisp apple fruit, finely balanced with attractive fresh clean lively acidity. Long finish.*	£5.50	NRW RDS TOS AUC	S
TATACHILLA SAUVIGNON BLANC SEMILLON 1997, TATACHILLA WINERY South Australia	*A biscuity nose with a creamy, gingery texture in the mouth. A spicy, peppery finish.*	£6.00	D&D ODD WTS	B
SAFEWAY'S AUSTRALIAN MARSANNE 1996, MURCHINSON VINEYARD COMPANY Victoria	*Ripe banana on the nose followed by a fresh full body with complexity. Attractively balanced but slightly phenolic.*	£6.50	SAF	S
CHATEAU TAHBILK MARSANNE 1997, CHATEAU TAHBILK Victoria	*Lots of tropical kiwi and apple fruit characters with a full gooseberry palate. Clean and finely balanced.*	£6.60	VDV G&M PLE ODD DBY PFT	S

CHATEAU TAHBILK MARSANNE 1996, CHATEAU TAHBILK Victoria	*Hints of lanolin, honey and spice on the nose. Full flavoured, balanced with crisp savory acidity good length, great finish.*	**£6.80**	Widely Available	**S**
CARLYLE MARSANNE SEMILLON 1996, CHRIS PFEIFFER Victoria	*Mildly aromatic nose with crisp lively citrus fruit on the palate and clean zingy acid.*	**£6.80**	IRV GNW	**B**
MITCHELTON THOMAS MITCHELL MARSANNE 1996, MITCHELTON WINERY Victoria	*Ripe fruits with hints of dried almonds, rich flavours, good length and well balanced acidity.*	**£6.90**	WCS ODD VIL	**B**
BEST'S VICTORIA COLOMBARD 1997, BEST'S GREAT WESTERN Victoria	*Zesty attractive fruit, this is a lively New World wine with honest crisp clean acidity.*	**£7.00**	JNW HOT WIN VWE TPE TOS	**B**
OXFORD LANDING ESTATE VIOGNIER 1996, YALUMBA WINERY South Australia	*Fresh lime and lemons on the nose followed by rich fruits and a spicy finish.*	**£7.00**	THS WRC BUP	**B**
PRIMO ESTATE COLOMBARD 1997, PRIMO ESTATE South Australia	*Bright aromatic nose with tropical herbaceous fruit. Crisp clean and simple palate, a refreshing drop.*	**£7.00**	WRC BUP	**B**
MITCHELTON PREECE SAUVIGNON BLANC 1997, MITCHELTON WINERY Victoria	*Intense fruit flavours on the creamy nose are backed up by zesty lime on the rich palate.*	**£7.30**	VDV VIL COK JEF NEI AWS AMW HVN	**B**
RIDDOCH SAUVIGNON BLANC 1997, WINGARA WINE GROUP South Australia	*Greengages and gooseberries on a pronounced forward nose and palate underpinned by fresh acidity*	**£7.40**	GGW BWL ODD	**B**

TIM KNAPPSTEIN SEMILLON SAUVIGNON BLANC 1997, TIM KNAPPSTEIN WINES South Australia	*Rich, nutty, yeasty nose with depth on the palate. Fruit is well rounded and the finish long and creamy with fresh acidity.*	£7.50	WCS MGN ODD	(S)
BRIDGEWATER MILL SAUVIGNON BLANC 1997, PETALUMA WINERY South Australia	*A tight and fragrant nose, well balanced with some leesy characteristics and developing fresh acidity.*	£7.60	WCR WCS MGN ODD	(B)
TIM KNAPPSTEIN SAUVIGNON BLANC SEMILLON 1996, TIM KNAPPSTEIN WINES South Australia	*This wine possesses a mineral and lime nose with good Semilion characters on the palate.*	£7.90	WCS MGN VIL ODD	(B)
HANGING ROCK "JIM JIM" SAUVIGNON BLANC 1997, HANGING ROCK WINERY Victoria	*Lively acidity on the nose is matched by a palate of some finesse with grassy, tangy fruit.*	£8.00	SEL	(B)
PLUNKETT BLACKWOOD GERWURZTRAMINER 1997, PLUNKETT WINES Victoria	*Orange zest on the nose, pineapples and nectarines balanced on the palate with racy acidity.*	£8.00	ALL	(B)
TALTARNI SAUVIGNON BLANC 1997, TALTARNI VINEYARDS Victoria	*Aromas of freshly mown grass and red peppers. Ripe but dry fruit with touches of sweetness on the fresh acidic finish.*	£8.20	FSW DIR HOH AVB	(S)
MITCHELTON GOULBURN VALLEY MARSANNE 1997, MITCHELTON WINERY Victoria	*Burnt toffee aromas and defined oak with smooth creamy touches followed by a huge finish.*	£8.20	MTL COK ODD VIL DBY CHH	(B)
CAPEL VALE VERDELHO 1997, CAPEL VALE Western Australia	*Vibrant mouthwatering fruit with herbal characters. Well-balanced with good length and high acidity.*	£8.30	NYW	(B)

MITCHELTON MARSANNE RESERVE 1994, MITCHELTON WINERY Victoria	*Figs and toasty oak aromas with distinctive oak on the palate finishing with astringent acidity.*	£8.80	JEF CPW VIL COK RVA HWL	B
KATNOOK ESTATE SAUVIGNON BLANC 1997, WINGARA WINE GROUP South Australia	*Forward nettly nose, while the palate reminded tasters of lemon and lime sherbet.*	£9.00	DIR BWL WRC VLW FUL	B
GEOFF MERRILL SAUVIGNON BLANC 1997, GEOFF MERRILL WINES South Australia	*A light fresh nose with delicate and subtle fruit flavours and a long powerful finish.*	£9.20	QWW DIR VIL	B
AMBERLEY MARGARET RIVER SAUVIGNON BLANC 1997, AMBERLEY ESTATE Western Australia	*Bright in colour, fresh and lively acidity with good use of primary fruit on its gooseberry palate.*	£9.70	HAS CNL DBY PFT THS	S
DEVIL'S LAIR FIFTH LEG WHITE 1997, DEVIL'S LAIR WINES Western Australia	*This wine personifies the girl next door with light fresh fruit flavour and honest acidity.*	£10.00	JNW SEL WIN GRT NYW	B
LENSWOOD SAUVIGNON BLANC 1997, LENSWOOD KNAPPSTEIN WINES South Australia	*Herbaceous, gooseberry nose with an elegant palate of full rounded flavours with grassy overtones.*	£11.00	BUP THS	S
CULLEN SAUVIGNON BLANC SEMILLON 1997, CULLEN WINES Western Australia	*This lively active wine pleases with melon and lemon bone dry fruit on the palate.*	£12.10	ADN DIR HAS DBY PFT NYW	B
MITCHELTON VIOGNIER ROUSANNE 1996, MITCHELTON WINERY Victoria	*The nose has ripe peach notes that follow onto the palate. Complex hints of spice complement the warm, ripe fruit.*	£14.90	JEF WCS NEI VIL DBY COK AMW	S

AUSTRALIA • SWEET WHITE

MIRANDA PIONEERS RAISINED MUSCAT 1996, MIRANDA WINES South Australia	*A honeyed nose bombards the senses, together with a luscious palate of rich orange marmalade.*	£4.70 (37.5cl)	WCR HOH VIL AVB BDR NYW	B
LINDEMANS BOTRYTIS RIESLING 1996, SOUTHCORP WINES South Australia	*With the appearance of sunrise, excellent acid balances this simply superb luscious style of wine.*	£5.90 (37.5cl)	Widely Available	S
RYMILL BOTRYTIS GEWÜRZTRAMINER 1997, RYMILL WINERY South Australia	*Kumquats and other citrus fruit aromas on the nose with a spicy sugar palate.*	£6.00 (37.5cl)	WCR VDV HVW PKR TOS	B
BROWN BROTHERS LATE HARVESTED RIESLING 1995, BROWN BROTHERS Victoria	*Honeysuckle on the nose with delicate honeyed citrus and tropical fruit combined with nutty tones.*	£7.30 (37.5cl)	VDV DIR MTL VIL TPE WTS	B
HEGGIES BOTRYTIS AFFECTED RIESLING 1997, YALUMBA WINERY South Australia	*A huge nose of fresh daisies and beeswax with an intense integrated botrytis palate.*	£7.60 (37.5cl)	BEN JNW EPO HVW HER ODD	B
YALUMBA BOTRYTIS SEMILLON SAUVIGNON BLANC 1997, YALUMBA WINERY South Australia	*Perfection on the nose as orange peel and sweet honey cling to the senses, long lasting.*	£7.70 (37.5cl)	JNW ODD MWW JNR	S
BROWN BROTHERS FAMILY RESERVE LATE HARVESTED NOBLE RIESLING 1994, BROWN BROTHERS Victoria	*Intense golden colour, a wonderful botrytis nose with acidity cutting through its rich interior. Fantastic length.*	£8.20 (37.5cl)	NRW DIR CPW VIL DBY TPE GNW	G

VASSE FELIX NOBLE RIESLING 1996, **VASSE FELIX** Western Australia	*Subtle combination of botrytis and oak with hints of honeyed fruit and acid.*	**£8.30** (37.5cl)	BEN HVW RBS VDV NYW	B
ELDERTON GOLDEN SEMILLON 1996, **ELDERTON WINES** South Australia	*Deep golden colour, wonderful nose with rich apricots, opulent sweet fruit with complexity and crisp clean acidity.*	**£8.40** (37.5cl)	ODF DBY	G
D'ARENBERG THE NOBLE RIESLING 1997, **D'ARENBERG WINES** South Australia	*Fresh baked citrus fruit on the nose and palate with soft lemon acidity and long lasting sweet finish.*	**£9.80** (37.5cl)	VDV ODD DBY BWL	S
DE BORTOLI NOBLE ONE 1995, DE BORTOLI WINES New South Wales	*Lemon and daisies on the nose with barley sugar sweetness making a rich and approachable wine.*	**£15.50**	Widely Available	S

AUSTRALIA • SPARKLING

SEAVIEW PINOT NOIR CHARDONNAY BRUT 1995, SOUTHCORP WINES South Australia	*A speedy stream of bubbles breaks into a doughy fruit outburst, nicely balanced with an elongated finish.*	**£8.50**	Widely Available	B WINE OF THE YEAR
SEAVIEW BLANC DE BLANCS BRUT 1995, SOUTHCORP WINES South Australia	*A green tinged grape with a hint of persistent mousse. Yeasty fruit but a little vertically challenged.*	**£9.00**	TBA VLW	B
YALUMBA CUVEE TWO PRESTIGE CABERNET SAUVIGNON NV, YALUMBA WINERY South Australia	*Berry fruit on the nose showing deep sweet big hedonistic blackberry fizz with refreshing soft tannic backbone.*	**£9.40**	VDV JNW ODD DBY TOS	B WINE OF THE YEAR

AUSTRALIA • SPARKLING – FORTIFIED

GREEN POINT BRUT VINTAGE 1994, DOMAINE CHANDON Victoria	*Has clean crisp fruit with a slightly dryer than usual edge to it, a clean finish.*	£11.80	Widely Available	S
GREEN POINT BRUT VINTAGE 1995, DOMAINE CHANDON Victoria	*A wine with a delicate nose, powerful palate, and a strong drying finish.*	£12.00	Widely Available	B
JANSZ SPARKLING BRUT VINTAGE 1993, HEEMSKERK WINE COMPANY Tasmania	Good rich nose with assertive bubbles, well structured but stops a bit short of the line.	£12.00	NEG	B
HASELGROVE SPARKLING GARNET BRUT NV, HASELGROVE WINES South Australia	Raspberry and vegetal aroma and palate with some sweetness but showing balancing acidity.	£12.80	NYW	B

AUSTRALIA • FORTIFIED

MICK MORRIS RUTHERGLEN LIQUEUR MUSCAT, MORRIS WINES Victoria	*An intensity of dried orange peel and raisin fruit remains wonderfully fresh thanks to lemon zest acidity.*	£5.40 (37.5cl)	Widely Available	S
YATES'S AUSTRALIAN WHITE WINE, BRL HARDY COMPANY South Australia	*Uplifted dry fruit nose with a touch of saltiness. Forward palate, lacking only a touch of depth.*	£6.00	YWL TOS CRS	B
PENFOLDS MAGILL TAWNY, SOUTHCORP WINES South Australia	*This Tawny is flavour - packed with butterscotch toffee and nut aromas and sweet ripe fruit.*	£6.10 (37.5cl)	Widely Available	B

STANTON & KILLEEN RUTHERGLEN MUSCAT, STANTON & KILLEEN Victoria	*Plenty of toffee and dried fruit flavours kept from being cloying by fresh citrus acidity.*	**£6.80** (37.5cl)	Widely Available	(B)
YALUMBA MUSEUM SHOW RESERVE MUSCAT, YALUMBA South Australia	*Rich, deep and sweet. The palate was intense with apricot and honey, showing good age.*	**£6.90** (37.5cl)	JNW CVR ODD MCW GRA	(B)
YALDARA RESERVE OLD TAWNY, YALDARA WINES South Australia	*Luscious raisined fruit exhibiting warm, round dried stonefruit with a fantastically long finish.*	**£7.00**	MTL CRS VIL HVW TPE HOU GLO WON	(B)
STANTON & KILLEEN RUTHERGLEN MUSCADELLE, STANTON & KILLEEN Victoria	*Sweet berries with a floral overview. Showing finesse on the palate with extrordinary length.*	**£7.80** (37.5cl)	WAW VDV SEL GON SAN AMW NYW	(S)
SEPPELT RUTHERGLEN SHOW MUSCAT DP63, SOUTHCORP WINES Victoria	*As stylish as the bottle it's in, this Muscat has dried currant flavours and great length.*	**£8.20** (37.5cl)	VDV WCS NEI ODD NYW AMW	(S)
STANTON & KILLEEN RUTHERGLEN MUSCAT COLLECTORS, STANTON & KILLEEN Victoria	*Luscious raisins, coffee and chicory atop a rich, warm mouthfeel of a palate.*	**£8.70** (37.5cl)	MIS NYW H&H SEL BOO	(S)
YALDARA FARMS SHOW TAWNY, YALDARA WINES South Australia	*Toffee and burnt butter aromas mingled with ripe fruit finishing with a broad sweet tangy palate.*	**£9.00**	SWS	(B)
CAMPBELL'S RUTHERGLEN MUSCAT, CAMPBELLS Victoria	*Benchmark Australian Muscat. Intensely sweet, warming, full on Christmas pudding in a glass.*	**£9.50** (37.5cl)	ADN BNK ODD DAV GNW	(B)

AUSTRALIA • FORTIFIED

YALDARA 15 YEAR OLD RESERVE TAWNY, YALDARA WINES South Australia	*This superb orange, gold tawny wine has a rich juicy raisin palate and beautiful length.*	**£9.90**	VDV VIL SWS GRT	**B**
CAMPBELL'S OLD RUTHERGLEN MUSCAT, CAMPBELLS Victoria	*Liqueur Muscat as only the Australians can make it. Spice and vanilla add depth to the liquid raisin flavours.*	**£10.70** (37.5cl)	WCR NIC BNK CPW ODD	**S**
BROWN BROTHERS LIQUEUR MUSCAT, BROWN BROTHERS Victoria	*Intensely aromatic chocolate orange nose and a palate awash with candied peel and treacle toffee.*	**£12.70**	Widely Available	**G**

AUSTRIA

With huge success once again in the sweet wine categories, Austria has proved itself above any past misdemeanors with a whole gamut of medals. The range of grape varieties used is amazing, it seems you just find a south facing piece of land plant anything you like and hey presto success can be yours. The only problem with these lush wines is they are difficult to find. However, they are worth seeking out mainly from small independent wine merchants. Look out also for the drier style whites. Prost!

AUSTRIA • RED

BLAUFRANKISCH - RIED GOLDBERG 1994, ENGELBERT PRIELER Burgenland	*Raspberry, stalky fruit on the nose followed by an enticing dry palate of ripe loganberries and soft acidity.*	£15.00	FWW	(S)

AUSTRIA • WHITE

WEINGUT DOLLE "OSCAR" 1996, PETER DOLLE Niederösterreich	*Intense youthful colour. Vegetal characters with a hint of sea shells. Well-balanced with good length.*	£7.00	NEI	(S)
SKOFF MORILLOU CHARDONNAY 1997, WALTER SKOFF Sud-Steiermark	*Crisp acidity and melon fruit on the palate and bouquet of this easy wine.*	£10.00	VLW	(B)
SKOFF WEISSBURGUNDER KABINETT 1997, WALTER SKOFF Sud-Steiermark	*If sweet and sour is your taste then don't let this wine go to waste.*	£10.00	VLW	(B)

AUSTRIA • SWEET

WELSCHRIESLING BOUVIER TROCKENBEERENAUSLESE 1995, JOHANN KAISERGARTEN Burgenland	*Honey and lemons infused with a delicate scent of tar. Wonderful weight and excellent finish.*	£8.50	RSN	S
SEEWINKLER IMPRESSIONEN TROCKENBEERENAUSLESE 1991, JOHANN KAISERGARTEN Burgenland	*Concentrated fruit combines with underlying acidity making this a well-balanced wine.*	£9.50	RSN	B
SÄMLING 88 TROCKENBEEREAUSLESE 1995, WEINGUT PANNONIA Burgenland	*A tropical fruit basket explodes from the glass. Smooth and velvety in the mouth with concentrated finish.*	£10.50	RSN	S
WELSCHRIESLING BEERENAUSLESE 1996, GERHARD NEKOWITSCH Burgenland	*Classic botrytised nose applauded by delectable sweetness and balance.*	£11.00	NYW	B
MUNZENRIEDER WELSCH-RIESLING TROCKENBEEREN-AUSLESE 1995, JOHANN MONZEUREIDER Burgenland	*Attractive botrytised fruit shines through with a touch of spicy oak underlying its unctuous texture.*	£16.50	RSN	S
BOUVIER MUSKAT ZWISCHEN DENSEEN TROCKENBEERENAUSLESE 1996, ALOIS KRACHER Burgenland	*Dive into the abyss and submerge into layers of rich, ripe fruit with lively acidity to balance.*	£18.00	NYW	S
SÄMLING 88 TROCKENBEERENAUSLESE 1996, GERHARD NEKOWITSCH Burgenland	*Lychees and tar on the nose, a raisin filled palate and a good clean finish.*	£18.00	NYW	B

THE RED ONE SCHILFWEIN STROHWEIN 1996, GERHARD NEKOWITSCH Burgenland	*Rosehip, strawberry and cherry aromas with intense sweet cherry fruit on palate and good length.*	£24.00	NYW	(B)
WELSCHRIESLING ZWISCHEN DENSEEN TROCKENBEERENAUSLESE 1996, ALÖIS KRACHER Burgenland	*This little star isn't afraid of being upfront, bursting with a multitude of flavours.*	£25.00	NYW	(B)
TRAMINER NO. 8 NOUVELLE VAGUE TROCKENBEERENAUSLESE 1995, ALÖIS KRACHER Burgenland	*A sherbet lemon nose with intense citrusy palate followed by an outstanding finish.*	£26.00	NYW	(G)
GRANDE CUVÉE NO.12 TROCKENBEERENAUSLESE 1995, ALÖIS KRACHER Burgenland	*This wine is one for the cellars with rich boneyed tones and ripe fruit balance.*	£26.00	NYW	(S)
CHARDONNAY WELSCHRIESLING NO.7 NOUVELLE VAGUE TBA 1995, ALÖIS KRACHER Burgenland	*Blooms almost at once to reveal a delightful multi-layered palate, with enthusiastic acid and good length.*	£28.00	NYW	(S)
SCHEUREBE NO.6 ZWISCHEN DENSEEN TROCKENBEERENAUSLESE 1995, ALÖIS KRACHER Burgenland	*A well-structured wine brimming with opulent fruit and mouth tingling acidity leading to a vivacious finish.*	£29.00	NYW	(S)
NOUVELLE VAGUE NO.10 TUES ADORABLE TROCKENBEERENAUSLESE 1995, ALÖIS KRACHER Burgenland	*Rich botrytis nose precedes a long lingering palate integrated with coarse orange marmalade.*	£29.00	NYW	(B)

Pinpoint who sells the wine you wish to buy by turning to the stockist codes. If you know the name of the wine you want to buy, use the alphabetical index. If the price is your motivation, refer to the invaluable price guide index; red and white wines under £5, sparkling wines under £12 and Champagne under £16. Happy hunting!

85

AUSTRIA • SWEET

SCHILFWEIN TRADITION STROHWEIN 1996, GERHARD NEKOWITSCH Burgenland	*Pale gold, spring fruit, figs and perfume. Palate displays lemon and butter with oily textures and good acidity.*	£30.00	NYW	**S**
KRACHER SCHEUREBE NO.14 ZWISCHEN DEN SEEN TBA 1995, ALÖIS KRACHER Burgenland	*Botrytis peach, lemon and a hint of spice on the nose, elegant fruit with sweet fresh marmalade characters.*	£32.00	NYW	**S**

EASTERN EUROPE

With added investment, better winemaking techniques are shining through in Eastern Europe. The influence of 'flying wine makers' has helped aid the transition from the more old fashioned styles leading to fresh commercial wines coming to the fore. Hungary continues to produce some lush Tokaji wines as well as a coveted Wine of The Year. Watch this space.

BULGARIA • RED

ASDA BULGARIAN MERLOT 1997, VINIPROM HASKOVO Haskovo	*Ripe jammy blackcurrant aromas are reflected on the balanced, attractive soft fruit dominated palate.*	£3.00	ASD	(B)
BVC IAMBOL MERLOT 1997, VINIS IAMBOL Iambol	*Minty notes on a jammy nose are carried over onto a concentrated black fruits' palate.*	£3.00	THS	(B)
IAMBOL BULGARIAN MERLOT 1997, IAMBOL WINERY Iambol	*Rich gamey aromas with hints of eucalyptus lead to a complex, slightly medicinal palate of jammy, black fruits.*	£3.20	WES UNS SMF THS WRC BUP	(S)
DOMAINE BOYAR CABERNET SAUVIGNON 1997, VINIS IAMBOL Iambol	*Attractive mulberry nose before a full blackcurrant palate with hints of eucalyptus and vanilla.*	£3.30	Widely Available	(B)
DOMAINE BOYAR MERLOT 1997, VINIS IAMBOL Iambol	*Light, fresh fruit and liquorice aromas lead to a jammy, plum palate with a green capsicum finish.*	£3.30	SMF THS WOW FUL THS WRC BUP	(B)

TESCO BULGARIAN RESERVE CABERNET SAUVIGNON 1993, VINIPROM HASKOVO	*Ripe, hot cassis aromas lead onto a rich, slightly oaked and minty, blackcurrant jam palate.*	£3.70	TOS	B
TESCO BULGARIAN RESERVE MERLOT 1992, VINIPROM HASKOVO	*Intense, ripe fruit and cinnamon aromas lead to hot, jammy, black fruit flavours on the ripe palate.*	£3.70	TOS	B
DOMAINE BOYAR CABERNET SAUVIGNON RESERVE 1995, VINIS IAMBOL Iambol	*Ripe raspberry aromas with hints of herby oak lead onto a well-structured red fruits palate.*	£3.80	JSM THS WOW THS WRC BUP	B
SELECTED RELEASE CABERNET SAUVIGNON 1996, VINIS LOVICO SUHINDOL Suhindol	*Rich jammy, blackcurrant aromas and flavours abound in this soft, easy drinking wine.*	£4.00	WOW JSM DBO	B
DOMAINE BOYAR CABERNET SAUVIGNON SPECIAL RESERVE 1990, VINIS IAMBOL Iambol	*Rich toasty aromas of ripe fruit with block-busting creamy black-currant fruit flavours and soft tannins.*	£4.20	THS	B
DOMAINE BOYAR CELLAR MASTERS RES ESTATE SELECT.CAB. SAUV. 1992, VINIS LOVICO SUNHINDOL Suhindol	*Clean morello cherry aromas lead to juicy blackcurrant fruit flavours with light vanilla notes.*	£9.00	WOW DBO	B

BULGARIA • WHITE

BVC ROUSSE SAUVIGNON BLANC 1997, VINIPROM ROUSSE Rousse	*A deliciously spicy and aromatic nose following onto a palate of supple, ripe fruits.*	£3.30	BVC	S

BULGARIA – HUNGARY • EASTERN EUROPE

BVC Hidden Valley Chardonnay 1997, Viniprom Rousse Rousse	Peachy, butter aromas lead onto a rich, slightly oily palate of melons and pears with some oak influence.	£3.50	CRS WCR	**S**
The Bulgarian Vintners Reserve Chardonnay 1996, Karamochev Rousse	Robust smooth fruit with sleek mouthfeel hints of mineral characters and slightly hot finish.	£4.00	BVC	**B**

HUNGARY • RED

Konyari Cabernet Sauvignon Reserve 1996, Vinarium St. Donatus Estate Lake Balaton	Intense cassis nose with hints of oak is followed by concentrated blackcurrant and vanilla flavours.	£5.00	WOW	**B**
Eger Bikaver Reserve 1996, Tibor Gal GIA North Hungary	Ripe, dark fruit aromas lead to a balanced palate of concentrated forest fruits and soft oak.	£7.50	WOW	**B**
Eger Kekfrankos Blaufrankisch Reserve 1995, Tibor Gal GIA North Hungary	Impressive mint and grass notes with fine lean tannins, blackberry fruit and good finish.	£7.50	WOW	**B**

HUNGARY • WHITE

Safeway's Woodcutter's White 1997, Neszmely Barsonyos	Spice on the nose, upfront fleshy soft fruit palate with fantastic crisp acidity leading to a clean finish.	£3.00	SAF	**S** WINE OF THE YEAR

89

SZOHOSKERT ZENIT OAKED 1997, NAGYREDE WINERY Mátraalja	*Refreshing citrus fruit with slightly steely characters. Good acid drawn into a long crisp finish.*	£3.00	SAF	(B)
CO-OP HUNGAROO PINOT GRIS 1996, INTERCONSULT Neszmely	*Lovely aromatic stone fruit characters with a touch of spice. Medium-bodied with firm acidity.*	£3.70	CWS	(B)
MISTY MOUNTAIN CHARDONNAY 1996, SYARAZ MINOSEGI FEHERBOR Tokaji	*Ripe tropical fruit flavours and a delicious zesty lime finish to this attractively balanced elegant wine.*	£3.70	SPR	(B)

HUNGARY • SWEET

CHÂTEAU MESSZELATO TOKAJI ASZÙ 5 PUTTONYOS 1988, MIKLOS GIA Tokaji	*Robed in deep gold with lashings of mouth-watering fruit. Builds into an unforgettable finish.*	£8.00	WOW	(G) TROPHY WINE
TOKAJI ASZÙ 5 PUTTONYOS 1992, HUNGAROVIN Tokaji	*A caramel nose leading to swirls of toffee and a storming finish.*	£10.80	ADN MTL JS MRN CWS	(B)
DOMAINE DISZNOKO 6 PUTTONYOS 1993, DOMAINE DISZNOKO Tokaji	*Tasters were impressed by the richly elegant palate and deserving finish of this lush wine.*	£16.40	DBY	(B)
ROYAL TOKAJI WINE COMPANY 5 PUTTONYOS 1991, ROYAL TOKAJI WINE COMPANY Tokaji	*Many levels of convoluted sweetness accompany the breathtaking acidity exquisitely. A perfect finish to a perfect wine.*	£19.00	SVT HOT MWW WTS BDR GNW	(G)

MONTENEGRO

MONTE CHEVAL VRANAC 1996, AGRIKOMBINAT JULY 13 South Montenegro	*Bright berry fruits and a big cherry flavour. Long and well-balanced with fine tannins.*	**£4.00**	ASD	(B)
MONTE CHEVAL VRANAC RESERVE 1993, PLANTAZE South Montenegro	*Big, dark and chewy with herbaceous notes on a very long finish with perfect balance.*	**£4.00**	SAF	(B)

ROMANIA • RED

IDLEROCK MERLOT RESERVE 1996, THE HANWOOD GROUP Dealul Mare	*Rich aromas and flavours of blackcurrant jam and mint on this soft, approachable wine.*	**£3.80**	JSM	(B)
DEALUL VIILOR MERLOT SPECIAL RESERVE BARREL MATURED 1994, VINEXPORT Severin	*Nose full of blackcurrants. Palate is big, sweet and rich with crème de cassis flavours and excellent length.*	**£4.50**	CWS TOS	(S)

ROMANIA • WHITE

MURFATLAR SPECIAL RESERVE LATE HARVEST PINOT GRIS 1962, SCV MURFATLAR Dobrodgea	*Intriguing. A lighter style wine but complex and rewarding. Luscious sweetness followed by a good lasting acidity.*	**£13.00**	LAW	(B)

FRANCE

This year sees France fighting back in the medal tables particularly in Burgundy, Champagne and Southern France. Improved vintages have lead to better quality wines. Some delicious Chablis, top class Pinot Noir and superb Champagnes are highlighted in the following pages. Look out also for some excellent Vins de Pays made from indigenous and unusual grape varieties. The French are really getting their act together and giving the rest of the vinous world a bit of healthy competition. Long may it continue. A votre santé!

FRANCE • ALSACE • RED

VAL ST GEOGOIRE PINOT NOIR 1997, CAVES VINICOLE DE TURKHEIM Alsace	*Ripe green strawberry fruits on a juicy cherry palate with light tannins and mineral character.*	£6.00	COK	B

FRANCE • ALSACE • WHITE

TOKAY PINOT GRIS PRESTIGE 1996, PIERRE SPARR Alsace	*Ripe apricots and peaches with a dash of spice. Firm acid and a lovely long finish.*	£6.00	SGL	B
TOKAY PINOT GRIS 1997, CAVE VINICOLE DE TURKHEIM Alsace	*This lively fun wine houses fresh pineapple and peach fruit characters with a refreshing acidity.*	£6.00	Widely Available	B
RIESLING SCHOENENBOURG GRAND CRU 1996, PIERRE SPARR Alsace	*Aromatic notes on a forward nose, the palate has honeysuckle and spice with a long finish.*	£7.00	SGL	B

GEWURZTRAMINER 1995, DOMAINE MITTNACHT-KLACK Alsace	*Golden coloured with petrol and warm spicy aromas. Elegant ripe fruit flavours and spicy acidity.*	£7.50	WIN	**B**
RIESLING HEIMBOURG 1996, CAVE VINICOLE DE TURKHEIM Alsace	*Quite light but with a lovely soft flinty feel. The palate is refreshing and long with subdued lemon acidity.*	£7.70	WES COK DBY HVW	**B**
TOKAY HEIMBOURG 1996, CAVE VINICOLE DE TURKHEIM Alsace	*This is a simple wine with moderate length, soft sweet fruit characters with crisp acidity.*	£8.40	COK DBY BOO	**B**
ALSACE GEWURZTRAMINER 1996, WOLFBERGER Alsace	*Lychees and limes on the nose with spices and green fruits. A rich, clean palate with well-balanced acidity.*	£8.50	CWS VIL	**S**
GEWÜRZTRAMINER FLEUR 1994, DOMAINES SCHLUMBERGER Alsace	*Sweet spicy fruit aromas. A viscous chewy mouthfeel complemented by luscious ripe fruit flavours and a stylish finish.*	£8.60	MMD POR	**S**
ALSACE GEWURZTRAMINER 1996, PAUL BUECHER Alsace	*Rose petal and lychee aromas with a good oily feel and a dry, spicy palate.*	£9.00	ELL	**B**
PINOT GRIS GRAND CRU BRAND 1994, CAVE VINICOLE DE TURKHEIM Alsace	*This is a pleasant little number with spicy figs and syrupy sweetness on the palate.*	£9.00	DBY	**B**
PINOT D'ALSACE 1996, DOMAINE ZIND HUMBRECHT Alsace	*Intense citrus burst with lemon grapefruit and honeysuckle, it is crisp clean and extremely tangy on the palate.*	£10.00	JNW ABY VLW WRC BUP	**B**

FRANCE • ALSACE • WHITE

PINOT GRIS LES PRINCES ABBES 1996, DOMAINES SCHLUMBERGER Alsace	*Delicate honeysuckle characters on the nose with crisp acidity and lovely honeyed fruit on the palate.*	£10.50	JNW SEL SHJ POR TPE	Ⓑ
GEWURZTRAMINER GUEBERSCHWIHR 1996, DOMAINE ZIND HUMBRECHT Alsace	*A classically spicy and aromatic nose, rich, spicy and tasty fruit with perfectly balanced fresh acidity.*	£10.70	JNW ABY VLW WRC BUP	Ⓑ
GEWÜRZTRAMINER TURCKHEIM 1994, DOMAINE ZIND HUMBRECHT Alsace	*A mature nose with honey and lychee aromas, dry, phenolic complexity and a beautiful finish.*	£11.70	JNW DBY VLW WRC	Ⓑ
HERRENWEG PINOT GRIS 1996, DOMAINE ZIND HUMBRECHT Alsace	*Youthful tangy citrus fruit with floral and honey characters, lemon acidity and some weight.*	£11.70	ABY VLW WRC BUP	Ⓑ
JOSMEYER "H" VIEILLES VIGNES 1996, JOS. MEYER & FILS Alsace	*An excellent wine with added flavours of ripe grapefruit and an underlying creaminess on the palate.*	£12.50	A&N	Ⓢ
RIESLING CLOS WINDSBUHL 1996, DOMAINE ZIND HUMBRECHT Alsace	*A gentle wine with intense ripe fruit having citrus and lychee nuances on a rich developed palate.*	£12.70	JNW ABY VLW WRC BUP	Ⓑ
PINOT GRIS CLOS JEBSAL 1996, DOMAINE ZIND HUMBRECHT Alsace	*Nut and honey flavours combine on the palate with fresh acidity to give a wonderful, slightly sweet, complex wine.*	£13.50	JNW ABY VLW WRC BUP	Ⓑ
RIESLING CLOS HAUSERER 1992, DOMAINE ZIND HUMBRECHT Alsace	*Lemon and lime nose with ripe strong fruit reminiscent of lychees and pineapples.*	£14.50	JNW ABY VLW WRC	Ⓢ

PINOT GRIS HEIMBOURG 1996, DOMAINE ZIND HUMBRECHT Alsace	*Very full bodied on the nose whilst the palate has cooked earthy fruits like apples and pears.*	**£14.80**	JNW ABY VLW WRC	(S)
PINOT GRIS VIEILLES VIGNES 1996, DOMAINE ZIND HUMBRECHT Alsace	*Pale gold colour with peach and gooseberry aromas, honeyed, oily texture, crisp acidity and a good finish.*	**£14.90**	JNW ABY VLW WRC	(S)
GEWÜRZTRAMINER KESSLER GRAND CRU 1994, DOMAINES SCHLUMBERGER Alsace	*A pronounced aromatic nose with crisp acidity, sappy fruit flavours and a spicy aftertaste.*	**£14.90**	MFS JNW MMD POR DBY TPE	(B)
RIESLING KITTERLE GRAND CRU 1993, DOMAINES SCHLUMBERGER Alsace	*Rich fruit with slate and lime feel with ripe overtones of lingering honeyed acidity.*	**£15.50**	MFS JNW SEL NIC MMD POR DBY	(S)
DOMAINE ALBERT MANN TOKAY PINOT GRIS GRAND CRU 1995, M. & J. BARTHELMÉ Alsace	*Complex aromatic peachy aromas develop into rich tropical fruit on the palate and an evolving length.*	**£15.60**	L&W NYW	(S)
GEWURZTRAMINER HENGST GRAND CRU 1996, DOMAINE ZIND HUMBRECHT Alsace	*A richly aromatic nose leads onto a rich palate with pronounced fruit flavours and acidity.*	**£16.80**	ABY VLW BUP	(B)
GEWURTZTRAMINER HENGST GRAND CRU 1992, JOS. MEYER & FILS Alsace	*Distinctive peach aromas followed by light and subtle fruit and a big burst of acidity.*	**£18.00**	A&N	(B)
RIESLING CUVÉE ST. CATHERINE 1995, DOMAINE WEINBACH-FALLER Alsace	*Exceptional wine with classic mineral floral notes, a lovely steely backbone and long finish.*	**£22.50**	J&B NYW	(S)

Tokay Pinot Gris Cuvée St Catherine 1996, Domaine Weinbach-Faller Alsace	*Vegetal characters with lots of asparagus, Lovely weight of fruit with good acidity, some sulphur.*	£23.50	J&B	(B)
Gewurztraminer Altenbourg Cuvée Laurence 1996, Dom. Weinbach-Faller Alsace	*A deep golden colour. Floral and spicy overtones, rich and elegant juicy fruit flavours with fresh acidity.*	£24.00	J&B NYW	(G)
Gewurztraminer Goldert Grand Cru 1996, Domaine Zind Humbrecht Alsace	*A slightly herbal nose with delicate spices. Excellent fruit and acid balance with a lingering finish.*	£24.90	JNW ABY VLW	(S)

FRANCE • ALSACE • SWEET

Gewurztram. Heimbourg Vendanges Tardive '96, Domaine Zind Humbrecht Alsace	*Intense ripe honeyed soft fruits on a sugared nose followed by a really weighty sweet palate.*	£24.40	JNW ABY	(G) TROPHY WINE
Clos des Capucins Riesling Cuvée d'Or Q. de Grains '91, Dom Weinbach-Faller Alsace	*Warm golden colour gives rise to raisins with a hint of tar. The lighter touch.*	£30.00	J&B	(B)
Riesling Grand Cru Vendanges Tardive '95, Domaine Zind Humbrecht Alsace	*Tight zesty zingy citrus fruit aromas with a fuller body and crisp clean acidity, and good length.*	£31.30	JNW ABY VLW	(B)
Pinot Gris Clos Jebsal SGN 1995, Domaine Zind Humbrecht Alsace	*Oak makes a guest appearance in this wine that hosts a destined match between sweet and sharp sensations.*	£47.30	JNW ABY VLW	(S)

PINOT GRIS HEIMBOURG SGN 1995, DOMAINE ZIND HUMBRECHT Alsace	*Tasters were impressed by rich lychee flavours and a savoury sweetness of lemon and lime jelly.*	**£71.80**	JNW ABY VLW	**B**

FRANCE • ALSACE • SPARKLING

CRÉMANT D'ALSACE CUVÉE PRESTIGE NV, RENE MURE Alsace	*This pale yellow wine has a grapey nose, backed up by a forward but subtle aftertaste of citrus fruit.*	**£9.50**	NIC	**B**
CRÉMANT D'ALSACE MAMBOURG CUVÉE DYNASTIE BRUT 1993, PIERRE SPARR Alsace	*A delightful wine graced with floral hints and an oiliness that backs its full bodied fruit.*	**£10.50**	SGL	**S**
CRÉMANT D'ALSACE TOKAY PINOT GRIS MAMBOURG BRUT 1993, PIERRE SPARR Alsace	*Shows persistent bubbles, complete in the mouth with rounded, floral flavours. Very drinkable. An elegant soft finish.*	**£10.50**	SGL	**S**

FRANCE • BEAUJOLAIS • RED

BEAUJOLAIS VILLAGES DOMAINE DE BACARRA 1996, PHILIPPE BONHOMME Beaujolais	*Chewy banana toffee nose ushers in a rich, honeyed, apple fruit base with great mouthfeel and length.*	**£5.40**	ABY	**B**
BROUILLY DOMAINE J. LOUGE 1997, EVENTAIL Beaujolais	*Fresh juicy cherries with low soft tannins and a quite austere finish.*	**£6.00**	GRT CWE WOC ESL	**S**

JULIÉNAS LES FOUILLOUSES 1997, EVENTAIL Beaujolais	*Perfumed fruit on the nose. The palate is jammy with some spice and herbal character.*	£6.00	VWE	(S)
MORGON CAVE BOCABARTEILLE 1997, E. LORON Beaujolais	*Raspberry jam fruit but nice and firm as well, tasters were impressed by this high class wine.*	£6.30	UNS	(S)
MORGON LES VERSAUDS 1996, DOMAINE PERRACHON Beaujolais	*Hints of violets and ripe bananas on a medium-weight succulent palate.*	£6.90	CPW	(B)
MORGON, DOMAINE LE TERRAIN ROUGE 1997, EVENTAIL Beaujolais	*An attractive fruity wine with soft berry fruits and warm strawberries on its excellent palate.*	£7.00	VWE	(S)
MORGON 1997, GEORGES DUBOEUF Beaujolais	*Vibrant cherry colour with a touch of plummy redcurrants sweet light tannins and good finish.*	£7.10	BWC MTL GDS MWW UNS	(S)
MALT HOUSE VINTNERS FLEURIE HENRI LA FONTAINE 1997, FAYE & CIE Beaujolais	*A fruity nose with soft jammy tannins, light acidity and a finish of lush red fruits.*	£7.30	MHV	(B)
MORGON LE CLACHET 1997, EVENTAIL Beaujolais	*Full bodied with rich juicy strawberry fruit. Silky on the palate with an enticing finish.*	£7.50	SHJ TPE CHH EPO	(S)
FLEURIE 1997, GEORGES DUBOEUF Beaujolais	*Deliciously juicy with light berry fruit, on a palate of seductive warm fruits.*	£8.30	Widely Available	(B)

MOULIN À VENT 1996, JACKY JANODET Burgundy	*Soft red fruits to the fore of this cherry wine. A gentle quaffing palate with balancing acidity.*	£8.80	DIR WIN AMW	B
FLEURIE DOMAINE VERT PRÉ 1996, PAUL BEAUDET Beaujolais	*Attractive cherries on the nose give rise to a fresh palate of crushed red fruit.*	£9.00	SGL NAD	B
MOULIN À VENT 1996, MAISON LOUIS JADOT Beaujolais	*Tasters enjoyed the rich fruit on this wine backed by perfumed elegance on a fine palate.*	£9.00	HOU NEI DBY TOS WTS	B

FRANCE • BORDEAUX • RED

MERLOT DE JACQUES ET FRANÇOIS LURTON 1996, J & F LURTON Bordeaux	*Ripe aromas of fresh blackcurrants with nuances of new oak and mint are reflected on the smooth palate.*	£4.80	JNW FUL THS WRC BUP	B
CHÂTEAU DU GRISON 1995, CHÂTEAU DU GRISON Bordeaux	*Rich aromas of dried fruits with nuances of creamy mint carry over onto the soft palate.*	£5.00	SAF	B
CO-OP PRESTIGE MÉDOC 1995, PRODUCTA Bordeaux	*Dry, tart aromas of fresh raspberries and redcurrants are reflected on the slightly green palate.*	£5.00	CRS	B
TESCO VINTAGE CLARET 1996, YVON MAU Bordeaux	*Tarry and herbaceous elements to a raspberry nose before a balanced blackcurrant palate with good length.*	£5.00	TOS	B

FRANCE • BORDEAUX • RED

MALT HOUSE VINTNERS MÉDOC 1997, LES CAVES ST GERMAIN Bordeaux	*Delicate aromas and flavours of ripe cassis and cigar box notes carry over onto the brisk palate.*	**£5.40**	MHV	Ⓑ
SAFEWAY'S OAK AGED MÉDOC 1996, VINYRAMA Bordeaux	*Creamy oak dominates the nose and palate of this fruity cassis wine with a soft finish.*	**£5.80**	SAF	Ⓑ
YVON MAU MAUREGARD BORDEAUX 1997, YVON MAU Bordeaux	*All that is good in this type of wine, brambly cassis fruit with lightish warm tannins.*	**£6.00**	YVM	Ⓑ
YVON MAU SAINT-ÉMILION 1996, YVON MAU Bordeaux	*A good generic wine with smooth supple tannins and rich juicy fruit and pleasing acidity.*	**£6.00**	WWI	Ⓑ
CHÂTEAU DE LA GARDE 1995, CHÂTEAU DE LA GARDE Bordeaux	*Some signs of age on this wine. Full of ripe fruit flavours with oak and tobacco notes.*	**£6.50**	NIC	Ⓑ
CHÂTEAU SUAU OAK AGED CLARET 1995, CHÂTEAU SUAU Bordeaux	*Rich aromas of black fruits carry over onto a full-bodied palate with oaky overtones.*	**£7.00**	THS WRC BUP	Ⓑ
CHÂTEAU LANGOIRAN PREMIÈRES CÔTES DE BORDEAUX 1995, CHÂTEAU LANGOIRAN Bordeaux	*Really good flavours of cassis and blackberry with pleasing lean tannins and soft acidity.*	**£7.70**	THS WRC BUP	Ⓑ
BARON PHILIPPE DE ROTHSCHILD MÉDOC 1995, BARON PHILIPPE DE ROTHSCHILD Bordeaux	*A mature juicy, mulberry and currant nose carries over onto the attractively structured palate.*	**£8.00**	NIC HOU VIL FEN DAB CWL	Ⓑ

CHÂTEAU BROWN LA MARTINE BORDEAUX SUPÉRIEUR 1995, COMPAGNIE MÈDOCAINE Bordeaux	*Restrained yet subtle aromas of spicy black fruits are followed by rich cassis and cream flavours.*	£8.60	ABY	**B**
CHÂTEAU D'AIGUILHE CÔTES DE CASTILLON 1993, RAVENTOS I BLANC Bordeaux	*Tasters found this quite light, but not thin and were enamoured by its vanillan character.*	£9.00	THS WRC BUP	**B**
CHÂTEAU D' AIGUILHE CÔTES DE CASTILLON 1995, RAVENTOS I BLANC Bordeaux	*Ripe aromas and flavours of sweet cassis and creamy oak with a soft finish to the palate.*	£9.00	WAW	**B**
RESERVE SPÉCIALE MEDOC 1995, DOMAINES BARON PHILIPPE DE ROTHSCHILD Bordeaux	*The lovely oaky flavours enhanced the obvious quality of this pleasing blackcurrant dominated wine.*	£9.50	NIC	**B**
BARTON & GUESTIER ST JULIEN TRADITION 1996, BARTON & GUESTIER Bordeaux	*Plummy nose with hints of cigar box leads onto a sweet cassis palate with soft oak nuances.*	£10.00	ODD SEA	**S**
BARTON & GUESTIER MARGAUX TRADITION 1996, BARTON & GUESTIER Bordeaux	*Blackcurrant and vanilla aromas on the nose with black fruits and spice notes on an earthy palate.*	£10.00	CWS ODD SEA CST	**B**
CHÂTEAU HAUT BAGES MONPELOU CRU BOURGEOIS 1994, BORIE MANOUX Bordeaux	*Fresh, herbal aromas on the black fruit bouquet with a delicate palate of soft fruits.*	£10.00	CDT FUL	**B**
CHÂTEAU HAUT SELVE MERLOT 1996, S. A. DU CHÂTEAU HAUT SELVE Bordeaux	*Deep aromas reminiscent of cough medicine lead to a minty palate with ripe currant flavours.*	£10.00	HDL VIW	**B**

CHÂTEAU LE CHARMAIL CRU BOURGEOIS 1995, ROGER SEZE Bordeaux	*This wine has a dry earthy style with black fruits and spice notes on a particularly attractive palate.*	£10.00	L&W	**B**
CHÂTEAU MAGNOL CRU BOURGEOIS 1995, CHÂTEAU MAGNOL Bordeaux	*Slightly jammy aromas of blackcurrant are reflected on the soft palate with hints of new oak.*	£10.00	ODD CLA SEA	**B**
CHÂTEAU LA CLARIÈRE - LAITHWAITE 1996, CHÂTEAU LA CLARIÈRE - LAITHWAITE Bordeaux	*Brambly fruit aromas with new oak nuances and jammy, blackcurrant fruit flavours with drying tannins.*	£10.20	BDR	**B**
CHÂTEAU PATACHE D'AUX CRU BOURGEOIS 1995, S.A. DU CHÂTEAU PATACHE D'AUX Bordeaux	*Raspberry aromas with hints of pencil shavings followed by herbaceous elements to the ripe red fruit flavoured palate.*	£10.30	NIC WCS WIN CPW POR	**B**
DOMAINE DE MARTIALIS 1994, MARTIALIS Bordeaux	*Rich oaky nose with ripe plum aromas leads to a soft blackcurrant and mint flavoured palate.*	£11.50	WRC	**B**
CHÂTEAU CORBIN GRAND CRU CLASSÉ 1995, CHÂTEAU CORBIN Bordeaux	*Complex blackberry aromas are followed by soft plum fruit flavours on a balanced palate.*	£11.80	NIC HOT MWW BDR FUL	**B**
CHÂTEAU CANUET 1995, COMPAGNIE MÈDOCAINE Bordeaux	*Rich aromas of blackcurrants with nuances of cedar, tobacco and spice are reflected on the structured palate.*	£12.00	ODD ABY	**B**
CHÂTEAU LA FLEUR CRAVIGNAC, ST ÉMILION 1994, CHÂTEAU LA FLEUR CRAVIGNAC Bordeaux	*Tasters enjoyed the full nose and palate of greenish berry fruits and delicate tannins.*	£12.00	BDR	**B**

CHÂTEAU FRANCK PHÉLAN 1995, SOCIETE DU CHÂTEAU PHÉLAN SÉGUR & GARDINIER ET FILS Bordeaux	*Ripe open aromas of soft black fruits are followed by blackcurrant fruit on the firm palate.*	£13.00	NIC	(B)
CHÂTEAU MALESCASSE CRU BOURGEOIS 1994, CHÂTEAU MALESCASSE Bordeaux	*Complex flavours of bitter cherries and raspberries on the nose and palate, with hints of cedary fruit.*	£13.00	COK	(B)
CHÂTEAU HAUT-BEAU-SÉJOUR CRU BOURGEOIS 1995, SOCIÉTÉ CIVILE LA SALLE ST ESTÈPHE Bordeaux	*A rich style of Bordeaux with generous fruit and strong flavours of cassis and damsons.*	£13.70	WIN MMD	(B)
CHÂTEAU BATAILLEY GRAND CRU CLASSÉ 1994, BORIE MANOUX Bordeaux	*Intense aromas of black fruits, spice and chocolate with rich flavours carrying over onto the smooth palate.*	£17.00	DIR WCS CDT	(S)
CHÂTEAU DE PEZ CRU BOURGEOIS 1995, SOCIÉTÉ CIVILE LA SALLE SAINT ESTÈPHE Bordeaux	*A superb wine with tobacco and cigar box notes on its silky palate with drying tannins.*	£17.70	MFS JNW MMD WRC BUP	(S)
CHÂTEAU MEYNEY CRU BOURGEOIS 1994, DOMAINES CORDIER Bordeaux	*Creamy vanilla with black fruit aromas and flavours on this concentrated and pleasant wine.*	£18.70	COK MMD WRC BUP	(B)
CHÂTEAU VILLEMAURINE GRAND CRU CLASSÉ 1995, ROBERT GIRAUD Bordeaux	*Light, delicate aromas of forest fruits and cedar wood with a medium palate of ripe cassis and vanilla.*	£19.50	HOH	(B)
CLOS DU MARQUIS 1994, S.C. DU CHÂTEAU LÉOVILLE-LAS-CASES Bordeaux	*Silky tobacco, cassis notes on a juicy oak dominated palate with lean tannins and lively acidity.*	£19.90	WCR JNW L&W RDS DBY NIC BDR	(S)

CHÂTEAU D'ARMAILHAC GRAND CRU CLASSÉ 1993, BARON PHILIPPE DE ROTHSCHILD Bordeaux	*This wine has a lovely cedary dustiness to its elegant palate of dark berry fruits.*	£20.20	BNK GDS TPE PAR LUC BDR	**B**
CHÂTEAU HAUT MARBUZET CRU BOURGEOIS 1996, HENRI DUBOSQ Bordeaux	*Blackberry nose, notes of cedar wood and menthol developing rich forest fruits on the approachable palate.*	£21.80	WCR JNW MTL COK WCS POR VWE HVW	**S**
CHÂTEAU CLERC MILON GRAND CRU CLASSÉ 1993, BARON PHILIPPE DE ROTHSCHILD Bordeaux	*Intense tobacco aromas with drying ripe sporty, spices and soft plummy cassis flavours on a glossy palate.*	£25.30	HOU DBY TPE EPO MTL BDR WRC	**S**
CHÂTEAU BEAUSÉJOUR GRAND CRU CLASSÉ 1994, DUFFAU LAGAROSSE Bordeaux	*A warm nose, classic blackberry and cedar with ripe fruit, toasty oak and grippy tannins.*	£30.90	DBY J&B	**B**
CHÂTEAU TROPLONG MONDOT GRAND CRU CLASSÉ 1993, GFA VALETTE Bordeaux	*Stalky blackcurrant fruit aromas on the nose and palate of this soft, easy drinking wine.*	£44.50	NIC L&W	**B**
CHÂTEAU PICHON COMTESSE DE LALANDE GRAND CRU CLASSÉ 1990, CHÂTEAU PICHON S.C. Bordeaux	*Intense black inky fruit with super structure and length. Lifted tannins and cedary cassis fruit.*	£74.50	JNW RES	**S**
CHÂTEAU MARGAUX 1993 GRAND CRU CLASSÉ, S.C.A. CHÂTEAU MARGAUX Bordeaux	*Fabulous strong tarry fruit with intense cinnamon and spice on an opulent blackberry palate.*	£180.00	NIC ABY	**G**

Pinpoint who sells the wine you wish to buy by turning to the stockist codes. If you know the name of the wine you want to buy, use the alphabetical index. If the price is your motivation, refer to the invaluable price guide index; red and white wines under £5, sparkling wines under £12 and Champagne under £16. Happy hunting!

FRANCE • BORDEAUX • WHITE

RIVERS MEET SAUVIGNON BLANC SÉMILLION 1997, GINESTET Bordeaux	*Mineral and smoky aromas. Underlying buttery, yeasty bouquet. Intense fruit and fresh lean acidity to match.*	£4.00	ODD SMF	(G)
MERCHANTS BAY SAUVIGNON BLANC SÉMILLON 1997, GINESTET Bordeaux	*Crisp quite green wine but with a lovely peachy ripeness in the finish which lasts and lasts.*	£4.00	WTS	(B)
YVON MAU GRAVES BLANC 1997, YVON MAU Bordeaux	*A well-structured wine with gooseberry fruit skilfully blended with harmonious acidity and medium length.*	£5.00	NEI FUL	(B)
CHÂTEAU PETIT-MOULIN 1997, VIGNOBLES SIGNE Bordeaux	*Cracking wine with ripe crushed soft fruit, a lovely crunchy nut acidity and spectacular finish.*	£5.80	DLA THS CHH WRC BUP	(G)
CHÂTEAU DU MAGNEAU 1997, CHÂTEAU DU MAGNEAU Bordeaux	*Violet and apricot aromas. A delicious creamy texture lifted by lime fruit followed by a long and alcoholic finish.*	£6.00	SAF	(S)
CHÂTEAU CARSIN CUVÉE PRESTIGE 1995, MANDY JONES Bordeaux	*Lifted vanillin oak and lemon aromas, a delicate, herbaceous palate and a fresh, crisp finish.*	£7.50	WTS	(B)
CHÂTEAU COUCHEROY RESERVE 1996, VIGNOBLES ANDRÉ LURTON Bordeaux	*A delicate and soft wine with green hints and restrained but balanced acidity to finish.*	£9.00	JNW	(B)

FRANCE • BORDEAUX • SWEET

CHÂTEAU DE LE CHARTREUSE 1994, FACCHETI RICARD Bordeaux	*Lemon is an outstanding contender in this wine shining through all the way to the finishing line.*	£9.80	WTS	(B)
CHÂTEAU DE CERONS 1989, JEAN PERROMAT Bordeaux	*A herbaceous nose precedes soft round fruit on the palate. The marriage of the two works well.*	£10.00	NIC	(B)
CHÂTEAU GRINOU 1996, GUY & CATHERINE CUISSET Bordeaux	*Wearing a golden robe, figs and apricots express themselves explicitly throughout this wine.*	£13.00	ALZ	(B)
CHÂTEAU DU VIEUX MOULIN CAZEAUX 1990, S. PERROMAT DAUNE Bordeaux	*A restrained lemon peel nose, candy floss sweetness with a touch of honey tempered by fresh citrus acidity.*	£16.30	NIC	(B)
CHÂTEAU LAFAURIE-PEYRAGUEY PREMIER GRAND CRU CLASSÉ '94, DOMAINES CORDIER Bordeaux	*Luscious rich honey broken up by a refreshing acidity on this attractive wine.*	£26.50	MMD DBY	(B)
CRU BARREJATS 1991, PHILLIPPE ANDURAND & MIREILLE DARET Bordeaux	*A concentrated orange nose with citrus fruit on the palate. A well-structured and attractive sweet wine.*	£30.00	J&B JOB	(S)
CHÂTEAU SIGALAS RABAUD PREMIER GRAND CRU CLASSÉ 1995, CHÂTEAU SIGALAS RABAUD Bordeaux	*This wine has a slight vegetal nose and lean palate with body and balance to match.*	£38.00	MMD	(B)

FRANCE • BURGUNDY • RED

MALT HOUSE VINTNERS MÂCON ROUGE SUP. HENRI LA FONTAINE 1997, FAYE & CIE Burgundy	*Light flavours of ripe cherries, strawberries and raspberries. A soft, smoothly balanced finish.*	£4.80	BNK MHV	(B)
BOURGOGNE ROUGE OAK AGED 1996, LOUIS CHEVALLIER Burgundy	*Ripe rich fruit with a touch of savoury character on the nose. Followed by a full fruit palate.*	£5.00	MAC	(B)
TESCO RED BURGUNDY 1997, MAISON VAUCHER Burgundy	*Aromatic fruit on the nose with structured well-defined fruit on the palate, moderate acidity.*	£5.50	TOS	(B)
DOMAINE PONT BOURGOGNE PINOT NOIR 1996, COTTIN FRÈRES Burgundy	*Fruits of the forest with toasty oak, round jammy fruit with slightly chalky tannins.*	£6.00	ASD	(B)
CÔTES DE NUITS VILLAGES 1994, JEAN PETITOT Burgundy	*Delicate, slightly jammy on the nose with soft flavoursome fruit and firm tannins, moderate acidity.*	£7.00	MVG	(B)
DOMAINE HAUTE CÔTES DES NUITS 1997, DOMAINE BERTAGNA EVA & MARK SIDDLE Burgundy	*Primary fruit characters with earthy tones on the nose, big rich fruit on the palate.*	£7.00	RSS JSM	(B)
HAUTES CÔTES DE NUITS VIEILLES VIGNES 1996, YVES CHALEY Burgundy	*Barny characters with primary fruit on the nose. Youthful fresh summer fruit with some good acidity.*	£7.00	PEC	(B)

MARANGES PREMIER CRU 1995, JOSEPH DROUHIN Burgundy	*Cherries and vanilla oak characters on the nose, excellent fruit with good structure and balance.*	£7.70	MGN NEI WCR	B
DOMAINE PILLOT MERCUREY 1996, JEAN-MICHEL & LAURENT PILLOT Burgundy	*Smoky oak with summer berry characters on the nose, delicate fruit flavours with integrated oak.*	£9.00	3DW	B
DOMAINE PILLOT, MERCUREY EN SAZENAY PREMIER CRU 1995, J. M. & L. PILLOT Burgundy	*Ruby red colour, meaty fruit with gamey characters and youthful cherry fruit on the palate.*	£9.30	3DW	G
DOMAINE CHEVROT, MARANGES LE BOIS DE CLEMENTINE F 1996, F. & C. CHEVROT Burgundy	*Intense red colour, rich berry fruit with meaty, leathery characters on the nose, palate has concentrated fruit.*	£9.30	3DW	S
RULLY ROUGE 1996, JOSEPH DROUHIN Burgundy	*Beetroot and fresh berry fruit on the nose with a good primary fruit palate, and balanced tannins.*	£9.50	WCR JNW MGN ODD	B
RULLY ROUGE 1995, MAISON LOUIS JADOT Burgundy	*Ripe fruit aromas with full-bodied fruit on the palate well-balanced and strong finish.*	£9.70	WCR HOU NEI FUL	B
FIXIN CLOS MARION 1996, DOMAINE FOUGERAY-BEAUCLAIR Burgundy	*Pale ruby colour, restrained fruit on the nose with elegant fresh fruit on the palate.*	£10.00	HWB	B
FIXIN PREMIER CRU 1995, MAISON LOUIS JADOT Burgundy	*Plums and jammy characters on the nose. Ripe full fruit balanced with good tannic structure.*	£10.00	NEI THR WRC BUP	B

SAVIGNY LES PEUILLETS PREMIER CRU 1993, CHÂTEAU DE MEURSAULT Burgundy	*Summer fruit with meaty characters on the nose, palate is complex with medium bodied fruit.*	£10.00	SAF	B
SOMERFIELD NUITS ST GEORGES 1996, GEORGES DESIRE Burgundy	*Primary fruit with hints of vegetal characters on the nose, moderate bodied primary fruit palate.*	£10.00	SMF	B
FIXIN 1995, MAISON JAFFELIN Burgundy	*Slightly vegetal barnyard and leathery characters on the nose with integrated firm tannins and balanced acidity.*	£10.50	WES HOH MWW AVB	S
MERCUREY CLOS L'EVÈQUE PREMIER CRU 1996, F. CHAUVENET Burgundy	*Plums, strawberries and a hint of vegetal character on the nose. Intense fruit and powerfully structured palate.*	£11.00	EHL	S
CÔTE DE BEAUNE 1995, JOSEPH DROUHIN Burgundy	*Ripe soft fruits on the nose with excellent strawberry fruit on the palate and integrated tannins.*	£11.20	FSW JNW MGN NEI ODD	B
BEAUNE LES AVAUX, DOMAINE JACOB PREMIER CRU 1996, JEAN-MICHEL JACOB Burgundy	*Soft ripe fruit on the nose with elegant summer fruit palate. Fine tannins and good length.*	£11.90	3DW	B
CHÂTEAU PHILIPPE LE HARDI BEAUNE PREMIER CRU 1996, GÉRARD FAGNONI Burgundy	*Upfront fruit with minty tones on the nose, palate has moderate complexity balance and acidity.*	£12.50	ABY	B
BEAUNE LES EPENOTTES PREMIER CRU 1995, DOMAINE PARENT Burgundy	*Brick red colour, slightly stalky characters on the nose. Excellent structure with ripe fruit and firm tannins.*	£13.00	SAF	S

FRANCE • BURGUNDY • RED

ALOXE CORTON 1996, CHÂTEAU DE SANTENAY Burgundy	*Spicy, peppery characters on the nose with a fruit dominated palate good structure and crisp acidity.*	£13.00	BDR	(B)
CHÂTEAU PHILIPPE LE HARDI POMMARD 1996, GÉRARD FAGNONI Burgundy	*Primary fruit characters on the nose with strawberries and loads of tannin to give structure.*	£13.80	ABY	(B)
MARANGES 1996, DOMAINE CHANSON PÈRE ET FILS Burgundy	*Hints of plum and soft red fruits on this full-bodied yet delicate wine.*	£14.00	NEI	(B)
CHOREY-LES-BEAUNE 1995, DOMAINE MAILLARD PERE & FILS Burgundy	*Strawberry, raspberry perfumed aroma with ripe fresh fruit palate. Firm tannins and good length.*	£14.50	NIC	(B)
BEAUNE PREMIER CRU LES GREVES 1992, PASCAL MAILLARD Burgundy	*Dark berry fruit with smoky bacon characters on the nose, full palate of complex fruit with gamey tones.*	£15.00	WTS	(S)
GEVREY CHAMBERTIN 1994, LES CAVES DES HAUTES-CÔTES Burgundy	*Ruby red with cherries on the nose, delicious balanced fruit with integrated fine tannins. A long finish.*	£15.50	COK SPR CWI	(S)
DOMAINE VOUGEOT VILLAGES CLOS BERTAGNA 1996, DOMAINE BERTAGNA E. & M. SIDDLE Burgundy	*Intense red fruits on the nose with berries on the palate. Grippy tannins and complexity.*	£16.00	RSS WEP	(B)
BEAUNE CLOS DES FEUES PREMIER CRU 1996, DOMAINE CHANSON PÈRE ET FILS Burgundy	*Gamey notes on a nose of ripe strawberries with layered tannins on a juicy finish.*	£16.40	CVR	(B)

RED • BURGUNDY • FRANCE

SAVIGNY LA DOMINODE PREMIER CRU 1994, DOMAINE BRUNO CLAIR Burgundy	*Fresh cherries and earthy characters on the nose with fleshy primary fruit and moderate acidity.*	**£18.50**	J&B	(B)
NUITS ST GEORGES LES VAUCRAINS PREMIER CRU 1992, DOMAINE ROBERT CHEVILLON Burgundy	*Ripe cherry fruit with a touch of mint. Palate is full-bodied with good length and some tannin.*	**£18.70**	MIS J&B	(B)
GEVREY CHAMBERTIN CAZETIERS PREMIER CRU 1989, BERNARD VALLET Burgundy	*Pale brick red colour, rich fruit aromas with meaty characters on the nose, smooth palate with full-bodied fruit.*	**£23.70**	HOU DBY	(S)
NUITS ST. GEORGES CLOS DES FORÊTS PREMIER CRU 1995, DOMAINE DE L'ARLOT Burgundy	*Rich ripe cherry characters on the nose, intense berry fruit on the palate. Fine tannin structure.*	**£24.20**	HOT ABY	(S)
NUIT ST GEORGES LES GRANDES VIGNES 1995, DOMAINE P & M RION Burgundy	*Rich spicy chocolate characters on the nose. Full bodied palate of sweet fruit with good tannin structure.*	**£24.30**	SEL M&V EBA	(S)
GEVREY CHAMBERTIN CLOS DES VAROILLES PREMIER CRU 1996, DOMAINE DES VAROILLES Burgundy	*Cherries, strawberries and raspberries on the nose. Mouth-watering fruit palate with slightly hard tannins.*	**£26.80**	VIL	(B)
CORTON-GRÈVES GRAND CRU 1995, MAISON LOUIS JADOT Burgundy	*Powerful fruit aromas mingled with mint. Weighty middle palate with excellent tannin structure and length.*	**£27.50**	WTS	(B)
CHARMES CHAMBERTIN GRAND CRU 1989, BERNARD VALLET Burgundy	*Wild berries on the nose with raspberries and strawberries on the palate and a smooth velvety finish.*	**£29.90**	MFS DBY BOO	(S)

FRANCE • BURGUNDY • RED & WHITE

VOSNE ROMANÉE LES CHAUMES 1995, DOMAINE P & M RION Burgundy	*Smoky oak and cherry fruit characters on the nose, complex fruit on the palate and good length.*	£30.00	M&V	**S**
GEVREY CHAMBERTIN CAZETIERS PREMIER CRU 1988, BERNARD VALLET Burgundy	*Rich berry fruit with leathery notes; palate has good structure with integrated firm fine tannins.*	£32.00	BPW	**B**
CORTON CLOS DE CORTONS GRAND CRU 1995, J FAIVELEY Burgundy	*Ruby red colour, ripe strawberries and cherries on the nose with berry fruit on the palate.*	£44.50	HRF DIR MMD POR	**S**
BONNES MARES GRAND CRU 1996, DOMAINE FOUGERAY-BEAUCLAIR Burgundy	*Rich spicy fruit with hints of liquorice on the nose. Dense fruit tightly packed on the palate.*	£45.00	EPO	**G**

FRANCE • BURGUNDY • WHITE

BOURGOGNE BLANC 1997, VAUCHER PÈRE ET FILS Burgundy	*Rich aromas of buttered apples lead onto a malic palate of crisp Granny Smith's and lime.*	£5.50	T&T CWS	**B**
ANDRÉ SIMON MÂCON LUGNY 1996, ALBERT BICHOT Burgundy	*Delicate chalky, mineral notes with cool melon flavours and a crisp zesty finish that cleans the palate.*	£6.00	MTL WRT	**B**
BOURGOGNE CHARDONNAY TÊTE DE CUVÉE 1996, DOMAINE LAROCHE Burgundy	*Honeydew melons dominate the nose and palate of this crisply tart wine.*	£6.40	DIR POR JSM THS WRC	**B**

BOURGOGNE CHARDONNAY SUR SOL JURASSIQUE 1996, JEAN-MARC BROCARD Burgundy	*Chalky, mineral characters on the dry nose with lemon, lime and grapefruit flavours on the balanced palate.*	**£7.00**	JBF MTR ODD	(B)
BOURGOGNE CHARDONNAY SUR SOL PORTLANDIEN 1996, JEAN-MARC BROCARD Burgundy	*Rich mineral aromas of chalk and slate carry over onto the lean palate of underripe lemons and limes.*	**£7.50**	JBF	(B)
CHABLIS LES VIGNERONS DE CHABLIS 1996, LA CHABLISIENNE Burgundy	*Light, aromatic floral nose with a crisply balanced, spicy palate of mixed citrus fruits.*	**£7.60**	WCR CWS MWW SMF VLW	(B) WINE OF THE YEAR
CHABLIS DOMAINE DES MANANTS 1996, JEAN-MARC BROCARD Burgundy	*A restrained nose with fruit and mineral character. Medium length but balanced in style and finish.*	**£8.10**	JBF G&M ADN HOT SHJ POR	(B)
ST VÉRAN LES DEUX ROCHES 1996, DOMAINE LES DEUX ROCHES Burgundy	*A dry minerally palate with citrus fruit overtones reflects the aromas on this attractive wine.*	**£8.10**	JNW GRT DBY WRC FUL ASD THS BUP	(B)
CHABLIS CHALMEAU CÔTE DE L'ETANG 1996, FRANCK CHALMEAU Burgundy	*A leesy richness to a tart palate of honeydew melon and limes with a crisp, clean finish.*	**£8.30**	3DW	(B)
ST VÉRAN 1995, FAIVELEY Burgundy	*Fruity, biscuity nose with lovely complex melon flavours and a lingering finish.*	**£8.30**	DIR WIN MMD	(B)
BOURGOGNE CHARDONNAY SUR SOL KIMMERIDGIEN 1996, JEAN-MARC BROCARD Burgundy	*A smoky, peachy nose with chalky notes is followed by a honeyed melon palate with a crisp finish.*	**£8.60**	MTR	(B)

CHÂTEAU DE MALIGNY CHABLIS VIEILLES VIGNES 1996, JEAN DURUP Burgundy	*Crisp, fruity nose with sweet peardrop overtones. Rich palate with zesty lime, ruby grapefruit and flinty, mineral notes.*	£8.90	ABY WRC BUP	(S)
CHABLIS CUVÉE LA CHABLISIENNE 1996, LA CHABLISIENNE Burgundy	*Crisp palate of lean melon and pineapple fruit with steely, flint and slate overtones.*	£9.00	WIN SGL NAD WSO SMF	(G)
BOURGOGNE ULTRA 35 CHARDONNAY 1996, DENIS PHILIBERT Burgundy	*Perfumed lime and citrus nose with light clean fresh fruit and slightly vegetal on palate.*	£9.00	FUL	(B)
CHABLIS DOMAINE DE CORBETON 1996, DOMAINE DE CORBETON Burgundy	*A clean rather austere nose with some zippy citric and melon flavours on the palate.*	£9.00	UNS	(B)
SAINT AUBIN CHÂTEAU PHILIPPE LE HARDI 1996, GÉRARD FAGNONI Burgundy	*Slightly confected with hints of marzipan, green apples mingled with sweet honey on the palate.*	£9.30	ABY	(B)
ST ROMAIN 1996, JOSEPH DROUHIN Burgundy	*Attractive apples and pears nose leads to an elegant, lean palate of melon and lime.*	£9.60	JNW MGN MWW WES	(B)
POUILLY FUISSÉ 1996, PAUL BOUTINOT Burgundy	*Polished wood and pastille sweet nose. Juicy fruit on the palate and sympathetic wood treatment.*	£9.80	NRW BUP COK WRC DBY AMW	(B)
CHABLIS PREMIER CRU 1995, LOUIS MOREAU Burgundy	*Sweet oak and grapefruit aromas carry over onto the vibrantly complex vanilla, white peach and citrus flavoured palate.*	£10.00	HOU WIM	(G)

WIN OF TH YEA

CHABLIS DOMAINE SAINT JULIEN PREMIER CRU BEAUREGARD 1997, JEAN-MARC BROCARD Chablis	*Green characters of lime and underripe redcurrants dominate this attractively balanced wine.*	£10.00	JBF WTS	(B)
POUILLY FUISSÉ DEPARDON 1997, EVENTAIL Burgundy	*A warm, vegetal nose leads onto a creamy lemon and lime mouth puckering finish.*	£10.00	HOL ESL	(B)
RULLY BLANC 1996, JOSEPH DROUHIN Burgundy	*A rich grapefruity nose with some floral notes leads to a similar palate and a crisp Granny Smith finish.*	£10.10	BEN JNW MGN ODD RTR LEA	(B)
CHABLIS DOMAINE LAURENT TRIBUT 1996, DOMAINE LAURENT TRIBUT Burgundy	*Clean citrus aromas with nuances of minerals and butter. The steely finish is quite refreshing.*	£10.20	LEA MIS J&B	(B)
CHABLIS CHEVALLIER 1996, LOUIS CHEVALLIER Burgundy	*Nutty, boneyed fruit aromas with a full, creamy luscious palate of mangos and peaches before a racy citrus finish.*	£10.30	BEN MAC	(S)
MALT HOUSE VINTNERS POUILLY FUISSÉ HENRI LA FONTAINE 1996, FAYE & CIE Burgundy	*Rich mineral flavours of chalk and slate with citrus overtones. Attractively austere nose of granite and tart fruit.*	£10.50	MHV	(S)
CHABLIS SAINT-MARTIN 1997, DOMAINE LAROCHE Burgundy	*A clean, fruity nose precedes an attractive citrus palate with a zappy finish.*	£10.50	DIR PFC THS WRC	(B)
LA COTE POUILLY FUISSÉ 1996, THIERRY & CORINNE DROUIN Burgundy	*Complex, flinty citrus aromas and flavours with a slightly green finish.*	£10.60	3DW	(S)

CHÂTEAU DE MALIGNY MONTÉE DE TONNERRE PREMIER CRU 1996, JEAN DURUP Burgundy	*Subtle mineral and citrus aromas with chalky characters to the light melon palate.*	**£10.80**	MIS ABY	B
CHABLIS VIEILLES VIGNES 1996, DANIEL DEFAIX Burgundy	*This is a zippy little number with subtle aromas and lean zingy citrus fruit characters.*	**£10.90**	SEL GON MIS CNL DBY BTH WRC BUP	B
CHABLIS LES VAILLONS PREMIER CRU 1996, DOMAINE SERVIN Burgundy	*Rich, buttery aromas with asparagus and lime characters precedes a concentrated melon palate.*	**£11.00**	TBC	S
CHABLIS MONTMAINS PREMIER CRU 1996, J. MOREAU & FILS Burgundy	*A richly complex nose of minerals, melon fruit and apricots with a creamy finish.*	**£11.00**	MTL HOU NEI	B
SAINT ROMAIN 1995, MAISON JAFFELIN Burgundy	*Crisp flavours of minerals and lemons with a mouthwatering finish of zesty lime.*	**£11.00**	AVB	B
CHÂTEAU DE MALIGNY VAU DE VEY PREMIER CRU 1996, JEAN DURUP Burgundy	*Delicate, floral and butter notes with a rich palate of pineapples and melons.*	**£11.20**	ABY	B
CHABLIS MONTMAIN PREMIER CRU 1997, DOMAINE PICO RACE Burgundy	*Fruity slightly aromatic aromas. Good herb and crisp dry citrus fruit with lovely long finish.*	**£11.40**	VIL DBY ENO	B
CHABLIS BEAUROY PREMIER CRU 1996, DOMAINE HAMELIN Burgundy	*Fresh creamy nose with honeyed aromas of ripe melons. Rounded palate full of clean grapefruit and lime flavours.*	**£12.10**	BEN MFS HOH VIL AVB	G

CHABLIS CHÂTEAU DE MALIGNY FOURCHAUME PREMIER CRU 1996, JEAN DURUP Burgundy	*A vegetal yet creamy nose precedes a buttery palate of chalky, minerally Granny Smith's apples.*	£12.10	MIS ABY THS WRC BUP	(B)
CHABLIS DOMAINE DES MANANT MONTMAINS PREMIER CRU 1996, JEAN-MARC BROCARD Chablis	*Peachy, lemon characters with hints of mineral influence on the nose and palate of this crisp wine.*	£12.20	JBF HOT SHJ ODD ADN	(B)
POUILLY FUISSÉ 1997, MAISON LOUIS JADOT Burgundy	*Toasty oak aromas with buttery almost creamy palate, lively fresh acid and good clean finish.*	£12.30	QWW HOU NEI TOS	(B)
MERCURY BLANC CLOS ROCHETTE 1996, BOURGOGNES FAIVELEY Burgundy	*This young wine needs time to develop; juvenile fruit bound in firm tannin and acid.*	£12.60	DIR FCA MMD FWL	(B)
DOMAINE DE LA BON GRAN MACON CLESSÉ 1996, JEAN THEVENET Burgundy	*Rich honey and coconut on the nose with plenty of rich ripe fruit, medium length.*	£13.00	Widely Available	(B)
PULIGNY-MONTRACHET 1996, JOSEPH DROUHIN Burgundy	*Clean apple and vanilla oak aromas, citrus fruit characters with very lively acidity and integrated oak balance.*	£16.10	WCR JNW MGN DBY	(S)
MEURSAULT 1996, COTTIN FRÈRES Burgundy	*Lovely tropical floral aromas, simple clean, slightly aromatic, fruit on the palate with moderate acidity.*	£18.00	BWL WTS FUL	(B)
CHABLIS MONTÉE DE TONNERRE PREMIER CRU 1996, DOMAINES VERGET Burgundy	*Rich, oaky nose with aromas of tropical fruits and a boneyed palate of melons, overripe pineapples and bananas.*	£19.60	L&W NYW	(G)

CHABLIS DOMAINE MOREAU LES CLOS GRAND CRU 1996, J. MOREAU ET FILS Burgundy	*Delicate aromas of yellow plums carry over onto the crisp palate of grapefruit and kumquats with a hint of vanilla.*	**£21.50**	MTL	**B**
CHASSAGNE MONTRACHET 1996, COTTIN FRÈRES Burgundy	*Apple spiced nose with creamy oak. Banana and custard on a palate cut by moderate acidity.*	**£21.50**	BWL FUL WTS	**B**
CHASSAGNE MONTRACHET PREMIER CRU 1995, MAISON LOUIS JADOT Burgundy	*Rich sweet toasty aromas, light fruit character finishing rich with a slighty hot acid bite.*	**£21.70**	NEI DBY THR BUP WRC	**B**
MEURSAULT 1993, DOMAINE DE CHÂTEAU DE MEURSAULT Burgundy	*Aromas of melon and creamy vanilla oak. The palate consists of lovely fleshy tropical fruit.*	**£23.20**	NRW HOU POR SAF VWC	**G**
PULIGNY MONTRACHET LES FOLATIÈRES PREMIER CRU 1995, GÉRARD CHAVY Burgundy	*Elegant fruit characters on the nose. The well-structured palate demonstrates fruit and acid complexity.*	**£23.60**	HRF BEN HOU CPW RDS WTS	**G**
NUITS ST. GEORGES PREMIER CRU 1996, DOMAINE DE L'ARLOT Burgundy	*Smoky vanilla oak aromas with delicate fruit mineral characters that finish with clean crisp acidity.*	**£27.70**	HRF HOT ABY	**B**
CHABLIS VAILLONS PREMIER CRU 1995, RAVENEAU Burgundy	*Mineral aromas of slatey chalk with nuances of lean melon fruit dominate the nose and palate.*	**£28.50**	BRI	**S**

TROPI WINI

Pinpoint who sells the wine you wish to buy by turning to the stockist codes. If you know the name of the wine you want to buy, use the alphabetical index. If the price is your motivation, refer to the invaluable price guide index; red and white wines under £5, sparkling wines under £12 and Champagne under £16. Happy hunting!

FRANCE • BURGUNDY • SPARKLING

CRÉMANT DE BOURGOGNE BRUT BLANC DE BLANCS PAUL DELANE NV, CAVES DE BAILLY Burgundy	*A pale colour with tip top mousse, clean flavours in the mouth and a strong finish.*	£7.30	T&T	B

FRANCE • CHAMPAGNE • WHITE

MALT HOUSE VINTNERS HOUSE CHAMPAGNE BRUT NV, F. BONNET Champagne	*Yeast autolysis integrated with soft supple floral style. Excellent persistence and a dry elegant finish.*	£11.00	MHV	B
CHAMPAGNE DEUTZ BRUT CLASSIC NV, DEUTZ Champagne	*Light toasty nose and fine mousse. Citrus, yeasty and nutty flavours harmonise around crisp acidity.*	£11.20	NIC NEI ODD BWC LNR PAG	S
CHAMPAGNE LE BRUN DE NEUVILLE CUVÉE SELECTION BRUT NV, LE BRUN DE NEUVILLE Champagne	*This pale yellow wine has a slightly nutty nose and toasty flavour. Good, well-balanced acidity.*	£12.00	WAW TRO	B
CHAMPAGNE DE TELMONT GRANDE RESERVE BRUT NV, DE TELMONT Champagne	*A rich gold colour, it shows finesse and style on the nose and in the mouth.*	£12.50	MWW	B
CHAMPAGNE LE BRUN DE NEUVILLE CUVÉE BLANC DE BLANCS BRUT NV, LE BRUN DE NEUVILLE Champagne	*Outstanding on the palate, well-balanced with a zesty finish of lime and grapefruit.*	£12.80	WAW TRO	S

WINE OF THE YEAR

SAFEWAY CHAMPAGNE ALBERT ETIENNE BRUT 1990, LANSON PÈRE ET FILS Champagne	*Lingering mousse with fresh biscuity nose. Palate filled with citrus fruit marinated in cream. A soft finish.*	£13.00	SAF	S
WAITROSE CHAMPAGNE BRUT NV, F. BONNET Champagne	*The tasters found a slightly appley, biscuity nose and palate leading to an elegant finish.*	£13.00	WTS	B
CHAMPAGNE A R LENOBLE GRAND CRU BLANC DE BLANCS BRUT NV, A. R. LENOBLE Champagne	*This young lively nose welcomes flavoursome grapefruit and gentle acidity onto the palate. Smashing bubbly!*	£14.00	JNW	B
CHAMPAGNE DRAPPIER DEMI-SEC NV, DRAPPIER Champagne	*Lovely, buttery nose indicates some bottle age. Subtle, sweet fruit flavours on the soft, nutty edged palate.*	£14.80	ABY	S
CHAMPAGNE DE CASTELLANE BRUT NV, DE CASTELLANE Champagne	*Pale gold with a buttery yeast nose, dry firm acid balanced out by citrus fruit.*	£15.00	POU NEI HZW BUD	B
CHAMPAGNE DEVAUX GRANDE RESERVE BRUT NV, DEVAUX Champagne	*A simple, fresh, fruity taste with wafting aromas of freshly baked bread. A long lingering finish.*	£15.10	WCR FSW MWW DBY VEX CER	S
CHAMPAGNE DRAPPIER CARTE D'OR BRUT NV, DRAPPIER Champagne	*Bread and yeast on the nose, fresh acid and fruit on the lengthy palate.*	£15.50	ABY DBY BUP THS WRC	S

Pinpoint who sells the wine you wish to buy by turning to the stockist codes. If you know the name of the wine you want to buy, use the alphabetical index. If the price is your motivation, refer to the invaluable price guide index; red and white wines under £5, sparkling wines under £12 and Champagne under £16. Happy hunting!

Wine	Notes	Price	Codes	
CHAMPAGNE RENAUDIN GRANDE RESERVE BRUT NV, R. RENAUDIN Champagne	*Dominated from start to finish by lemons. Soft citrus flavours are well-integrated with refreshing acidity.*	£15.50	VIL	(S)
CHARLES DE CAZANOVE BRUT CLASSIQUE NV, CHARLES DE CAZANOVE Champagne	*A good mousse with developed characteristics on the nose. A creamy palate and clean finish.*	£16.00	HER	(S)
CHAMPAGNE VEUVE GALIEN BRUT NV, GEORGES GOULET Champagne	*A huge mousse presenting clean fruit on the nose and palate and a strong finish.*	£16.00	NIC	(B)
CHAMPAGNE DEMOISELLE BRUT VINTAGE 1990, VRANKEN Champagne	*Lovely citrus fruit flows through this clean bready style Champagne with a refreshingly crisp finish.*	£16.20	NIC COK NEI	(B)
CHAMPAGNE HENRIOT BRUT SOUVERAIN NV, HENRIOT Champagne	*This wine has plenty to offer including a digestive biscuit nose and a lovely creamy palate.*	£16.20	ABY SKW	(B)
CHAMPAGNE LANSON DEMI-SEC NV, LANSON PÈRE ET FILS Champagne	*Biscuits and apples fight it out for supremacy on the nose, with a malic flavour on the soft palate.*	£16.30	WCR ABY	(B)
CHAMPAGNE LE MESNIL BLANC DE BLANCS BRUT NV, LE MESNIL Champagne	*This is a wine with attitude and a full palate. Lemony flavours with a stylish finish.*	£16.40	ADN NEI SHJ BUP NYW THS WRC	(B)
CHAMPAGNE LE BRUN DE NEUVILLE CUVÉE ROI CLOVIS BRUT NV, LE BRUN DE NEUVILLE Champagne	*A fine bead with biscuity nose. Dry crispness to balance the medium intensity and long finish.*	£16.50	WAW	(B)

FRANCE • CHAMPAGNE • WHITE

CHAMPAGNE PHILIPPONNAT ROYAL RESERVE BRUT NV, PHILIPPONNAT Champagne	*This has a subdued, yeasty nose, a more expressive palate of lime and digestive biscuits.*	£16.50	CDT	**B**
CHAMPAGNE MARTEL PRESTIGE BRUT NV, G.H.MARTEL Champagne	*Great staying power, get fresh with its fruity palate that sticks around for the duration.*	£17.00	WSP	**S**
CHAMPAGNE BARON EDOUARD MASSÉ BRUT MILLÉSIME 1992, LANSON PÈRE ET FILS Champagne	*Bullish and yeasty autolysis on the nose with a bready, toasty palate and a touch of pepper.*	£17.50	MCD	**S**
CHAMPAGNE H. BLIN. BRUT VINTAGE 1990, H. BLIN ET CIE Champagne	*A golden hue with sound mousse, the young buttery nose leads to a stringent finish.*	£17.50	JBF ODD	**B**
CHAMPAGNE PIPER-HEIDSIECK DEMI-SEC NV, PIPER-HEIDSIECK Champagne	*Yeasty, summer-fruit nose followed by lovely, strawberry flavours and luscious, lime acidity for a refreshing finish.*	£17.70	BTH VLW TOS WTS	**B**
CHAMPAGNE HENRIOT BLANC DE BLANCS BRUT NV, HENRIOT Champagne	*A fine mousse on a confectionery dominated nose. Crisp acidity supports pleasant biscuity and citrus palate.*	£17.90	NIC ABY SKW	**S**
CHAMPAGNE CHARLES DE CAZANOVE BRUT AZUR PREMIER CRU NV, CHARLES DE CAZANOVE Champagne	*Clearly golden, this wine offers a slightly herbal nose with light fruit on the palate.*	£18.00	HER	**B**
CHAMPAGNE PIPER-HEIDSIECK BRUT NV, PIPER-HEIDSIECK Champagne	*Golden in colour, lightly crumbled bread crumbs dominate the palate. Well-balanced with a prime length.*	£18.20	Widely Available	**B**

Wine	Description	Price	Stockists	
CHAMPAGNE BRUNO PAILLARD BRUT NV, BRUNO PAILLARD Champagne	*The well-balanced blend of fruit and oak gives elegance and finesse to this wine.*	£18.50	BWC NIC GON BDR L&W NYW BOO	**B**
CHAMPAGNE DEVAUX CUVÉE DISTINCTION BRUT VINTAGE 1990, DEVAUX Champagne	*An apple dominated palate follows an elegant toasty nose. A well-balanced wine with an appealing finish.*	£19.00	WCR FSW VEX	**S**
CHAMPAGNE JOSEPH PERRIER CUVÉE ROYALE BRUT VINTAGE 1990, JOSEPH PERRIER Champagne	*The crisp fresh acidity and attractive critrusy fruit flavours with yeasty notes make this a refreshing Champagne.*	£19.20	CVR GRT NEI WWI FSA ESL GNW	**B**
CHAMPAGNE FLEUR DE CHAMPAGNE BRUT VINTAGE 1990, DUVAL-LEROY Champagne	*Delicate aromas of bread and lemon carry over onto the crisp, zesty palate displaying good length.*	£19.70	TPE BDR	**B**
CHAMPAGNE JOSEPH PERRIER CUVÉE ROYALE BRUT NV, JOSEPH PERRIER Champagne	*Clean aggressive nose with good length and citrus fruit flavours resulting in a pleasant complexity.*	£19.80	GRT NEI WWI FSA ESL JOB FUL GNW	**B**
CHAMPAGNE GERMAIN BRUT PRESTIGE VINTAGE 1990, GERMAIN Champagne	*Full lemon yellow in colour with a sumptuous bready nose. A viscous, honey and lemon curd palate.*	£20.00	TWB	**S**
CHAMPAGNE DE CASTELLANE BRUT VINTAGE 1990, DE CASTELLANE Champagne	*A toasty nose followed by mouth watering fruit creates a simple yet elegant drink.*	£20.00	POU NEI HZW BUD	**B**

Pinpoint who sells the wine you wish to buy by turning to the stockist codes. If you know the name of the wine you want to buy, use the alphabetical index. If the price is your motivation, refer to the invaluable price guide index; red and white wines under £5, sparkling wines under £12 and Champagne under £16. Happy hunting!

123

CHAMPAGNE DEVAUX CUVÉE MILLÉSIME BRUT VINTAGE 1992, DEVAUX Champagne	*Medium yellow with fine bubbles, soft malic flavours with cooking apples acidity and a creamy finish.*	**£20.00**	WCR VEX CER FSW	B
CHAMPAGNE PIPER-HEIDSIECK BRUT VINTAGE 1989, PIPER-HEIDSIECK Champagne	*Mid yellow. Good mousse with an appley nose and palate leading to a sharp yet strong finish.*	**£20.60**	WCR SHJ BUP VLW MHV WRC	B
CHAMPAGNE LE MESNIL GRAND CRU BLANC DE BLANCS BRUT VINTAGE 1990, LE MESNIL Champagne	*A pale green look with lively yeast on the nose and rich creamy fruit flavours.*	**£20.70**	ADN NEI SHJ BUP NYW THS WRC	B
CHAMPAGNE JACQUART BLANC DE BLANCS BRUT VINTAGE 1990, JACQUART Champagne	*Pale gold with a full mousse. Toffee nose, excellent intensity on the crisp apple palate.*	**£22.00**	PCC ORA	S
CHAMPAGNE CHARLES HEIDSIECK BRUT RÉSERVE "MIS EN CAVE 1994" NV, CHARLES HEIDSIECK Champagne	*Golden hay, minute bubbles with a biscuity nose. Well-integrated honeyed fruit finishing on a strong note.*	**£22.20**	Widely Available	B
CHAMPAGNE CHARLES HEIDSIECK BRUT RÉSERVE "MIS EN CAVE 1993" NV, CHARLES HEIDSIECK Champagne	*Deep gold colour, a yeasty biscuity nose. Tropical fruit flavours, even acidity and good length.*	**£22.50**	Widely Available	G TROPHY WINE
CHAMPAGNE VEUVE CLICQUOT YELLOW LABEL BRUT NV, VEUVE CLICQUOT Champagne	*Superb biscuity aromas and creamy complexity which all contribute to an unforgettable citric lime finish.*	**£22.60**	Widely Available	S

Pinpoint who sells the wine you wish to buy by turning to the stockist codes. If you know the name of the wine you want to buy, use the alphabetical index. If the price is your motivation, refer to the invaluable price guide index; red and white wines under £5, sparkling wines under £12 and Champagne under £16. Happy hunting!

CHAMPAGNE VILMART GRAND CELLAR NV, VILMART Champagne	*A hint of citrus and toast on the nose. Weighty in the mouth with good acidity.*	£23.50	DIR SEL GON GRO	(B)
CHAMPAGNE PERRIER-JOUET BRUT VINTAGE 1992, PERRIER-JOUET Champagne	*Introverted nose with a palate dominated by citrus fruit and autolysis. Good mousse and acidity.*	£24.60	CPW ODD MWW THS WRC BUP SEA	(B)
CHAMPAGNE "R" DE RUINART BRUT VINTAGE 1992, RUINART Champagne	*A restrained nose and palate with green and citrus fruits to the fore. Well-balanced.*	£26.10	WCR L&W RUK BUP LVN WRC	(B)
CHAMPAGNE MOËT & CHANDON BRUT IMPÉRIAL VINTAGE 1992, MOËT & CHANDON Champagne	*Lovely toasty nose and fine mousse rises from a ripe maple syrup palate with refreshing crisp acidity.*	£26.50	Widely Available	(G)
CHAMPAGNE CHARLES HEIDSIECK BRUT RÉSERVE "MIS EN CAVE 1992" NV, CHARLES HEIDSIECK Champagne	*Apple and bread aromas with creamy chocolate and malt to the fore of the palate.*	£26.70	WSP MTL NEI CPW BUP TOS WRC	(S)
CHAMPAGNE MUMM CORDON ROUGE VINTAGE 1989, G H MUMM & CIE Champagne	*A fine and subtle nose, delicate mousse. A good balance of freshness and flowers on the palate.*	£26.90	NEI ODD DBY THS WRC BUP SEA	(S)
CHAMPAGNE CHARLES HEIDSIECK BRUT VINTAGE 1990, CHARLES HEIDSIECK Champagne	*Bright lemon yellow appearance. Autolysis apparent on the nose with apples and digestives in the background.*	£29.10	WSP MTL NEI CPW BUP WRC	(B)
CHAMPAGNE BEAUMONT DES CRAYERES CUVÉE SPEC. BRUT NOST. 1990, BEAUMONT DES CRAYERES Champagne	*Deep yellow with some weight and nutmeg on the nose, a subtle base with a graceful finish.*	£30.20	HOH RES	(B)

FRANCE • CHAMPAGNE • WHITE

CHAMPAGNE MUMM DE CRAMANT BLANC DE BLANCS BRUT NV, G. H. MUMM & CIE Champagne	*Bubbles as far as the eye can see with bready aromas and lime fruit on the palate.*	**£31.40**	ODD VIL THS SEA	**B**
CHAMPAGNE ALFRED GRATIEN BRUT VINTAGE 1989, ALFRED GRATIEN Champagne	*A delicate nose with a toasty palate and good clean, crisp acidity with a long finish.*	**£31.50**	VIC WSO	**B**
CHAMPAGNE POL ROGER BRUT VINTAGE 1988, POL ROGER Champagne	*Mature nose and rich depth combined with citrus fruits, well-rounded and full of quality.*	**£31.80**	Widely Available	**B**
CHAMPAGNE VEUVE CLICQUOT RESERVE BRUT VINTAGE 1990, VEUVE CLICQUOT Champagne	*Melon and tangerine fruit with autolysis notes grace the soft delicate palate boasting zippy acidity.*	**£32.60**	Widely Available	**B**
CHAMPAGNE VEUVE CLICQUOT RICH RESERVE VINTAGE 1990, VEUVE CLICQUOT Champagne	*Toasty nose leading to a balanced structure of honeyed apple and citrus with a clean finish.*	**£32.70**	Widely Available	**B**
CHAMPAGNE POL ROGER BRUT CHARDONNAY VINTAGE 1990, POL ROGER Champagne	*Ripe bready nose leading to a full palate of biscuit, crunchy acidity and a developing toasted nut finish.*	**£35.20**	LEA BEN WSP BDR BNK ODD VIL	**B**
CHAMPAGNE CANARD-DUCHÊNE CHARLES VII BRUT GRAND CUVÉE NV, CANARD-DUCHÊNE Champagne	*A rich yeasty nose with a gold to greenish tinge in colour, complex and bready.*	**£35.90**	VIL EDC HOF	**S**
CHAMPAGNE BOLLINGER GRANDE ANNÉE BRUT VINTAGE 1990, BOLLINGER Champagne	*Deep gold colour with dedicated mousse. Developed ripe fruit on the palate and splendid sharpness. Superb finish.*	**£38.40**	Widely Available	**G**

CHAMPAGNE LANSON NOBLE CUVÉE BRUT VINTAGE 1989, LANSON PÈRE ET FILS Champagne	*Ripe and mature floral notes on the palate, upbeat acidity and powerful density. Long finish.*	£46.70	SEL VWE THS WRC BUP	(G)
CHAMPAGNE PHILIPPONNAT CLOS DES GOISSES BRUT 1986, PHILIPPONNAT Champagne	*Yeasty lemons with toasty oak influence, a lively and vigorous mousse with a creamily balanced finish.*	£47.50	CDT	(G)
CHAMPAGNE PERRIER-JOUËT BELLE EPOQUE BRUT 1990, PERRIER-JOUËT Champagne	*Lovely balance and mousse throughout with lime fruit and yeasty, mineral flavours to the fore.*	£48.60	SEL HOU CPW ODD MWW BDR	(S)
GRAND CORDON DE MUMM BRUT VINTAGE 1990, G H MUMM & CIE Champagne	*A creamy rich yeast and biscuit aroma with ripe fruit on the palate.*	£51.20	WCR ODD MWW SEA	(B)
CHAMPAGNE LANSON NOBLE CUVÉE BRUT VINTAGE 1988, LANSON PÈRE ET FILS Champagne	*Melons and fresh green fruit, a good complex palate with a full body and delightful end.*	£52.20	SEL THS WRC BUP CST	(B)
CHAMPAGNE LANSON BLANC DE BLANCS BRUT VINTAGE 1990, LANSON PÈRE ET FILS Champagne	*Clean fresh palate with zippy citrus fruits and creamy, honeyed flavours to the fore. Good persistent mousse.*	£53.00	MCD	(S)
CHAMPAGNE DOM RUINART BLANC DE BLANCS BRUT VINTAGE 1990, RUINART Champagne	*Pale yellow hue and a medium mousse combine with an attractive yeasty nose. A complex, balanced palate.*	£53.20	WCR LEA RUK LVN ARM HAR	(S)

Pinpoint who sells the wine you wish to buy by turning to the stockist codes. If you know the name of the wine you want to buy, use the alphabetical index. If the price is your motivation, refer to the invaluable price guide index; red and white wines under £5, sparkling wines under £12 and Champagne under £16. Happy hunting!

CHAMPAGNE CUVÉE DOM PÉRIGNON BRUT VINTAGE 1990, MOËT & CHANDON Champagne	*A classic structure with prominent nose and ripe fruit on the palate. Finishes well with length.*	**£59.50**	Widely Available	(S)
CHAMPAGNE VEUVE CLICQUOT LA GRANDE DAME BRUT VINTAGE 1990, VEUVE CLICQUOT Champagne	*Weighty, stylish and full of ripe fruit this wine has an attractive level of acidity. Displaying further ageing potential.*	**£59.90**	Widely Available	(B)
CHAMPAGNE GOSSET CÉLÉBRIS BRUT VINTAGE 1990, GOSSET Champagne	*Bread crumbs and red apples are matched by substantial acidity. A hint of butter softens the components.*	**£63.30**	LEA DIR NYW	(S)

FRANCE • CHAMPAGNE • ROSÉ

CHAMPAGNE PAUL LANGIER BRUT ROSÉ NV, F. BONNET Champagne	*Pale pink in colour with a buttery, yeasty nose, very dry palate and some zesty acidity.*	**£13.50**	MHV	(B)
CHAMPAGNE LE BRUN DE NEUVILLE BRUT ROSÉ NV, LE BRUN DE NEUVILLE Champagne	*Shimmering rose hip fruit on a nose which leads onto strawberries and delicate acidity.*	**£14.00**	WAW	(S)
CHAMPAGNE DUVAL LEROY FLEUR DE CHAMPAGNE BRUT ROSÉ DE SAIGNÉE NV, DUVAL-LEROY Champagne	*Summer pudding nose with a finely balanced palate of crisp, clean fruits with delicate florally tones.*	**£16.20**	TPE	(S)
CHAMPAGNE DEVAUX CUVÉE MILLÉSIME ROSÉ 1990, VINTAGE DEVAUX Champagne	*Attractive salmon pink colour that gives rise to a typically autolytic nose with a long finish.*	**£17.20**	WCR FSW COK VEX WNS CWL	(B)

CHAMPAGNE DEVAUX CUVÉE ROSÉ BRUT NV, DEVAUX Champagne	*A salmon pink, lightly sparkling Champagne, with clean, biscuity aromas, gentle fruits and crisp acidity to balance.*	**£17.50**	WCR FSW DBY CER EVE	(B)
CHAMPAGNE PIPER-HEIDSIECK BRUT ROSÉ NV, PIPER-HEIDSIECK Champagne	*A classic yeasty nose with hints of apples. A finely structured palate of zesty fruits and citrus acidity.*	**£19.70**	WS MTL TOS	(S)
CHAMPAGNE JACQUART BRUT ROSÉ 1990, VINTAGE JACQUART Champagne	*A complex, interesting Champagne with a dry, nutty nose, ripe fruit flavours and hints of toasty oak.*	**£20.00**	PAT	(B)
CHAMPAGNE DEVAUX CUVÉE DISTINCTION BRUT ROSÉ VINTAGE 1988, DEVAUX Champagne	*Rich, biscuity, vegetal nose then dry almost hidden fruit with a sharp acidic palate and dry finish.*	**£24.50**	VEX FTH	(B)
CHAMPAGNE "R" DE RUINART BRUT ROSÉ NV, RUINART Champagne	*Creamy, biscuity nose with a refined blend of strawberries, apples and balancing acidity on the palate.*	**£27.60**	Widely Available	(S)
CHAMPAGNE MOËT & CHANDON BRUT IMPÉRIAL ROSÉ VINTAGE 1990, MOËT & CHANDON Champagne	*A leesy, biscuity nose precedes a clean, zesty palate with touches of melons and a refreshing finish.*	**£31.30**	G&M SEL HOU UNS DBY TOS VLW	(B)
CHAMPAGNE CHARLES HEIDSIECK BRUT ROSÉ VINTAGE 1985, CHARLES HEIDSIECK Champagne	*Smooth, toasty aromas open out to juicy, summer fruit flavours mixed with fresh acidity and a medium finish.*	**£31.80**	WSP NEI CPW HAR FEN	(B)
CHAMPAGNE VEUVE CLICQUOT ROSÉ RESERVE VINTAGE 1989, VEUVE CLICQUOT Champagne	*An earthy, yeasty nose. Hints of class evident in the complex appley, biscuity flavours on the fine palate.*	**£32.30**	Widely Available	(B)

CHAMPAGNE POL ROGER BRUT ROSÉ VINTAGE 1990, POL ROGER Champagne	*Elegant mousse with full on delicate strawberry fruit, lovely soft acidity and a voluptuous finish.*	£33.50	BEN CNL VIL ODF DBY	(S)
CHAMPAGNE CUVÉE DOM PÉRIGNON ROSÉ VINTAGE 1986, MOËT & CHANDON Champagne	*A stunningly complex nose with notes of toast and caramel heralds a palate of immense structure.*	£149.3	MTL HOU ABY VLW CST	(G)

FRANCE • LANGUEDOC • RED

SOMERFIELD SYRAH VDP D'OC NV, JEANJEAN Languedoc Roussillon	*Quite light but with juicy fruit, softish tannins and a pretty good finish.*	£3.00	SMF	(B)
CHEVAL D'OR MERLOT VDP D'OC 1997, LES CAVES DU SIEUR D'ARQUES Languedoc Roussillon	*Vibrant, juicy, cherry fruit but quite smoky tannins and leafy acidity. Nice!*	£3.50	WRT	(B)
FORTANT DE FRANCE GRENACHE VDP D'OC 1997, SKALLI Languedoc Roussillon	*Nicely perfumed this is a soft, very fruity, clean wine that is very easy to appreciate.*	£3.80	BNK WTS HOU MWW DBY PWI PEA CEN	(B)
MARKS & SPENCER BIN 80 MINERVOIS 1996, PIERRE DE PASSENDALE Languedoc Roussillon	*Fresh and juicy with good acidity and firm tannins.*	£3.99	M&S	(B)
B&G CABERNET SAUVIGNON VDP D'OC 1997, BARTON & GUESTIER Languedoc Roussillon	*On the nose quite dry blackberry fruit but with nice woody tannins and a lean stalkiness.*	£4.00	CWS ODD SEA CST	(B)

CAMAS BLANC CABERNET SAUVIGNON VDP D'OC 1997, FREDÈRIC ROGER Languedoc Roussillon	*Chunky and rich with good length. A firm fruity wine with fine chalky tannins.*	£4.00	VER	(B)
ERMITAGE DU PIC ST. LOUP 1996, MAUREL VEDEAU Coteaux du Languedoc	*Quite light, a well structured wine showing minty, spicy, fruit characters in the mouth.*	£4.00	T&T WTS FUL	(B)
CABERNET SAUVIGNON MERLOT VDP D'OC 1997, FREDERIC ROGER Languedoc Roussillon	*Smooth palate of black cherry puree and spicy black pepper with a silky creamy finish.*	£4.00	VER	(B)
FORTANT DE FRANCE SYRAH CABERNET SAUVIGNON VDP D'OC 1997, SKALLI Languedoc Roussillon	*Hot, ripe, chewy and spicy fruit on the palate with good oaky and vegetal overtones.*	£4.10	BNK VWE DBY PWI	(B)
DOMAINE CABRAIRAL ORGANIC RED VDP D'OC 1997, JACQUES FRELIN Languedoc Roussillon	*Meaty, smoky bacon, nose followed by game notes and a palate of drying tannins and spice.*	£4.30	VER	(B)
FORTANT DE FRANCE SYRAH VDP D'OC 1997, SKALLI Languedoc Roussillon	*A green pepper nose and vibrant raspberry palate with not too aggresive tannins in support.*	£4.30	WCR HOU DBY	(B)
TERRASSES DE GUILHEM ROUGE VDP D'OC 1997, MOULIN DE GASSAC Languedoc Roussillon	*With pepper and fruit on the nose, this is a clean wine. Good mouthfeel, fruit and tannins.*	£4.40	JNW BEN ADN DBY HVW PFT CHF	(B)
ASH RIDGE MERLOT VDP D'OC 1997, MAUREL VEDEAU Languedoc Roussillon	*This Merlot is a big rounded juicy wine that is very well-structured and demands attention.*	£4.50	T&T UNS	(S)

SYRAH LES BATEAUX VDP D'OC 1996, JACQUES ET FRANÇOIS LURTON Languedoc Roussillon	*A meaty nose with a hint of coffee leads to a fleshy, cherry dominated palate with excellent acidity.*	**£4.50**	JNW FUL	**S**
CHÂTEAU BEAUVOISIN 1997, VIGNERONS DE CERRESOU Languedoc Roussillon	*Tasters were impressed by lively hints of cedar and tobacco on this rustic but charming wine.*	**£4.50**	VWE	**B**
CHÂTEAU DE PENNAUTIER VDQS CABADÉS 1995, LORGERIL Languedoc Roussillon	*A lean, quite Bordelais style wine with black cassis fruit and a tarry finish.*	**£4.50**	WCR PTR	**B**
CHÂTEAU VALOUSSIÈRE VDP D'OC 1996, JEANJEAN Languedoc Roussillon	*Brooding dark fruit and lifted tannins in this intense wine with lively vanilla notes.*	**£4.50**	SMF	**B**
MARKS & SPENCER DOMAINE JEUNE COUNOISE VDP D'OC 1997, PAUL JEUNE Languedoc Roussillon	*Rounded and packed with fruit, a well balanced, uncomplicated wine, sure to please.*	**£4.50**	M&S	**B**
RICHEMONT CABERNET SAUVIGNON VDP D'OC 1996, HUGH RYMAN Languedoc Roussillon	*Complex aromas of redcurrant fruit with nuances of tar, cedar and caramel develop on the firm palate.*	**£4.50**	RYW	**B**
OAKED CABERNET SAUVIGNON VDP D'OC 1997, CAVE DE VALVIGNERES Languedoc Roussillon	*Rich attractive aromas of currants and mint carry over onto the fresh palate of this wine.*	**£4.80**	BDR	**B**
MAS DE LA GARRIGUE ROUSSILLON 1996, J P HENRIQUES Languedoc Roussillon	*Jammy raspberry fruit on the nose and palate. A clean wine with good tannins and pleasing acidity.*	**£4.90**	NRW	**B**

MARKS & SPENCER VIGNE ANTIQUE SYRAH BARRIQUE AGED VDP D'OC 1996, PIERRE DE PASSENDALE Languedoc Roussillon	*A complex wine with animal, fruit aromas and excellent acidity on its broad vanillan spiced palate.*	£4.99	M&S	B
CHÂTEAU LA BOUTIGNANE CLASSIQUE 1996, OLIVIER FAIURE Languedoc Roussillon	*Concentrated yet delicate with masses of personality. Delicious rich chocolatey flavours and a superb mouthfeel.*	£5.00	WCR	S
GOUTS ET COULEURS SYRAH MOURVÈDRE VDP D'OC 1997, CAZAL VIEL Languedoc Roussillon	*Deep ruby colour with a vegetal nose and tones of truffles. Brambles and loads of ripe fruit flavours.*	£5.00	SMF	S
CHÂTEAU DE PARAZA MINERVOIS 1996, M. PASSERIEUX Languedoc Roussillon	*Soft and dry. A well put together, balanced, wine showing good fruit and acidity.*	£5.00	WCR	B
CHÂTEAU ROUMANIÉRES 1996, CHÂTEAU ROUMANIÉRES Coteaux du Languedoc	*A soft and fresh wine with hints of spice and an attractive, complex nose.*	£5.00	MWW	B
TRAMONTANE RESERVE OAKED CABERNET SAUVIGNON 1996, VDP D'OC MAUREL VEDEAU Languedoc Roussillon	*A gamey palate with sinewy fruit balanced by delicious oak notes on a strong finish.*	£5.00	T&T	B
BARON PHILIPPE DE ROTHSCHILD MERLOT VDP D'OC 1996, BARON PHILIPPE DE ROTHSCHILD Languedoc Roussillon	*Medicinal aromas of clove and eucalyptus dominate the bouquet. The palate is full of rich plummy fruit flavours.*	£5.20	MTL CRS VIL BAB COE TOS MHV CST	B
LA BAUME MERLOT VDP D'OC 1997, BRL HARDY WINE COMPANY Languedoc Roussillon	*This is quite lean and dry on the palate with lean tannins and pleasing stalky fruit.*	£5.30	WCR SPR DBY JSM FUL	B

133

FRANCE • LANGUEDOC • RED

Château de Segure 1995, Producteurs du Mont Tauch Fitou	*Deeply coloured with a wonderfully complex, mature leathery nose this is a clean well-balanced wine.*	£5.60	NIC T&T JSM	**G**
Château Grand Caumont 1996, Château Grand Caumont Languedoc Roussillon	*Soft and light but with animal and spicy fruit aromas. Well-balanced with a fine structure.*	£5.60	BDR	**B**
Château de Calce 1994, Château de Calce Languedoc Roussillon	*A nice mouthful of fruit nicely balanced by the tannins and acidity. Soft, long and good.*	£5.70	BDR	**B**
Château Les Pins Barrique Aged 1996, Cave des Vignerons des Baixas Languedoc Roussillon	*Deeply coloured, this is an elegant, rounded, well-made wine that is very easy to appreciate.*	£6.00	FUL	**S**
Château Mire L'Etang 1996, Château Ventenac Languedoc Roussillon	*Soft and fruity with some spice. A very pleasant wine that feels succulent on the palate.*	£6.00	STG	**B**
Domaine de Granoupiac 1996, Claude Flauard Coteaux de Languedoc	*Well balanced and structured. A spicy wine with a good chewy mouthfeel and depth.*	£6.00	JNW	**B**
Mas de Bressades 1995, Mas de Bressades Languedoc Roussillon	*A lovely warm nose leads onto brambly fruit with some spice and mineral notes.*	£6.00	WIN MWW	**B**
Château de Flaugergues Cuvée Sélection 1996, Château de Flaugergues Coteaux de Languedoc	*Rich dark and brooding this is fine sleek kit that will repay cellaring.*	£6.50	MWW SGL NAD	**B**

CHÂTEAU L' AMARINE 1996, CHÂTEAU L'AMARINE Languedoc Roussillon	*Finishing well, this is quite a tough wine with a full fruit palate and good nose.*	£6.50	BPW	(B)
SEIGNEUR DE SIRAN MINERVOIS 1996, SCV DE SIRANAISE Languedoc Roussillon	*A darkly coloured wine with leather and spice fruit characters. Excellently crafted with good acidity and length.*	£6.60	BDR	(S) WINE OF THE YEAR
CHÂTEAU DE LASTOURS ÉLEVÉ EN FUTS DE CHÊNE 1994, CHÂTEAU DE LASTOURS Languedoc Roussillon	*Juicy and plump. Quite a firm wine possessing good spicy ripe fruit characters and length.*	£6.70	NRW WES COK POR DBY HVW TSE	(B)
CHÂTEAU L'EUZIERE PIC SAINT LOUP 1996, CHÂTEAU L'EUZIERE Languedoc Roussillon	*Ripe, concentrated mulberry and big bramble character. Round, earthy and flavoured with rich fruit and pepper.*	£7.10	BTH LIB NYW FUL	(G)
CHÂTEAU HELENE CUVÉE HELENE DE TROIE 1995, MARIE-HELENE GAU Languedoc Roussillon	*Cassis, lavender and roses on the nose with flavours of dry and bitter cherries.*	£7.80	WAW	(S)
DOMAINE DE LAVABRE PIC SAINT LOUP 1995, DOMAINE DE LAVABRE Languedoc Roussillon	*Rich, ripe fruit merging with dark cherry fruits, evident new oak with concentrated fruit palate.*	£7.80	JNW NYW	(S)
FITOU, 50TH ANNIVERSARY CUVÉE 1996, LES PRODUCTEURS DU MONT TAUCH Languedoc Roussillon	*Deep cherry in colour, a softish wine showing good berry fruit and wood charaters.*	£8.00	T&T	(B)
DOMAINE DE VILLEMAJOU 1995, GERARD BERTRAND Languedoc Roussillon	*A deliciously complex wine. Delivers a good juicy mouthful of flavours that lasts so well.*	£8.50	NIC	(S)

FRANCE • LANGUEDOC • RED

LES HAUTS DE FORCAREAL 1996, J P HENRIQUES Languedoc Roussillon	*Stylishly made, this wine has a deep purple colour and attractive ripe fruit aromas.*	£9.70	DBY	**B**
MAS DE DAUMAS GASSAC ROUGE VDP DE L'HÉRAULT 1996, MOULIN DE GASSAC Languedoc Roussillon	*Although quite young this has a meaty backbone with layers of condensed fruit and grippy tannins.*	£15.90	Widely Available	**S**

FRANCE • LANGUEDOC • WHITE

LES MARIONETTES MARSANNE VDP D'OC 1997, TERROIR CLUB Languedoc Roussillon	*Rich aromas of peaches with perfumed, floral notes. Ripe tropical fruits follow with an attractively zesty overtone.*	£4.00	VER	**G** TROPHY WINE
MAUREL VEDEAU GRENACHE VIOGNIER VDP D'OC 1997, MAUREL VEDEAU Languedoc Roussillon	*An enticing wine with rhubarb and custard on the nose and lovely tropical fruit palate.*	£4.00	T&T UNS	**B**
DOMAINE DE VALENSAC CHARDONNAY VDP D'OC 1997, GFA DE VALENSAC Languedoc Roussillon	*Pronounced melon fruit nose carries over to give some complexity to a citric palate.*	£4.50	FCA FWL	**B**
LES FRÈRES SCARAMOUCHE CHARDONNAY VDP D'OC 1997, LES VIGNOBLES LA REZE Languedoc Roussillon	*Sweet pineapple and herb aromas with fresh lemon and lime fruit on a palate of integrated oak.*	£4.50	CRS	**B**
LES MARIONETTES CHARDONNAY ROUSANNE VDP D'OC 1997, TERROIR CLUB Languedoc Roussillon	*Clean fresh fruit with light aromatic characters resulting in a pleasant and easy drinking wine.*	£4.50	VER	**B**

CUCKOO HILL VIOGNIER VDP D'OC 1996, NICK BUTLER Languedoc Roussillon	*This medium-bodied simple wine is full of fruit with grapefruit tropical and guava characters.*	£4.70	CRS WTS ASD	(B)
LAPEROUSE ASSEMBLAGE BLANC VDP D'OC 1996, PENFOLDS & VAL D'ORBIEU Languedoc Roussillon	*Delicate flavours comprising a medley of fruit, hints of spice and a soft finish.*	£4.80	GGW ODD	(B)
HUGH RYMAN ROUSSANNE VDP D'OC 1996, HUGH RYMAN Languedoc Roussillon	*Soft ripe peachy fruit which results in a supple wine with hints of vanilla oak.*	£4.90	RYW WTS	(B)
MARKS & SPENCER VIGNE ANTIQUE CHARDONNAY BARREL VDP D'OC 1997, PIERRE DE PASSENDALE Languedoc Roussillon	*Honeyed slightly minty nose. Dominant oak with full-bodied tropical fruit flavours and good acid balance.*	£4.99	M&S	(B)
DOMAINE LA CHEVALIÈRE CUVÉE SPÉCIALE BLANC VDP D'OC 1996, DOMAINE LA CHEVALIÈRE Languedoc Roussillon	*Ripe tropical aromas of guava and melon with some perfumed notes to the nose and palate.*	£5.20	DIR PFC	(B)
TESCO FRENCH VIOGNIER VDP D'OC 1997, LES DOMAINES VIENNET Languedoc Roussillon	*Pears combined with spicy tomato plant characters. The palate is full with clean, moderate, acidity.*	£5.50	TOS	(B)
CHARDONNAY "L" GRAND CUVÉE VDP D'OC 1997, DOMAINE LAROCHE Languedoc Roussillon	*Lemon and oak aromas. Crisp, very dry citrus palate, subtle oak and good lengthy finish.*	£5.60	DIR PFC MWW BEL WTS	(B)
DOMAINE LA CHEVALIÈRE CHARDONNAY OAK RESERVE VDP D'OC '97, DOMAINE LA CHEVALIÈRE Languedoc Roussillon	*Pungent, spicy, fruit and toasty oak on the nose with a palate of soft clean acidity.*	£5.70	DIR PFC CWL	(B)

FRANCE • LANGUEDOC • WHITE

DOMAINE DE FORCAREAL 1997, J P HENRIQUES Languedoc Roussillon	*Impressively strong nose of flowers and vanilla lead onto a structured wine with splendid acidity and zingy citrus fruit.*	£6.00	BOO	**B**
CHÂTEAU DE LANCYRE "LA ROUVIERE" 1997, BERNARD DURAND Languedoc Roussillon	*Herbaceous notes to a citrus nose with hints of asparagus on a clean, lemony palate.*	£8.00	TOS FUL	**B**
MAS DE DAUMAS GASSAC BLANC VDP DE L'HÈRAULT 1997, MOULIN DE GASSAC Languedoc Roussillon	*Opulent, creamy nose. An elegant palate with warm, spicy overtones and extremely flavoursome fruit.*	£16.00	Widely Available	**S**

FRANCE • LANGUEDOC • ROSÉ

DOMAINE LA TOUR BOISÉE 1997, JEAN-LOUIS POUDOU Languedoc Roussillon	*Delightful colour with rich cherry fruit. Slightly peppery but has lovely jammy fruit in a delicate sweet finish.*	£4.30	WAW	**B**

FRANCE • LOIRE • RED

LA CHAPELLE DE CRAY RED 1996, CHAPELLE DE CRAY Loire	*Vegetal edge to this soft fruit nose with hints of boiled sweets. Light with a balanced palate.*	£4.00	WCR NEI NRW WES DBY COK AMW	**B**
TOURAINE CABERNET FRANC 1995, DOMAINE DE LA BERGÈRIE Loire	*An earthy, plummy nose. The palate has a soft strawberry base with some interesting complexity.*	£5.00	GRT	**B**

CHINON DOMAINE DESBOURDES 1996, M. R. DESBOURDES Loire	*Peppery nose with a vegetal edge reflected in a mouth of spicy, brambley fruits and firm tannins.*	£5.10	ABY	(B)
BOURGUEIL 1995, DOMAINE PIERRE GAUTHIER Loire	*Subdued berry fruit on the nose, with green tannins on a well-balanced and lengthy palate.*	£6.00	NRW COK HVW	(B)
ANJOU DOMAINE LEDUC-FROUIN 1996, GEORGES LEDUC Loire	*Deep, attractive colour and light, spicy, aroma. A palate full of blackcurrant fruits and ripe tannins.*	£6.30	ALZ	(B)
BOURGUEIL DOMAINE DE LA CHEVALIÈRE VIEILLES VIGNES 1996, PIERRE CASLOT Loire	*A leathery, almost sour cherries aroma. Weighty fruit and drying green tannins on the palate.*	£6.50	3DW	(B)
ANJOU-VILLAGES DOMAINE DE LA MOTTE 1995, ANDRÉ & GILLES SORIN Loire	*A sharp, stone-fruit perfume becomes a spicy, almost hot palate of medium fruit intensity and length.*	£6.50	3DW	(B)
SAUMUR-CHAMPIGNY DOMAINE DE LA CUNE 1996, JEAN-LUC & JEAN-ALBERT MARY Loire	*Soft, slightly jammy nose precedes a lightly fruited, herbal palate with soft tannins and some length.*	£7.50	3DW	(B)
CHINON EXCEPTIONAL 1996, PAUL BUISSE Loire	*A punchy, berry and herb nose. A soft, juicy body with balancing, ripe tannins. A delicious aftertaste.*	£8.00	EVI	(S)
SAUMUR CHAMPIGNY 1996, CAVE DES VIGNERONS DE SAUMUR Loire	*This smoky, cedary nose is intriguing and is complemented by its cherry and oak flavours.*	£8.70	NIC	(B)

SAUMUR CHAMPIGNY DOMAINE DE LA CUNE LES 3 JEAN 1995, JEAN-LUC & JEAN-ALBERT MARY Loire	*Hot, fruity aromas rise out of a palate dominated by berry fruits and fleshy tannins.*	£9.00	3DW	**B**
SAUMUR CHAMPIGNY CHÂTEAU DE VARRAINS ROUGE 1996, LANGLOIS CHATEAU Loire	*Big, ripe, blackberry aromas lead to meaty, full-bodied wine with smooth oak tones and tannins.*	£10.50	NEI	**B**
CHÂTEAU DE LA GRILLE 1995, LAURENT GOSSET Loire	*Spicy, almost mushroomy nose with a leafy, lean palate. Light on fruit but with some structure.*	£13.00	CFT	**B**
ANJOU CHATEAU DE LA ROULERIE 1996, S.A. DE FESLES Loire	*Ripe, fruity nose and vegetal tones, complex palate of powerful brambly fruit with minty notes.*	£14.00	DIR NIC	**S**
SAUMUR CHAMPIGNY MARIGNALE 1995, THIERRY GERMAIN Loire	*A smoky, minty nose produces a peppery, oaky, fruit-laden wine accompanied by attractively ripe tannins.*	£15.80	DIR TPE ALL	**B**

FRANCE • LOIRE • WHITE

CHENIN BLANC VDP DE LA JARDIN DE FRANCE 1997, ACKERMANN Loire	*Fresh green fruits on the nose develop into zingy, citrus flavours with an elegant minerally edge.*	£3.70	CVR IWS KWI	**B**
MUSCADET CLOS DES ORFEUILLES 1997, MARCEL SAUTEJEAU Loire	*A tangy and fruity nose, with a good weight of minerally, stone-fruit flavours and pleasant acidity.*	£4.30	WWI	**B**

TOURAINE SAUVIGNON CHAPELLE DE CRAY 1996, CHAPELLE DE CRAY Loire	*Classic musty wet wool and honey aromas with clean dry grassy characteristics on the palate.*	**£4.30**	Widely Available	(B)
TOURAINE SAUVIGNON BLANC 1997, ROCHEMARTAIN Loire	*An earthy, appley nose with lean acids and unripe apple flavours, a mouthwatering finish.*	**£4.99**	SAF	(B)
POUILLY FUMÉ LE CHANT DES VIGNES 1997, JOSEPH MELLOT Loire	*Chalky mineral notes, honeyed nutty aromas of smoke and currants carry over onto the citrus palate.*	**£5.50**	NEI MWW GRA FRT	(S)
VOUVRAY COTEAUX TUFFIER 1996, CHAPELLE DE CRAY Loire	*Citric, green nose with honeyed tones. Pronounced apples and stone-fruit on the mid-palate, medium length.*	**£5.60**	NRW WCS VWE DBY AMW	(B)
MONTLOUIS CHAPELLE DE CRAY 1997, CHAPELLE DE CRAY Loire	*Zesty nose hints at the appley, peardrop flavours and fresh acidity that give this wine a superb mouthfeel.*	**£5.80**	Widely Available	(S)
MONTLOUIS CHAPELLE DE CRAY 1995, CHAPELLE DE CRAY Loire	*A peachy, citrus bouquet with classic wet wool overtones precedes a lemon and apples palate.*	**£5.80**	NRW NYW COK WCS DBY MWW	(B)
DOMAINE DES HUARDS CHEVERNY 1996, MICHEL & JOCYLENE GENDRIER Loire	*A soft and floral nose with vanilla hints. The palate has distinctive crushed gooseberry flavours.*	**£5.80**	ALZ	(B)
CHÂTEAU CHASSELOIR MUSCADET DE SÈVRE ET MAINE SUR LIE 1997, CHÉREAU-CARRÉ Loire	*A pleasant leesy, appley perfume is followed by a zesty prickle in the mouth.*	**£6.10**	DLA QWW HOH TPE	(S)

MENETOU-SALON CLOS DU PRESSOIR 1997, JOSEPH MELLOT Loire	*Delicate mineral notes lead to a floral bouquet and a palate with some citrus overtones and a clean finish.*	£6.30	GRA FRT	(B)
MALT HOUSE VINTNERS POUILLY FUMÉ DOMAINE DES VALLÉES 1997, MICHEL BAILLY Loire	*Mineral notes on a gooseberry nose with elements of smoke before the palate, which displays the influence of "terroir".*	£6.90	MHV	(B)
POUILLY FUMÉ LES AUBÉPINES 1997, PIERRE FOUASSIER Loire	*A chalky and vegetal nose followed by a dry, fresh palate with a zesty finish.*	£6.90	MTB	(B)
SANCERRE DOMAINE LES GRANDS GROUX 1997, PIERRE FOUASSIER Loire	*Ripe fruit aromas and a rich concentration of fruit balanced by zesty, fresh acidity.*	£7.00	MTB	(B)
SANCERRE CUVÉE LA CLEMENCE 1997, VINCENT PINARD Loire	*Dry and balanced savoury flavours with some apricot fruit and grassy, crisp, fresh acidity.*	£7.10	MIS GRT ABY	(S)
POUILLY FUMÉ 1997, DOMAINE MASSON-BLONDELET Loire	*A mature and elegant nose with excellent fruit and acid balance. A well rounded wine.*	£7.50	WTS	(B)
SANCERRE LES COLLINETTES 1997, JOSEPH MELLOT Loire	*Gun flint aromas on the herbaceous nose with nuances of minerally chalk on the gooseberry palate.*	£8.00	WIN NEI GRA FRT	(S)
POUILLY FUMÉ CUVÉE DU TRONCSEE 1997, JOSEPH MELLOT Loire	*Delicate gooseberry flavours follow a herbaceous nose of freshly mown lawn with nuances of chalk.*	£8.00	WIN NEI GRA FRT	(B)

SANCERRE LES BONNES BOUCHES 1997, DOMAINE HENRI BOURGEOIS Loire	*A sharp, grainy nose matched with steely fruit and complex mineral notes on the palate.*	**£8.50**	CNL SAF	(B)
SANCERRE DOMAINE DU CARROIR PERRIN 1997, PIERRE RIFFAULT Loire	*A promising nose of zesty fruit that follows onto a palate of apples and pears.*	**£8.80**	3DW	(B)
POUILLY FUMÉ DOMAINE DES CHANTBINES 1996, JEAN PABIOT ET FILS Loire	*Attractive apples and pear aromas lead onto a weighty and balanced palate with gooseberry flavours.*	**£9.00**	BDR	(B)
SANCERRE CUVÉE FLORES 1996, VINCENT PINARD Loire	*Rich mineral notes to a grapefruit palate with nuances of herbaceous grass and asparagus.*	**£9.00**	MIS GRT L&W FUL	(B)
DOMAINE DU CHATENOY SAUVIGNON BLANC 1997, PIERRE CLEMENT Loire	*Smoky Sauvignon nose with a balanced palate, grassy flinty notes and an excellent racy finish.*	**£9.20**	DIR NIC ENO	(S)
POUILLY FUMÉ CHÂTEAU FAVRAY 1997, QUENTIN DAVID Loire	*Smoky aromas of gooseberry and flinty minerals carry over onto a lemon and lime palate with a zippy finish.*	**£9.30**	ENO	(B)
POUILLY FUMÉ DEZAT 1996, ANDRÉ DEZAT Loire	*Aromas of gooseberries and grass carry over onto the balanced palate wub nuances of limes and grapefruit.*	**£9.70**	SHJ JNW GNW	(B)
POUILLY FUMÉ CHÂTEAU DE TRACY 1996, COMTE HENRI D'ESTUTT D'ASSAY Loire	*A boneyed nose that is complemented on the palate with lemony acidity and even balance.*	**£10.50**	Widely Available	(B)

POUILLY FUMÉ DE LADOUCETTE 1996, DOMAINE DE LADOUCETTE Loire	*Steely acid with asparagus and pears. The palate has gooseberries and sharp green fruits with a delicious aftertaste.*	**£13.00**	FSW DIR SEL NEI MWW COE HVN HOF	(S)
SANCERRE BLANC LE CHENE MARCHAND 1996, PASCAL JOLIVET Loire	*A subtle nose with mineral notes. Delicate palate of gooseberry fruit and well matched acidity.*	**£13.50**	MMD	(S)

FRANCE • LOIRE • SWEET

BONNEZEAUX CHÂTEAU DES FESLES 1996, VIGNOBLES GERMAIN Loire	*Crammed with barley sugar, apples and toffees this wine leaves you reminiscing of halcyon schooldays.*	**£25.50** (37.5cl)	WSP DIR TPE ALL	(S)
LE HAUT LIEU VOUVRAY MOELLEUX PREMIER TRIE 1990, GASTON HUET Loire	*A blend of strawberries and cream, rich buttered honey and marmalade. Has crisp acidity and fresh finish.*	**£28.10**	RDS NYW WTD	(G)

FRANCE • PROVENCE • RED

DOMAINE DU JAS D'ESCLANS CRU CLASSÉ ORGANIC 1994, DOMAINE DU JAS D'ESCLANS Côtes de Provence	*With its smoky and berry fruit aromas this is a complex wine that is not too overpowering.*	**£5.00**	VER	(B)
CHÂTEAU ROUTAS INFERNET 1995, ROUVIER PLANE Côtes de Provence	*Dry and lean with spicy pepper fruit in a wine of great length and weight.*	**£6.20**	GGW M&V DBY F&M BOO HVN	(B)

Wine	Description	Price	Codes	
CHÂTEAU MINUTY ROUGE CUVÉE PRESTIGE 1996, MATTON-FARNET Côtes de Provence	*Full rich and complex. A very well-balanced wine with firm tannins and excellent fruit.*	£6.90	ABY	B
LES BAUX DE PROVENCE 1994, CHAPELLE DE ROMANIN Les Baux de Provence	*Fresh plum nose leading to a palate of lifted tannins and prickly acidity.*	£8.50	ADN	B
DOMAINE DE TRIENNES LES AURELIENS 1995, DOMAINES DE TRIENNES Côtes de Provence	*Deeply coloured with enticingly mingling oak and plum fruit flavours developing beautifully in the mouth.*	£9.00	A&N	S
DOMAINES LES BEATES 1996, MARC CHAPOUTIER Côtes de Provence	*Has quite a Rhône feel, spicy fruit and warm tannins mingle with tar and dark brambly fruit.*	£9.20	GON MGN NEI WCR MWW	B
DOMAINES DE TRIENNES RESERVE 1995, DOMAINES DE TRIENNES Côtes de Provence	*A young tightly structured, cherry red wine that shows elegant herbaceous characters.*	£9.50	BEN A&N	B
MAS DE LA ROUVIÈRE 1995, DOMAINE BUNAN Bandol	*Spicy fruit on both the nose and palate, a nicely coloured soft wine showing some oak.*	£10.90	SEL DBY FLM	B
CHÂTEAU DE PIBARNON 1995, COMTE DE ST. VICTOR Bandol	*Intense and concentrated, this wine has a very complex structure in its chewy palate.*	£13.30	GON WIN ABY DBY	B
RABIEGA CLOS D'IÉRE CUVÉE II 1994, RABIEGA VINS Côtes de Provence	*Another medal winning wine proves this producer is onto a good thing. A clean and complex wine.*	£19.00	LEA	S

FRANCE • PROVENCE • ROSÉ

CHÂTEAU MINUTY ROSÉ CUVÉE PRESTIGE 1997, MATTON-FARNET Côtes de Provence	*Delicious with slightly spicy strawberry fruit and subtle underlying tannins on a broad palate.*	**£9.30**	ABY	B

FRANCE • RHÔNE • RED

TESCO'S CÔTES DU RHÔNE VILLAGES 1997, PRINCES DE FRANCE Rhône	*A good fruit nose, quite sharp palate with integrated tannins and a good finish.*	**£4.00**	TOS	B
VAUCLUSE LE JOANIS 1997, JEAN-LOUIS CHANCEL Rhône	*This wine had fragrant berry fruit some spice and pepper notes and dancing tannins.*	**£4.20**	ABY	B
CÔTES DU RHÔNE CARTE NOIR 1995, CELLIER DES DAUPHINS Rhône	*This high profile producer can be proud of this clean, quite lean wine which showed well.*	**£4.90**	WES HOT	B
CÔTES DU LUBÉRON CHÂTEAU VAL JOANIS 1995, JEAN-LOUIS CHANCEL Rhône	*Lighter cuvée but bursting with fresh, vibrant fruit with ripe tannins and spice notes.*	**£5.00**	ABY	B
CÔTES DU RHÔNE DOMAINE DE LA PRÉSIDENTE 1997, DOMAINE MAX AUBERT Rhône	*Clean, light and fruity on the nose. This is a delicate, balanced, subtle wine.*	**£5.00**	SGL NAD	B

VACQUERAS DOMAINE DE LA SOLEIADE 1997, J P SELLES Rhône	*A slightly perfumed nose with good ripe sweet fruit flavours in ascendency and a decent length.*	£5.00	UNS SMF	B
MARKS & SPENCER LA TOUR DU PRÊVÔT 1996, JEAN-PIERRE ET FRANÇOIS PERRIN Rhône	*Jammy boiled fruit. Deep bramble and creamy mulberry palate. Nicely balanced, thoroughly velvety and voluptuous.*	£5.00	M&S	B
CAIRANNE CÔTES DU RHÔNE VILLAGES 1996, DOMAINE BRUSSET Rhône	*An attractive blackberry nose with nice fruit, tannins and acidity. A hint of smoke and spiciness.*	£5.30	DBY ENO	B
CHÂTEAUNEUF-DU-PAPE CHÂTEAU SIMIAN 1996, SERGUIER ET FILS Rhône	*A minty, spicy nose leads to a well-balanced, fruity and peppery palate with a decent finish.*	£5.50	ALZ	B
CHÂTEAU DE LA TUILÈRIE 'CARTE BLANCHE' ROUGE 1996, CHÂTEAU DE LA TUILÈRIE Rhône	*Ripe gamey notes with soft spicy tannins on an underlying palate of cinnamon.*	£5.90	WES SGL NAD	B
CÔTES DU LUBÈRON CUVÉE CHATAIGNIER 1997, DOMAINE DE LA CITADELLE Rhône	*A well-coloured wine, very well-structured with a good palate and good finish.*	£6.00	NIC	B
CÔTES DU RHÔNE LAURENT BRUSSET 1996, DOMAINE BRUSSET Rhône	*A clean and aromatic wine that has spicy fruit anda good finish with medium colour.*	£6.00	ENO	B

Pinpoint who sells the wine you wish to buy by turning to the stockist codes. If you know the name of the wine you want to buy, use the alphabetical index. If the price is your motivation, refer to the invaluable price guide index; red and white wines under £5, sparkling wines under £12 and Champagne under £16. Happy hunting!

CÔTES DU LUBÈRON CHÂTEAU L'ISOLETTE 1996, LUC PINATEL Rhône	*A lovely fruit nose carries to the palate and meets pepper and tobacco tones.*	**£6.30**	WES	**B**
CÔTES DU RHÔNE BOUQUET DE GARRIGUES 1996, VACHERON POUIZIN Rhône	*A rich brambley nose leads on to a complex fruity palate with a hint of tobacco.*	**£6.70**	HVW	**B**
CÔTES DU LUBÈRON CHÂTEAU CONSTANTIN CHEVALIER 1995, ALLEN CHEVALIER Rhône	*A lovely perfumed nose. It is balanced and complex with ripe soft berry and savoury characters.*	**£6.80**	WSA	**S**
RASTEAU CÔTES DU RHÔNE VILLAGES 1996, MARC CHAPOUTIER Rhône	*A ripe, rich and warm wine. It develops well in the mouth and has a good finish.*	**£7.10**	WCR ADN DIR HOT MGN NEI CNL ODD	**S**
DOMAINE ST ANNE CUVÉE NOTRE DAME 1996, LES CELLETTES Rhône	*A spicy, peppery nose, with blackberries and jammy fruit flavours on the palate and a long finish.*	**£7.90**	GON	**S**
CAIRANNE CÔTES DU RHÔNE VILLAGES 1997, DOMAINE RICHAUD Rhône	*Good fruit structure with minty, peppery overtones. Spicy acidity and well developed tannins blend into a good finish.*	**£8.00**	HOU LIB	**B**
CÔTES DU LUBÈRON CHÂTEAU VAL JOANIS LES GRIOTTES 1993, JEAN-LOUIS CHANCEL Rhône	*Bright cherry colour with stacks of fine berry fruit, juicy tannins and a whizz finish.*	**£8.00**	ABY	**B**
CÔTES DU LUBÈRON CHÂTEAU VAL JOANIS LES GRIOTTES 1995, JEAN-LOUIS CHANCEL Rhône	*Tasters were suitably impressed by the fine quality of this lovely wine with elegant tannins and chunky fruit.*	**£8.00**	ABY	**B**

CROZES HERMITAGE PETITE RUCHE 1996, MARC CHAPOUTIER Rhône	*Ripe strong fruit with grippy drying tannins on a layered palate with an elegant finish.*	**£8.40**	Widely Available	**B**
ST JOSEPH 1996, LOUIS MOUSSET Rhône	*Quite austere on the nose but has warm generous fruit on a peppered, tar palate.*	**£8.50**	UNS	**B**
GIGONDAS 1996, CHÂTEAU DU TRIGNON Rhône	*One of the southern Rhône's more robust wines this is a wonderfully powerful example of its type.*	**£9.10**	DLA GRT MWW TPE BDR WRC	**S**
CHÂTEAUNEUF-DU-PAPE LES OLIVIERS 1996, CAVES ST PIERRE Rhône	*Do we not like this? Leathery, tar notes big fruit cake flavours and tannins.*	**£9.10**	SVT WCR ODD WTS THS WRC BUP	**B**
CROZES HERMITAGE LES MEYSONNIERS 1995, MARC CHAPOUTIER Rhône	*This Syrah is quite firm has a pleasant nose, big fruit characters and a good finish.*	**£9.40**	Widely Available	**B**
GIGONDAS TRADITION 1996, DOMAINE BRUSSET Rhône	*Excellent on the nose this wine has power, structure, equilibrium and a very good finish.*	**£9.90**	ENO	**B**
CÔTES DU LUBÈRON CHÂTEAU L'ISOLETTE AQUARELLE 1989, LUC PINATEL Rhône	*Luscious nose and a huge fruit palate with considerable acidity and introverted tannins.*	**£10.00**	BPW	**B**
GIGONDAS 1995, DOMAINE SANTA DUC Rhône	*Deeply coloured, this warm complex wine shows spirity, leathery characters and has a long rounded finish.*	**£10.20**	DIR GON MIS POR NYW	**S**

CROZES HERMITAGE DOMAINE DE THALABERT 1995, PAUL JABOULET Rhône	*A spicy, leathery nose. Chocolatey, oaky palate with raspberry fruit and softish tannins in support.*	£11.40	Widely Available	**S**
CHÂTEAUNEUF-DU-PAPE DOMAINE CHANTE CIGALE 1996, DOMAINE CHANTE CIGALE Rhône	*A rich chewy wine with open tannins and a strong, spicy but lean finish.*	£11.70	NRW CVR COK WIN POR DBY BOO	**B**
DOMAINE DE CABASSE SEGURET ROUGE CUVÉE CASA BASSA 1995, DOMAINE DE CABASSE Rhône	*Inky red colour and subtle nose with a fruity and spicy tobacco palate.*	£12.00	HWL HW SVT	**B**
CHÂTEAUNEUF-DU-PAPE DOMAINE FONT DE MICHELLE 1996, JEAN & MICHEL GONNET Rhône	*This has quite delicious fruit ripe spicy tannins and a slightly jammy finish.*	£12.10	Widely Available	**B**
DOMAINE RICHEAUME CUVÉE COLUMELLE 1996, HENNING HOESCH Rhône	*Juicy black cherry, spice and leather aromas. Fruit, mint and a warm alcohol liquorice palate with good tannins.*	£12.90	DBY VER TOS	**S**
CHÂTEAUNEUF-DU-PAPE DOMAINE FONT DE MICHELLE 1995, JEAN & MICHEL GONNET Rhône	*Light and fruity nose, but with some age and mature fruit. Elevated oak length and complexity.*	£13.60	DBY L&W AMW THS WRC BUP	**B**
CHÂTEAUNEUF-DU-PAPE 1995, MARC CHAPOUTIER Rhône	*A concentrated warm and generous wine. Intensely fruity. Develops wonderfully in the mouth. Very well-structured.*	£13.80	Widely Available	**S**
DOMAINE FONT DE MICHELLE, CUVÉE ETIENNE GONNET 1995, JEAN & MICHELLE GONNET Rhône	*Spicy and rustic with balanced acidity and pronounced fruit. Medium tannins and length.*	£14.80	DBY BUP HVW BKT UBC NYW THS WRC	**B**

HERMITAGE **J VIDAL- FLEURY 1991,** **BRUNO THIERRY** Rhône	*Mature gamey flavours on the nose, fantastic colour, big spicy fruit and underlying tannins.*	**£15.00**	BDR	(B)
GIGONDAS TRADITION **LES HAUTES DE** **MONTMIRAIL 1996,** **DOMAINE BRUSSET** Rhône	*A lovely nutty and smoky bacon nose with strong tannins and acid supporting subtle fruits.*	**£16.50**	ENO	(B)
CHÂTEAUNEUF-DU-PAPE **DOMAINE DE LA JANASSE** **VIEILLES VIGNES 1996,** **DOMAINE DE LA JANASSE** Rhône	*Herbaceous nose leads to good fruit and warm spicy oak. Creamy with a long finish.*	**£20.60**	ENO	(B)
CORNAS LES RUCHETS **1995, JEAN-LUC** **COLOMBO** Rhône	*An earthy farmyard nose uncomplicated juicy blackberry fruit. It finishes well with some taut wood tannins.*	**£23.50**	MFS JNW NYW	(B)

FRANCE • RHÔNE • WHITE

CHARDONNAY VIN DE **PAYS DES COTEAUX DE** **L'ARDECHE,** **VIGNERONS ARDECHOIS** Rhône	*Light floral bouquet with fresh lively fruit on the palate and a soft adequate finish.*	**£4.80**	NIC CPW	(B)
CHÂTEAU DE LA TUILÈRIE **"CARTE BLANCHE"** **BLANC 1997, CHÂTEAU** **DE LA TUILÈRIE** Rhône	*This has spicy fruit, lovely acidity and tip top sherbet zip on a soft palate.*	**£5.00**	SGL NAD	(B)
CHÂTEAU VAL JOANIS **CÔTES DU LUBÈRON** **1997, CHRISTIAN** **CHANCEL** Rhône	*Perfumed nose with a mouth full of luscious ripe fruit with nice acid and length.*	**£5.00**	ABY	(B)

LAURUS CÔTES DU RHÔNE BLANC 1997, GABRIEL MEFFRE Rhône	*Delicate perfumed fruit on the nose with lifted acidity and slight lanolin character on the finish.*	£5.00	GYW	(B)
CONDRIEU LES CHAILLETS VIEILLES VIGNES 1997, DOMAINE CUILLÈRON Rhône	*Grassy and floral hints on the nose, complex flavours and sweetness, a crisp pleasant finish.*	£20.00	ODD ENO	(B)

FRANCE • SOUTH WEST • RED

MERLOT VDP DE CÔTES DE GASGOGNE 1997, YVON MAU South West France	*Hot, baked flavours of plums and damsons with a grippy finish. An attractive, quaffing wine.*	£3.99	YVM	(B)
CÔTES DE ST. MONT ROUGE VDQS 1996, PRODUCTEURS PLAIMONT South West France	*Ripe, fruity flavours with grippy tannins from local grape varieties mark this wine out.*	£4.30	NIC HOT SHJ L&W ABY JSM ALZ	(B)
BERGERAC ROUGE 1997, CHÂTEAU DE LA COLLINE South West France	*An enticing mingling of oak and plum fruit flavours, with an attractively tannic finish.*	£5.40	GRT	(S)
CAHORS CLOS DE LA COUTALE 1995, BERNEDE & FILS South West France	*This wine has tremendous character with a herby Garrigue nose and develops superbly in the mouth.*	£6.70	WCR NIC	(B)
MADIRAN CHÂTEAU BOUSCASSÉ 1995, ALAIN BRUMONT South West France	*A dark, beautifully coloured wine. Well-balanced with a concentration and finish that is hard to beat.*	£9.10	WIN RDS ABY DBY NYW	(S)

FRANCE • SOUTH WEST • WHITE

DOMAINE DU TARIQUET SAUVIGNON BLANC VDP DE CÔTES DE GASGOGNE 1997, DOMAINES GRASSA South West France	*A gentle, sophisticated nose with earthy, ripe tropical fruit flavours and an easy youthful finish.*	£4.70	WCR JNW THS WRC BUP	(B)
JURANÇON SEC SÈVE D'AUTOMNE 1996, DOMAINE SÈVE D'AUTOMNE South West France	*Lots of mango and tropical fruit characters with a hint of grass and integrated oak.*	£6.00	JNW SGL NAD EBA	(B)
DOMAINE DU TARIQUET SAUVIGNON BLANC VDP DE CÔTES DE GASGOGNE 1996, DOMAINES GRASSA South West France	*Mineral, limestone notes to a zippy gooseberry palate with a refreshingly clean, citrus finish.*	£6.20	WCR L&W T&T BUP THS WRC	(B)
LES JARDINS DU BOUSCASSÉ 1996, DOMAINE DU BOUSCASSÉ Pacherenc du Vic - Bilh	*Spicy fragrant fruit with banana and vanilla on the nose combined with excitingly zingy acid.*	£6.30	ABY	(B)
DOMAINE DE LUZANET VDP DE CÔTES DE GASGOGNE 1997, F. & J. RIGAL South West France	*Ripe flavours of melons, tart gooseberries and grapefruit on a clean, lingering and zappy palate.*	£6.50	ENO BUP	(B)
JURANÇON SEC 1996, DOMAINE CASTERA South West France	*Floral gooseberry and grapefruit aromas with lots of fresh clean fruit on the palate, great length.*	£8.10	SEL GRT	(S)

Pinpoint who sells the wine you wish to buy by turning to the stockist codes. If you know the name of the wine you want to buy, use the alphabetical index. If the price is your motivation, refer to the invaluable price guide index; red and white wines under £5, sparkling wines under £12 and Champagne under £16. Happy hunting!

FRANCE • SOUTH WEST • SWEET

JURANÇON CHÂTEAU LE PAYRAL CUVÉE MARIE JEANNE 1995, CHÂTEAU LE PAYRAL South West France	*Rich apricots and butter on the nose, followed by an even fatter palate of freshly cooked toffee.*	**£11.50**	ENO NYW

(S)

GERMANY

Germany continues to produce award winning wines at all quality and price levels, from delicious Eisweins to the quaffing QbAs. The judges also noted that there was a general increase in quality across the board from supermarket own labels to the produce of individual vineyards. Some stunningly attractive wines are in this section from classic grape varieties and locations as well as the increasingly popular "New World" style wines from forward thinking producers. Pröst!

GERMANY • WHITE

TESCO NIERSTEINER KABINETT 1997, ZGM ZELL-MOSEL Rheinhessen	*Starts with a subtle, honeyed aroma and continues to impress with a palate of concentrated, lemony pear drops.*	**£3.20**	TOS	**B**
KENDERMANN NORTHERN STAR MEDIUM 1997, WEINGUT KENDERMANN Pflaz	*Peachy nose and delicate aromatics lead on to a well-balanced mouth of soft fruit and sherbet like acidity.*	**£3.50**	ASD	**B**
CO-OP OWN LABEL SPÄTLESE 1996, PETER MERTES Pfalz	*Medium dry, vegetal and spicy aromas bringing on the honey and lemon flavours, and a little acidity.*	**£4.00**	CWS	**B**
SOMERFIELD RHEINHESSEN SPÄTLESE 1994, RHEINBERG KELLEREI Rheinhessen	*Ripe fruit nose, palate of honey and pineapple flavours follows through with some complexity and depth.*	**£4.00**	SMF	**B**
ZELTINGER HIMMELREICH RIESLING KABINETT 1997, MOSELLAND EG Mosel-Saar-Ruwer	*Powerful lime fruit on nose; a hint of petillance underlines the pronounced spicy, zesty flavours.*	**£4.00**	JSM	**B**

MALT HOUSE VINTNERS BLAUMEISTER AÜSLESE '96, WEINGUT REICHSGRAFIN VON MEDEM Pfalz	*Honeyed mature nose, rich floral palate of sweet lychee flavours which linger in a long pleasant finish.*	£4.80	MHV	B
GRANS FASSIAN RIESLING 1995, WEINGUT GRANS FASSIAN Mosel-Saar-Ruwer	*Slatey, flinty mineral notes on the honeyed pineapple flavoured palate with lots of crunchy lemon acidity.*	£6.00	SPR	S
SCHLOSS SCHONBORN RIESLING KABINETT 1987, SCHLOSS SCHONBORN Rheingau	*Honeyed beeswax nose; pleasing soft fruits with a touch of residual sugar and good acidity.*	£6.00	SMF	B
OCKFENER BOCKSTEIN RIESLING 1996, VON KESSELSTATT Mosel-Saar-Ruwer	*Beautiful sweet green apples on the nose hint at the zingy fresh acidity and fruit in the mouth.*	£6.20	JNW CWS ODD	B
NIERSTEINER OELBERG RIESLING SPÄTLESE 1991, BURGERMEISTER BALBACH ERBEN Rheinhessen	*Delicate floral aromas and flavours of honeysuckle with notes of petroleum. A refreshing, clean finish.*	£7.20	BDR	B
BERNKASTELER BADSTUBE RIESLING KABINETT 1996, WEINGUT VON KESSELSTATT Mosel-Saar-Ruwer	*The classic mineral, grapefruit bouquet heralds a stately yet subtle wine of clean fresh floral flavour.*	£7.50	FSW JNW CWS MWW	S
HATTENHEIMER PFAFFENBERGER RIESLING SPÄTLESE 1989, SCHLOSS SCHONBORN Rheingau	*A ripe petroly Riesling nose floats out of this supremely well-balanced ripe, sweet fruit mature palate.*	£7.60	WTS BDR CST	S
BRAUNEBERGER JUFFER RIESLING SPÄTLESE 1994, WEINGUT LICHT-BERGWEILER Mosel-Saar-Ruwer	*Citrus notes of lemon and zesty lime on a floral palate of honeysuckle and roses.*	£7.70	BDR	B

WHITE • GERMANY

Wine	Description	Price	Codes	
JOHANNISBERGER KLAUS RIESLING SPÄTLESE 1990, SCHLOSS SCHONBORN Rheingau	*Mineral notes giving complexity to a ripe pineapple and citrus palate. Floral highlights on the refreshing finish.*	£9.30	BDR	(S)
REICHSGRAF VON KESSELSTATT RIESLING SPÄTLESE 1996, WEINGUT REICHS. VON KESSELSTATT Mosel-Saar-Ruwer	*Delicate floral bouquet, a finely balanced palate of ripe apples and fresh peach, balancing acidity and superb finish.*	£9.40	JNW CPW MWW HVW SAF	(S)
ROBERT WEIL RIESLING KABINETT 1996, WILLHELM WEIL Rheingau	*Crisp floral notes lead to fresh, zippy, appley flavours which are delicately balanced by a medium-dry acidity.*	£10.00	WTS	(B)
SCHLOSS JOHANNISBERG RIESLING KABINETT 1996, SCHLOSS JOHANNISBERG Rheingau	*Light floral nose, leads to a mineral, honey palate with refreshing acidity and a balanced finish.*	£10.40	WIN DBY GNW	(B)
RUDESHEIMER BERG ROSENECK SPÄTLESE 1997, JOSEF LEITZ Rheingau	*Ripe pineapple and honey flavours with a zesty grapefruit finish to a classic Riesling.*	£13.00	WSG	(B)
SCHLOSS JOHANNISBERG RIESLING SPÄTLESE 1995, SCHLOSS JOHANNISBERG Rheingau	*Smoky, honeyed bouquet. Spicy, mouthwatering citrus fruit characters given added complexity by mineral tones.*	£13.30	WIN DBY GNW	(S)
GRAACHER HIMMELREICH RIESLING SPÄTLESE 1994, J. J. PRÜM Mosel-Saar-Ruwer	*Delicate nose with some mineral notes underlines the rich Spätlese style with classic petrol notes.*	£13.50	WTS	(B)
HOCHHEIMER KIRCHENSTUCK RIESLING SPÄTLESE 1996, WEINGUT FRANZ KÜNSTLER Rheingau	*Fruity nose with rich honeyed tones develops into ripe strawberry fruit with icing sugar sweetness.*	£15.00	DIR J&B	(S)

157

GERMANY • WHITE – SWEET

BERNKASTELER DOCTOR RIESLING KABINETT 1996, ZIMMERMANN, GRAEFF & MULLER Mosel-Saar-Ruwer	*A perfumed fruity nose precedes this simple but likeable, spritzy palate of good fruit and low acidity.*	£16.00	UNS	(B)
WEHLENER SONNENUHR RIESLING SPÄTLESE 1994, J. J. PRUM Mosel-Saar-Ruwer	*Lemon lime tones on the nose with clean, honey and citrus characters balanced by a refreshing acidity.*	£16.90	J&B	(S)

GERMANY • SWEET

SOMERFIELD RHEINHESSEN AÜSLESE 1997, RHEINBERG KELLEREI Rheinhessen	*Complex caramelly nose, rich ripe Riesling character on palate, clean honey, floral flavours with good acidity.*	£4.30	SMF	(B)
TESCO PFALZ AÜSLESE NV, GEBIETS-WINZERGENOSS-ENSCHAFT DEUTSCHES WEINTOR IIBESHEIM Pfalz	*Floral nose with a hint of caramel; good ripe fruit concentration and some pleasant acidity.*	£5.00	TOS	(B)
GRAACHER HIMMELREICH RIESLING AÜSLESE 1993, WEINGUT LICHT-BERGWEILER ERBEN Mosel-Saar-Ruwer	*Sweet nose of kerosene and roses with ripe pineapples and cleansing green apples on the finish.*	£8.90	BDR	(G)
WEINGUT VON SCHLEINITZ RIESLING AÜSLESE 1995, WEINGUT VON SCHLEINITZ Mosel-Saar-Ruwer	*Rich, honeyed fruits, pineapples and lemons, on a floral palate full of roses and honeysuckle.*	£9.40	WSP BBO	(S)
URZIGER WÜRZGARTEN RIESLING AÜSLESE GOLD CAPSULE 1997, WEINGUT BENEDICT LOOSEN-ERBEN Mosel-Saar-Ruwer	*Pear and burnt toast on nose with simple barley-sugar sweetness make this an enjoyable wine.*	£17.70	JNW HVW	(B)

ITALY

Gone are the days when no self respecting party would be complete without a large bottle of inexpensive Italian wine. While top quality producers such as Gaja and Frescobaldi continue to set the standard the rapid increase of IGT wines can only help to release enthusiastic winemakers from the constraining shackles of the DOC system and encourage new styles of wines using different grape varieties. However Italy is still unsurpassed in the production of stunning Recioto and Amarone wines. Salute!

ITALY • PIEDMONT

BARBERA D'ASTI BRICCO ZANONE 1996, TERRE DA VINO Piedmont	*Refined fruit and toasty are apt descriptions, tasters suggested this may open up in time.*	£5.00	ODD SMF	B
DOLCETTO D' ALBA VIGNA SANTA ANNA 1996, GIACOMO ASCHERI Piedmont	*A violet ruby colour offers crunchy, under ripe plums along with hints of leafy brambles.*	£8.10	DIR WCS ENO	B
DOLCETTO D' ALBA PRIAVINO 1996, ROBERTO VOERZIO Piedmont	*Rich flavours of liquorice and almonds with ripe currants and cherries are balanced by good acidity.*	£8.90	DIR V&C ENO NYW	S
BARBERA D' ALBA VIGNA FONTANELLE 1995, GIACOMO ASCHERI Piedmont	*Smoky hints with a gamey liquorice palate with earthy tannins and lean acidity.*	£9.00	DIR ENO	B
ALASIA PINOT NERO 1997, ALASIA Piedmont	*Green pea, vegetal nose with ripe, vibrant Pinot Noir fruit character on the palate. Good length.*	£9.30	LIB	B

Wine	Notes	Price	Stockist	
BARBERA D'ALBA 1996, CORDERO DI MONTEZEMOLO Piedmont	Upfront and youthful, with crisp minty aromas. Fresh plummy fruit with balanced tannins and acidity.	£10.00	BBR WIM CCL	B
CROUTIN BARBERA D'ASTI SUPERIORE RISERVA PERSONALE '95, CANTINE F. & M. SCRIMAGLIO Piedmont	Spectacular Christmas cake flavours, with a wild array of cherries, toasted nuts, plump raisins.	£14.00	IWS	S
BAROLO SERRALUNGA D'ALBA 1993, FONTANNAFREDA Piedmont	Nose shows good complexity. Liquorice, rosehip and stewed red fruit flavours predominate.	£14.90	V&C	B
BAROLO MONVIGLIERO 1990, CANTINE TERRE DEL BAROLO Piedmont	A slightly oxidised nose is carried through to the cold tea tannins and biting acidity.	£16.50	IWS TOS	B
SITOREY GAJA 1994, ANGELO GAJA Piedmont	Hard to believe that this is Barbera. Gaja has worked magic in this heady mint and blackcurrant wonder.	£17.20	DIR V&C L&W RDS DBY JAR	G
BAROLO SORI GINESTRA 1994, CONTERNO FANTINO Piedmont	A strong herbal, medicinal quality on the nose is translated into a light fresh Barolo.	£26.50	DIR ENO	B

ITALY • TUSCANY

Wine	Notes	Price	Stockist	
CHIANTI SUPERIORE LA CINQUANTINA BURCHINO 1996, CASTELLANI Tuscany	Big ripe fruit nose, a little confected but good flavours and structure on the finish.	£4.50	YWL	B

VILLA TESEO 1995, CASTELLANI Tuscany	*A moderate use of oak adds richness and finesse to an already full, fruity palate.*	£5.00	YWL	(B)
CHIANTI 1997, CANTINE LEONARDO Tuscany	*Light, florally perfumed fruit on the nose. Well reflected in the structured, rounded palate.*	£5.70	BEN	(B)
CHIANTI VILLA SOVESTRO 1996, BARONCINI Tuscany	*Displays great finesse on the nose and palate. Ripe fruit is masked by still youthful tannins.*	£6.00	BDR	(S)
CHIANTI CLASSICO REMOLE 1996, MARCHESI DE' FRESCOBALDI Tuscany	*Ripe flavours of cherries with nuances of liquorice, spice and violets. A drying bitter finish with good length.*	£6.30	SEL GNW MWW ODD WCR GRA	(B)
CHIANTI 1997, RENZO MASI Tuscany	*Lots of primary fruit aromas of blackcurrant and cherries make it great to drink now or later.*	£6.40	BDR	(S)
TESCO CHIANTI CLASSICO RISERVA 1995, CASTELLI DEL GREVEPESA, MERCATALE VAL DI PESA Tuscany	*A lighter but still fragrant style of Chianti Classico. May open up more with time.*	£6.50	TOS	(B)
CHIANTI CLASSICO 1996, PICCINI Tuscany	*Characteristic almond and bitter cherry nose. Light body showing great finesse with an elegantly long finish.*	£6.60	WRT SMF CST	(S)
CHIANTI CLASSICO VILLA ARCENO VIGNA LA PORTA 1995, TENUTA DI ARCENO Tuscany	*Obvious ripe fruit appeal to this wine. Palate not overtly complex yet, just give it a year or two.*	£7.00	BPW	(S)

Brisco Dei Barbi 1996, Fattoria dei Barbi Tuscany	*Dry, fresh lively and peppery with bountiful, herbacious fruit. Well-balanced tannins and fresh acidity.*	£7.30	DIR V&C HVW ENO VIL	**S**
Chianti Classico 1996, Villa La Pagliaia Tuscany	*Chianti Classico showing its quality with a little more depth of flavour than the norm.*	£7.50	AMW	**B**
Barco Reale di Carmignano 1997, Capezzana Tuscany	*Full of summer fruits with just a tinge of violets. Rounded off by well-structured tannins.*	£7.80	HOT CWI	**B**
Castello di Nippozzano Riserva 1994, Marchesi de' Frescobaldi Tuscany	*Delights the nose with savoury spice and ripe fruit flavours backed by a palate of crushed cherries.*	£8.00	CPW CRS ODD MWW GRA	**S**
Chianti Rufina 1996, Selvapiana Tuscany	*Attractive gamey nose with wood hints and generous fruit on a baked cherry palate.*	£8.00	V&C GGW HVW LIB NYW	**B**
Poggio Alla Badiola Rosso di Toscana 1996, Castello di Fonterutoli Tuscany	*Closed nose, but showing potential for the future. Fresh blackcurrant flavours with good oak balance.*	£8.00	ENO VLW	**B**
Vino Nobile de Montepulciano 1994, Santa Sabina Tuscany	*Still youthful, the good concentration of fruit and tannin will enable this wine to age gracefully.*	£8.00	FAB	**B**
Chianti Rufina Riserva 1993, Villa Di Vetrice Tuscany	*Gently medicinal nose, with redcurrants and oak flavours. Tannins are softening, so drink now.*	£8.10	Widely Available	**B**

VINO NOBILE DI MONTEPULCIANO 1994, AVIGNONESI Tuscany	*Well developed with an open toasty oak and butterscotch nose. Firm but approachable now.*	£9.00	WTS	(B)
PARRINA RISERVA 1995, FATTORIA LA PARRINA Tuscany	*Smooth and mature with chocolate, creamy cherry fruit, coffee and toffee flavours emerging.*	£9.20	Widely Available	(S)
CHIANTI CLASSICO BARRIQUE 1995, TENIMENTI PILE LAMIOLE Tuscany	*Burnt cherry aromas with liquorice and vanilla notes on a chewy palate with lifted tannins.*	£9.30	ALI	(B)
CHIANTI CLASSICO 1995, FATORIA VALTELLINA Tuscany	*A more full bodied style, well deserving of its Classico status. Needs some laying down.*	£9.50	ABA	(B)
CHIANTI CLASSICO 1996, CASTELLO DI FONTERUTOLI Tuscany	*Tobacco and plum hints on a lean nose dive into a generous palate of burnt cherries.*	£9.50	JNW V&C RDS DBY VLW NYW	(B)
CHIANTI CLASSICO 1996, FONTODI Tuscany	*Inky, with a touch of iodine. Firm palate with well-balanced tannins, acidity, smoky fruit and oak.*	£10.00	V&C HOT DBY VLW FUL LIB	(S)
POMINO ROSSO 1994, MARCHESI DE' FRESCOBALDI Tuscany	*An interesting blend of Pinot Noir, Sangiovese and Cabernet Sauvignon produces this dry elegant red.*	£10.00	ODD GRA FRT	(B)
CHIANTI CLASSICO 1996, FELSINA BERARDENGA Tuscany	*Those berby black cherry aromas come to the fore, with just a sprinkling of black pepper.*	£10.20	SVT V&C CPW GGW DBY SAN	(B)

Wine	Description	Price	Stockists	
CHIANTI RISERVA DUCALE 1993, TENIMENTI RUFFINO Tuscany	*Assaults the senses with medicinal, savoury and fruit aromas. Ripe cherry fruit on the palate and balanced acidity.*	£10.40	V&C POR ALI LLY	G
CHIANTI CLASSICO RISERVA LAMOLE DI LAMOLE 1994, TENIMENTI PILE LAMOLE Tuscany	*Rich with black cherry, burnt almond and mint flavours. A perfect partner to roast venison.*	£10.70	ALI	B
CHIANTI RUFINA RISERVA VIGNETO BUCERCHIALE 1994, SELVAPIANA Tuscany	*Ripe black cherries and dark chocolate balance perfectly on the palate with firm, grainy tannins.*	£10.90	BEN V&C GGW DBY NYW RES LIB	S
CHIANTI CLASSICO 1996, ISOLE E OLENA Tuscany	*Smoky, quite leafy aromas with bright cherry fruit on a medium weight palate.*	£11.40	Widely Available	B
CHIANTI RUFINA RISERVA VIGNETO FORNACE 1994, SELVAPIANA Tuscany	*Deep concentrated colour and a palate that doesn't disappoint. Powerful and well structured with smoky redberry fruit.*	£11.70	V&C COK GGW NYW RES LIB	S
VINO NOBILE DI MONTEPUCIANO 1995, POLIZIANO Tuscany	*Vibrant fruit, well-balanced oak and green spices with well matched tannins.*	£12.30	DIR V&C COK SHJ ENO VIL VIL	B
CHIANTI CLASSICO RISERVA VIGNETO RANCIA 1994, FELSINA BERARDENGA Tuscany	*Slightly prickly nose, and depth and development on the palate. Retains plenty of fruit and tannin.*	£13.30	Widely Available TROPI WIN]	G
PROMIS ROSSO 1994, PIEVE DI SANTA ROSTITUTA Tuscany	*Nice balance of fruit, acidity and tannin rounded off with a subtle use of oak.*	£13.40	DIR L&W DBY JAR	B

BRIGANTE 1994, FATTORIA DEI BARBI Tuscany	*Showing development on the toasty oak nose, but the palate is still packed with plums and damsons.*	£13.70	DIR ENO VIL	(B)
FARNITO CABERNET SAUVIGNON 1995, CARPINETO Tuscany	*Massive rich ripe berry fruits and spice aromas before fresh raspberry flavours appear on the medium soft palate.*	£14.10	V&C HOH AVB DIR BDR	(S)
CASAL FERRO SANGIOVESE DI TOSCANA 1995, CASTELLO DI BROLIO Tuscany	*Initially bitter almonds on the palate spills into an open chasm of red cherries, vanilla and spice.*	£14.20	JNW V&C NEI DBY ENO NYW VIL	(G)
CHIANTI CLASSICO RISERVA LAMOLE DI LAMOLE 1993, TENIMENTI PILE LAMOLE Tuscany	*Subdued chocolatey nose that still needs time. The rich, complex palate shows how good it could be.*	£14.60	ALI	(S)
TORRIONE 1995, FATTORIA PETROLO Tuscany	*The great concentration of elegant fruit from 40-year-old vines gives this wine its superb structure.*	£14.70	V&C RES LIB	(S)
SPARGOLO ROSSO 1995, CASA VINICOLA CECCHI Tuscany	*The judges called this wine "delicious", with its broad range of lush, juicy flavours.*	£15.00	IWS	(S)
CHIANTI CLASSICO RISERVA VIGNA DEL SORBO 1995, FONTODI Tuscany	*Pungent slightly leathery oak with masses of spicy fruit aromas. Soft and spicy blackcurrant flavours.*	£15.00	V&C HOT DBY LIB VLW	(B)
I GRIFI 1994, AVIGNONESI Tuscany	*Bountiful aromas of mint and oak. Solid fruit structure, with bitter black cherry fruit.*	£15.40	RDS HVW WRC	(G)

CHIANTI CLASSICO RISERVA 1994, BADIA A COLTIBUONO Tuscany	*Tobacco and leather hints with dark cherries and woody tannins on the palate.*	**£17.20**	V&C HOH AVB	S
CHIANTI CLASSICO RISERVA 1995, CASTELLO DI FONTERUTOLI Tuscany	*Mint, violets and spice on the nose, spicy berries and sweet vanilla oak on the palate.*	**£17.50**	JNW V&C RDS DBY ENO VLW NYW CWI	G
CABREO RUFFINO IL BORGO 1995, TENIMENTI RUFFINO Tuscany	*Concentration of ripe, raisiny fruit is given layers of complexity by liquorice, spice and dark chocolate flavours.*	**£18.30**	DBY ALI V&C LLY	S
BRUNELLO DI MONTALCINO 1993, COL D'ORCIA Tuscany	*Displaying some characteristic notes. The full bitter chocolate and morello cherry finish is pure Brunello.*	**£18.50**	LUC V&C	B
ELEGIA 1995, POLIZIANO Tuscany	*Heady Belgian chocolate truffle aromas continue onto the palate with endlessly concentrated fruit.*	**£20.40**	DIR V&C RDS ENO VIL	S
LE STANZE 1995, POLIZIANO Tuscany	*Aromas of cassis and flavours of fresh blackberries with elements of oak, herbs and tobacco on the palate.*	**£20.40**	DIR V&C RDS ENO VIL	S
BRUNELLO DI MONTALCINO 1993, FATTORIA DEI BARBI Tuscany	*Complex earthy nose. Medium weight palate, with developed, even flavour and some solid tannins.*	**£20.80**	DIR DBY HVW ENO VIL CWI	B
FONTALLORO BERARDENGA 1994, FELSINA BERARDENGA Tuscany	*Good nutty nose, with lots of pepper and spice on the well-structured finish.*	**£22.70**	GGW DBY CWI LIB	B

CABERNET DI TOSCANA 1994, OLMAIA Tuscany	*Redcurrants and vanilla dominate the nose before concentrated forest fruits appear on the firm palate.*	**£23.50**	MWW WIM LUC	(B)
CEPPARELLO 1995, ISOLE E OLENA Tuscany	*Soft and round spicy nose, showing some maturity. Nice fruit balance with firm tannins and acidity.*	**£24.40**	Widely Available	(B)

ITALY • OTHER RED

VENIER MONTEPULCIANO D'ABRUZZO 1996, GIV Abruzzo	*A dusty nose with beady eucalyptus, well developed and mature with a healthy acidic finish.*	**£3.00**	KWI	(B)
NERO D'AVOLA 1997, FIRRIATO Sicily	*New World, herbal overtones greet the taster and guide to a softly structured finish.*	**£4.00**	SAF ODD FUL	(B)
NERO DI TROIA PRIMITIVO 1997, BRIGHT BROTHERS Puglia	*Very deep colour. Attractive nose and a rich, full palate make for an enjoyable wine.*	**£4.00**	SMF	(B)
D'ISTINTO SANGIOVESE MERLOT 1997, BRL HARDY WINE COMPANY Sicily	*A meaty, bitter sweet Sangiovese, Merlot blend. The characteristic morello cherry and plums are perfectly matched.*	**£4.10**	Widely Available	(S)
COLORI PRIMITIVO 1996, CASALBAIO Puglia	*Smoky raisin nose with cherry fruit palate and a hint of gameyness on the finish.*	**£4.40**	NRW NEI GGW BWL SMF	(G)

ITALY • OTHER RED

MERLOT TRENTINO 1995, CONCILIO VINI S.P.A Trentino	*Wild mulberry fruit, balanced by tightly packed tannins and earthy wood with a biting finish.*	£4.50	IWS	S
MERLOT TRENTINO 1997, CONCILIO VINI S.P.A Trentino	*A surprising softness beneath the folds of tannin. Lush black cherries should develop with time.*	£4.90	IWS TOS BDR FUL	S
ALLORA PRIMITIVO 1997, CASALBAIO Puglia	*Rich purple colour. Succulent with lots of sweet berry fruit, balanced acidity and good length.*	£4.90	GGW BWL JSM	B
L'ARCO FRIULI GRAVE CABERNET FRANC 1996, CANTINA DI BERTIOLO Friuli-Venezia-Giulia	*Herbaceous notes on a currant and summer fruits nose. Vanilla highlights on the palate with nuances of liquorice.*	£5.00	SMF TOS	G
ROSSO CONERO RISERVA 1995, TERRE CORTESI MONCARO Marche	*Chocolate and mocha nose with a savoury complexity. The mouth fills with oodles of forest fruits.*	£5.00	WIM CCL TOS	G
MONTEPULCIANO D'ABRUZZO CHIARO DI LUNA 1997, MGM MONDO DEL VINO Abruzzo	*Slightly closed on the nose, but opening out into a grassy medicinal red with an aggressive herby acidity.*	£5.00	SAF FUL	S
DUE MONTE NERO DI TROIA CABERNET SAUVIGNON 1996, CANTINA DI BERTIOLO Puglia	*A tight long length is preceded by artificial raspberries and hollow tannins. Heavy commercial style.*	£5.00	EHL	B
MARCA TREVIGIANA MERLOT 1997, LA GIOISA Veneto	*Confected on the nose but is rescued by subtle hints of cedar and green peppers.*	£5.00	D&D	B

OTHER RED • ITALY

RONCHI DI VILLA CABERNET SAUVIGNON REFOSCO 1997, RONCHI DI VILLA Friuli-Venezia Giulia	*A minty, ripe nose and approachable tannins allow full enjoyment of the beady, bubblegum flavours.*	£5.00	WIM CCL	B
VILLA PIGNA ROZZANO 1996, VILLA PIGNA Marche	*A flirty, firey wine with hot tannins and burning scents of tar. Weighty and warm.*	£5.00	ASD	B
VALPOLICELLA CLASSICO SUPERIORE 1995, ZENATO Veneto	*A mature damson nose is accompanied by green, slightly bitter tannins and sharp racey acidity.*	£5.10	SVT L&W DVD THS WRC BUP	B
CABERNET SAUVIGNON MERLOT BASILICATA 1997, BASILUM Basilicata	*This great Cabernet Merlot displays wonderful gamey aromas with rich dark fruit and chocolate flavours.*	£5.20	HOH AVB WTS	G
RIPAROSSO MONTE-PULCIANO D'ABRUZZO 1997, AZIENDA AGRICOLA DINO ILLUMINATI Abruzzo	*Easy drinking, youthfully, full and fruity Montepulciano. Made to be drunk with Gnocchi Al Forno.*	£5.20	V&C SHJ F&M L&W SMF	B
SANGIOVESE DI ROMAGNA LUGO SUPERIORE 1996, GRUPPO COLTIVA Emilia Romagna	*Some slightly oxidised, gamey fruit which adds to the very Italian feel of this flavoursome Sangiovese.*	£5.50	BPW	B
BIZANTINO ROSSO DEL SALENTO 1996, PERVINI Puglia	*A complex nose of violets and baked cherries evolve into an explosion of fruit, tightly wrapped up in drying tannins.*	£5.70	BPW	S
I PORTALI AGLIANICO DEL VULTURE 1996, BASILUM Basilicata	*Big wafts of ginger and cinnamon matched beautifully with black-currant and cigar box flavours.*	£6.00	HOH AVB	S

169

CARAMIA NEGROAMARO 1996, AZIENDA VINICOLA CANTELE Puglia	*The Negroamaro grape can often produce gems like this concentrated little jewel of a wine.*	**£6.00**	IWS THS TOS WRC BUP	B
PINOT NERO 1994, FRIUIVINI Friuli-Venezia-Giulia	*Showing some classic Pinot Noir maturity of stewed red fruits, vegetal and farmyardy aromas.*	**£6.00**	GRA FRT	B
ROSSO DEL SALENTO NOTARPANERO 1993, AZIENDA AGRICOLA TAURINO Puglia	*Negromaro and Malvasia Nera in perfect harmony. Herby and cherry-tomato packed, each vintage just gets better and better.*	**£6.10**	WIN CRS ODD DBY MWW SMF GRA	S
SALICE SALENTINO RISERVA 1994, FRANCESCO CANDIDO Puglia	*A refreshingly light wine with a cleanness to it that makes it perfect for picnics.*	**£6.10**	Widely Available	B
COPERTINO RISERVA 1994, CANTINA SOCIALE COPERTINO Puglia	*The nose and palate is awash with sun-dried tomatoes, spice and tobacco. Ideal to drink now.*	**£6.20**	Widely Available	G
CIRO CLASSICO ROSSO 1996, LIBRANDI Puglia	*Take a sip of this wine and be transported to a sunny Salento summer.*	**£6.40**	DIR V&C WIN CWI HVW ENO VIL NYW	B
VALPOLICELLA CLASSICO 1997, ALLEGRINI Veneto	*A bursting, young ruby wine which shouts bubblegum flavours with a touch of stalkiness.*	**£6.50**	WCR V&C ENO JSM VIL NYW CWI	S
COLLI DEL TRASIMENO ROSSO 1997, PIEVE DEL VESCOVO Umbria	*Concentrated nose, pungent with chocolate and cherries. A beautifully crafted wine which will get better.*	**£6.70**	V&C LIB	G

OTHER RED • ITALY

Wine	Tasting Note	Price	Stockists	
MONTEPULCIANO D'ABRUZZO JORIO 1995, UMANI RONCHI Abruzzo	*Intensely structured, brick red wine. Rich, with savoury red fruit which continues to linger on the finish.*	£6.80	WCR NYW V&C WCS NEI ENO VLW VIL	(S)
VELLETRI ROSSO RISERVA 1994, CONSORZIA VINI DI VELLETRI Lazio	*Minty, toffee nose. Made predominantly from Sangiovese and Montepuliciano this wine is unmistakably Italian.*	£6.90	LUC	(S)
CAPPELO DI PRETE ROSSO DEL SALENTO 1994, FRANCESCO CANDIDO Puglia	*An ambiguous wine; with its hot medicinal nose and intense green flavours in the mouth.*	£6.90	Widely Available	(B)
VALADORNA VIGNA LA PORTA PRIMITIVO DI PUGLIA 1997, TENUTA DI ARCENO Puglia	*Hot alcohol aromas fail to mask the spicy notes of cinnamon and nutmeg on this full bodied Italian red.*	£7.00	BPW	(B)
LA SEGRETA ROSSO 1997, PLANETA Puglia	*From such an arid climate this wine stands out as a testimony to inspired wine making.*	£7.20	DIR V&C CPW DBY ENO VLW VIL CWI	(S)
CAPITEL SAN ROCCO VINO DI RIPASSO 1995, FRATELLI TEDESCHI Veneto	*Intense, rich truffle nose, creamy and sweet with great length on the bitter cherry fruit finish.*	£7.20	HOH MWW AVB ADN	(B)
GORGO TONDO ROSSO 1996, CARLO PELLEGRINO Sicily	*Solid fruit on the front palate if a little cloying, with a green stalky length.*	£7.20	DIR HOH AVB	(B)
TORNAMAGNO 1994, COLONNARA Marche	*Mature, slightly animal nose. Crisp palate remains herbaceous, with developed fruit and oak flavours.*	£7.80	ALI	(B)

171

ITALY • OTHER RED

BAROCCO 1994, TERRE CORTESI MONCARO Marche	*Smoky vapours emerge while hot alcohol blends with warm cherries. Juicy currants lie in wait.*	£8.00	WIM CCL	(S)
VIGNETI CASTERNI AMARONE CLASSICO 1992, FLLI. PASQUA Veneto	*Reeking of wet wool, bitter cherries assail the palate before gentle spice and tannin lead to a full finish.*	£8.50	WTS	(B)
AGONTANO ROSSO CONERO RISERVA 1995, CASA VINICOLA GIOACCHINO GAROFOLI Marche	*Impressive aromas of bitter cherries, almonds and alcohol with a complex palate of raspberries, leather and tar.*	£8.90	DIR WIN IWS ODD	(G)
DONNAFUGATA IL ROSSO 1996, TENUTA DI DONNAFUGATA Sicily	*Fruit to the fore in this jam packed red. Thick with plums, strawberries and cherries.*	£8.90	V&C PSC CCL BUT	(S)
DON ANSELMO RISERVA AGLIANICO DEL VULTURE 1993, PATERNOSTER Basilicata	*Perfumed with violets, plums and dark chocolate, the whole package is encapsulated in velvety tannins.*	£9.80	DIR WCS ENO	(B)
DUCA SAN FELICE CIRO CLASSICO RISERVA 1993, LIBRANDI Southern Italy	*Slight prickle on the tongue, gives way to rich orange peel and concentrated dark cherries.*	£9.90	Widely Available	(B)
VALPOLICELLA CLASSICO SUPERIORE 1994, CORTEFORTE Veneto	*Great complexity to be found on the nose and palate of this above average Valpolicella.*	£10.40	BEN GGW LIB	(B)
GAMBINI PRIMITIVO ROSSO NV, DUCA DI GABBANI, PUGLIA Salento	*An improvement on previous offerings from this little known producer. A tobacco smoked nose with a rustic palate.*	£11.50	Widely Available	(B)

DUCA DI ARAGONA ROSSO DEL SALENTO 1992, FRANCESCO CANDIDO Puglia	*A faintly dusty flavour which moves towards an elegant palate of herbs and cedar flavours.*	£11.80	DIR V&C CPW DBY ENO NYW VIL	(S)
ROSSO CONERO CÙMARO 1994, UMANI RONCHI Marche	*A feast of every known berry. Well-rounded palate, with rich tobacco and bitter liquorice finish.*	£11.80	Widely Available	(S)
LIANO 1995, UMBERTO CESARI Emilia Romagna	*Lovely summer fruit character with good balance on the palate and a long nutty finish.*	£11.80	LUC NYW	(B)
DOMINI VENETI VALPOL-ICELLA AMARONE CLASSICO 1993, CANTINA SOCIALE VALPOLICELLA NEGRAR Valpolicella	*Complex orange peel and spice aromas. Palate of tar, savoury plums and brazil nuts. Concentrated, long finish.*	£12.00	GRA FRT	(G)
TANCREDI 1996, TENUTA DI DONNAFUGATA Sicily	*A chewy, nutty taste follows with sweet fruit appearing on the back palate. Structurally sound for future years.*	£12.00	V&C PSC BUT	(S)
TORRACCIO SANGIOVESE DELLA UMBRIA 1995, CANTINA COLLI AMERINI Umbria	*Aromatic cedary nose, dry fruits on the palate with upfront tannins and a long fruit finish.*	£12.00	IWS ENO VIL	(B)
AMARONE DELLA VALPOLICELLA CLASSICO 1995, FRATELLI TEDESCHI Veneto	*A lovely satisfying mouthfeel of morello cherries, warming to a finish of dark espresso coffee.*	£13.10	WCR AVB V&C ADN HOH WIN POR MWW	(B)
SFORZATO VALTELLINA 1994, CASA VINICOLA NERA Valtellina	*Cherries in a vat of hot tar sink into the mature drying tannins. Magnificient length.*	£14.70	V&C LUC	(B)

AMARONE DELLA VALPOLICELLA CLASSICO 1993, CESARI OF AZ AGRICOLA BRIGALDARA Veneto	*Lush chocolate and cherry aromas. Full bodied, the palate reflects flavours found on the nose.*	£15.00	V&C MWW BUT BTH DBY	**B**
VIGNA MARA VINO DA RIPASSO CLASSICO 1995, CESARI Veneto	*A zealous, lively Italian keen to push its baked cherry flavours and beautifully structured acidity.*	£15.00	AFI	**B**
GRAVELLO 1991, LIBRANDI Calabria	*Deep and earthy with truffles, rich spice and herby red fruit on a non-stop finish.*	£15.50	DIR V&C NEI VLW NYW VIL CWI	**G**
CAPITEL MONTE FONTANA 1995, FRATELLI TEDESCHI Veneto	*The sweet flavours of sun dried cherries and ripe fruits have a balancing acidity giving a clean finish.*	£15.50	DIR HOH AVB	**S**
AMARONE DELLA VALPOLICELLA CLASSICO 1990, ZENATO Veneto	*Attractive dusty nose contains a surprising, subtle juicy edge which develops into a powerful, harmonious length.*	£15.70	V&C FCA BUP FWL WRC	**S**
GRATICCIAIA 1992, AGRICOLE VALLONE Puglia	*A little unfocused but with a certain rustic charm. Old style wine making, but pleasant.*	£16.60	NRW ADN COK NEI DBY IND	**B**
VIGNETO SGARZON TEROLDEGO ROTALIANO 1995, FORADORI Trentino-Alto-Adige	*Rich velvety fruit to the fore on the bitter sweet palate promises greater things to come.*	£16.70	JNW DIR V&C ENO	**S**

Pinpoint who sells the wine you wish to buy by turning to the stockist codes. If you know the name of the wine you want to buy, use the alphabetical index. If the price is your motivation, refer to the invaluable price guide index; red and white wines under £5, sparkling wines under £12 and Champagne under £16. Happy hunting!

TERRE BRUNE 1994, SANTADI Sardinia	*Tangy, sweet and sour, raisiny, fruit developing tea and caramel coffee complexity on the persistent palate.*	£17.30	Widely Available	(S)
ARGIOLAS TURRIGA RESERVA 1992, GIACOMO TACHIS Sardinia	*Has a distinctly New World style with sweet new oak and upfront damson fruit palate.*	£17.50	L&W WTS	(S)
LUCCIAIO ROSSO 1996, PIEVE DEL VESCOVO Umbria	*Bright cherry red colour reflects the overtly youthful palate packed with fresh black cherry fruit.*	£17.50	LIB CLP RES	(B)
MONTE OLMI CAPITEL AMARONE 1995, FRATELLI TEDESCHI Veneto	*A touch of spritzy fruit awakens the mouth to an array of warm, complex, spices.*	£17.80	DIR V&C HOH AWB	(B)
IL RONCAT ROSSO 1993, GIOVANNI DRI Friuli-Venezia-Giulia	*Immerse yourself in a sea of blueberries and float among spice and chocolate flavours. Awesome finish.*	£18.00	ALI	(S)
AMARONE CLASSICO DELLA VALPOLICELLA 1993, ALLEGRINI Veneto	*A little volatile acidity on the nose which transforms to sweet, heady Kirsch flavours on the palate.*	£18.30	Widely Available	(B)
PELAGO 1995, UMANI RONCHI Marche	*Bright summer fruit pudding nose. Rich fruit flavours integrating beautifully with dusty youthful tannins.*	£19.10	Widely Available	(S)
LUMEN MONTEPULICIANO D'ABRUZZO 1993, AZIENDA AGRICOLA DINO ILLUMINATI Abruzzo	*Soft leathery nose belies a fairly robust palate of firm plum and cherry fruit.*	£19.80	DIR BLN	(S)

AMARONE DELLA VALPOLICELLA IL BOSCO CLASSICO 1990, CESARI Veneto	*Full and concentrated as all good Amarones should be. Will benefit from some quality cellar time.*	£20.00	AFI	**B**
AMARONE della VALPOLICELLA CLASSICO 1994, CORTEFORTE Veneto	*Classic black bitter cherries predominate a whole host of complex aromas and flavours.*	£20.70	FSW BEN GGW LIB NYW	**S**
GRANATO ROSSO 1995, FORADORI Trentino-Alto-Adige	*Floral aromas are in perfect harmony with warm ripe black cherry flavours. Greenish tannins suggest ageing potential.*	£20.70	JNW V&C ENO	**S**
AMARONE CLASSICO DELLA VALPOLICELLA 1988, ZENATO Veneto	*Bitter chocolate flavours, laden with overripe fruit, all pulled together with tight tannins.*	£24.50	WIM	**S**
MARCHESE DI VILLA MARINA 1993, SELLA MOSCA Sardinia	*Warm medicinal aromas with a sweet jammy palate of black fruits on an elegantly structured wine.*	£24.50	E&B LUC	**B**
LA POJA 1993, ALLEGRINI Veneto	*Intense aromas of morello cherries with complex nuances of leather, tar and roasted almonds carry over onto the palate.*	£25.30	FSW DIR ENO NYW VIL CWI RES	**G** TROP WIN
MONTIANO ROSSO 1996, CANTINA FALESCO Lazio	*New World style wine with baked plums, mulberry fruit and hints of creamy oak on the palate.*	£26.20	V&C DBY LIB SOM NYW	**S**

Pinpoint who sells the wine you wish to buy by turning to the stockist codes. If you know the name of the wine you want to buy, use the alphabetical index. If the price is your motivation, refer to the invaluable price guide index; red and white wines under £5, sparkling wines under £12 and Champagne under £16. Happy hunting!

ITALY • ROSÉ

LA SORTE BARDOLINO CHIARETTO CLASSICO 1997, CANTINA SOCIALE VALPOLICELLA NEGRAR Veneto	*Fun picnic wine with lovely soft fruit pleasing light acidity and a touch of tannin.*	£4.80	GRA FRT	(B)
CAMPIROSA CERASUOLO MONTEPULCIANO D'ABRUZZO 1997, DINO ILLUMINATI Abruzzo	*Unusual with liquorice and tar underlying a palate of red fruits and morello cherries.*	£5.50	V&C	(B)
CHIARRETTO DI BARDOLINO L'INFINITO 1997, SANTI Veneto	*Splendid strawberry fruit with slight bitterness on a fine, ripe and juicy palate.*	£6.50	DIR ENO VIL	(B)

ITALY • WHITE

CHARDONNAY GARGANEGA 1997, CANTINA DI SOAVE Veneto	*Attractive hot bread and creamy buttery characters. Who needs breakfast with a wine like this?*	£3.80	VER ASD	(B)
PONTE VECCHIO OAKED SOAVE 1997, CANTINA DI SOAVE Veneto	*Lemon and peach on the nose with hints of butter. Citrusy palate and astringent acidity.*	£4.00	CRS MRN ASD	(B)
SOMERFIELD CHARDONNAY DELLE VENEZIE 1997, GRUPPO ITALIANO VINI Veneto	*Clean citrus aromas lead onto a fresh palate of grapefruits, lime zest and a mouthwatering finish.*	£4.00	SMF	(B)

LE TRULLE CHARDONNAY 1997, AZIENDA VINICOLA CANTELE LECCE Puglia	*A full pear and peach nose carries over onto the balanced creamy palate with good length.*	£4.30	IWS CWS CRS THS SMF TOS FUL	**B**
MALT HOUSE VINTNERS VERDICCHIO DEI CASTELLI DI JESI 1997, SCHENK SPA Marche	*Elegant, clean and zippy. This is a textural wine rather than one driven by fruit.*	£4.30	MHV	**B**
SOMERFIELD FRASCATI 1997, GRUPPO ITALIANO VINI Lazio	*A lush wine full of pineapple, honey and almondy richness. Moderate acidity and good depth.*	£4.30	SMF	**B**
LA SORTE SOAVE CLASSICO 1997, CANTINA SOCIALE VALPOLICELLA NEGRAR Veneto	*This well-structured wine consists of apricot and lime fruit characters with nicely integrated acid.*	£4.70	TPE GRA FRT	**B**
SAN SIMONE SAUVIGNON BLANC 1997, SAN SIMONE Fruili-Venezia-Giulia	*An aromatic, grassy and nettley nose. Chewy acidity and some creamy oak. The fruit arrives as a burst at the back of the palate.*	£4.80	WTS GIS CCL	**S**
SAUVIGNON BLANC GRAVE DEL FRIULI 1997, BIDOLI VINI Fruili-Venezia-Giulia	*Attractive fruit aromas follow onto the palate which balances the racy acidity with ripe fruit.*	£4.80	SMF ODD TPA FUL	**B**
VERDICCHIO CLASSICO 1997, CASA VINICOLA GIOACCHINO GAROFOLI Marche	*Pale lemon colour with refreshing aromatic characters. Subtle tropical fruit, a hint of nuts and good acidity.*	£4.90	DIR TOS	**S**
LE VELE VERDICCHIO CLASSICO 1997, TERRE CORTESI MONCARO Marche	*Pineapple, citrus and gooseberry characters encased in a delicate shell of moderate acidity and length.*	£4.90	THS BEL MRN	**B**

CORTESE ALTO MONFERRATO 1997, ARALDICA Piedmont	*Tangy richness and cream cleaned up with good acidity. The perfect match for an authentic Italian meal.*	**£5.00**	DIR V&C WCS NEI CPW ENO	(S)
CORTECHIARA SOAVE CLASSICO 1997, SERGIO ZENATO Veneto	*Crisp clean wine with concentrated limes and gooseberries on the palate. Great balance and length.*	**£5.00**	WTS L&W DVD	(B)
FONTANABIANCA 1996, CONCILIO VINI SpA Trentino	*Fat, buttery nose with some toasty elements carry over onto a creamy palate of ripe tropical fruits.*	**£5.00**	IWS	(B)
PRIMAVERA SPRING NV, VINICOLA CANTELE LECCE & KYM MILNE Puglia	*Full bodied with ripe interesting fruit, tangy acid and a hint of creaminess.*	**£5.00**	IWS THS WRC BUP	(B)
SOAVE VIGNETI DI SELLA CLASSICO SUPERIORE 1997, CASA VINICOLA CAV P SARTORI Veneto	*Tropical fruit characters balanced with vanilla oak and medium acidity on a palate of apples and pears.*	**£5.00**	IWS	(B)
BARREL FERMENTED CATARRATTO 1996, FIRRIATO Sicily	*Rich and intense pineapple and lychee aromas with oak overtones. Buttery, full palate, crisp acidity, long finish.*	**£5.20**	IWS ODD	(S)
VILLA FLORA LUGANA 1996, SERGIO ZENATO Lombardy	*A little spice on the nose and soft ripe fruit palate with moderate depth and boneyed finish.*	**£5.30**	WTS	(S)
LUGANA CRU SAN BENEDETTO 1997, SERGIO ZENATO Lombardy	*Peach and almonds on the nose followed by delicate melon and apples on the palate.*	**£5.30**	JSM WIM C&B BUP WRC	(B)

ITALY • WHITE

Wine	Description	Price	Codes	
VERDICCHIO VILLA BIANCHI 1997, UMANI RONCHI Marche	*A light style wine with lots of apple, citrus characters. A perfect food wine.*	£5.50	JNW V&C WCS NEI ENO VIL	B
ALASIA PIEMONTE CHARDONNAY 1997, ALASIA Piedmont	*Grassy bouquet of tinned pineapple chunks leads onto a balanced palate of ripe tropical fruit flavours.*	£5.60	FSW BEN GGW UNS V&C NYW LIB	B
CHARDONNAY ZENATO 1996, SERGIO ZENATO Veneto	*Coffee bean and lychees aromas before complex, Chinese gooseberry, flavours on the lingering, clean palate.*	£5.90	BBR WIM CCL	B
SOAVE CLASSICO VIGNETO COLOMBARA 1997, SERGIO ZENATO Veneto	*A rather shy nose with green apple fruit on palate bound in a lean structure.*	£5.90	SVT L&W WTS DVD	B
PASSITO DI PANTELLERIA, ALVIS Sicily	*Deep amber colour with honeyed nuts and raisins on the nose and palate. Lengthy finish.*	£6.00	GRA FRT	S
VERDICCHIO RISERVA 1995, UMANI RONCHI Marche	*Tropical fruit with nicely integrated malo characters a moderate length pleasing acidity and a creamy finish.*	£6.30	JNW V&C NEI RDS DBY VLW HVW ENO	S
FRASCATI SUPERIORE TERRE DEI GRIFI 1996, FONTANA CANDIDA Lazio	*Warm floral fruit combined with almonds and aromatic fruit characters. The finish is a little light.*	£6.30	DIR RDS ENO JOB VIL NYW	B

Pinpoint who sells the wine you wish to buy by turning to the stockist codes. If you know the name of the wine you want to buy, use the alphabetical index. If the price is your motivation, refer to the invaluable price guide index; red and white wines under £5, sparkling wines under £12 and Champagne under £16. Happy hunting!

FRASCATI SUPERIORE VIGNETO SANTA TERESA 1997, FONTANA CANDIDA Lazio	*Fragrant herbs and aromatic fruit with hints of peach and marzipan. A flavour packed wine.*	£6.40	V&C WCS ENO VLW VIL CWI	B
VIGNA NOVALI 1996, TERRE CORTESI MONCARO Marche	*Nose consists of aromatic spice and the palate pleases with creamy round lychees and grapefruit.*	£6.50	MWW WIM CCL	S
SOAVE CLASSICO SUPERIORE 1997, PRA Veneto	*Pale golden colour, ripe, pungent and concentrated fruit on the nose carried through onto the palate.*	£6.60	COK GRT POR DBY TSE BOO	S
VERDICCHIO CLASSICO CASAL DI SERRA 1997, UMANI RONCHI Marche	*Peach melon and citrus fruit with medium body. This wine gets better towards the finish.*	£6.60	Widely Available	B
ROERO ARNESI MARGHERITA ROSA 1997, ARALDICA Piedmont	*Fresh almonds and peardrops on the nose. Crisp citric acidity with almonds on the palate.*	£7.70	DIR ENO VIL	S
ALASIA LANGHE ARNEIS 1996, ALASIA Piedmont	*This is a wine of the land with earthy, slightly saline characters and nutty overtones.*	£7.70	FSW HOT GGW SAF LIB V&C CWI	B
VERDICCHIO CLASSICO PODIUM 1996, GIOACCHINO GAROFOLI Marche	*Delicate rose water on the nose and subtle complexity. Intense peach flavours with good length.*	£8.00	DIR	S
VIGNA DI GABRI 1997, TENUTA DI DONNAFUGATA Sicily	*Clean ripe fruit with a slight stalkiness on the nose. Lots of ripe banana fruit on the palate.*	£8.00	PSC CCI	S

SOLALTO 1996, FATTORIA LE PUPILLE Tuscany	*Delicious peach, pear and dried fruit aromas with pronounced ripe citrus fruit on the palate.*	£8.50	BEN	B
PLANETA ALASTRO 1996, PLANETA Sicily	*This is an oaky wine with simple fruit, nutty, toasty, characters and a creamy palate.*	£8.60	DIR V&C L&W HVW ENO VLW VIL NYW	B
SAUVIGNON TRENTINO AL POGGIO 1996, LE MERIDIANE Trentino-Alto-Adige	*Crisp and fresh with lovely zingy acidity and slight liquorice notes.*	£9.00	ALI	B
LUGANA BROLETTINO 1996, DAL CERO Lombardy	*Big toasty nose which follows onto the palate. Well-integrated fruit and a buttery finish.*	£10.00	V&C CPW ENO NYW CWI	B
PINOT GRIGIO ISONZO 1997, GIOVANNI PUIATTI Friuli-Venezia-Giulia	*A mix of apricots and winegums. This wine has moderate body balanced with a salty finish.*	£10.00	DIR ENO	B
PINOT GRIGIO COLLIO 1997, BARGO CONUENTI Friuli-Venezia-Giulia	*Aromatic herbaceous fruit with grapefruit characters. Upfront acidity draws out into a long balanced finish.*	£11.80	V&C LUC	B
PLANETA CHARDONNAY 1996, PLANETA Sicily	*Deep golden colour with grapefruit and tropical fruit aromas. Complex fruit palate with an integrated oak finish.*	£11.90	Widely Available	S
LANGHE CRU LA MORRA CHARDONNAY 1994, BENI DI BATASIOLO Piedmont	*Honeyed nose with fresh, rich creamy slightly vegetal palate balanced with good lingering finish.*	£12.40	MON	B

Wine	Tasting Notes	Price	Stockists	
POMINO BENEFIZIO 1995, MARCHESI DE' FRESCOBALDI Tuscany	*A defined oak nose, good fruit extract and touches of sweet oak. Sharp, racy acidity.*	£13.00	V&C CPW GRA FRT	B
PLANETA CHARDONNAY 1995, PLANETA Sicily	*Voluptuous tropical fruit aromas with full bodied soft tropical fruit on the palate. Balanced acidity.*	£13.30	DIR V&C VLW VIL WRC	B
PINOT BIANCO 1996, JERMANN Friuli-Venezia Giulia	*Spicy and aromatic with tangy acid. This wine has good length and persistence of flavour.*	£13.80	JNW V&C WCS WIN RDS ENO VLW VIL	B
SELLA DEL BOSCONE CHARDONNAY 1995, BADIA A COLTIBUONO Tuscany	*Slightly aromatic with zippy citrus flavours on a clean dry palate that makes the mouth water.*	£13.90	HOH AVB	B
TERRE DI TUFI 1997, TERRUZI E PUTHOD Tuscany	*Intense nose with slightly tart citrus fruit on the palate and a hint of steeliness.*	£14.10	BEN DIR V&C ABY ENO VLW CWI	B
CHARDONNAY ISONZO 1995, VIE DI ROMANS Friuli-Venezia-Giulia	*Butterscotch aromas lead onto a tropical fruit and fig flavoured palate with a clean finish.*	£17.50	ENO	B
CAPO MARTINO BIANCO 1996, JERMANN Friuli-Venezia-Giulia	*Spicy with some complexity. Hints of fresh pine resin and clean slate. Finishes slightly astringent.*	£21.00	WCS RDS ENO VIL	B
DREAMS 1996, JERMANN Friuli-Venezia-Giulia	*Full round fruit with clean acid and slightly spicy nose. Slightly bitter on the finish.*	£30.50	Widely Available	B

ITALY • SPARKLING

BORELLI ASTI SPUMANTE NV, FRATELLI MARTINI Asti	Light, frothy, delicate and floral. A soft sparkle in the mouth with honeyed apple flavours.	£5.20	WRT	(B)

ITALY • FORTIFIED

RALLO MARSALA SUPERIORE - DOLCE, ALVIS Sicily	Ripe sweet fruit on the nose with a palate of rich cooked notes and an intriguing finish.	£5.00	GRA FRT	(B)
OPERA UNICA NV, TENUTA DI DONNAFUGATA Sicily	Concentrated caramel and toffee flavours with a slightly burnt, figgy edge.	£6.00	PSC	(S)
BEN RYE PASSITO DI PANTELLERIA 1996, TENUTA DI DONNAFUGATA Sicily	Grapey sweetness with lush fruit flavours, fleshy acidity and overiding Muscat notes.	£8.00	PSC	(B)
MARSALA VERGINE 12 YEAR OLD, ALVIS Sicily	Wonderful rich cooked coffee notes on this attractive wine which enthralled the panel with its subtle flavours.	£11.00	GRA FRT	(S)

Pinpoint who sells the wine you wish to buy by turning to the stockist codes. If you know the name of the wine you want to buy, use the alphabetical index. If the price is your motivation, refer to the invaluable price guide index; red and white wines under £5, sparkling wines under £12 and Champagne under £16. Happy hunting!

NEW ZEALAND

New Zealand was one of the stars of this year's WINE Challenge. Delicious Sauvignon Blancs as expected, yes but also delicate, subtle Chardonnays, fresh Rieslings and more surprisingly, to some, fantastic Bordelais style reds. The maritime climate is an added element, in some years a help, in others, a hinderance. One thing is sure, as far as sparkling wine is concerned New Zealand seems to have got it right. Quality is ever improving and can only get better with further viticultural advances. Cheers.

NEW ZEALAND • CABERNET SAUVIGNON

COOKS CABERNET SAUVIGNON MERLOT 1997, CORBANS WINES Hawkes Bay	*Light, delicate aromas lead to a similar palate dominated by minty, blackcurrant flavours.*	£5.40	WES MTL HOU DBY SPR UNS VLW	**B**
DELEGAT'S PROPRIETOR'S RESERVE CABERNET SAUVIGNON 1996, DELEGAT'S WINE ESTATE Hawkes Bay	*Ripe, jammy, simple fruit aromas and flavours with hints of oak, cedar and tobacco.*	£8.00	FRT	**B**
SAINTS CABERNET SAUVIGNON MERLOT 1995, MONTANA WINES Hawkes Bay	*Ripe chocolatey black fruit nose with rich spicy fruit cake flavours on the balanced palate.*	£8.00	M&S	**B**
THE BAYS CABERNET SAUVIGNON MERLOT 1995, VIDAL ESTATE Hawkes Bay	*Smoky nose, ripe black fruits and hints of pencil shavings develop on a rich blackcurrant flavoured palate.*	£8.50	GRA MWW	**S**
LINCOLN HOME VINEYARD CABERNET SAUVIGNON MERLOT 1995, LINCOLN VINEYARDS Auckland	*Leafy mint, nuances of cough medicine and creamy aromas of summer fruits carry over onto the balanced palate.*	£8.70	HVW RBS SWS VIL	**S**

NEW ZEALAND • RED • CABERNET SAUVIGNON

CORBANS PRIVATE BIN CABERNET SAUVIGNON 1995, CORBANS WINES Hawkes Bay	*Soft black fruits with new oak give a creamy finish to intense New World flavours.*	**£8.70**	DBY PEA CEN	B
CHURCH ROAD CABERNET SAUVIGNON MERLOT 1995, MONTANA WINES Hawkes Bay	*Herbaceous aromas of crushed blackcurrant leaves compliment a ripe berry fruit flavour on the palate.*	**£8.90**	SEL MTW ABY VLW WTS	B
CHURCH ROAD CABERNET SAUVIGNON MERLOT 1996, MONTANA WINES Hawkes Bay	*Plums and damsons on the nose and palate with hints of creamy herbs. Good length.*	**£8.90**	MTW THS CPW ODD BUP VWC WRC	B
ESK VALLEY MERLOT CABERNET SAUVIGNON 1996, ESK VALLEY WINES Hawkes Bay	*Attractive baked fruit aromas with herbaceous notes lead onto a light palate with hints of toasted oak.*	**£9.10**	WCR TPE BAB EBA COE	B
TE MATA ESTATE CABERNET SAUVIGNON MERLOT 1996, TE MATA ESTATE WINERY Hawkes Bay	*Herby notes to a palate full of redcurrant and raspberry flavours with hints of vanilla cream.*	**£10.60**	Widely Available	B
FAIRHALL ESTATE CABERNET SAUVIGNON 1996, MONTANA WINES Marlborough	*Spicy notes to the ripe black fruit aromas lead to rich creamy blackberry flavours.*	**£11.00**	MTW ODD VLW	S
CORBANS COTTAGE BLOCK CABERNET SAUVIGNON CABERNET FRANC MERLOT 1995, CORBANS WINES Hawkes Bay	*Minty, blackcurrant nose. Ripe forest fruit flavoured palate with elements of menthol, eucalyptus and vanilla.*	**£11.30**	DBY CEN CDE	S
LINCOLN PRESTIGE SELECTION CABERNET SAUVIGNON MERLOT 1995, LINCOLN VINEYARDS Hawkes Bay	*Raspberry aromas develop into fresh tayberry and cream flavours and an attractive almondy finish.*	**£13.00**	SWS	B

VIDAL RESERVE CABERNET SAUVIGNON 1995, VIDAL ESTATE Hawkes Bay	*Deep toasted oak notes on this approachable wine with ripe, leafy cassis fruit flavours.*	**£15.00**	GRA FRT	B

NEW ZEALAND • PINOT NOIR

WAIPARA WEST PINOT NOIR 1996, TUTTON SIENKO & HILL Canterbury	*Ripe fruit on the nose with some signs of complexity. Palate has delicate fruit finish.*	**£9.20**	WAW DIR FNZ	B
GROVE MILL PINOT NOIR 1997, GROVE MILL Marlborough	*Strawberries and hints of coconut on the nose with sweet berry fruit and firm tannins.*	**£9.50**	LAW ALE	B
PALLISER ESTATE PINOT NOIR 1996, PALLISER ESTATE WINES Martinborough	*Spicy barnyard characters on the nose; sweet berries on the palate with good length and tannins.*	**£10.00**	JNW ABY DBY TOS NYW WRC BUP	S
NEUDORF MOURTERE PINOT NOIR 1997, TIM & JUDY FINN NEUDORF VINEYARD Nelson	*Strawberries and raspberries abound on the palate with crisp, green apple acidity giving balance.*	**£13.00**	DBY	B
ATA RANGI PINOT NOIR 1996, CLIVE PATON Marlborough	*Vegetal characters and oak on the nose, A full-bodied ripe fruit palate, lots of oak, and a lingering finish.*	**£18.20**	Widely Available	S

Pinpoint who sells the wine you wish to buy by turning to the stockist codes. If you know the name of the wine you want to buy, use the alphabetical index. If the price is your motivation, refer to the invaluable price guide index; red and white wines under £5, sparkling wines under £12 and Champagne under £16. Happy hunting!

PINOT NOIR LA STRADA 1996, FROMM VINEYARDS Marlborough	*Ruby red colour with plump ripe fruit. Lots of firm tannins and a lovely flavoursome finish.*	**£23.50**	L&W	(B)

NEW ZEALAND • OTHER RED

DELEGAT'S PROPRIETORS RESERVE MERLOT 1996, DELEGAT'S WINE ESTATE Hawkes Bay	*Herbaceous, green tobacco notes on the mulberry nose of this rich, plum fruit dominated wine.*	**£8.00**	DEL	(B)
MONTANA RESERVE MERLOT 1996, MONTANA WINES Marlborough	*Complex damson fruit aromas with nuances of cedar and pencil are displayed on the rich clean nose.*	**£8.70**	MTW ODD EPO VLW	(B)
COOPERS CREEK MERLOT RESERVE 1995, COOPERS CREEK VINEYARD Hawkes Bay	*Flavours of concentrated soft black fruits on a balanced palate follow rich fruit and cedar aromas.*	**£9.00**	DIR	(B)
TE MATA ESTATE BULLNOSE SYRAH 1996, TE MATA ESTATE WINERY Hawkes Bay	*Classic style. Nice vanilla fruit and vegetal nose. Juicy fruit in an easy drinking style.*	**£13.70**	JEF ESL	(B)
ESK VALLEY RESERVE MERLOT MALBEC CAB. SAUVIGNON RESERVE 1995, ESK VALLEY WINES Hawkes Bay	*Dense, complex vanilla and cassis aromas lead onto a youthful yet intensely creamy, summer fruit pudding palate.*	**£14.00**	DBY COE IRV	(S)
SACRED HILL BROKEN STONE MERLOT 1995, SACRED HILL Hawkes Bay	*Minty, blackcurrant nose and soft New World flavours of vanilla and sweet ripe black fruits.*	**£15.00**	ODD SEL	(B)

NEW ZEALAND • CHARDONNAY

MARKS & SPENCER KAITUNA HILLS CHARDONNAY 1997, MONTANA WINES Gisborne	*Peaches with creamy new oak aromas. Ripe fruit on the palate with an apple lift.*	£5.50	M&S	S
MONTANA MARLBOROUGH CHARDONNAY 1997, MONTANA WINES Marlborough	*Herbaceous notes to the lifted palate of rich lemon meringue pie, pears and green apples.*	£5.70	Widely Available	S
TWIN ISLANDS UNWOODED CHARDONNAY 1997, NEGOCIANTS NEW ZEALAND Marlborough	*Honeysuckle aromas lead on to a ripe palate of creamy greengages. An elegant zesty, lemon finish.*	£6.10	JNW HVW	S
VIDAL CHARDONNAY 1997, VIDAL ESTATE Hawkes Bay	*Delicate nose of creamy peaches, palate of buttery apricots and almonds with hints of herby minerals.*	£6.10	HVW BDR	S
FALL HARVEST CHARDONNAY 1996, HOUSE OF NOBLIO Gisborne	*Creamy tropical fruits on the nose and palate and a crisp finish to this approachable wine.*	£6.80	WCR WES DIR BNK HOH AVB	B
STONELEIGH CHARDONNAY 1996, CORBANS WINES Marlborough	*Lime, tropical fruit and toasty oak aromas. Rich ripe fruit on the palate resulting in an elongated finish.*	£7.00	Widely Available	S WINE OF THE YEAR
MATUA VALLEY EASTERN BAYS CHARDONNAY 1996, MATUA VALLEY WINES Waimaku	*Lush toffee and banana aromas. Full-bodied peach characters with sweet oak and moderate acidity.*	£7.20	JNW JSM WCS MGN WES WSO VIL	B

NEW ZEALAND • WHITE • CHARDONNAY

KIM CRAWFORD UNWOODED CHARDONNAY 1997, KIM CRAWFORD South Island	*A fresh nose of pineapple chunks lead into a palate of lifted tropical fruit with a gentle touch of citrus acidity.*	**£7.40**	SAF	(B)
BABICH MARA ESTATE CHARDONNAY 1995, BABICH WINES Hawkes Bay	*Nutty and cheesy aromas with ripe simple fruit, Straightforward wine with good length and finish.*	**£7.60**	BNK SEL TBO VIL	(B)
GROVE MILL CHARDONNAY 1996, GROVE MILL Marlborough	*Subtle vegetal and biscuity aromas with light creamy fruit on the palate and moderate acidity.*	**£7.60**	NRW LAW HVW	(B)
KIM CRAWFORD MARLBOROUGH UNOAKED CHARDONNAY 1997, KIM CRAWFORD Marlborough	*Ripe bananas and vanilla aromas with lively fresh fruits and acids on the clean finish.*	**£7.70**	WCR DBY NYW FUL LIB	(B)
MONTANA RESERVE MARLBOROUGH CHARDONNAY 1997, MONTANA WINES Marlborough	*Honeyed buttery aromas with sweet guava on the palate. High acidity and resiny oak finish.*	**£7.80**	BNK MTW CRS MWW ODD WRC	(B)
JUDD ESTATE CHARDONNAY 1997, MATUA VALLEY WINES Auckland	*Aromatic fruit characters mingle with vanilla oak. Well combined grapefruit and melon on the palate.*	**£7.90**	JNW WCS MGN PTR HAR	(S)
ESK VALLEY CHARDONNAY 1997, ESK VALLEY ESTATE Hawkes Bay	*Rich, creamy, star fruit notes on a coconut, ripe tropical mango and melon palate.*	**£8.00**	WCR NEI DBY TPE DEN BAB EOR	(G)
DELEGAT'S PROPRIETOR'S RESERVE CHARDONNAY 1996, DELEGAT'S WINE ESTATE Hawkes Bay	*Rich warm tropical fruit on the nose. Plenty of citrus fruit and integrated buttery vanilla oak.*	**£8.00**	WCR DEL DBY FRT	(S)

SAINTS CHARDONNAY 1996, MONTANA WINES Gisborne	*Ripe flavours of mangos, melons and pineapples abound on a palate displaying creamy, vanilla oak characters.*	**£8.00**	MTW M&S	(S)
NOBILO ICON CHARDONNAY 1996, HOUSE OF NOBILO Gisborne	*Delicate, slightly floral on the nose with lean fruit and a soft silky palate. Well-balanced.*	**£8.00**	DIR AVB	(B)
VILLA MARIA CELLAR SELECTION CHARDONNAY 1997, VILLA MARIA ESTATE Hawkes Bay	*Slightly perfumed pineapple notes with hints of oak on the nose. and clean citrus fruit on palate.*	**£8.00**	ODD	(B)
MONTANA RESERVE GISBORNE CHARDONNAY 1997, MONTANA WINES Gisborne	*Grapefruit and tangerine with waxy oak. Attractive floral, well balanced, fruit and integrated oak palate.*	**£8.30**	DBY	(B)
CORBANS PRIVATE BIN CHARDONNAY 1996, CORBANS WINES Marlborough	*Subtle yet powerful aromas with citrus and tropical fruit on a dry smooth palate. Integrated oak.*	**£8.70**	DBY JAV PEA CEN	(B)
GIESEN CHARDONNAY 1996, GIESEN WINE ESTATE Marlborough	*Fresh, creamy aromas of melons and pineapple are followed by a rich palate of bananas and avocado.*	**£8.70**	MOR JNW EPO BOO GNW	(B)
VILLA MARIA LIGHTLY OAKED CHARDONNAY 1996, VILLA MARIA ESTATE Auckland	*Full citrus fruit on the nose carries over onto a creamy palate of honeyed melon.*	**£8.70**	BUP THS WRC	(B)
CHURCH ROAD CHARDONNAY 1996, MONTANA WINES Hawkes Bay	*Creamy, oak characters on this cool climate Chardonnay full of melon flavours and a citrus finish.*	**£8.80**	Widely Available	(B)

NEW ZEALAND • WHITE • CHARDONNAY

CHURCH ROAD CHARDONNAY 1997, MONTANA WINES Hawkes Bay	*Floral and fresh lemon characters on the nose with harmonised fruit and lively balanced acidity.*	**£9.00**	Widely Available	**S**
CORBANS PRIVATE BIN CHARDONNAY 1995, CORBANS WINES Marlborough	*Melon, pineapple and kiwi fruit flavours playfully gambol with each other on this rounded palate.*	**£9.00**	VWE BUP	**B**
RONGOPAI UNWOODED CHARDONNAY 1997, RONGOPAI Waikato	*Fresh aromas of kiwi fruit, limes and mangos carry over onto the zesty palate.*	**£9.00**	VLW	**B**
GROVE MILL LANSDOWNE CHARDONNAY 1996, GROVE MILL Marlborough	*Grapefruit and aromatic aromas, loads of fruit with creamy integrated oak and a crisp finish.*	**£9.10**	LAW HVW	**S**
MANSION HOUSE BAY CHARDONNAY 1997, MANSION HOUSE BAY Marlborough	*Rich and juicy flavours of tinned fruit cocktail on this crisply citric clean wine.*	**£9.50**	ENO VIL	**B**
CORBANS PRIVATE BIN OAKED CHARDONNAY 1996, CORBANS WINES Gisborne	*Rich flavours of toasted oak, ripe tropical fruits and limey, kiwi fruit highlights on the palate.*	**£9.60**	DBY THR BUP TOS WRC	**G**
ALLAN SCOTT CHARDONNAY 1996, ALLAN SCOTT Marlborough	*Stylish on the nose with marmalade fruit characters lots of acid, subtle integrated oak.*	**£10.00**	NEI L&W	**B**

Pinpoint who sells the wine you wish to buy by turning to the stockist codes. If you know the name of the wine you want to buy, use the alphabetical index. If the price is your motivation, refer to the invaluable price guide index; red and white wines under £5, sparkling wines under £12 and Champagne under £16. Happy hunting!

Wine	Description	Price	Stockist	
DASHWOOD CHARDONNAY 1996, VAVASOUR WINES Marlborough	*Lemon and melon on the nose, creamy citrus fruit on palate with slight tannic edge.*	£10.00	JNW	(B)
PALLISER ESTATE CHARDONNAY 1996, PALLISER ESTATE WINES Martinborough	*Buttered croissants and tropical fruit characters combined with integrated, toasty vanilla oak and moderate acidity.*	£10.00	ABY DBY	(B)
RIFLEMANS CHARDONNAY 1995, SACRED HILL Hawkes Bay	*Lemon and banana on the nose with lots of heavy vanilla oak characters, high acidity.*	£10.00	ODD SEL FUL	(B)
SANCTUARY CHARDONNAY 1996, GROVE MILL Marlborough	*A gobful of ripe lemons and bananas with good cleansing acidity in a long finish.*	£10.00	LAW SEL JSM	(B)
VIDAL RESERVE CHARDONNAY 1995, VIDAL ESTATE Hawkes Bay	*Butter and lemon on the nose with a hint of oak. Buttery and smooth palate.*	£10.00	GRA FRT	(B)
JACKSON ESTATE RESERVE CHARDONNAY 1996, JACKSON ESTATE Marlborough	*Light citrus aromas with buttery ripe fruit and fresh acidity. Finishing toasty and dry.*	£10.40	HWL SVT WSP VIL	(B)
LAWSON'S DRY HILLS MARLBOROUGH CHARDONNAY 1996, LAWSON'S DRY HILLS WINES Marlborough	*Tropical fruit with buttery charred oak aromas. Elegant lemon and pineapple fruit characters on palate.*	£10.50	VDV BWL	(S)
MONTANA ORMOND ESTATE CHARDONNAY 1996, MONTANA WINES Gisborne	*Lime spice and toasty oak on the nose with body and weight from soft lush fruits giving delightful balance.*	£10.50	Widely Available	(S)

NEW ZEALAND • WHITE • CHARDONNAY

TE MATA ESTATE CHARDONNAY 1997, TE MATA ESTATE WINERY Hawkes Bay	*Restrained new oak and citrus fruit aromas with supple juicy fruit and soft creamy palate.*	£10.50	G&M JEF ESL HAR AMW WRC BUP	(B)
MORTON ESTATE HAWKES BAY CHARDONNAY 1996, MORTON ESTATE Hawkes Bay	*Butterscotch and full fruit characters on the nose, excellent structure and a clean crisp finish.*	£10.60	BWC DBY LNR PAG NYW	(G)
MONTANA RENWICK ESTATE CHARDONNAY 1996, MONTANA WINES Marlborough	*Buttery pears combined with caramel aromas. Ripe fruit characters toffee and integrated oak, with racy acidity.*	£10.70	G&M MTW ODD DBY VLW WCR	(S)
ESK VALLEY RESERVE CHARDONNAY 1995, ESK VALLEY Hawkes Bay	*Buttery lemon aromas with concentrated creamy citrus fruit on the palate and good persistent length.*	£11.00	BAB COE EBA	(B)
ESK VALLEY RESERVE CHARDONNAY 1996, ESK VALLEY ESTATE Hawkes Bay	*Ripe fruit mingled with controlled oak on the nose. Zingy citric acid with full-bodied fruit.*	£11.00	BAB COE EBA	(B)
STONECROFT CHARDONNAY 1996, STONECROFT Hawkes Bay	*Tropical fruit aromas combine with smooth creamy fruit and a crisp citric acid finish.*	£11.00	LEA	(B)
STONECROFT CHARDONNAY 1997, STONECROFT Hawkes Bay	*Lots of toasty oak on the nose. Grapefruit and ripe tropical palate with high acidity.*	£11.00	LEA	(B)
CHURCH ROAD RESERVE CHARDONNAY 1996, MONTANA WINES Hawkes Bay	*Cool, crisp flavours of melon and passion fruit with nuances of creamy vanilla and spice.*	£11.20	MTW ODD BUP VLW WRC	(B)

CORBANS COTTAGE BLOCK MARLBOROUGH CHARDONNAY 1996, CORBANS WINES Marlborough	*Big waxy wood aromas. Ripe lemon and peach fruit, high acidity and big buttery oak.*	£11.30	DBY PEA CAP CEN SEL	(B)
HUNTER'S CHARDONNAY 1996, HUNTER'S WINES Marlborough	*Slightly restrained lime and tropical fruit aromas and palate with creamy malo characters with a tingly finish.*	£11.40	DIR CVR GRT CPW DBY NYW WRC BUP	(B)
HUNTER'S CHARDONNAY 1994, HUNTER'S WINES Marlborough	*Tropical fruit and vanilla on the nose, the palate has ripe fruit and integrated oak.*	£11.60	DIR CVR HOT GRT CPW DBY BUP CFT	(S)
MARTINBOROUGH CHARDONNAY 1996, MARTINBOROUGH VINEYARD Martinborough	*Fresh floral fruit with toasty oak aromas. Sweet, slightly nutty characters on the palate.*	£11.80	Widely Available	(B)
RONGAPAI CHARDONNAY VINTAGE RESERVE 1996, RONGOPAI Waikato	*Smoky, peachy nose. Tropical fruit palate with mineral nuances. Crisp finish of sun ripened kiwi and citrus fruits.*	£12.00	VLW TOS	(G)
TASMAN BAY CHARDONNAY 1997, PHIL JONES Marlborough	*Lots of lemon and citrus aromas, fresh tropical fruit palate and a touch of oak.*	£12.00	FNZ FSW	(B)
VAVASOUR CHARDONNAY 1997, VAVASOUR WINES Marlborough	*Simple with lots of character, this wine consists of tropical fruit and new sappy oak.*	£12.60	JNW HOT NYW FUL	(B)

Pinpoint who sells the wine you wish to buy by turning to the stockist codes. If you know the name of the wine you want to buy, use the alphabetical index. If the price is your motivation, refer to the invaluable price guide index; red and white wines under £5, sparkling wines under £12 and Champagne under £16. Happy hunting!

NEW ZEALAND • WHITE • CHARDONNAY

KIM CRAWFORD TIETJIEN GISBORNE CHARDONNAY 1996, KIM CRAWFORD Gisborne	*Overt buttery nose, peach and pineapple fruit with lime acidity, integrated oak, complex stylish wine.*	£13.80	WCR RDS DBY LIB NYW RES	(S)
SPENCER HILL EVAN'S VINEYARD CHARDONNAY 1996, SPENCER HILL Nelson	*Subtle buttery nose with light apple and citrus fruit combined with fine oak. Moderate acidity.*	£14.00	FNZ	(B)
COOPERS CREEK SWAMP RESERVE CHARDONNAY 1996, COOPERS CREEK VINEYARD Hawkes Bay	*Rich, peachy tropical fruit characters, toasty oak and nutty hints on the nose and palate.*	£14.40	DIR NEI CNL	(G)
RONGAPAI WINEMAKERS SELECTION 1996, RONGOPAI Waikato	*Toasty buttery apricots on the palate with sweet medium body fruit and spirally acid finish.*	£15.00	VLW	(B)
BABICH THE PATRIARCH CHARDONNAY 1996, BABICH WINES Hawkes Bay	*Cool climate Chardonnay with light fragrant elegant fruit palate and herbal characters on the nose.*	£15.50	PFC DIR VIL	(B)
NEUDORF MOURTERE CHARDONNAY 1997, NEUDORF VINEYARD Nelson	*Put this wine away and wait for it to develop. Buttery with restrained citrus fruit.*	£18.40	DBY	(B)

NEW ZEALAND • SAUVIGNON BLANC

CORBANS WAIMANU DRY WHITE 1997, CORBANS WINES Gisbourne	*Floral citrus fruit on the nose with a zippy lemon lime palate and medium body.*	£4.00	Widely Available	(B)

SAUVIGNON BLANC • WHITE • NEW ZEALAND

MALT HOUSE VINTNERS NEW ZEALAND WHITE NV, SACRED HILL Hawkes Bay	*A creamy and grassy nose with oak hints and some good acidity on the finish.*	£4.70	MHV	B
CORBANS ESTATE SAUVIGNON BLANC 1997, CORBANS WINES Marlborough	*A lifted nose and palate of bracing lemons and limes with smacking but balanced acidity. A lean and stylish finish.*	£4.90	WES MGN DBY PEA CAP	S
KOHI POINT SAUVIGNON SEMILLON 1997, MONTANA WINES Marlborough	*Blue cheese with hints of grapefruit on the nose. Palate shows some weight with peach, apricot and herbaceous characters.*	£5.00	MTW SAF	S
COOKS SAUVIGNON BLANC 1997, CORBANS WINES South Island	*Bright pale lemon. Intense, elegant unsugared gooseberries on the nose. Some elegance on the palate.*	£5.10	Widely Available	S
KAITUNA HILLS SAUVIGNON BLANC 1997, MONTANA WINES Marlborough	*Pale straw coloured with a restrained nose and attractive herbaceous characters. A simple clean style.*	£5.50	MTW M&S HVW	B
MONTANA PATUTAHI ESTATE SAUVIGNON BLANC 1997, MONTANA WINES Marlborough	*Slight aromas of ripe guava. Good solid fruit with finely balanced tangy acidity behind it.*	£5.50	Widely Available	B
MONTANA SAUVIGNON BLANC 1997, MONTANA WINES Marlborough	*An elegant and intense nose of gooseberry fruits. The mineral elements on the nose follow onto the palate.*	£5.60	Widely Available	S

Pinpoint who sells the wine you wish to buy by turning to the stockist codes. If you know the name of the wine you want to buy, use the alphabetical index. If the price is your motivation, refer to the invaluable price guide index; red and white wines under £5, sparkling wines under £12 and Champagne under £16. Happy hunting!

STONELEIGH SAUVIGNON BLANC 1997, CORBANS WINES Marlborough	*Light golden colour with green apples on the nose, a fresh palate with an oily texture and good all-round balance.*	£6.00	Widely Available	**S**
HAWKES BAY SAUVIGNON BLANC 1997, DELEGAT'S WINE ESTATE Hawkes Bay	*An unusual rich aroma with lots of ripe gooseberries on the palate. A rounded style.*	£6.00	DEL	**B**
HIGHFIELD ESTATE SAUVIGNON BLANC 1997, HIGHFIELD ESTATE Marlborough	*Nettles and light gooseberries on the nose. Green fruit and an attack of lean acidity.*	£6.00	FUL	**B**
MILLS REEF SAUVIGNON BLANC 1996, MILLS REEF WINERY Hawkes Bay	*A minerally, peachy nose. The creamy fruit has strong alcoholic support and a boneyed finish.*	£6.20	COK HVW FTH	**B**
STONELEIGH SAUVIGNON BLANC 1996, CORBANS WINES Marlborough	*A pleasing wine with easy fruit and drying acidity on its broad palate.*	£6.30	WCR VLW G&M BNK HOU WIN BUP	**B**
TWIN ISLANDS SAUVIGNON BLANC 1997, NEGOCIANTS NEW ZEALAND Marlborough	*Pale lemon yellow, lime aromas followed by a chalky mouthfeel and a citrusy burst of flavour.*	£6.50	JNW QWW CPW HVW	**S**
VIDAL SAUVIGNON BLANC 1997, VIDAL ESTATE Hawkes Bay	*Green grass and blackcurrants on the nose. The fruit is balanced with lots of acidity.*	£6.50	GRA FRT	**B**
BABICH MARLBOROUGH SAUVIGNON BLANC 1997, JOE BABICH Marlborough	*Pale yellow with intense gooseberries on the nose. Good weight and length. Distinct varietal characteristics.*	£6.60	PFC DIR GAG BDR VIL AMW	**B**

SAUVIGNON BLANC • WHITE • NEW ZEALAND

MATUA VALLEY SAUVIGNON BLANC 1997, MATUA VALLEY WINES Waimaku	*Very soft asparagus aromas. Acid comes through on the mid-palate. Balanced, easy drinking.*	£6.60	WCR JNW WCS MGN GRT GCL HAL VIL	(B)
FALL HARVEST SAUVIGNON BLANC 1997, NOBILO Marlborough	*Pale green hues. Aromas of fresh peas and asparagus. Quite sharp acidity but not rasping.*	£6.70	WCR WES BOD QWW DIR BNK HOH AVB	(B)
OYSTER BAY SAUVIGNON BLANC 1997, DELEGAT'S WINE ESTATE Marlborough	*Pale lemon grass colour with some lemon and citrus on the nose, a zesty, clean palate.*	£6.70	Widely Available	(B)
VILLA MARIA PRIVATE BIN SAUVIGNON BLANC 1997, VILLA MARIA ESTATE Marlborough	*Pale yellow with lovely spicy fruit on the nose. Excellent fruit concentration and complex spicy flavours.*	£6.90	Widely Available	(S)
CORBANS ESTATE MARLBOROUGH SAUVIGNON BLANC 1997, CORBANS WINES Marborough	*A full almost meaty nose with lots of unripe gooseberries and asparagus on the palate.*	£7.00	DBY PEA CAP	(B)
LINCOLN HAWKES BAY SAUVIGNON BLANC 1997, LINCOLN VINEYARDS Hawkes Bay	*Lemons and limes on the nose that flows onto a palate bursting with sharp greengages.*	£7.00	MHA SWS	(B)
MORTON ESTATE HAWKES BAY SAUVIGNON BLANC 1997, MORTON ESTATE Hawkes Bay	*Splendid creamy rich fruit with gooseberry and nettle character on a rewarding palate.*	£7.00	BWC LNR PAG	(B)
SEIFRIED ESTATE SAUVIGNON BLANC 1997, SEIFRIED ESTATE Nelson	*Hot and grassy flavours with tart green pepper fruits followed by a zesty finish.*	£7.10	COK UNS EWD CWA WSO PON	(B)

NEW ZEALAND • WHITE • SAUVIGNON BLANC

Wine	Tasting Notes	Price	Stockists	
NGATARAWA STABLES OAK AGED SAUVIGNON BLANC 1997, NGATARAWA WINERY Hawkes Bay	*Delicious aromas of creamy fruit and apple peel. Refreshing green appley fruit with creamy hints on the palate.*	£7.20	BNK STE NYW AMW	S
VILLA MARIA PRIVATE BIN SAUVIGNON BLANC 1996, VILLA MARIA Marlborough Estate	*Grapefruits and peaches burst from the nose. Palate has bags of youthful citrusy fruits matched with zippy acidity.*	£7.20	Widely Available	S
VIDAL LIGHTLY OAKED SAUVIGNON BLANC 1997, VIDAL ESTATE Hawkes Bay	*A grapey and aromatic nose with gooseberries on the palate. A pronounced and oaky finish.*	£7.20	QWW BDR	B
GROVE MILL SAUVIGNON BLANC 1997, GROVE MILL Marlborough	*A rich, fat herbaceous nose. The palate has good weight and a delicious oily texture.*	£7.40	NRW LAW BNK CNL JSM ODD HVW LLV	S
PONDER ESTATE SAUVIGNON BLANC 1997, PONDER ESTATE Marlborough	*A clean fresh herbaceous nose with a touch of wet wood. A rich and full palate with green gooseberry fruit.*	£7.40	A&A CPW GGW	S
BABICH MARA ESTATE SAUVIGNON BLANC 1995, JOE BABICH Hawkes Bay	*Flavours of intense fruit sherbet and creamy green fruits on a rich and rewarding palate.*	£7.50	PFC CNL EPO VIL	B
GIESEN SAUVIGNON BLANC 1997, GIESEN WINE ESTATE Canterbury	*Dry, with ripe fruit reminiscent of nettles and gooseberry purée with crunchy acidity.*	£7.50	POR MOR ODD BOO	B
MATUA VALLEY RESERVE SAUVIGNON BLANC 1997, MATUA VALLEY WINES Waimaku	*Rich and well-integrated oak nose. Balanced palate of asparagus, red peppers and mouth watering acidity.*	£7.70	JNW WCS MGN PTR WES VIL CST	S

FORREST ESTATE SAUVIGNON BLANC 1997, FORREST ESTATE Marlborough	*Distinctive smoky and grassy aromas follow onto the palate. An elegant well-balanced wine with clean zesty acidity.*	£7.80	ADN HAS DBY PFT BEN NYW	**B**
SHINGLE PEAK SAUVIGNON BLANC 1997, MATUA VALLEY WINES Marlborough	*Ripe, juicy green apple flavours marry with complex buttery notes giving a well-balanced and full-bodied style.*	£7.90	WCS MGN CPW VWE VIL	**S**
VILLA MARIA CELLAR SELECTION SAUVIGNON BLANC 1997, VILLA MARIA ESTATE Marlborough	*Tropical fruit on the nose. The palate balances the grapefruit and pineapple with crisp mouth watering acidity.*	£8.00	ODD	**S**
NOBILO ICON SAUVIGNON BLANC 1997, HOUSE OF NOBILO Marlborough	*A fine herbaceous nose carries onto the palate. Astringent and fresh acidity refreshes the mouth.*	£8.00	DIR AVB	**B**
SELAKS MARLBOROUGH SAUVIGNON BLANC 1997, SELAKS Marlborough	*A nose of citrus fruit followed by a palate of tropical fruit and lime floral notes.*	£8.00	ODD SGL NAD WSO	**B**
KIM CRAWFORD MARLBOROUGH SAUVIGNON BLANC 1998, KIM CRAWFORD Marlborough	*Lemon and lime aromas. Delicate but concentrated palate with citrus fruit, green apples and some complex leafy overtones.*	£8.10	WCR HOU NEI DBY TOS NYW FUL LIB	**G**
COOPERS CREEK MARLBOROUGH SAUVIGNON BLANC 1997, COOPERS CREEK Marlborough	*Greengage and prickly nose to a palate of lime, green fruits and tangy citrus acidity.*	£8.10	DIR NIC CNL	**S**
KIM CRAWFORD MARLBOROUGH SAUVIGNON BLANC 1997, KIM CRAWFORD Marlborough	*A rich light and inviting nose with soft and distinctive honeyed notes. A well-made wine with good texture.*	£8.10	WCR DBY NYW FUL RES LIB	**S**

WHITCLIFFE SAUVIGNON BLANC 1997, SACRED HILL Hawkes Bay	*Almost water white with subtle nettle aromas, a lean and citrusy palate with balancing acidity.*	£8.20	ODD SEL MHV	B
CASTLE HILL SAUVIGNON BLANC 1997, TE MATA ESTATE WINERY Hawkes Bay	*Pale straw coloured with green hues, the nose has fresh grassy aromas followed by a clean and lively palate.*	£8.30	Widely Available	S
DASHWOOD SAUVIGNON BLANC 1997, VAVASOUR WINES Marlborough	*Impressive green leaf fruit with herbaceous overtones and excellent balancing acidity.*	£8.30	Widely Available	S
WAIRAU RIVER SAUVIGNON BLANC 1996, WAIRAU RIVER WINES Marlborough	*Excellent rich green and grassy fruit with a full palate of ripe apples and pears.*	£8.30	LEA MIS RDS BUP NYW WRC CFT	S
LAWSON'S DRY HILLS MARLBOROUGH SAUVIGNON BLANC 1997, LAWSON'S DRY HILLS WINES Marlborough	*An unusual meaty grass aroma. A powerful and fruity wine with good length and acidity.*	£8.50	VDV BWL WTS	B
WAIPARA WEST SAUVIGNON BLANC 1997, TUTTON SIENKO & HILL Canterbury	*Watery green in colour. Fresh and zippy with bags of fruit to balance the acidity.*	£8.60	WAW DIR FNZ	B
CAIRNBRAE SAUVIGNON BLANC 1997, CAIRNBRAE WINES Marlborough	*A lightly tropical and gooseberry nose with sappy fruits mid-palate and a lean concentrated finish.*	£8.70	NEI ENO RES	B
ISABEL ESTATE SAUVIGNON BLANC 1997, SAM WEAVER Marlborough	*Ripe citrus and nettles on the nose. A very elegant and well-balanced palate with a good core of flavour and backbone.*	£8.80	HOU GGW M&V DBY RBS NYW	S

SAUVIGNON BLANC • WHITE • NEW ZEALAND

ALLAN SCOTT SAUVIGNON BLANC 1997, ALLAN SCOTT Marlborough	*A herbaceous and grassy nose with a good, ripe body full of intense fruit flavours.*	£8.90	SHJ L&W NYW	**B**
JACKSON ESTATE SAUVIGNON BLANC 1997, JACKSON ESTATE Marlborough	*Herbal and grassy nose with a light lifted fresh palate and a clean finish.*	£8.90	Widely Available	**B**
REDWOOD VALLEY SAUVIGNON BLANC 1997, HERMANN SEIFRIED Nelson	*This has good minty leaf character on its rewarding palate which impressed the tasters.*	£8.90	FNZ ODF FSW DDT	**B**
PALLISER ESTATE SAUVIGNON BLANC 1997, PALLISER ESTATE WINES Martinborough	*An intense nose followed by an explosion of acidity and fruit on the mid-palate.*	£9.00	Widely Available	**G** TROPHY WINE
COOPERS CREEK OAKED SAUVIGNON BLANC RESERVE 1996, COOPERS CREEK VINEYARD Marlborough	*Touches of bananas on the nose. A well textured, savoury palate with well-balanced acids.*	£9.00	TOS	**B**
NAUTILUS ESTATE SAUVIGNON BLANC 1997, NEGOCIANTS NEW ZEALAND Marlborough	*A classic, restrained nose with elegant chalk and flint overtones. A light, clean palate with refreshing acidity.*	£9.20	BEN VDV JNW DBY QWW WIN HVW	**S**
SELAKS DRYLANDS SAUVIGNON BLANC 1997, SELAKS Marlborough	*A wonderfully ripe and citrussy nose that leads onto a palate of depth and elegance.*	£9.20	WSP ODF SGL NAD	**S**

Pinpoint who sells the wine you wish to buy by turning to the stockist codes. If you know the name of the wine you want to buy, use the alphabetical index. If the price is your motivation, refer to the invaluable price guide index; red and white wines under £5, sparkling wines under £12 and Champagne under £16. Happy hunting!

NEW ZEALAND • WHITE • SAUVIGNON BLANC

VILLA MARIA CLIFFORD BAY SAUVIGNON BLANC RESERVE 1997, **VILLA MARIA ESTATE** Marlborough	*A ripe rounded wine with soft acidity. Full on green fruits with hints of vanilla.*	£9.49	COK NEI ODD VWE MCW	**B**
RONGOPAI OAK AGED SAUVIGNON BLANC 1996, RONGOPAI Waikato	*An intense nose of caramel and toasted oak. Good peach and lime fruit and balanced acidity.*	£9.50	FSW VLW	**S**
VILLA MARIA WAIRAU VALLEY SAUVIGNON BLANC RESERVE 1997, VILLA MARIA ESTATE Marlborough	*Delicate fruit flavours permeate from this lovely wine with its soft acidity and notes of gooseberries.*	£9.60	QWW UNS DBY BUP THS WRC	**S**
DE REDCLIFFE ESTATE RESERVE SAUVIGNON BLANC 1996, DE REDCLIFFE ESTATE Marlborough	*An aromatic almost herbal nose with good fruit and a slight spritz on the palate.*	£10.00	COK CTH	**B**
HUNTER'S SAUVIGNON BLANC 1997, HUNTER'S WINES Marlborough	*Quite full fruit nose with a grassy creamy palate of lime green fruits.*	£10.10	Widely Available	**S**
VAVASOUR SAUVIGNON BLANC 1997, VAVASOUR WINES Marlborough	*Lean fruits on a gooseberry and steely fruit palate, quite light in texture.*	£10.30	JNW BNK CVR HOT DBY BTH AMW NYW	**S**
MONTANA BRANCOTT ESTATE SAUVIGNON BLANC 1996, MONTANA WINES Marlborough	*Well crafted, full bodied, with soft creamy fruit and gentle acidity on its full palate.*	£10.30	BNK VLW MTW ODD DBY WCR	**B**

Pinpoint who sells the wine you wish to buy by turning to the stockist codes. If you know the name of the wine you want to buy, use the alphabetical index. If the price is your motivation, refer to the invaluable price guide index; red and white wines under £5, sparkling wines under £12 and Champagne under £16. Happy hunting!

VAVASOUR SAUVIGNON BLANC 1996, **VAVASOUR WINES** Marlborough	*The nose is grassy with herbaceous notes. The citrus fruit is balanced with fresh acidity.*	£10.30	JNW BNK ODD BTH NYW	B
HUNTER'S SAUVIGNON BLANC OAK AGED 1996, **HUNTER'S WINES** Marlborough	*Peaches and nectarines burst from the nose and lead onto the ripe palate.*	£10.50	DIR MIS DBY NYW	S
NEUDORF MOURTERE SAUVIGNON BLANC 1997, TIM & JUDY FINN **NEUDORF VINEYARD** Nelson	*One of the best examples of this wine. Rich, green, creamy fruits matched by taut acidity.*	£10.50	SEL	S

NEW ZEALAND • OTHER WHITE

MONTANA MARLBOROUGH RIESLING 1997, MONTANA WINES Marlborough	*Lemon, grapefruit and citrus aromas with a broad palate of soft fruits and lychees.*	£5.20	BNK COK MTW GDS TOS VLW	B
VILLA MARIA PRIVATE BIN RIESLING 1997, **VILLA MARIA ESTATE** Marlborough	*Fresh lime fruits on a quite forward nose with a creamy soft mouthfeel of lychees.*	£5.40	HOU NEI DBY BUP WTS THS WRC	B
MATUA VALLEY PINOT GRIS 1997, **MATUA VALLEY WINES** Marlborough	*Freshly picked delicate stone fruit mingled with spice followed by pleasing acid and good length.*	£6.00	JSM	B
JACKSON ESTATE MARLBOROUGH RIESLING 1997, JACKSON ESTATE Marlborough	*Ripe, tropical fruit on the nose with a palate of citrusy lime and melon flavours.*	£6.90	HWL SVT BNK TAN NYW	B

PALLISER ESTATE RIESLING 1996, PALLISER ESTATE WINES Martinborough	*Impressive lemon sherbet notes from this well made wine with gentle acidity.*	**£7.10**	ABY	B
GROVE MILL RIESLING 1997, GROVE MILL Marlborough	*A peachy, honeyed nose gives up an austere apple fruit palate with a minerally edge and sharp undertones.*	**£7.50**	NRW LAW WTS	S
MONTANA RESERVE VINEYARD SELECTION RIESLING 1997, MONTANA WINES Marlborough	*A lovely rich nose with a palate to match. Ripe peachy citrus fruit and a long finish.*	**£8.00**	MTW ODD	B
LAWSON'S DRY HILLS MARLBOROUGH GEWURZTRAMINER 1997, LAWSON'S DRY HILLS WINES Marlborough	*A delicate perfumed nose with crisp ripe mouth-filling fruit and a full, long finish.*	**£8.30**	VDV GGW BWL	B
CORBANS PRIVATE BIN RIESLING 1995, CORBANS WINES Marlborough	*Lovely sherbet and lime nose, uplifted acidity and ripe melon fruit.*	**£8.70**	DBY CDE CAP	B
MILLTON BARREL FERMENTED CHENIN BLANC 1997, THE MILLTON VINEYARD Gisborne	*An attractive buttery nose. The palate has apple and lemon notes with a buttery finish.*	**£8.70**	ADN WTS VER	B
WAIPARA WEST RIESLING 1997, TUTTON SIENKO & HILL Canterbury	*Fine fruit notes on the nose, leads to zippy acidity on a lovely palate of melon and tropical fruit.*	**£8.90**	WAW VDV DIR	S
NOBILO ICON GEWURZTRAMINER 1997, HOUSE OF NOBILO Marlborough	*An attractive warm and spicy nose leads to a very delicate, sappy and floral palate.*	**£9.00**	DIR HOH AVB	B

VILLA MARIA RESERVE RIESLING 1997, VILLA MARIA ESTATE Marlborough	*Ripe fruit with soft acidity, flavours of lemon and pink grapefruit on a palate of richness.*	£9.00	ODF	**B**
STONECROFT GEWURZTRAMINER LATE HARVEST 1997, STONECROFT Hawkes Bay	*Intense fruit with a hint of spice on the nose. Sweet fruit and oily texture.*	£24.00 (37.5cl)	LEA	**B**

NEW ZEALAND • SPARKLING

HUNTER'S MIRU MIRU MARLBOROUGH BRUT 1995, HUNTER WINES Marlborough	*Excellent mousse. Dry and powerful flavours grip the mouth and it has wonderful fruit flavours.*	£9.70	DIR CVR NEI MWW NYW	**G**
NAUTILUS ESTATE MARLBOROUGH CUVÉE BRUT NV, NEGOCIANTS NEW ZEALAND Marlborough	*A quick dissipating mousse leads to a complex nose and palate including yeast, toasty and lemons.*	£10.90	VDV JNW WIN MWW DBY HVW JNR	**B**
DEUTZ MARLBOROUGH CUVÉE BRUT NV, MONTANA WINES Marlborough	*Pale straw, ripe and toasty nose this fresh and zippy wine has a long pleasant finish.*	£11.00	Widely Available	**B** WINE OF THE YEAR
DEUTZ BLANC DE BLANCS BRUT VINTAGE 1994, MONTANA WINES Marlborough	*This fruity little number doesn't shy away from a large crowd. Lively acidity with a brisk finish.*	£12.00	MTW ODD	**B**
DANIEL LE BRUN BRUT NV, CELLIER LE BRUN Marlborough	*A toasty nose with tropical citrus fruit marrying well with the oak content. Excellent long finish.*	£12.80	Widely Available	**B**

NEW ZEALAND • SPARKLING

DANIEL LE BRUN BLANC DE BLANCS BRUT 1991, CELLIER LE BRUN Marlborough	*A large buttery wine with masses of oak and bags of fruit emulating in a huge finish.*	**£16.40**	HWL SVT VIL

NORTH AMERICA

A curate's egg of a WINE Challenge for North America this year. It was good in parts, especially the reds, but for some Chardonnay producers the line "over-blown, over-oaked and over here" may be too close to the truth for comfort. On the other hand, Canadian winemakers continued to impress with Eiswiens and a super Pinot Gris. California and the North West States have produced impressive red and white wines displaying subtlety and complexity, all good examples of the winemaker's art. Set 'em up Joe!

CALIFORNIA • CABERNET SAUVIGNON

REDWOOD TRAIL CABERNET SAUVIGNON 1995, STERLING VINEYARDS California	*Rich aromas of blackberries and herbs lead to ripe jammy flavours on the balanced palate.*	£5.60	COK CPW ODD FUL SEA	B
FIRESTONE CABERNET SAUVIGNON 1996, FIRESTONE VINEYARDS California	*Sandlewood notes to the rich aromas of black fruits and creamy oak. A balanced finish to the full-bodied palate.*	£6.00	CPW MWW GRA FRT	B
FETZER VINEYARDS VALLEY OAKS CABERNET SAUVIGNON 1995, FETZER VINEYARDS California	*Big aromas of American oak dominate the plum jam nose before a soft minty palate of damson fruit.*	£6.90	Widely Available	B
DE LOACH PLATINUM CABERNET SAUVIGNON 1996, DE LOACH VINEYARDS California	*Light, herbaceous redcurrant nose with creamy new oak notes leads to a stewed rhubarb palate.*	£7.10	LIB NYW	B
SUTTER HOME CABERNET SAUVIGNON RESERVE 1994, SUTTER HOME WINERY California	*A leafy, blackcurrant nose is followed by a soft jammy palate full of cassis and bramble flavours.*	£7.80	MTL COK DAV EPO PAR VIL	B

JEKEL VINEYARDS CABERNET SAUVIGNON 1996, JEKEL VINEYARDS California	*Deep aromas of cherries and vanilla develop into intense flavours of blackcurrants and blueberries.*	£8.00	BRF MWW FRT	(S)
BONTERRA VINEYARDS CABERNET SAUVIGNON 1995, BONTERRA VINEYARDS California	*Ripe black fruits aromas with hints of toffee oak lead to a rich palate of spicy minty cassis.*	£8.80	WIN BRF ODD DBY FRT JSM WTS FUL	(B)
HEUBLEIN AITKEN NAPA CABERNET SAUVIGNON 1994, JOEL HEUBLEIN AITKEN California	*Blackcurrants and cream on the nose and palate with nuances of cedar wood and spice.*	£9.00	PFC	(B)
SEVEN PEAKS CABERNET SAUVIGNON 1996, SOUTHCORP WINES California	*Creamy oak, rich cassis with balanced acids and tannins combine beautifully on this wine.*	£9.00	PEF	(B)
STONEGATE CABERNET SAUVIGNON 1995, STONEGATE WINERY California	*Attractive, warm cedary element to this richly flavoured wine. The palate is full of blackberries and spicy oak.*	£9.50	POU BUD	(B)
BENZIGER CABERNET SAUVIGNON 1995, BENZIGER OF GLEN ELLEN California	*Jammy fruit aromas with hints of new oak lead onto ripe sweet flavours of creamy blackcurrants and vanilla.*	£10.00	WCR CDT	(S)
VICHON CALIFORNIAN SELECTION CABERNET SAUVIGNON 1994, VICHON California	*New oak and blackcurrant aromas are reflected on a structured palate. Complex notes of spicy, creamy vanilla.*	£10.00	REM	(S)
KENDALL-JACKSON CAB. SAUVIGNON VINTNER'S RESERVE 1994, KENDALL-JACKSON VINEYARDS California	*Huge aromas of ripe black fruits carry over onto a soft, creamy palate of berries, brambles oak and mint.*	£10.00	G&M DIR DBY CPW	(B)

FETZER VINEYARDS BARREL SELECT CABERNET SAUVIGNON 1995, FETZER VINEYARDS California	*Cream and summer fruits with figgy elements to the sweet fruity palate. The lingering finish is well-balanced.*	£10.70	SHJ BRF SMF FRT	B
KENWOOD VINEYARDS YULUPA CABERNET SAUVIGNON 1994, KENWOOD VINEYARDS California	*Fruity, eucalyptus and spice notes on the nose and palate of this fresh, easy drinking wine.*	£11.00	COK VNO GLY P&R	B
SEVEN OAKS CABERNET SAUVIGNON 1995, J. LOHR California	*Vanilla and chocolate notes on the blackcurrant nose carry over onto the richly flavoured, creamily smooth palate.*	£11.00	ENO VLW	B
ST. SUPERY NAPA VALLEY CABERNET SAUVIGNON 1994, ST. SUPERY VINEYARDS & WINERY California	*Ripe forest fruits with hints of spice, eucalypt and loads of vanilla pod. Good length.*	£11.20	LIB THS WRC BUP	B
GALLO SONOMA FREI RANCH CABERNET SAUVIGNON 1994, ERNEST & JULIO GALLO WINERY California	*Elements of spice and herbs on a sweet blackberry palate. New oak and balanced acids give length.*	£11.50	TOS	B
VICHON NAPA VALLEY CABERNET SAUVIGNON 1990, VICHON California	*Ripe plummy fruits with complex layers of figs, spice and dried fruits develops into a palate of forest berries.*	£13.80	WSP REM	G TROPHY WINE
MONDAVI NAPA VALLEY CABERNET SAUVIGNON 1995, ROBERT MONDAVI WINERY California	*A spicy aromatic nose with a sweet forest fruits palate and hints of mint and chocolate.*	£13.80	JNW MGN MWW THS FTH PTR VIL	B
DRY CREEK VINEYARD MERITAGE 1995, DRY CREEK VINEYARDS California	*Ripe aromas of blackberry and strawberry lead to soft flavours of plummy fruit and oak.*	£14.50	DIR DNL	B

FETZER VINEYARDS CHALK HILL CABERNET SAUVIGNON 1995, FETZER VINEYARDS California	*Rich, creamy flavours of oak with fresh juicy blackcurrants and nuances of peppery spice and figs.*	£15.00	BRF	G
FETZER VINEYARDS PRIVATE COLLECTION CABERNET SAUVIGNON 1994, FETZER VINEYARDS California	*Spicy, minty black-currant fruit aromas carry over to the palate with some oak nuances.*	£15.00	BRF ODD	B
MONDAVI OAKVILLE CABERNET SAUVIGNON 1993, ROBERT MONDAVI WINERY California	*Nose dominated by new oak but the palate displays fruit complexity of ripe juicy blackberries, pepper and vanilla.*	£15.90	JNW MGN DBY THS	S
JADE MOUNTAIN LES JUMEAUX 1995, JADE MOUNTAIN WINERY California	*A smoky and light palate with sweet wild strawberry notes and a dry oaky finish.*	£17.10	BEN JNW WIN RDS M&V NYW	B
CHALK HILL ESTATE CABERNET SAUVIGNON 1994, CHALK HILL ESTATE California	*Complex aromas of leafy cassis with liquorice and oak notes followed by a full bodied palate of ripe blackcurrants.*	£17.50	J&B NYW	G
CLOS DU VAL CABERNET SAUVIGNON 1993, CLOS DU VAL WINE COMPANY California	*Herbaceous notes to the rich forest fruits aromas. Oak to the fore on the intense, balanced palate displaying length.*	£17.60	FSW HOH AVB	B
KENDALL-JACKSON CAB. SAUVIGNON GRAND RESERVE 1994, KENDALL-JACKSON VINEYARDS California	*A sweet, concentrated palate of blackcurrants and cream with complex cedar wood and herbaceous notes.*	£18.50	G&M DIR EPO	B
MONDAVI OAKVILLE CABERNET SAUVIGNON 1995, ROBERT MONDAVI WINERY California	*Intensely complex flavours of cassis, brambles and damsons with nuances of vanilla, cedar wood, mint and spice.*	£19.30	Widely Available	S

CABERNET SAUVIGNON • CALIFORNIA • N. AMERICA

DURNEY VINEYARDS CABERNET SAUVIGNON 1992, DURNEY VINEYARDS California	*Creamy oak dominates the nose and palate with sweet and spicy black fruit flavours and a chocolatey finish.*	£20.00	SOB PAR	(S)
WHITE ROCK MERITAGE 1993, WHITE ROCK VINEYARDS California	*Blackcurrants, plums and figs with new oak and minty nuances. The lengthy palate displays a complex elegance.*	£20.00	WIN	(B)
CECCHETTI SEBASTIANI CABERNET SAUVIGNON 1993, CECCHETTI SEBASTIANI CELLARS California	*Blackcurrant leaves and spice aromas with rich raspberry flavours displaying vanilla, menthol and eucalypt notes.*	£24.00	TWB UNS	(S)
DURNEY VINEYARDS CABERNET SAUVIGNON RESERVE 1992, DURNEY VINEYARDS California	*Ripe blackcurrants with spicy oak and hints of mint, cedar wood and fig. A juicy palate with good length.*	£25.00	SOB F&M PAR	(B)
CAIN FIVE CABERNET SAUVIGNON CABERNET FRANC MERLOT 1994, CAIN ESTATE California	*Spicy oak with creamy currants and plums. A sweet palate with juicy cassis and balancing acidity.*	£28.00	J&B	(B)
ERNEST & JULIO GALLO ESTATE BOTTLED CAB. SAUVIGNON 1993, ERNEST & JULIO GALLO WINERY California	*Smoky, ripe fruits on the nose with creamy, oak notes and hints of mint and fig on the palate.*	£30.00	E&J	(B)
MONDAVI NAPA VALLEY CABERNET SAUVIGNON RESERVE 1994, ROBERT MONDAVI WINERY California	*Vanilla spice notes to a rich nose and palate of berries, cigar box, mint and dried fig.*	£39.70	Widely Available	(S)
RIDGE MONTEBELLO 1993, RIDGE VINEYARDS California	*Rich flavours of berries and currants with new oak and hints of cough medicine and figgy spice.*	£54.70	Widely Available	(S)

OPUS ONE 1994, BARON PHILIPPE DE ROTHSCHILD & ROBERT MONDAVI California	*Concentrated flavours of jammy berries and brambles. Complex nuances of oak, menthol, cedar wood, fig and spice.*	**£66.90**	Widely Available	**G**

CALIFORNIA • PINOT NOIR

FETZER VINEYARDS BARREL SELECT PINOT NOIR 1996, FETZER VINEYARDS California	*Beetroot and ripe berry fruit on the nose. Moderately complex palate with ripe fruit characters.*	**£8.90**	WCR SHJ BRF ODD FRT TOS	**S**
MONDAVI COASTAL PINOT NOIR 1996, ROBERT MONDAVI WINERY California	*Smoky oak and fragrant berry fruit characters on the nose. Soft and round palate with integrated tannins.*	**£9.50**	JNW VIL MGN DBY JSM MWW FEN THS	**S**
KENDALL-JACKSON PINOT NOIR VINTNERS RESERVE 1995, KENDALL-JACKSON VINEYARDS California	*Intense new oak, developed fruit and smoky meaty characters on the nose. Firm integrated tannins.*	**£9.80**	G&M DIR GDS DBY LUC	**S**
MONDAVI COASTAL PINOT NOIR 1995, ROBERT MONDAVI WINERY California	*Ruby red with meaty bacon aromas. Complex, dense berry fruit on the palate with a tight structure.*	**£12.00**	Widely Available	**G**
BYRON SANTA BARBARA PINOT NOIR 1994, ROBERT MONDAVI WINERY California	*Ripe fruit with hints of barnyard characters on the nose. Full fruit with balanced tannins.*	**£12.40**	JNW MGN HAR BEL VIL	**B**
SANFORD PINOT NOIR 1996, SANFORD WINERY California	*Youthful berry fruit with toasty oak on the nose. Strawberries and herbaceous characters on the palate.*	**£12.50**	DBY VLW	**S**

PINOT NOIR – ZINFANDEL • CALIFORNIA • N. AMERICA

SAINTSBURY PINOT NOIR 1996, SAINTSBURY California	*Intense meaty aromas with a touch of greenness. Full bodied fruit, soft tannins and length.*	£13.30	Widely Available	**B**
MARIMAR TORRES ESTATE PINOT NOIR 1995, MARIMAR TORRES VINEYARDS California	*Violets and rich oak on the nose. Fleshy fruit with lots of oak. Good length.*	£17.30	COK JEF GGW POR SCA PLA JCB	**B**
BYRON PINOT NOIR RESERVE 1995, ROBERT MONDAVI WINERY California	*Hints of vegetal and meaty characters. Full-bodied sweet berry fruit on the palate. Integrated tannins.*	£18.80	JNW MGN WCR UNC VIL WRC BUP	**S**
KENDALL-JACKSON PINOT NOIR GRAND RESERVE 1994, KENDALL-JACKSON VINEYARDS California	*Slight vegetal and savoury characters on the nose. Excellent full-bodied fruit with good weight and tannins.*	£19.50	G&M DIR EPO	**S**
MONDAVI NAPA VALLEY PINOT NOIR RESERVE 1996, ROBERT MONDAVI WINERY California	*Fruits of the forest on the palate with velvety mouth feel and good weight, moderate acidity.*	£21.00	Widely Available	**S**

CALIFORNIA • ZINFANDEL

BERINGER VINEYARDS ZINFANDEL 1995, BERINGER VINEYARDS California	*Ripe, plummy lifted aromas with grainy spices. Good warm fruit and a long dry finish.*	£6.70	BWC UNS MWW LNR MMW	**B**
DUNNEWOOD NORTH COAST ZINFANDEL 1994, CANADAIGUA California	*A heavy dark palate with plenty of spice and oak beautifully married together. A good, dry finish.*	£7.00	SAF REM	**S**

NORTH AMERICA • CALIFORNIA • ZINFANDEL

Wine	Tasting Note	Price	Stockist	
PEDRONCELLI ZINFANDEL 1996, J. PEDRONCELLI WINERY California	*Strawberry aromas with overtones of herbs and furniture polish. Green and spicy fruit with excellent oak integration.*	£7.30	DIR L&W NYW	S
BERINGER VINEYARDS NORTH COAST ZINFANDEL 1995, BERINGER VINEYARDS California	*Toasted oak dominates the nose. A tightly structured palate with sweet oak characteristics and green fruit flavours.*	£7.90	BWC SEL MWW DBY LNR NYW	S
BONTERRA VINEYARDS ZINFANDEL 1996, BONTERRA VINEYARDS California	*Dark plum colours lead to a very plummy palate with a spicy kick to finish.*	£8.00	BRF ODD FRT	B
SEBASTIANI SONOMA CASK OLD VINE ZINFANDEL 1996, SEBASTIANI VINEYARDS California	*A peppery nose reminiscent of pine needles. Tannins coat the mouth nicely and finish sweetly.*	£8.00	FBG	B
DE LOACH PLATINUM ZINFANDEL 1996, DE LOACH VINEYARDS California	*Well-structured tannins support a big, blackcurrant and clove palate with fine acidity and a great finish.*	£9.40	GGW LIB UNS TOS NYW	S
GALLO SONOMA FREI RANCH ZINFANDEL 1995, ERNEST & JULIO GALLO WINERY California	*Succulent nose with tobacco hints that follow onto the powerful and balanced palate with mulberry and spice.*	£9.50	ASD E&J	S
KENDALL-JACKSON ZINFANDEL VINTNERS RESERVE 1995, KENDALL-JACKSON VINEYARDS California	*An upfront and spicy nose with liquorice overtones. Excellent balance and depth of flavour on the palate.*	£9.90	G&M DIR DBY SHJ	S

Pinpoint who sells the wine you wish to buy by turning to the stockist codes. If you know the name of the wine you want to buy, use the alphabetical index. If the price is your motivation, refer to the invaluable price guide index; red and white wines under £5, sparkling wines under £12 and Champagne under £16. Happy hunting!

DRY CREEK VINEYARD ZINFANDEL 1995, DRY CREEK VINEYARDS California	*Mulberry and raisins on the nose with big ripe chewy fruit following onto the palate.*	£11.00	DIR DNL	(S)
GALLO SONOMA FREI RANCH ZINFANDEL 1994, ERNEST & JULIO GALLO WINERY California	*Awesome nose full of rich, spicy, plummy fruits. Balanced by sweet liquorice notes and hints of aniseed.*	£11.50	QWW SEL	(G)
VILLA MT EDEN SONOMA VALLEY GRAND RESERVE ZINFANDEL 1994, VILLA MT. EDEN California	*A nice complex nose with good peppery and velvety fruit and a big crunchy finish.*	£14.80	LIB NYW	(B)
RIDGE GEYSERVILLE ZINFANDEL 1995, RIDGE VINEYARDS California	*Rich blackcurrant, almost Port-like aromas follow onto the palate and mingle with coffee and spice notes.*	£17.50	BEN ADN MIS HAS CPW DBY PFT JNW	(S)
RIDGE LYTTON SPRINGS ZINFANDEL 1995, RIDGE VINEYARDS California	*Big, tarry, spicy oaked nose. Rich and powerful palate with complex ripe jammy flavours and smooth vanilla notes.*	£17.50	Widely Available	(G)

CALIFORNIA • OTHER RED

ASDA ARIUS CALIFORNIAN CARIGNANE 1997, CALIFORNIA DIRECT California	*Hot sweet and spicy flavours of rich fruit cake dominate this full-bodied wine.*	£4.30	ASD	(B)
ASDA ARIUS CALIFORNIAN SYRAH 1997, CALIFORNIA DIRECT California	*A vegetal nose and ruby appearance with lots of sweet fruit on the palate. Well-balanced.*	£5.00	ASD	(B)

FETZER VINEYARDS SYRAH 1996, FETZER VINEYARDS California	*Smoky, sweet ripe flavours of baked black fruits. A balanced, clean finish of good length.*	**£8.00**	WIN UNS BRF ODD TOS FRT FUL	**B**
PARDUCCI PETITE SIRAH 1995, PARDUCCI WINE CELLARS California	*Soft fruit with an interesting gamey nose. Tasty fruit flavours, delicate structure and finish.*	**£8.00**	COK PIM HDL	**B**
CLOS DU VAL LE CLOS RED 1994, CLOS DU VAL WINE COMPANY California	*A deep red with a subdued nose. The palate has light fruit and good acids.*	**£8.50**	WCR FSW HOH CPW AVB	**B**
CA' DEL SOLO IL FIASCO 1996, RANDALL GRAHM California	*Ripe cherries and blackcurrants, tobacco and smoke mellow out to a full and lingering finish.*	**£9.10**	Widely Available	**B**
FETZER VINEYARDS BARREL SELECT MERLOT 1996, FETZER VINEYARDS California	*Attractive stewed plums with balancing oak vanilla and spicy herbaceous notes on the nose and palate.*	**£9.20**	WIN BRF MWW FRT	**B**
KENDALL-JACKSON MERLOT VINTNERS RESERVE 1995, KENDALL-JACKSON VINEYARDS California	*Attractive black fruits nose with a vegetal edge precedes a sweet fruit palate with minty highlights.*	**£10.70**	G&M CPW DBY WRC BUP CFT	**B**
FIRESTONE MERLOT 1995, FIRESTONE VINEYARDS California	*Smoky, spicy notes to the plummy nose with complex flavours of summer fruits and cinnamon.*	**£11.00**	MWW GRA FRT	**B**
BONNY DOON LE CIGARE VOLANT 1995, RANDALL GRAHM California	*Mouth watering fruit with dry wood textures. Complex fresh and crisp style with reasonable length.*	**£11.10**	Widely Available	**B**

VINO NOCETO SANGIOVESE 1995, VINO NOCETO California	*Tarry, spicy aromas with overtones of leather, mint and vanilla oak. The rich, cherry like palate is full of complex flavours.*	£11.40	Widely Available	**G**
SEVEN PEAKS SHIRAZ 1996, SOUTHCORP WINES California	*Soft and oaky on the nose. Vibrant spicy fruit flavours on the palate and a long finish.*	£12.00	PEF	**S**
STONEGATE MERLOT 1995, STONEGATE WINERY California	*Inky, dense soft black fruits and vanilla aromas lead to ripe juicy cassis flavours with good structure.*	£12.00	POU BUD	**S**
QUPÉ SYRAH BIEN NACIDO 1996, BOB LINDQUIST California	*The palate is almost overwhelmed by concentrated flavours of smoked black fruits and white pepper spice.*	£12.10	BEN WIN GRT RDS M&V DBY NYW HVN	**S**
GALLO SONOMA BARRELLI CREEK VALDIGUIE 1995, ERNEST & JULIO GALLO WINERY California	*Big spicy aromas and flavours with mint and creamy, vegetal notes from this rare grape variety.*	£13.00	E&J	**B**
SILVERADO HILL MERLOT 1995, SILVERADO HILL CELLARS California	*Herbaceous notes of rosemary and thyme on the cassis driven nose and palate of this wine.*	£14.00	WIN	**B**
VILLA MT. EDEN GRAND RESERVE SYRAH 1996, VILLA MT. EDEN California	*Oak and spicy pepper, raspberry and earthy flavours develop on the palate. Finish is almost smoky.*	£15.00	LIB	**S**
FETZER VINEYARDS CHALK HILL PRIVATE COLLECTION MERLOT 1996, FETZER VINEYARDS California	*Rich prune aromas and flavours with nuances of grass, cedarwood and spice. A smooth finish to this attractive wine.*	£15.00	BRF ODD	**B**

KENDALL-JACKSON MERLOT GRAND RESERVE 1994, KENDALL-JACKSON VINEYARDS California	*Aromas of blackcurrant and vanilla lead to warm, creamy ripe black fruit flavours which linger.*	£18.50	G&M DIR EPO
CLOS DU VAL MERLOT STAG'S LEAP DISTRICT 1994, CLOS DU VAL WINE COMPANY California	*Mint and cedar notes to the nose and palate of this concentrated blackberry wine.*	£20.80	FSW HOH AVB

CALIFORNIA • CHARDONNAY

SUTTER HOME CHARDONNAY 1997, SUTTER HOME WINERY California	*Creamy, lactic characters come over onto the rich melon palate with a balanced finish.*	£4.80	Widely Available
ERNEST & JULIO GALLO EST. BOTT. CHARDONNAY 1995, ERNEST & JULIO GALLO WINERY California	*Marmalade and honey on toast with crisp dry fruit mingled with malt and yeast characters.*	£5.00	CRS
STONYBROOK VINEYARDS CHARDONNAY 1997, STONYBROOK VINEYARDS California	*Herbaceous, slightly spicy nose is followed by a well balanced palate of peppered pineapple.*	£5.00	UNS MRN
ZUNINO RANCH CHARDONNAY 1997, ASSOCIATED VINTAGE GROUP California	*Fresh citrus and pear drops on the nose. Lots of lime fruit with moderate acidity.*	£6.00	BWL
FETZER VINEYARDS SUNDIAL CHARDONNAY 1997, FETZER VINEYARDS California	*Rich creamy aromas with clean, crisp flavours of pink grapefruit and zest of lime.*	£6.40	Widely Available

Wine	Tasting Notes	Price	Stockists	
ERNEST & JULIO GALLO EST. BOTT. CHARDONNAY 1994, ERNEST & JULIO GALLO WINERY California	*Creamy nuances of toasty oak dominate a palate full of ripe tropical mangos.*	£6.50	CRS JSM	Ⓢ
MONTEVIÑA CHARDONNAY 1995, MONTEVIÑA WINERY California	*Soft rounded flavours of ripe citrus fruits with a balanced, easy drinking finish.*	£7.00	TPE DAV UNS	Ⓑ
STERLING CHARDONNAY 1996, STERLING VINEYARDS California	*Big creamy nose with soft round full-bodied fruit on the palate and toasty oak.*	£7.50	ODD SEA	Ⓑ
BONTERRA VINEYARDS CHARDONNAY 1996, BONTERRA VINEYARDS California	*Pineapple and banana mingle with sweet vanilla oak on the nose and palate with melon characters.*	£8.00	WIN BRF ODD DBY FRT JSM WTS FUL	Ⓢ
VILLA MT. EDEN CHARDONNAY 1996, VILLA MT. EDEN California	*Pale yellow with green hue. Peach aromatic fruit and oak aromas, light creamy fruit on the palate.*	£8.20	WCR HOU CPW LIB NYW	Ⓢ
BONTERRA VINEYARDS CHARDONNAY 1995, BONTERRA VINEYARDS California	*Rich oak and nutty aromas combined with full-bodied tropical fruit and high balanced acidity.*	£8.50	WCR SEL WIN BRF DBY JSM FUL	Ⓑ
FETZER VINEYARDS BARREL SELECT CHARDONNAY 1996, FETZER VINEYARDS California	*Toasty oak on the nose with tropical citrus fruit characters. Well-balanced with a good finish.*	£8.70	WIN SHJ BRF MWW DBY FRT TOS	Ⓑ
HERMAN WENTE RIVA RIVER RIVER CHARDONNAY 1995, WENTE BROS. California	*Tropical fruit mingled with subtle oak aromas, some complexity with balanced acidity and good length.*	£9.00	GRA FRT	Ⓑ

SEVEN PEAKS CHARDONNAY 1996, SOUTHCORP WINES California	*Big oaky nose with lots of tropical fruit some complexity balanced with crisp clean acidity.*	£9.00	PEF
FIRESTONE BARREL FERMENTED CHARDONNAY 1996, FIRESTONE VINEYARDS California	*Hints of lemon and lime on the nose. Ripe fruit with fresh citrus finish on palate.*	£9.60	MWW GRA FRT
BENZIGER CHARDONNAY 1994, BENZIGER California	*Big, attractive butter and fig aromas with creamy full body and good acidic clean finish.*	£9.60	WCR CDT
MONDAVI CENTRAL COAST CHARDONNAY 1995, ROBERT MONDAVI WINERY California	*Caramel, toffee toasty oak and melon on the nose, pineapple and caramel toffee characters on the palate.*	£9.90	Widely Available
GALLO SONOMA LAGUNA RANCH CHARDONNAY 1996, ERNEST & JULIO GALLO WINERY California	*Toasted biscuit, bacon and citrus characters on the nose. Complex palate of lemon fruit and oak.*	£10.00	Widely Available
SILVERADO HILL CHARDONNAY ART CUVEE 1996, SILVERADO HILL CELLARS California	*Leesy, yeasty nose with hints of toast. Complex palate of sun-ripened mangos, pineapples and ogen melons.*	£10.00	WIN WRC
VICHON CALIFORNIAN SELECTION CHARDONNAY 1995, VICHON California	*Apricots and stone fruits dominate the nose and palate of this attractive wine with a fresh citrus finish.*	£10.00	REM
KENDALL-JACKSON CHARDONNAY VINTNERS RESERVE 1996, KENDALL-JACKSON VINEYARD California	*Pale straw with green tinge. Lemon and fig aromas with subtle oak and well-balanced fruit.*	£10.10	G&M DIR GDS LUC WRC BUP

CHARDONNAY • CALIFORNIA • NORTH AMERICA

MONDAVI CENTRAL COAST CHARDONNAY 1996, ROBERT MONDAVI WINERY California	*Rich buttery oak aromas and sweet ripe peachy fruit. Simple style with lots of body.*	£10.10	Widely Available	(B)
KENWOOD VINEYARDS YULUPA CHARDONNAY 1996, KENWOOD VINEYARDS California	*Attractive floral perfumed nose with hints of grass clippings, lovely soft fruit and moderate acidity.*	£10.50	VNO GLY P&R	(B)
BROCK EDNA VALLEY CHARDONNAY 1995, CLAY BROCK California	*Creamy aromas of oak and ripe tropical fruits are reflected on the smoothly sensuous palate.*	£10.60	DBY WTS	(B)
BERINGER VINEYARDS CHARDONNAY 1996, BERINGER VINEYARDS California	*Toasted oak flavours, wrapped up in a slice of ripe mango. A clean mouthwatering finish follows.*	£10.70	BWC MWW DBY LNR	(B)
CHARDONNAY HERMAN WENTE RESERVE 1995, WENTE BROS. California	*Creamy oak and melon flavours combine with refreshing lime and lemon acidity in this wine.*	£11.00	GRA FRT	(B)
J. LOHR RIVERSTONE CHARDONNAY 1996, J. LOHR California	*Rich vanilla oak with hints of mint on the nose. Well-structured citrus fruit.*	£11.00	ENO VLW	(B)
GALLO SONOMA STEFANI VINEYARD CHARDONNAY 1995, ERNEST & JULIO GALLO WINERY California	*Ripe glazed fruit with buttery oak aromas, soft full round palate with slightly bitter finish.*	£11.20	QWW SEL MWW TOS	(B)
ST. SUPERY NAPA VALLEY CHARDONNAY 1996, ST. SUPERY VINEYARDS California	*Sweet coconut aromas. Apple and peach fruit flavours, powerful oak balanced by good weighty fruit.*	£11.30	LIB	(B)

SAINTSBURY CHARDONNAY 1996, SAINTSBURY California	*Rich, toasty oak dominates the nose and palate of this creamy smooth ripe melon wine.*	£12.70	Widely Available	(B)
GALLO SONOMA LAGUNA RANCH CHARDONNAY 1995, ERNEST & JULIO GALLO WINERY California	*Cinnamon, toasty oak and cigar box hints on the nose, ripe tropical fruit on palate.*	£13.00	QWW	(S)
CLOS DU VAL CHARDONNAY CARNEROS DISTRICT 1996, CLOS DU VAL WINE COMPANY California	*Pale gold with green highlights. Opulent fruit with integrated new oak moderate acidity and elegant finish.*	£13.50	HOH AVB	(S)
SANFORD CHARDONNAY 1996, SANFORD WINERY California	*Floral, tropical and citrus fruit aromas. Lovely citrus fruit on the palate and integrated oak.*	£14.00	GRT DBY VLW	(B)
BYRON SANTA MARIA VALLEY CHARDONNAY 1996, ROBERT MONDAVI WINERY California	*Huge flavours of charred oak barrels fill the palate. Ripe melon fruits and crisp citrus acidity give balance.*	£14.80	JNW MGN THS BEL HAR JSM VIL	(S)
CLOS LA CHANCE CHARDONNAY 1996, CLOS LA CHANCE WINERY California	*Peaches and blossoms on the nose. Citrus fruit and honeyed texture with a slightly mineral finish.*	£15.00	BBR	(B)
MARIMAR TORRES ESTATE CHARDONNAY 1995, MARIMAR TORRES VINEYARDS California	*Inviting biscuity vegetal nose with lovely ripe fruit hazelnuts and butter with firm balanced acidity.*	£15.00	COK JEF GGW POR SCA PLA JCB	(B)
VILLA MOUNT EDEN GRAND RESERVE CHARDONNAY 1996, VILLA MOUNT EDEN California	*Pale straw with green hue. Citrus fruit with toasty oak on the nose, soft fruit, and creamy vanilla on the palate.*	£15.70	CPW LIB	(S)

CHARDONNAY – OTHER WHITE • CALIF. • N. AMERICA

KENDALL-JACKSON CHARDONNAY GRAND RESERVE 1995, KENDALL-JACKSON VINEYARDS California	*Lemon and buttery toasty oak on the nose. Creamy vanilla palate with tropical fruit characters.*	**£15.90**	G&M DIR	(S)
CHALK HILL ESTATE BOTTLED CHARDONNAY 1995, CHALK HILL ESTATE California	*Bold oak on the nose and palate. Sweet round fruit with good acid and finish.*	**£15.90**	J&B	(B)
MONDAVI NAPA VALLEY CHARDONNAY RESERVE 1996, ROBERT MONDAVI WINERY California	*Pale yellow with ripe citrus characters and toasty crispy oak aromas. Full body with ripe fruit.*	**£23.00**	Widely Available	(S)

CALIFORNIA • OTHER WHITE

RANCH SERIES PINOT BLANC 1997, ASSOCIATED VINTAGE GROUP California	*Peaches and cream bound in a perfumed bouquet, the fruit is ripe with adequate length.*	**£6.00**	BWL	(B)
DRY CREEK VINEYARDS CHENIN BLANC 1997, DRY CREEK VINEYARDS California	*A creamy, resinous nose with a well-rounded, juicy acidity in the mouth.*	**£7.70**	DIR SEL L&W DNL GNW	(B)
BERINGER VINEYARDS FUMÉ BLANC 1996, BERINGER VINEYARDS California	*Cream soda with nuances of gooseberry. The sweet oak palate is balanced by a ripe citric acid finish.*	**£7.80**	BWC MWW ODD LNR MMW	(S)
FETZER VINEYARDS VIOGNIER 1996, FETZER VINEYARDS California	*A nose of petrol and oak with rich pineapples and peaches on a spicy finish.*	**£7.80**	WIN BRF MWW TOS WTS WRC BUP	(B)

NORTH AMERICA • CALIFORNIA • OTHER WHITE

FIRESTONE VINEYARDS SAUVIGNON BLANC 1996, FIRESTONE VINEYARDS California	*Ripe herbaceous aromas and flavours of gooseberries and asparagus with some creamy notes and a cleansing finish.*	£8.00	GRA FRT	S
DRY CREEK VINEYARDS FUMÉ BLANC 1997, DRY CREEK VINEYARDS California	*A green, asparagus nose matched with chewy green fruit and good acidity on the palate.*	£8.90	DIR L&W DNL PIM GNW	B
KENWOOD VINEYARDS SAUVIGNON BLANC 1996, KENWOOD VINEYARDS California	*Sweet citrus and mineral notes with a lean fresh finish and lingering green fruit flavours.*	£9.00	COK VNO GLY WRK	B
ROBERT MONDAVI NAPA VALLEY FUMÉ BLANC 1996, ROBERT MONDAVI WINERY California	*A perfumed, smoky nose with ripe limes and well integrated, smoky oak on the palate.*	£10.30	JNW WCS MGN MWW THS FTH PTR VIL	B
CHALK HILL ESTATE SAUVIGNON BLANC 1995, CHALK HILL ESTATE California	*Coconuts and butter on the nose. An oaky palate giving touches of spice and warmth.*	£11.30	J&B	B
GALLO SONOMA BARRELLI CREEK SAUVIGNON BLANC 1995, ERNEST & JULIO GALLO WINERY California	*Fresh tropical fruit flavours mingle with the smoky flavours to give a delicious, gutsy wine.*	£13.00	E&J	S
VILLA MT. EDEN GRAND RESERVE PINOT BLANC 1996, VILLA MT. EDEN California	*Deep, rich and concentrated fruit flavours with elderflower overtones. The finish is well-balanced and clean.*	£15.00	LIB	S

Pinpoint who sells the wine you wish to buy by turning to the stockist codes. If you know the name of the wine you want to buy, use the alphabetical index. If the price is your motivation, refer to the invaluable price guide index; red and white wines under £5, sparkling wines under £12 and Champagne under £16. Happy hunting!

CALIFORNIA • SPARKLING

QUARTET BRUT NV, ROEDERER ESTATE California	*Good yeasty nose with a hint of earth. Excellent fruit, nicely balanced with a crisp palate.*	**£14.60**	Widely Available	(S)

CALIFORNIA • FORTIFIED

ELYSIUM BLACK MUSCAT 1996, ANDREW QUADY WINERY California	*A dark brooding beast waiting to assault your tastebuds with figs, mocha and sun-dried raisins.*	**£6.80**	Widely Available	(B)
QUADY STARBOARD 88 NV, ANDREW QUADY WINERY California	*Dark, slightly orange in colour this had bitter sweet candied peel fruit on a dense prune palate.*	**£8.10**	WCR FSW JNW ADN HOH AVB L&W RBS	(B)
QUADY STARBOARD 1990, ANDREW QUADY WINERY California	*Intense stewed fruit on a lifted cinnamon and nutmeg palate with delicious lean fruits.*	**£13.10**	HOH MIS AVB JOB	(B)

OREGON • RED

WILLAMETTE VALLEY WHOLE BERRY FERMENTED PINOT NOIR 1995, WILLA-METTE VALLEY VINEYARDS Oregon	*Spicy and jammy fruit on the nose, raspberry and plums on the palate. Firm tannins.*	**£9.00**	COK	(B)

NORTH AMERICA • OREGON – WASHINGTON STATE

REX HILL PINOT NOIR 1995, REX HILL VINEYARDS Oregon	*Ripe berry fruit with caramel overtones and vegetal characters on the nose. Fruit palate with moderate acidity.*	£14.50	JNW MOR HVN	Ⓢ
ARGYLE PINOT NOIR RESERVE 1996, ARGYLE WINERY Oregon	*Fresh fruit with a touch of mint on the nose. Good body, with soft tannins.*	£15.00	DIR CRV PAV	Ⓑ
REX HILL PINOT NOIR RESERVE 1994, REX HILL VINEYARDS Oregon	*Pungent fruit with barnyard and slightly vegetal aroma. Deep fruit palate has good tannin acid balance.*	£26.00	JNW MOR	Ⓢ

OREGON • WHITE

ARGYLE HIDEOUT BLOCK CHARDONNAY 1996, ARGYLE WINERY Oregon	*Rich aromas of melons and oak carry over onto the palate of cool pineapples and vanilla.*	£13.00	DIR HAR ABY	Ⓑ

WASHINGTON STATE • RED

COLUMBIA CREST VALLEY ESTATE MERLOT 1994, COLUMBIA CREST WINERY Washington State	*Complex fruit flavours of berries and cherries with nuances of vanilla oak and herbs.*	£10.20	WCR HOU RDS LIB	Ⓢ
COLUMBIA CREST ESTATE SERVICES CABERNET SAUVIGNON 1993, COLUMBIA CREST WINERY Washington State	*Black fruit aromas with nuances of capsicum and smoke progress onto powerful flavours with integrated oak.*	£10.70	WCR LIB NYW	Ⓑ

228

WASHINGTON STATE – CANADA • NORTH AMERICA

COLUMBIA CREST **COLUMBIA VALLEY** **MERLOT 1995,** **COLUMBIA CREST WINERY** Washington State	*Ripe soft fruits with hints of caramel and cream on the nose and palate of this wine.*	£11.50	RDS LIB WRT	(B)
CHATEAU STE. MICHELLE **COLUMBIA VALLEY** **MERLOT 1995,** **CHATEAU STE. MICHELLE** Washington State	*Wild berry aromas lead onto sweet, jammy black fruit and new oak flavours on the well-balanced palate.*	£16.10	CPW LIB CWI	(S)
CHATEAU STE. MICHELLE **COLD CREEK CABERNET** **SAUVIGNON 1995,** **CHATEAU STE MICHELLE** Washington State	*Warm nose of oaky baked fruit. Confected palate of juicy blackcurrants and spicy vanilla that lingers.*	£16.30	CWI LIB	(S)

WASHINGTON STATE • WHITE

CHATEAU STE. MICHELLE **COLUMBIA VALLEY** **CHARDONNAY 1996,** **CHATEAU STE. MICHELLE** Washington State	*Lemon butter and toasty oak on nose and palate. Good clean finish with persistent length.*	£7.00	LIB THS WRC BUP	(B)
CHATEAU STE. MICHELLE **COLD CREEK** **CHARDONNAY 1995,** **CHATEAU STE. MICHELLE** Washington State	*Lots of new vanilla oak combined with rich ripe tropical fruit and good persistent length.*	£18.50	LIB	(B)

CANADA • RED

PELEE ISLAND CABERNET **FRANC 1995,** **WALTER SCHMORANZ** Ontario	*Green, vegetal nose with a slight marzipan edge. Has an angular palate; fruity with good acidity.*	£6.00	QWW ALL	(B)

MISSION HILL BARREL SELECT PINOT NOIR GRAND RESERVE 1996, MISSION HILL WINERY British Colombia	*Cherry red with fresh raspberry aromas. Mouth filling raspberries on the palate with complexity and balance.*	£9.80	WCR GDS DBY	(B)
FOUNDERS' SHOW RESERVE PINOT NOIR 1995, INNISKILLIN OKANAGAN British Colombia	*Smoky aromas with developed fruit on the nose, palate has beetroot characters, balance and length.*	£15.00	VLW	(B)

CANADA • WHITE

MISSION HILL BARREL SELECT PINOT GRIS GRAND RESERVE 1996, MISSION HILL WINERY British Colombia	*Well-pronounced nose with hints of spicy oak. A complex palate of mango, pineapple, lychee and tropical fruits.*	£8.00	NEI	(G)
MISSION HILL PINOT BLANC GRAND RESERVE 1994, MISSION HILL WINERY British Colombia	*Hints of buttery oak on the nose. Citrus fruit complimented by a creamy, long finish.*	£8.20	TPE EOO	(B)
INNISKILLIN PINOT BLANC 1996, INNISKILLIN OKANAGAN British Colombia	*This wine is rich with lots of toffee and butterscotch and a ripe weighty palate.*	£8.50	WCR DIR HOH VLW	(B)
INNISKILLIN CHARDONNAY RESERVE 1995, INNISKILLIN OKANAGAN Niagara	*Creamy oak and delicate fruit aromas. Light style Chardonnay with subtle fruit and integrated oak.*	£9.30	DIR HOH VLW	(B)
CHARDONNAY KLOSE VINEYARD 1995, INNISKILLIN OKANAGAN Ontario	*Honeyed, subtle fruit aromas with delicate fruit and oak on the palate. Balanced acidity.*	£10.80	DIR HOH VLW	(B)

CANADA • FORTIFIED

SOUTHBROOK FARMS FRAMBOISE NV, SOUTHBROOK FARMS Ontario	*Stewed sweet raspberries in a rich coulis of mint and strong red berry fruit gum flavours.*	**£8.00** **(37.5cl)**	WTS ADN CRS	(S)
SOUTHBROOK FARMS CASSIS NV, SOUTHBROOK FARMS Ontario	*Fantastic! Strong black fruit flavours on a sweet alcoholic palate. Try pouring it over ice cream.*	**£8.20** **(37.5cl)**	ADN DIR CRS WTS MWW	(B)

PORTUGAL

P ortugal continues to produce lighter styles of red wine to meet the demands of the modern wine consumer. As evidence one has only to look at the number of Port producers now making good quality table wines such as Quinto do Crasto, a Gold medal winner this year to add to its Silver medal and Red Wine of the Year award last year. This is not to say that winemakers are forgetting their more traditional wines. Some super Ports impressed our judges, as did the Madeira and Garafeira entries.

PORTUGAL • RED

FALUA 1997, SOCIEDADE DE VINHOS LTDA Ribatejo	*Simple perhaps, but with juicy fruit aromas and a forward cherry palate, little tannin and good acidity.*	£3.00	KWI	B
J P TINTO BARREL SELECTION 1992, J P VINHOS Alentejo	*Spicy gamey elements on its ripe vanillan nose lead to rich oaky notes on an easy going palate.*	£3.60	TOS	B
CO-OP DÃO 1996, V.I.S.O Dão	*Simply but well put together with pleasing brambly fruit, light acids and some evident tannins.*	£3.70	CWS	B
TERRA BOA 1997, ALIANCA Tras-Os-Montes	*Vanilla and plum tones mingle on the nose. Palate exudes a complex mix of ripe fruit flavours.*	£3.80	NEI ODD VWE DBY THS WRC BUP	S
ESPIGA 1997, QUINTA DA BOAVISTA Estremadura	*Quality wine with cedar on the full nose with drying stalky fruit and an excellent finish.*	£4.50	BUP THS WRC	S

MONTE VELHO 1997, HERDADE DO ESPORAO Alentejo	*Spicy, cherry and oak nose develops in the mouth with lush, dark cherry flavours and a dusting of pepper.*	£4.80	THS	Ⓑ
QUINTA DAS SETENCOSTAS 1996, QUINTA DA BOAVISTA Alenquer	*Minty, blackfruit aromas rise from this succulent, wine gum flavoured palate with some depth.*	£4.90	QWW UNS ODD BTH PFT	Ⓑ
TUELLA DOURO TINTO 1996, COCKBURN SMITHIES Douro	*Cedar and dark cassis aromas lead to a palate of earthy gamey fruit and woody tannins.*	£4.90	COK NEI CNL LOH WNS BOO AMW	Ⓑ
FIUZA CABERNET SAUVIGNON 1996, BRIGHT BROTHERS Douro	*Forward cedar nose with drying berry fruit on a smoky palate with woody tannins and some acidity.*	£5.00	DBY THS SMF FUL WRC BUP	Ⓢ
MONSARAZ 1997, ADEGA COOPERATIVE DE REGUENGOS DE MONSARAZ Redondo	*Excellent red with soft primary fruits all wrapped in a lush combination of brambley acidity and tannin.*	£5.00	WHS	Ⓑ
QUINTA DE LAGOALVA 1994, QUINTA DE LAGOALVA Alpiarca	*Slightly tarry nose, rich burnt cherry fruit, slightly cooked, but with flavours of black fruits and damsons.*	£5.20	WCR QWW ODD	Ⓑ
PERIQUITA TERRAS DO SADO 1995, JOSE MARIA DA FONSECA Vinho Regional de Alantejo	*Plums and cassis on the nose with juicy fruit, some acidity and fleshy tannins on the palate.*	£5.30	G&M DBY TOS NYW	Ⓑ
CHAMINE TINTO 1997, HANS JORGENSEN Alentejo	*A restrained nose in contrast to the full-bodied, blackfruit palate and well-balanced tannins.*	£5.40	HWL SVT	Ⓑ

FEIST TINTO 1995, H & C.J.FEIST Douro	*Strong notes of black fruit with dry tannins and acidity that makes for a rewarding result.*	£5.50	D&F	**B**
VINHA DO MONTE 1996, SOGRAPE Alentejo	*A powerful, brambley, plummy nose follows onto a smoky, tarry palate with a pleasant rustic structure.*	£5.50	NAD SGL L&W VLW GNW	**B**
BAIRRADA GARRAFEIRA 1995, ALIANÇA Bairrada	*Rich mellow fruit, The palate shows blackberry and cherry fruit with layered tannins and pleasing acidity.*	£6.00	DIR ODD	**B**
DÃO RESERVA 1989, CAVES VELHAS Dão	*This has soft ripe berry fruits on both the nose and palate with its soft tannins and acidity.*	£6.00	WHS	**B**
FALCOARIA 1995, RAMOS Almeirim	*A zippy, raspberry nose. Balanced tannins mingle with raspberry ripple and hickory wood in the mouth.*	£6.00	WSP WTS	**B**
TINTO DA ANFORA 1992, JOSE MARIA DA FONSECA Alentejo	*Tasters liked the lovely smooth fruit with slight wood notes, dusty soft tannins and pleasing acidity.*	£6.00	MWW DBY NYW	**B**
QUINTA DE PANCAS CABERNET SAUVIGNON 1996, P.V.Q. LTDA Estremadura	*Ripe loganberry fruit with lashings of fresh creamy oak on the nose and palate of this well-integrated wine.*	£6.10	PFT CWS SMF WCR THS WRC BUP	**S**
REGUENGOS 1997, ADEGA COOPERATIVE DE REGUENGOS DE MONSARAZ Redondo	*A ripe juicy wine with cassis and spice on a palate of juicy tannins and crunchy acidity.*	£6.20	WSP MGN WHS	**B**

RED • PORTUGAL

QUINTA DOS ROQUES ALFROCHEIRO PRETO 1996, QUINTA DOS ROQUES ão	Tobacco and woody notes on the nose are followed by dry black fruit and tannins on a generous palate.	£6.30	MFS WSO GEL P&R	(B)
QUINTA DE ABRIGADA NTO 1996, QUINTA DE ABRIGADA enquer	Peppery, fruit aromas precede a body rich in firm tannins but with solid, ripe-fruit flavours.	£6.40	SEL MIS POR DBY WNS DXC BOO HOU	(B)
QUINTA DE LA ROSA ED 1996, M BERQUIST ouro	Strong elements of tarry fruit aromas on a chewy rich palate of blackberries and lifted tannins.	£6.40	Widely Available	(B)
ORTES DE CIMA 1996, ANS JORGENSEN lentejo	An interesting, gamey nose signals a fresh and fruity red wine with a touch of green tannins.	£6.50	HWL SVT CPW	(B)
QUINTA DA MAIAS 996, SOCIEDADE GRICOLA FALDAS DA ERRA ão	Spice and banana-skin nose, followed by a dry, savoury palate with a subtle, sweet woody edge.	£6.50	IWS POR DBY BBR P&R BOO	(B)
OMEIRA GARAFEIRA 993, CAVES VELHAS almela	Lovely subtle wine, quite mature with mellow damson fruits, softening tannins and pleasant acidity.	£6.50	WHS	(B)
ORTES DE CIMA 1997, ANS JORGENSEN lentejo	Bursting with fruity, ripe aromas. Smooth rich palate and a hint of a minerally edge from the balanced tannins.	£6.60	HWL SVT CPW NYW	(S)
UQUE DE VISEU 1995, OGRAPE ão	Smoky, preserved fruits waft from a full-on blueberry, tarry cigar-box palate with a smooth finish.	£6.60	CWS L&W PFT NAD SAF CEN	(B)

235

LUIS PATO TINTO 1996, **LUIS PATO** Bairrada	*Pinewood and vegetal aromas emanate from this elegantly structured redcurrant and cranberry dominated palate.*	£6.60	L&W
QUINTA DO CRASTO DOURO RED 1997, **QUINTA DO CRASTO** Douro	*Fantastic, still a baby, has intense black fruit, chunky tannins and acidity. This will keep for some time.*	£6.90	Widely Available
VINHA GRANDE 1995, **A.A.FERREIRA** Douro	*Strong fruit aromas lead onto a dense mulberry palate with blackcurrant and cassis notes.*	£7.00	NAD SGL VLW
ARAGONES 1997, **RAMOS PINTO** Alentejo	*A delicate berryfruit nose leads to a rustic palate with a staggering array of succulent flavours.*	£7.00	NOW
ESPORAO CABERNET SAUVIGNON 1994, **ESPORAO** Alentejo	*Creamy aromas of sweet ripe fruit lead onto a mellow well balanced palate of mature berries and brambles.*	£7.00	THS
QUINTA DE CAMARATE TINTO 1992, **JOSÉ MARIA DA FONSECA** Terras do Sado	*An intriguing cedar and prune nose almost overwhelms an old-style, oaky palate with delicate fruit flavours.*	£7.20	G&M COK NEI CPW DBY
SOGRAPE DOURO RESERVA 1995, SOGRAPE Douro	*Ripe cassis and cedar fruit with woody notes and intense flavours of cherries and vanillan oak.*	£7.80	DBY NAD SAF CEN BOO
VILA SANTA 1997, **RAMOS** Alentejo	*Gentle herbaceous nose and a rich mixture of flavours backed up by fresh tannins.*	£8.00	JNW

QUINTA DE LA ROSA RESERVE 1995, IM BERGQUIST Douro	*Dark fruits on the nose, with ripe berry wood flavours on a rich, opulent raisin palate.*	£8.10	SEL M&V DBY EBA BOO VLW	(S)
QUINTA DO FOJO RED VINHAS VELHAS 1996, MARGARIDA SERODIO BORGES Douro	*Impressive red with quality primary fruit on the nose. A palate of broody fruit with dark woody elements.*	£8.30	DBY HWL	(B)
QUINTA DOS ROQUES 1996, QUINTA DOS ROQUES Dão	*This has lovely woody aromas leading onto a rich palate of oaked fruit and ripe, nutty tannins and acidity.*	£8.50	SEL WSO GEL P&R BOO	(B)
QUINTA VALE DONA MARIA 1996, QUINTA DO CRASTO Douro	*Rich toasty vanilla oak, cherry fruit with damsons and excellent balanced tannin and acidity.*	£9.50	ODF ENO	(S)
QUINTA DOS ROQUES TOURIGA NACIONAL 1996, QUINTA DOS ROQUES Dão	*A cedary, smoky, multi-faceted nose. Palate of classy, blackcurrant and tobacco tones with a rich, smooth finish.*	£10.00	WSO GEL P&R	(S)
TRINCADEIRA 1997, RAMOS Alentejo	*A lightly perfumed, spicy aroma introduces the ripe, baked-fruit flavours well-balanced by firm tannins.*	£12.70	JNW ADN HOT ODF CWS NYW	(B)
QUINTA DA GAIVOSA 1995, DOMINGOS ALVES E SOUSA Douro	*Dark brooding fruit and dry tannins but with a delicious underlying fruit and chewy richness.*	£13.70	SEL WCS JBR HWB EPO	(B)
TRA MANCA 1994, FUNDACAO EUGENIO DE ALMEIDA Evora	*Intense ruby in colour. A rich woody nose and a palate of berry fruit. Quite firm tannins and good acidity.*	£20.00	L&W ARM WFL	(B)

PORTUGAL • WHITE

PORTA DA RAVESSA 1997, ADEGA COOPERATIVE DE REDONDO Redondo	*Pineapple on the nose followed by plentiful fruit cleaned up with moderate acid and length.*	£3.70	BTH WHS
BRIGHT BROS ATLANTIC VINES WHITE 1997, JP VINHOS Ribateio	*Hints of tropical fruit mingled with lemon and ripe melon. Lovely fresh and well-balanced.*	£4.00	TOS FUL
QUINTO DE AZEVEDO 1997, SOGRAPE Vinho Verde	*Delicate floral nose with lemon fruit on the palate and acidity that stands to the fore.*	£5.00	SEL SGL NAD VLW
QUINTA DE SIDRO CHARDONNAY 1997, REAL COMPANHIA VELHA Tras os Montes	*A clean, lemony delicate nose is reflected on the palate of tropical fruit flavours of galia melon and sun-ripened mango.*	£5.50	PLB
LUIS PATO BRANCO VINHAS VELHAS 1997, LUIS PATO Bairrada	*Clean lemon nose with creamy fruit on the palate, balanced with oak overtones and fine acid.*	£5.80	WFD
CATARINA CHARDONNAY 1996, J. P. VINHOS Ribatejo	*Yellow with green tinges. Rich toasty oak and ripe pineapple and mango on the nose.*	£5.90	CPW ASD CWS
QUINTA DE PEDRALVITES 1997, SOGRAPE Bairrada	*Floral and citrus flavours resulting in a medium bodied wine with moderate length and acidity.*	£6.00	SEL EBA SGL

PORTUGAL • MADEIRA

BLANDY'S DUKE OF CLARENCE FULL RICH MADEIRA, BLANDY'S MADEIRA Madeira	*A pleasant wine with toffee and fig characters on a rich sweet nose and palate.*	£9.20	Widely Available	**B**
BLANDY'S DUKE OF SUSSEX SPECIAL DRY SERCIAL, BLANDY'S MADEIRA Madeira	*Fresh with warm toasty character. Apricot and marmalade favours with a touch of gentle acidity.*	£9.40	Widely Available	**G**
BLANDY'S FIVE YEAR OLD MALMSEY NV, BLANDY'S MADEIRA Madeira	*Sweet nutty flavours on the nose. The palate has lingering flavours of honey and molasses.*	£11.70	Widely Available	**S**
BLANDY'S FIVE year Old BUAL, BLANDY'S MADEIRA Madeira	*Medium sweet with a slight citrus twist to its sweet palate with a touch of acidity.*	£11.70	Widely Available	**B**
BLANDY'S FIVE YEAR OLD VERDELHO, BLANDY'S MADEIRA Madeira	*Medium-bodied with its pale colour and a taste of fruity lifted acidity and sweetness.*	£11.70	BEN JNW G&M JEF ODD VIL CST	**B**
COSSART GORDON FIVE YEAR OLD SERCIAL, COSSART GORDON Madeira	*Drier style with pleasing citrus acidity running through the sweet fruit flavours which predominate.*	£13.30	Widely Available	**B**
COSSART GORDON FIVE YEAR OLD MALMSEY, COSSART GORDON Madeira	*Rich, quite opulent but not over sweet still retaining flavours of burnt sugared apples.*	£13.80	Widely Available	**B**

HENRIQUES & HENRIQUES 10 YEAR OLD BUAL MADEIRA, HENRIQUES & HENRIQUES Madeira	*Lovely wine with toffee, caramel and fig notes. Some gentle underlying acidity and a really balanced palate.*	£16.40	Widely Available	G
COSSART GORDON TEN YEAR OLD BUAL, COSSART GORDON Madeira	*Darker colour with generous fruit on a medium sweet palate of fig and apricots.*	£16.40	Widely Available	B
BLANDY'S 10 YEAR OLD MALMSEY, BLANDY'S MADEIRA Madeira	*Golden brown in colour, lush sweet fruit, with toffee and nut flavours. Some oak hints.*	£16.50	Widely Available	S
BLANDY'S FIFTEEN YEAR OLD MALMSEY, BLANDY'S MADEIRA Madeira	*Ripe, full-bodied. Intensely sweet with rich, smoky fruit on a layered palate of honeyed caramel.*	£21.40	JNW JEF DBY BDR	G

PORTUGAL • PORT

QUINTA DO SAGRADO VINTAGE CHARACTER PORT, A.A. CÁLEM & FILHO Douro	*Slightly lighter but has impressive open fruit on its palate of spiced plum and cinnamon.*	£6.00	LAU	B
CO-OP VINTAGE CHARACTER PORT, SMITH WOODHOUSE Douro	*Excellent opulent fruit aromas with pleasant full bodied fruit on the palate. Slightly nutty with prune characters.*	£6.50	CWS	B
CÁLEM RUBY PORT, A A CÁLEM & FILHO Douro	*Lovely ripe fruit on the nose with plums on the palate and a tobacco finish.*	£6.50	UNS WIM JEH	B

CO-OP NO.1 VINTAGE CHARACTER PORT, SMITH WOODHOUSE Douro	*Well made, spicy, figgy fruit with a quite generous mellow palate and enticing finish.*	**£6.80**	CRS	**B**
NOVAL OLD CORONATION RUBY PORT, QUINTA DO NOVAL Douro	*Berry fruit on the nose with ripe cherry richness and a lovely lingering clove finish.*	**£7.10**	ETV FUL L&W VIL GNW	**B**
MALT HOUSE VINTNERS REGIMENTAL VINTAGE CHARACTER PORT, SILVA & COSENS Douro	*Dark ruby in colour. The nose is of rich stewed fruits, plums and spices.*	**£7.20**	MHV	**B**
TAYLOR FIRST ESTATE RESERVE PORT, TAYLOR, FLADGATE & YEATMAN Douro	*This Port is reminiscent of Christmas with fruit cake flavours, nutty complexity and raisin fruit.*	**£7.20**	Widely Available	**B**
CO-OP LATE BOTTLED VINTAGE PORT 1992, SMITH WOODHOUSE Douro	*Apricot and fruit peel aromas with an intense fruit driven palate. Slightly sweet with pleasing nuances.*	**£7.30**	CWS	**B**
TESCO LATE BOTTLED VINTAGE PORT 1992, SMITH & WOODHOUSE Douro	*Soft berry fruit on the nose with a fleshy ripe fruit palate and moderate balanced acidity.*	**£7.50**	TOS	**B**
ROZÉS VINTAGE PORT 1995, ROZÉS Douro	*Jammy fruit characters with chocolate and spice all wrapped up in a simple enjoyable fruit laden palate.*	**£8.00**	ROZ	**B**
WAITROSE LATE BOTTLED VINTAGE PORT 1991, SMITH WOODHOUSE Douro	*Intense raisin aromas with rich, ripe fruit on the palate of balanced spirit and good length.*	**£8.00**	WTS	**B**

SMITH WOODHOUSE LODGE RESERVE PORT, SMITH WOODHOUSE Douro	*A Port blend with delicate fruit but some power in its rich, full-bodied damson palate.*	£8.30	JEF DBY WRI C&B HOU (S)
WARRE'S WARRIOR RESERVE PORT, WARRE & Ca Douro	*Strawberry, cherry and a touch of mint on the nose with a nutty complex palate.*	£8.40	Widely Available (B)
CHURCHILL'S WHITE PORT, CHURCHILL GRAHAM Douro	*Ripe fruit mingled with lots of nutty characters on the palate and nose. Good length.*	£8.80	HWL SVT IRV WTS VIL (B)
CÁLEM LATE BOTTLED VINTAGE PORT 1993, A A CÁLEM & FILHO Douro	*Intense colour with ripe fruit characters on the nose. The palate is full of elegant dried fruits.*	£9.00	MTL UNS WIM JEH (S)
SAFEWAY'S 10 YEAR OLD TAWNY PORT, SMITH WOODHOUSE Douro	*Sweet, cherry vanilla and nuts on the nose with harmonious balance between fruit and fibrous tannins.*	£9.00	SAF (B)
FONSECA BIN NO 27 PORT, FONSECA GUIMARAENS Douro	*A bit lean but with pleasing apricot and fig character on a balanced palate.*	£9.10	Widely Available (B)
NOVAL LB HOUSE RESERVE PORT, QUINTA DO NOVAL Douro	*Enticing fruit on the nose. Plentiful fruit palate good structure with moderate acidity*	£9.20	SHJ TPE FUL JFR JOB VIL (B)
FERREIRA LATE BOTTLED VINTAGE PORT 1990, A.A. FERREIRA Douro	*Tasters were attracted to the warm apricot and orange skin fruit of this delicate wine.*	£9.30	WES (S)

Wine	Tasting Note	Price	Availability	
NOVAL TRADITIONAL LATE BOTTLED VINTAGE PORT 1991, QUINTA DO NOVAL Douro	*Intense raisins on the nose with lovely palate weight and slightly oily texture providing extra flavour.*	£9.60	MTL CVR UNS HVN MAR VIL NYW	B
QUINTA DA URTIGA VINTAGE CHARACTER PORT, ADRIANO RAMOS-PINTO Douro	*Ripe fruit is prevalent on the nose. The palate has masses of fruit with hints of liquorice.*	£10.30	Widely Available	S
QUINTA DO CRASTO LATE BOTTLED VINTAGE PORT 1994, QUINTA DO CRASTO Douro	*This Port doesn't give a lot away on the nose but the palate is full of rich fruit and chocolate.*	£10.60	ADN ODD ENO CWI	S
TESCO 10 YEAR OLD TAWNY PORT, SMITH & WOODHOUSE Douro	*Intense raisin characters on the nose and palate with overlying alcohol and fairly high acidity.*	£10.60	TOS	B
GRAHAM'S LATE BOTTLED VINTAGE PORT 1992, W & J GRAHAM & CO Douro	*Meaty characters on the nose with a ripe round fruit palate and lingering long finish.*	£10.70	Widely Available	B
TAYLOR'S LATE BOTTLED VINTAGE PORT 1992, TAYLOR, FLADGATE & YEATMAN Douro	*Intense fruit on the nose. The palate is full of ripe and dried fruit characters with nutty overtones.*	£10.80	Widely Available	S
QUINTA DE LA ROSA LATE BOTTLED VINTAGE PORT 1991, TIM BERGQUIST Douro	*Powerful, intense and fruit packed this Port has concentrated characters with a fairly sweet finish.*	£11.00	SEL FCA M&V TPE THC FWL BOO NYW	B
CHURCHILL'S TRADITIONAL LATE BOTTLED VINTAGE PORT 1992, CHURCHILL GRAHAM Douro	*This wine has a lovely ripe berry nose with orange spiced middle palate and ripe sweet tannins.*	£11.20	Widely Available	S

GRAHAM'S SIX GRAPES VINTAGE CHARACTER PORT, W & J GRAHAM & CO Douro	*Lovely well-made wine with a toasty nose of black fruits, warmth of flavour with chocolate almond notes.*	£11.60	Widely Available	**G**
BERRY'S OWN SELECTION WELLINGTON PORT, QUINTA DO NOVAL Douro	*Nutty aromas with soft, fairly sweet dark fruit characters housed in a simple balanced wine.*	£12.00	BBR	**B**
QUINTA DE LA ROSA VINTAGE PORT 1994, TIM BERGQUIST Douro	*Deep purple in colour representative of a young port with fresh fruit characters on the splendid palate.*	£12.50	Widely Available	**S**
DOW'S CRUSTED (BOTTLED 1991) PORT, SILVA & COSENS Douro	*Purple with red tinges. This Port has crusted complex characters on the nose with rich ripe mature fruit on the palate.*	£12.70	VWE DBY WTS VIL CST	**S**
NOVAL 10 YEAR OLD TAWNY PORT, QUINTA DO NOVAL Douro	*Fruit cake characters hints of coffee and hazlenut on the nose. The palate has concentrated flavours.*	£12.90	HVW TPE F&M DEN QRW WTS	**S**
WARRE'S SIR WILLIAM 10 YEAR OLD TAWNY PORT, WARRE & CA Douro	*Nut and figs on the nose with a slightly spirited palate and good creamy texture.*	£13.00	JEF HHC CES AVB	**B**
CHURCHILL'S 10 YEAR OLD TAWNY PORT, CHURCHILL GRAHAM Douro	*Dried fruit with spice and nut characters on the nose and full, ripe fruit palate.*	£13.40	HWL SVT WSP QWW DBY TAN VIL	**B**
WARRE'S BOTTLE MATURED LATE BOTTLED VINTAGE PORT 1986, WARRE & CA Douro	*Quite full bodied and austere for this style of Port. Drying fruit and strong but pleasing tannins.*	£14.50	JEF SAF TOS WTS VIL AMW	**B**

GRAHAM'S 10 YEAR OLD TAWNY PORT, W & J GRAHAM & CO Douro	*Dried apricots, raisined fruit and nuts. The palate is balanced with a fabulous long finish.*	£14.90	Widely Available	(B)
WARRE'S TRADITIONAL LATE BOTTLED VINTAGE PORT 1984, WARRE & CA Douro	*Smoky and lean on the nose. The palate consists of fairly rich moderately concentrated spiced plums.*	£15.00	Widely Available	(B)
CÁLEM QUINTA DA FOZ VINTAGE PORT 1987, A A CÁLEM & FILHO Douro	*Has attractive fruit on a spicy, plum nose. Intense flavours of cooked damsons and raisins.*	£15.00	UNS WIM JEH	(B)
CÁLEM QUINTA DA FOZ VINTAGE PORT 1992, A A CÁLEM & FILHO Douro	*Dark in colour this has attractive black fruit and a slighlty cooked feel to its strong palate.*	£15.00	UNS WIM JEH	(B)
DOW'S 10 YEAR OLD TAWNY PORT, SILVA & COSENS Douro	*Chocolate and raisin on the nose and palate. Delicate structure with a long nutty finish.*	£15.10	Widely Available	(S)
SMITH WOODHOUSE TRADITIONAL LATE BOTTLED VINTAGE PORT 1984, SMITH WOODHOUSE Douro	*Fantastic warm fig and prune character on this attractive wine with lasting bouquet.*	£15.20	COK JEF SMF C&B GAR	(S)
NOVAL 20 YEAR OLD TAWNY PORT, QUINTA DO NOVAL Douro	*Rich raisin and honeyed aromas with a slightly spicy and nutty palate. Smooth and long.*	£15.20	TPE F&M VIL	(B)
TAYLOR'S 10 YEAR OLD TAWNY PORT, TAYLOR, FLADGATE & YEATMAN Douro	*One taster wrote of orange peel and prune. A delicate wine with some finesse.*	£15.80	Widely Available	(B)

PORTUGAL • RED

OSBORNE VINTAGE PORT 1995, OSBORNE Douro	*Packed with tarry spice and big inky dark fruit flavours. There is plenty of brooding tannin waiting for maturity.*	£16.00	HBJ ODD	G
QUINTA DE TERRA FEITA VINTAGE PORT 1986, TAYLOR, FLADGATE & YEATMAN Douro	*This Port presents itself well in the glass with a lovely rich colour and prune characters on the spicy palate.*	£16.60	BEN MGN VWE MWW JSM	S
SMITH WOODHOUSE QUINTA DA MADALENA VINTAGE PORT 1988, SMITH WOODHOUSE & CO Douro	*Baked fruit characters on the nose followed by an intense dried fruit palate with a touch of spice.*	£17.50	JEF	S
FONSECA GUIMARAENS LATE BOTTLED VINTAGE PORT 1983, FONSECA GUIMARAENS Douro	*Mature with rich developed fruit, this has full flavours of damson, woody hints and opulence.*	£17.60	DIR VLW WTS VIL	B
FERREIRA VINTAGE PORT 1987, A.A. FERREIRA Douro	*Bronze in colour with chocolate and fig characters on the nose and palate.*	£18.70	HOU HVW AMW	S
QUINTA DE LA ROSA VINTAGE PORT 1996, TIM BERGQUIST Douro	*Young and slightly unsettled with lovely fruit. This Port has promise for those who wait.*	£18.80	JNW M&V BOO	B
QUINTA DE VARGELLAS VINTAGE PORT 1986, TAYLOR, FLADGATE & YEATMAN Douro	*Raisin tobacco and candied peel provide plenty of flavour to mull over. Finishes rather well.*	£19.60	Widely Available	S
FERREIRA VINTAGE PORT 1995, A.A. FERREIRA Douro	*Class act, despite its youth this is already showing promise in its thick plum palate.*	£19.70	HVW	B

FONSECA GUIMARAENS VINTAGE PORT 1984, **FONSECA GUIMARAENS** Douro	*Intense fruit with slight volatility on the nose. Palate has good weighty plum fruit and length.*	£19.80	Widely Available	B
FORTNUM & MASON SILVAL VINTAGE PORT 1995, QUINTA DO NOVAL Douro	*Top blend for putting in your cellar. Intense black dark berry fruit and chewy tannins.*	£20.00	F&M	S
DOW'S QUINTA DO BOMFIM VINTAGE PORT 1984, SILVA & COSENS Douro	*This Port is more mature in style with delicate fruit characters on the nose. Elegant in the mouth too.*	£20.00	Widely Available	S
QUINTA DO RORIZ VINTAGE PORT 1995, QUINTA DO NOVAL Douro	*Ripe dark berries on the nose and palate with lovely depth and a long smooth finish.*	£20.00	PRG	B
WARRE'S QUINTA DO CAVADINHA VINTAGE PORT 1984, WARRE & CA Douro	*A more developed Port with delicate fruit characters on the nose. The palate is dark and brooding with sweet fruit.*	£20.10	Widely Available	S
DOW'S QUINTA DO BOMFIM VINTAGE PORT 1986, SILVA & COSENS Douro	*Slightly spirity nose with dried fruit and hints of chocolate. The palate has full-bodied plum and spice.*	£20.30	NRW G&M JEF ODD TOS JSM	S
GRAHAM'S QUINTA DO MALVEDOS VINTAGE PORT 1986, W & J GRAHAM & CO Douro	*This Port has a fantastically inviting nose with chocolate, dried fruit and spice characters.*	£20.50	Widely Available	S

Pinpoint who sells the wine you wish to buy by turning to the stockist codes. If you know the name of the wine you want to buy, use the alphabetical index. If the price is your motivation, refer to the invaluable price guide index; red and white wines under £5, sparkling wines under £12 and Champagne under £16. Happy hunting!

QUINTA DO CRASTO VINTAGE PORT 1995, QUINTA DO CRASTO Douro	*Deep bricky colour. Huge fruit mingled with chocolate and spice on the nose. The palate is intense and rich.*	£20.50	ADN ODD ENO	S
WARRE'S QUINTA DA CAVADINHA VINTAGE PORT 1986, WARRE'S & CA Douro	*Christmas cake characters on the nose followed by a rich creamy texture with lots of ripe spiced plums.*	£20.60	Widely Available	S
FONSECA GUIMARAENS VINTAGE PORT 1982, FONSECA GUIMARAENS Douro	*This has wonderful mature almost chocolate flavours on a base of dark blackcurrant and prune.*	£20.60	Widely Available	B
WARRE'S QUINTA DA CAVADINHA VINTAGE PORT 1987, WARRE & CA Douro	*Dark ruby colour with a slightly shy nose. The palate contains lovely rich dark berry fruit.*	£21.60	CPW ODD SAF BUP VIL AMW	S
SMITH WOODHOUSE VINTAGE PORT 1983, SMITH WOODHOUSE Douro	*A lovely aged Port showing some maturity, it has a dried fruit and slightly vegetal character.*	£22.70	Widely Available	S
DOW'S 20 YEAR OLD TAWNY PORT, SILVA & COSENS Douro	*Dark caramel in colour. The nose has caramalised toffee characters mingled with mint and sweet fruit.*	£22.80	G&M JEF CWS VWE VIL	S
SANDEMAN'S 20 YEAR OLD TAWNY PORT, SANDEMAN Douro	*A delight with its cooked apricot nose, elegant refined palate of woody scent and plum spice.*	£23.10	LEA MTL ODD SEA CST	G
GRAHAM'S 20 YEAR OLD TAWNY PORT, W & J GRAHAM & CO Douro	*Coffee and walnuts on the nose with opulent glazed fruit palate.*	£23.90	JNW JEF DBY TOS HAR HVN VIL	B

FONSECA TRADITIONAL LATE BOTTLED VINTAGE PORT 1983, FONSECA GUIMARAENS Douro	*Full, ripe fruit mingled with lovely mushroom characters and plenty of spirit on the nose.*	**£24.10**	DIR VLW VIL	**B**
CHURCHILL'S VINTAGE PORT 1996, CHURCHILL GRAHAM Douro	*Very closed but underneath there is some excellent intense primary fruit showing through the thick tannins.*	**£25.00**	HWL SVT IRV	**B**
CHURCHILL'S VINTAGE PORT 1982, CHURCHILL GRAHAM Douro	*Delicious figgy nut character with deep smooth cooked fruits on a long lasting palate.*	**£25.20**	HWL SVT WSP CVR NEI IRV VIL	**B**
RAMOS-PINTO VINTAGE PORT 1994, ADRIANO RAMOS-PINTO Douro	*Lovely colour, ripe prune fruit, quite sweet with a juicy finish and not too spirity.*	**£27.50**	QWW POR VLW	**S**
QUINTA DO BOM RETIRO 20 YEAR OLD TAWNY PORT, ADRIANO RAMOS-PINTO Douro	*Toffee and fig aromas with nuts and a savoury edge providing a warm inviting Port.*	**£29.10**	FSW SEL MMD VLW	**B**
QUINTA DO NOVAL VINTAGE PORT 1995, QUINTA DO NOVAL Douro	*Quite closed but showing promise on its densely packed youthful palate of black opaque fruit.*	**£30.00**	AVB EDC F&M	**B**
QUINTA DO VESUVIO VINTAGE PORT 1996, SOC. AGRIC. DA QUINTA DO VESUVIO Douro	*For its precocious youth this wine is packed with voluptuous firm fruit dense tannins and rich alcohol.*	**£33.00**	COK JEF NEI	**G**
TAYLOR'S 20 YEAR OLD TAWNY PORT, TAYLOR, FLADGATE & YEATMAN Douro	*Mid-brown with a orange hue the nose is delicate with herb character, the palate has apricot and toasted fruit.*	**£33.40**	Widely Available	**S**

PORTUGAL • PORT

RAMOS-PINTO 30 YEAR OLD TAWNY PORT, ADRIANO RAMOS-PINTO Douro	*Nutty savoury nose. The palate has plummy sweetness with a creamy texture.*	£38.60	SEL CVR VLW	S
NOVAL 40 YEAR OLD TAWNY PORT, QUINTA DO NOVAL Douro	*This is a sweet ripe style Port with lots of chocolate, nut and fig characters.*	£59.00	QRW F&M VIL	B

SOUTH AFRICA

South Africa continues to meet the challenges of the post-apartheid era. Large investments in modern wineries and vineyard techniques are beginning to pay off. A new breed of winemakers is now producing the fruit driven wines demanded by the modern wine buyer and the current exchange rate with the Rand against Sterling can only help South African wines find their niche in the UK market. We look forward to seeing more of these "boutique" wines on our shelves in the near future.

SOUTH AFRICA • RED

TESCO CAPE CINSAULT 1996, VINFRUCO Western Cape	*A subtle, complex and harmonious wine. One of the few New World countries to grow this grape.*	**£3.50**	TOS	(S)
KUMALA CINSAULT PINOTAGE 1997, SONOP Western Cape	*Soft, light and stylish. Hints of oak and bags of rich plum and cherry fruits.*	**£4.00**	ODD BTH MRN SAF HZW FUL	(B)
MALT HOUSE VINTNERS SOUTH AFRICAN CABERNET SAUVIGNON 1997, SONOP Western Cape	*Cedarwood and minty spice with rich cassis flavours and smooth, silky tannins on a lingering palate.*	**£4.40**	MHV	(B)
SOMERFIELD SOUTH AFRICAN PINOTAGE 1997, SONOP Western Cape	*A rich, powerful palate of soft, squashed summer fruits with good depth, development and length.*	**£4.50**	SMF	(B)
OAK VILLAGE PINOTAGE MERLOT 1996, VINFRUCO Coastal Region	*An elegant and complex style with ripe and earthy fruit. Jammy elements, youthful and delicious.*	**£4.50**	TOS	(B)

LONG MOUNTAIN CABERNET SAUVIGNON 1996, LONG MOUNTAIN WINES Western Cape	*Cassis and green raspberries dominate the palate of this sweet, juicy wine with a tart finish.*	£4.60	Widely Available	**B**
PINOTAGE IMPALA 1997, GOUE VALLEI Western Cape	*Slightly medicinal nose gives way to big black-currant and apple flavours. Complex over-tones of nuts and spice.*	£4.80	CDT	**S**
MOUNT DISA CAPE SALUT 1997, COPPOOLSE & FINLAYSON Stellenbosch	*An intense blackcurrant nose matched with juicy berry flavours on the palate, hints of oak.*	£5.00	WOI SEA	**B**
BELLINGHAM PINOTAGE 1996, BELLINGHAM WINES Paarl	*Soft jammy fruit nose with green hints lead onto a palate of stalky bramble fruit and a spiced finish.*	£5.20	HVW SMF NYW FUL WRC BUP	**S**
ALTUS CABERNET SAUVIGNON 1996, BOLAND WYNKELDER Paarl	*Light, green aromas of raspberries and currants carry over onto the palate. A smooth finish with a slight tannin grip.*	£5.20	NRW COK WCS DBY FUL BOO	**B**
GROOT CONSTANTIA PINOTAGE 1995, GROOT CONSTANTIA Constantia	*A warm spicy nose. Well-rounded palate with good tannins and delicate fruit flavours.*	£5.50	DBY BBU G&M	**B**
PINOT NOIR SIMSBERG 1997, MICHAEL BACK Paarl	*Mature ripe fruit on the nose, lovely cherries on the palate with slightly drying tannins.*	£5.60	L&W GNW	**B**

Pinpoint who sells the wine you wish to buy by turning to the stockist codes. If you know the name of the wine you want to buy, use the alphabetical index. If the price is your motivation, refer to the invaluable price guide index; red and white wines under £5, sparkling wines under £12 and Champagne under £16. Happy hunting!

KWV MERLOT 1995, KWV Western Cape	*Figgy plums and minty eucalyptus on the nose and palate. A soft clean finish.*	£5.60	G&M GDS SEL BCL WMK FUL CST	**B**
FAIRVIEW ESTATE ZINFANDEL CINSAULT 1997, CHARLES BACK Paarl	*A slightly yeasty ripe blackberry nose, a smooth jammy palate and a woody, long finish.*	£5.80	ADN ODD FUL	**B**
RIEBEEK CELLARS PINOTAGE 1997, RIEBEEK CELLARS Coastal Region	*Very oaky. This wine has good fruit, tannins and a delicately balanced finish.*	£5.80	SHJ CPW CNL DIL	**B**
KANONKOP KADETTE 1996, KANONKOP ESTATE Stellenbosch	*Heavy, savoury nose with rich, well-structured fruit. Distinctive flavours develop on the long finish.*	£6.00	RSS SAF	**S**
PINNACLE CABERNET SAUVIGNON SHIRAZ 1996, VINFRUCO Stellenbosch	*A light style with strawberries and cherries on the palate. A spicy and tart finish.*	£6.00	IWS VWE TOS FUL	**B**
MOUNT DISA CABERNET SAUVIGNON 1996, COPPOOLSE & FINLAYSON Stellenbosch	*Aromas of fresh black-currants with a minty highlight carry over onto a smoothly balanced palate of creamy cassis.*	£6.00	WOI SEA	**B**
MOUNT DISA PINOTAGE 1996, COPPOOLSE & FINLAYSON Stellenbosch	*Rich dark chocolate aromas with a fairly big meaty palate and a dusty, lingering finish.*	£6.00	WOI SEA	**B**
WINELANDS SHIRAZ CABERNET SAUVIGNON 1996, KYM MILNE Western Cape	*Ripe aromas of blackcurrants, mint and vanilla carry over onto a raspberry palate with a crisp finish.*	£6.40	IWS WRC BUP	**B**

SOUTH AFRICA • RED

KUMALA CABERNET SAUVIGNON RESERVE 1997, STELLENBOSCH FARMERS Stellenbosch	*Complex medicinal, blackcurrant nose leads to a palate full of ripe berry fruit and creamy vanilla oak.*	£6.70	CRS ODD SMF TOS WTS FUL	S
CATHEDRAL CELLAR TRIPTICH 1995, KWV Coastal Region	*Concentrated flavours of cassis and tart currants. Hints of mint and pencil shavings carry over onto the attractive palate.*	£6.70	G&M BNK WIL SEC JEH DBY	B
FAIRVIEW ESTATE PINOTAGE 1997, CHARLES BACK Paarl	*A wonderfully aromatic nose. Rich and thick fruit, tar and raspberries finishing with firm tannins.*	£6.80	ADN BNK COK GRT CWS JSM	B
FAIRVIEW ESTATE CABERNET FRANC MERLOT 1995, CHARLES BACK Paarl	*Herbaceous aromas with hints of mint and grass. A clean palate with nuances of underripe currants. Good length.*	£7.00	WTS	B
FAIRVIEW ESTATE SHIRAZ RESERVE 1996, CHARLES BACK Paarl	*A lovely wine. Although light in body, it has minty, spicy and attractively sweet mulberry fruit.*	£7.00	GRT WTS FUL	B
STELLENZICHT SHIRAZ GRENACHE 1996, STELLENZICHT VINEYARD Stellenbosch	*A classic Rhone blend from South Africa. This example has quite high acidity.*	£7.50	HOH	B
LEEF OP HOOP CABERNET SAUVIGNON 1996, ETIENNE LE RICHE Stellenbosch	*Rich aromas of cough medicine, menthol, cedarwood and oak. Ripe forest fruits fill the mouth.*	£7.60	Widely Available	S
CLOS MALVERNE PINOTAGE RESERVE 1996, CLOS MALVERNE Stellenbosch	*A spicy, minty, oaky nose. Big fruit and powerful alcohol follows to a long finish.*	£7.70	CNL ODD VWE WTS FUL GNW	B

Wine	Tasting Notes	Price	Stockists	
SAXENBURG CABERNET SAUVIGNON 1996, SAXENBURG Stellenbosch	*Concentrated green pepper and currant aromas with cedar notes are reflected on the rich palate.*	£7.70	G&M BBR IRV	(B)
CATHEDRAL CELLAR CABERNET SAUVIGNON 1995, KWV Coastal Region	*Rich aromas and flavours of blackcurrant with nuances of minty grass, cigar box and new oak.*	£7.80	G&M DBY FUL	(S)
MEERENDAL PINOTAGE 1995, MEEREDAL ESTATE Stellenbosch	*Soft and ripe fruit on the nose with a good clean palate and berry flavours.*	£7.90	CVR MMD MWW DBY	(B)
GROOT CONSTANTIA CABERNET SAUVIGNON 1995, GROOT CONSTANTIA Constantia	*Creamy blackcurrants with nuances of green apples, tobacco and spicy oak on this attractive wine.*	£7.90	G&M DBY BBU CAP	(B)
WOODLANDS CABERNET SAUVIGNON 1997, SAVANA WINES Stellenbosch	*Concentrated palate of medicinal blackcurrants with nuances of menthol and fig. A smooth, balanced finish.*	£8.00	TOS	(S)
SIMONSIG CABERNET SAUVIGNON 1995, SIMONSIG ESTATE Stellenbosch	*Clean, plummy chocolate aromas lead to ripe flavours of black fruits with mint notes.*	£8.00	SOA CAP SEL	(B)
MOOIPLAAS CABERNET SAUVIGNON 1996, UVA MIRA ESTATE Stellenbosch	*Rich savoury nose with hints of oak and cedar develops into ripe fruits of the forest flavours.*	£8.00	VWE THS WRC BUP	(B)

Pinpoint who sells the wine you wish to buy by turning to the stockist codes. If you know the name of the wine you want to buy, use the alphabetical index. If the price is your motivation, refer to the invaluable price guide index; red and white wines under £5, sparkling wines under £12 and Champagne under £16. Happy hunting!

SOUTH AFRICA • RED

CATHEDRAL CELLAR MERLOT 1994, KWV Coastal Region	*Soft plums and figgy mint notes to the nose of this attractively flavoured wine.*	**£8.10**	G&M QWW CAP SOA	(S)
CATHEDRAL CELLAR MERLOT 1995, KWV Coastal Region	*Pronounced blackcurrant and cedar aromas on the nose with ripe minty summer fruits on the balanced palate.*	**£8.30**	G&M CAP	(S)
VILLIERA ESTATE MERLOT 1995, VILLIERA WINE ESTATE Paarl	*A soft fruity nose leads to a light plummy palate with sweet new oak elements.*	**£8.30**	WRC BUP	(B)
HARTENBERG ESTATE ZINFANDEL 1995, HARTENBERG ESTATE Stellenbosch	*Bags of warm spices on the nose. Amazing fruit flavours matched with sherbet and spicy notes.*	**£8.50**	WRC	(S)
CATHEDRAL CELLAR PINOTAGE 1995, KWV Coastal Region	*Delicious cedar aromas follow onto a palate of complex flavours opening up to reveal fruit and spicy oak.*	**£8.90**	G&M CAP SOA	(S)
VEENWOUDEN CLASSIC PRIVATE CELLAR 1995, VEENWOUDEN PRIVATE CELLAR Northern Paarl	*Pencil shavings to the fore of this attractive cassis flavoured wine with nuances of oak and minty herbs.*	**£9.00**	ODD	(S)
HARTENBERG ESTATE SHIRAZ 1995, HARTENBERG ESTATE Stellenbosch	*Delicious sweaty fruit characters. Deep with good length and mysteriously complex fruit and wood flavours.*	**£9.00**	WRC	(S)

Pinpoint who sells the wine you wish to buy by turning to the stockist codes. If you know the name of the wine you want to buy, use the alphabetical index. If the price is your motivation, refer to the invaluable price guide index; red and white wines under £5, sparkling wines under £12 and Champagne under £16. Happy hunting!

BOSCHENDAL MERLOT 1995, BOSCHENDAL ESTATE Franschhoek	*Plummy, herbaceous aromas of grass and herbs. A full palate of jammy black fruits with a green finish.*	£9.20	ADN GDS TPE PHI	(B)
BRENTHURST CABERNET SAUVIGNON MERLOT 1995, BRENTHURST WINERY Paarl	*Plummy currants with hints of methol and eucalyptus. Balanced palate with elements of pencil shavings.*	£9.40	ENO NYW	(B)
BOUCHARD FINLAYSON GALPIN PEAK PINOT NOIR 1996, BOUCHARD FINLAYSON Walker Bay	*Intense fruit. Slight sulphide characters on the nose. Good fruit with balance and some complexity.*	£10.00	BWL FUL	(B)
BELLINGHAM CABERNET FRANC 1997, BELLINGHAM WINES Coastal Region	*Cassis aromas followed by an intense youthful blackcurrant taste. Soft tannins with warming herbal notes.*	£10.00	FUL	(B)
UITKYK ESTATE CARLONET CABERNET SAUVIGNON 1992, UITKYK ESTATE Stellenbosch	*Spicy overtones to the blackcurrant palate with nuances of cedar wood and mint. A clean and pleasant finish.*	£10.30	BEN MVD DBY	(B)
MÔRESON MERLOT 1995, MÔRESON-MATIN SOLEIL Franschhoek	*Green flavours of underripe redcurrants and raspberries, creamy notes and a clean, lingering finish.*	£11.30	EPO	(B)
BEYERSKLOOF CABERNET SAUVIGNON 1995, BEYERS TRUTER BEYERSKLOOF Stellenbosch	*Deep rich nose of currants and oak carries over onto a concentrated palate of creamy summer fruits.*	£11.70	RSS ODD VLW	(B)
MEERLUST MERLOT 1994, MEERLUST ESTATE Stellenbosch	*A concentrated palate of plums and damsons with medicinal notes of herbs and eucalyptus.*	£12.70	BEN JNW CVR COK MMD POR TPE	(S)

HAMILTON RUSSELL WALKER BAY PINOT NOIR 1997, HAMILTON RUSSELL VINEYARDS Walker Bay	*Slightly jammy fruit with a touch of five spice. Redcurrants on the palate and up front tannins.*	£14.10	Widely Available	B
KLEINBOSCH YOUNG VATTED PINOTAGE 1997, CAPE WINE CELLARS Paarl	*Soft and attractive wine with bags of cranberry fruit, jammy flavours and hints of maraschino cherries.*	£15.00	IWS SAF	S
RUSTENBERG CABERNET SAUVIGNON MERLOT 1996, RUSTENBERG ESTATE Stellenbosch	*Soft plummy flavours of cassis and cream with herbal and oak edges. A clean, concentrated palate with good length.*	£15.00	L&W	B

SOUTH AFRICA • WHITE

ASDA CAPE CHARDONNAY RESERVE 1997, DE WETSHOF ESTATE Robertson	*Green, herby notes to a crisp, tart nose and palate of underripe Williams pears.*	£5.50	ASD	B
SPRINGFIELD ESTATE SAUVIGNON BLANC 1997, ABRIE BREWER Robertson	*Intense green gooseberries on the nose. Excellent fruit and acid balance and a biting finish.*	£5.60	GGW BWL JSM	B
VILLIERA ESTATE GEWÜRZTRAMINER 1997, VILLIERA WINE ESTATE Paarl	*Lime and lemon aromas with a well balanced viscous palate and a long, lingering finish.*	£5.80	WRC BUP	B
NEETHLINGSHOF GEWÜRZTRAMINER 1997, NEETHLINGSHOF ESTATE Stellenbosch	*Hay and straw aromas with touches of residual sugar on the palate and refreshing acidity.*	£6.00	CPW CWS DBY CRS	B

VILLIERA BUSH VINE SAUVIGNON BLANC 1997, VILLIERA WINE ESTATE Paarl	*Asparagus on the nose. An opulent and spicy body with clean, complex milky tones.*	£6.50	WRC BUP	(S)
LABORIE CHARDONNAY 1996, LABORIE ESTATE Paarl	*Slightly closed nose with ripe tropical fruit palate moderate acidity and a hot finish.*	£6.80	G&M SHJ SEL SOA	(B)
RUSTENBERG ESTATE BRAMPTON SAUVIGNON BLANC 1997, RUSTENBERG ESTATE Stellenbosch	*Freshly squashed gooseberry aromas and big, well-rounded lime and gooseberry fruit on the palate.*	£6.90	HOT L&W NYW	(S)
RUSTENBERG ESTATE BRAMPTON CHARDONNAY 1997, RUSTENBERG ESTATE Stellenbosch	*Soft nose and palate on this wine, Complex notes of grapefruit, lemon, lime and ripe tropical fruits.*	£7.00	L&W	(S)
SPRINGFIELD ESTATE SAUVIGNON BLANC SPECIAL CUVÉE 1997, ABRIE BREWER Robertson	*A big nose of fresh gooseberries and greengages. Mouth watering acidity and a biting finish.*	£7.10	GGW BWL HAR JSM WTS	(B)
KLEIN CONSTANTA SAUVIGNON BLANC 1997, KLEIN CONSTANTA ESTATE Coastal Region	*Nettle and grass aromas behind a palate of attractive perfume and sappy green, dry fruits.*	£7.20	MGN SHJ VWE DBY WTS GCL F&M VIL	(B)
BACKSBERG CHARDONNAY 1996, BACKSBERG ESTSTE Paarl	*Yeasty, mineral aromas are followed by a fat palate of ripe bananas and a buttercream vanilla finish.*	£7.30	Widely Available	(B)
PLASIR DE MERLE SAUVIGNON BLANC 1996, STELLENBOSCH FARMERS WINERY Paarl	*A restrained nose flows onto an Old World style weighty palate with complexity and length.*	£7.60	DBY CAP EPO MWW	(B)

SOUTH AFRICA • WHITE

Wine	Description	Price	Stockist	
L'AVENIR CHARDONNAY 1996, L'AVENIR Stellenbosch	*Pine resin elements to a citrusy palate of grapefruits and limes with hints of oak.*	£7.70	QWW	B
PAUL CLUVER SAUVIGNON BLANC 1997, PAUL CLUVER Nederburg	*A delightful nose of fruit and minerals. A fat and spicy palate with steely acidity.*	£8.00	TOS	B
MÓRESON PREMIUM CHARDONNAY 1996, MÓRESON-MATIN SOLEIL Franschoek	*Rich buttery fruit aromas with simple balanced palate, integrated oak and moderate acidity. Good finish.*	£8.30	CAP IRV	B
JORDAN CHARDONNAY 1997, JORDAN VINEYARDS Stellenbosch	*Leafy nose, juicy very sweet fruit with complex berry flavours leading to a deep peppery finish.*	£8.40	Widely Available	S
BOUCHARD FINLAYSON CHARDONNAY 1996, BOUCHARD FINLAYSON Overberg	*Citrus fruit and buttery oak on the nose. Palate has toasty characters and crisp apple acidity.*	£9.20	WTS FUL	S
HAMILTON RUSSELL WALKER BAY CHARDONNAY 1997, HAMILTON RUSSELL VINEYARDS Walker Bay	*Toasty charred nose. Zingy lively acidity with lime fruit and integrated creamy oak on palate.*	£10.90	WES DIR HOH MIS AVB VLW	B
MISSION VALE ESTATE RESERVE CHARDONNAY 1997, BOUCHARD FINLAYSON Walker Bay	*Dense palate of tropical fruits with creamy oak overtones and a zesty finish on a vanilla palate.*	£11.00	BWL	B

Pinpoint who sells the wine you wish to buy by turning to the stockist codes. If you know the name of the wine you want to buy, use the alphabetical index. If the price is your motivation, refer to the invaluable price guide index; red and white wines under £5, sparkling wines under £12 and Champagne under £16. Happy hunting!

SOUTH AFRICA • SPARKLING

DOUGLAS GREEN SOUTH AFRICAN SPARKLING NV, MADEBA WINERY Robertson	*Toasty and attractive with nutty aromas caressing the ever persistent mousse. Long and complex.*	£7.00	TOS	(B)

261

SOUTH AMERICA

The strength of wine making in South America continues to gather pace in leaps and bounds. The quality level from Argentina impressed the judges this year, as did Chile once more. Wineries are investing in quality vinification methods and using exciting grape varieties such as Bonarda and Sangiovese as well as the more traditional French varieties. There is also much cross fertilisation of ideas from both European and American so called flying wine makers which can only enhance these efforts. Salud!

ARGENTINA • RED

ASDA ARGENTINIAN BONARDA 1997, LA AGRICOLA Mendoza	*Herbaceous, jammy nose. The palate is fruity and full of soft, sweet fruits yet light and quaffable.*	£3.50	ASD	(B)
MARANON MALBEC 1997, VIÑAS MARANON Mendoza	*Intense red berry fruit gives this a mouth-watering palate matched with great body and length.*	£3.70	D&D KWI	(B)
RAFAEL ESTATE TEMPRANILLO 1997, HUGH RYMAN Mendoza	*Uplifted nose showing rich berry fruit. Clean palate with fruit broadness and length. Integrated oak.*	£3.80	WCR RYW SAF	(B)
RAFAEL ESATE TEMPRANILLO 1997, HUGH RYMAN Mendoza	*Floral and herb nose, showing ripe fruit. Clean with good fruit length and finish.*	£3.80	WCR RYW	(B)
SAFEWAY'S MENDOZA OAK AGED TEMPRANILLO 1996, LA AGRICOLA Mendoza	*Damsons and blackcurrants. Vanilla and spice with a solid mouthfeel, exhibiting good fruit.*	£4.00	SAF	(B)

UNWINS ARGENTINIAN SANGIOVESE BONARDA 1997, LA AGRICOLA Mendoza	*Spicy uplifted nose, showing berries and damsons. Complex fruit palate with good length.*	£4.00	UNS	(B)
BODEGA J. & F. LURTON MENDOZA BONARDA 1997, BODEGA J. & F. LURTON Mendoza	*A leathery, spicy nose leading to a juicy and currany palate with superb length.*	£4.20	JNW IWS THS WRC BUP	(B)
ISLA NEGRA BONARDA 1997, VIÑA PATAGONIA Mendoza	*A bright purple wine with delicious ripe plum and raspberry fruit. Excellent balance and length.*	£4.50	ODD SAF	(B)
MARQUES DE GRIÑON TEMPRANILLO CRIANZA 1997, ARCO BODEGAS UNIDAS Mendoza	*Fresh, appealing strawberry nose which is superseded by the firm tannin structure and dense vanilla.*	£4.50	D&D CWS MWW ODD	(B)
SANTA JULIA SANGIOVESE 1997, LA AGRICOLA Mendoza	*Warm aromas of soft cherries. The palate has vanilla touches, bramble fruit and shows finesse.*	£4.50	T&T	(B)
SANTA JULIA MALBEC OAK RESERVE 1996, LA AGRICOLA Mendoza	*Mellow tobacco and cedar aromas. A luscious oaky, spicy wine with rich dark damson fruits.*	£4.80	UNS T&T TOS	(B)
SANTA JULIA MALBEC 1997, LA AGRICOLA Mendoza	*Succulent ripe berry fruits, tart acids and firm tannins. Stylish with a persistent, long finish.*	£4.90	T&T	(B)
BALBI CABERNET SAUVIGNON BARREL RESERVE 1997, BODEGA BALBI Mendoza	*Cassis nose with spicy oak. Lengthy palate of ripe leafy blackcurrant, cinnamon and vanilla.*	£5.00	WCR	(S)

BRIGHT BROTHERS SHIRAZ RESERVE 1997, BRIGHT BROTHERS San Juan	*Perky strawberry hot nose whilst dry ripe and concentrated. Excellent fruit palate and fine tannins.*	£5.00	CWS TOS	B
NIETO Y SENETINER CABERNET SAUVIGNON 1995, NIETO Y SENETINER Mendoza	*Liquorice nose and intense fruit flavours, juicy blackcurrants, firm tannins and a vanilla finish.*	£5.30	Widely Available	S
ISLA NEGRA SYRAH 1997, VIÑA PATAGONIA Mendoza	*Deep garnet in colour with a rich, spicy, ripe cherry palate and excellent finish.*	£5.50	FUL WSO ODD WRC BUP	B
ISLA NEGRA MALBEC RESERVE 1997, VIÑA PATAGONIA Mendoza	*Pepper and spice aromas following onto a medium-bodied, fruity palate matched with racy acidity.*	£5.50	SAF WRC BUP RES	B
VISTA ANDES MERLOT 1997, VIÑA MORANDE Mendoza	*Light fresh fruit aromas with some medicinal notes then a mouthful of sweet black fruits and creamy vanilla.*	£5.60	MFS DIR VIL HVW ENO	B
SANTA JULIA TEMPRANILLO OAK RESERVE 1997, LA AGRICOLA Mendoza	*Vivid purple with sweet oak on the nose. The palate bursts with strawberries and cream.*	£5.60	UNS T&T	B
BODEGAS Y VIÑEDOS MICHEL TORINO CAB. SAUVIGNON SIN CRIANZA 1996, MICHEL TORINO Salta	*Herbs, chocolate and liquorice are followed by flavours of ripe currants and spice on the lingering palate.*	£5.80	JEF	S
HUMBERTO CANALE MALBEC 1996, HUMBERTO CANALE Rio Negro	*Purple in colour with aromas of damsons and spice. Some fine tannins with good structure.*	£5.90	HWL SVT QWW VIL	B

MARQUES DE GRIÑON DOMINIO DE AGRELO MALBEC 1996, ARCO BODEGAS UNIDAS Mendoza	*A leafy yet chocolatey nose with high acids balanced by jammy fruit and metallic notes.*	**£6.00**	D&D CWS ODD MWW	(B)
HUMBERTO CANALE MALBEC 1997, HUMBERTO CANALE Rio Negra	*Bright purple, youthful appearance. Young, inky black fruits on the palate, and a considerable finish.*	**£6.10**	HWL VIL SVT	(B)
RESERVE SYRAH VALLE DE VISTALBA 1996, NIETO Y SENETINER Mendoza	*Firm rich nose with gentle fruit and a touch of oak. Balanced long finish.*	**£6.10**	Widely Available	(B)
SANTA JULIA CABERNET SAUVIGNON OAK RESERVE 1996, LA AGRICOLA Mendoza	*Black fruits and firm oak develop into rich plummy herbaceousness. Long, spicy, balanced palate.*	**£6.50**	T&T TOS	(S)
GRAN LURTON CABERNET SAUVIGNON 1996, BODEGA J. & F. LURTON Mendoza	*Concentrated berries, liquorice, oak, cedar and spice. Palate of juicy, jammy blackcurrants, vanilla and spice.*	**£6.70**	JNW IWS THS FUL	(G)
VISTA ANDES SYRAH 1997, VIÑA MORANDE Mendoza	*Nose has some spice, bramble fruit, cherries and crispy bacon. Lots of fruit on the palate.*	**£6.90**	DIR ENO	(S)
TRAPICHE MERLOT 'OAK CASK' RESERVE 1996, BODEGA TRAPICHE Mendoza	*Ripe fruit aromas with hints of spice before rich flavours of oak and blackberries.*	**£7.00**	DIR UNS VIL SGL NAD	(B)
ARLNALDO B. ETCHART CABERNET SAUVIGNON MERLOT 1994, BODEGA ETCHART Cafayate	*Subtle nose showing soft aromas. Well formed palate of berry fruit and spice. Good length.*	**£7.20**	WIN DBY CAP PEA CEN	(B)

CATENA MALBEC 1995, BODEGA NICOLAS CATENA Mendoza	*Aromas of leather and spice follow on the palate where they are matched with flavours of sweet oak and cherries.*	**£7.60**	CPW GGW RDS DBY BWL WSO FUL	(S)
BODEGA Y CAVAS DE WEINERT CARRASCAL 1994, BERNARDO WEINERT Mendoza	*Uplifted fruit with spicy aromas. Berries on the palate with fair length and depth.*	**£7.80**	Widely Available	(B)
BODEGA NORTON PRIVADA 1996, BODEGA NORTON Mendoza	*An intense nose of violet and leather. Generous redcurrant, complex liquorice and spice. Excellent balance.*	**£7.90**	WCR LNR ODD NYW BWC JNW PAG	(S)
LUIGI BOSCA MALBEC 1993, LEONCIO ARIZU Mendoza	*Bitter cherries on the nose. Damsons and cherries with good tannins and a powerful finish.*	**£8.30**	ADN HAS HVW PFT	(B)
BODEGA Y CAVAS DE WEINERT MERLOT 1994, BERNARDO WEINERT Mendoza	*Leafy, cough syrup aromas with a nice oak finish to the soft fruity palate.*	**£9.00**	Widely Available	(B)
BALBI BARBARO BLEND 1997, BODEGA BALBI Mendoza	*Deep plum. The palate has intense plum and cherry, the tannins are firm but showing maturity.*	**£10.00**	GYW	(S)
BODEGA Y CAVAS DE WEINERT GRAN VINO 1992, BERNARDO WEINERT Mendoza	*Leathery, tarry notes and hot cassis aromas carry over onto the intense ginger spice palate of black fruits.*	**£11.50**	WSP DIR SHJ LEA WFD CNL NYW CFT	(B)

Pinpoint who sells the wine you wish to buy by turning to the stockist codes. If you know the name of the wine you want to buy, use the alphabetical index. If the price is your motivation, refer to the invaluable price guide index; red and white wines under £5, sparkling wines under £12 and Champagne under £16. Happy hunting!

ARGENTINA • WHITE

PICAJUAN PEAK CHARDONNAY NV, LA AGRICOLA Mendoza	*Soft Nevers oak aromas with citrus and tropical fruits flavours and a rich buttery finish.*	**£4.00**	T&T TOS	(B)
ALAMOS RIDGE CHARDONNAY 1996, BODEGA NICOLAS CATENA Mendoza	*Earthy and citrus fruit aromas with savoury palate, juicy fresh lively acidity and good finish.*	**£5.40**	CPW GGW DBY BWL SAF FUL CHF	(B)
SANTA JULIA OAKED CHARDONNAY 1997, LA AGRICOLA Mendoza	*A wine of great length with lots of smoky vanilla oak. Needs age to develop.*	**£6.70**	HOU UNS T&T	(B)
ETCHART BARREL FERMENTED CHARDONNAY 1997, BODEGA ETCHART Cafayate	*Hot ripe buttery aromas with lovely balanced fruit, moderate acidity and subtle integrated oak characters.*	**£7.40**	MFS HOU WIN DBY BUP SLM THR	(B)
CATENA CHARDONNAY 1996, BODEGA NICOLAS CATENA Mendoza	*A freckly juvenile with intense complex oak and good weighty fruit. Wait until it blossoms.*	**£8.70**	GGW BWL WSO FUL ASD	(B)

CHILE • RED

TIERRA DEL FUEGO CABERNET SAUVIGNON 1996, TIERRA DEL FUEGO Maule Valley	*Ripe aromas of stewed plums are followed by intense flavours of soft sweet blackcurrants on a lengthy palate.*	**£4.50**	GAR	(B)

CANEPA CABERNET SAUVIGNON 1997, JOSÉ CANEPA Maipo Valley	*Strong aromas of mint and herbs lead to rich flavours of blackberries and creamy butterscotch.*	£4.90	SPR T&T	**B**
LAS LOMAS MERLOT 1997, C.A.U. CAUQUENES BARRIA Maule Valley	*Spicy, leafy herbaceous aromas are followed by jammy fruits of the forest and vanilla flavours.*	£5.00	AMU	**B**
VIÑA CARTA VIEJA MERLOT ANTIGUA RESERVE 1996, VIÑA CARTA VIEJA Maipo Valley	*Plummy damsons dominate the creamy palate. Hints of spicy oak and mint. Beautiful balance and finish.*	£5.00	MWW PIM ARM	**B**
VIÑA CARTA VIEJA CABERNET SAUVIGNON ANTIGUA RESERVE 1996, VIÑA CARTA VIEJA Maule Valley	*Rich cinnamon spiced fruit cake aromas are reflected on the simple flavours of the lengthy palate.*	£5.00	MWW PIM ARM MHV	**B**
SOLECA CABERNET SAUVIGNON 1997, VIÑA BISQUERTT Rapel Valley	*Lifted aromas of spiced fruit and oak lead to peppery, blackberry fruit flavours on the soft welcoming palate.*	£5.10	PLE ODD PFT	**B**
ISLA NEGRA SYRAH 1997, VIÑA CONO SUR Rapel Valley	*Pleasant gamey nose introduces warm vibrant fruit palate with loads of pepper and good finish.*	£5.40	ODD FUL WRC BUP	**B**
MONT GRAS MERLOT 1996, MONT GRAS VINEYARDS Rapel Valley	*Rich, stewed bramble fruit flavours are preceded by aromas of new oak and soft fruits.*	£5.40	JNW VIL HVW ENO VLW TOS NYW	**B**
CASA LEONA MERLOT RESERVE 1997, VIÑA PEUMO Rapel Valley	*Ripe blackcurrant aromas with nuances of spice and oak are reflected on the clean, juicy berry fruit palate.*	£5.50	HWL M&S	**S**

VIU MANENT MALBEC 1997, VIU MANENT Colchagua	*Some herbal, hoppy aromas with hints of sage and thyme. A big juicy fruit concentration.*	£5.50	HWL	(S)
ROWAN BROOK CABERNET SAUVIGNON RESERVE 1995, JOSÉ CANEPA Central Valley	*Jammy cassis fruit on the nose and palate with hints of spicy plums and smoke.*	£5.50	ASD	(B)
CASA LEONA CABERNET SAUVIGNON RESERVE 1996, VIÑA PEUMO Rapel Valley	*Jammy, herby, currant nose with sweet black fruits flavours on a balanced palate.*	£5.50	HWL M&S	(B)
CALIBORO CABERNET SAUVIGNON RESERVA 1995, VIÑA SEGU OLLE Maule Valley	*Ripe, sweet fruit on the nose followed by good fruit extract and balanced tannins for a firm structure.*	£5.50	HWL	(B)
AVENTURA MALBEC 1997, VIÑA MORANDE Maipo Valley	*Distinctive aromas of straw and herbs tightly constructed with savoury fruits and a complex finish.*	£5.50	ODD	(B)
AVENTURA CARIGNAN 1997, VIÑA MORANDE Curico Valley	*Garnet coloured with smoky oak and damson aromas. Some tight tannin with green fruit flavours.*	£5.50	ODD	(B)
ERRAZURIZ CABERNET SAUVIGNON 1996, ERRAZURIZ Aconcagua Valley	*Medicinal, minty notes to the nose and palate of this blackberry flavoured wine. Good length, soft finish.*	£5.60	Widely Available	(B)
TRIO MERLOT 1997, VIÑA CONCHA Y TORO Rapel Valley	*Ripe bramble aromas with cigar box and oak elements. Balanced palate of plum jam and cinnamon spice.*	£5.70	CWA BOO VLW THS WRC BUP	(S)

SOUTH AMERICA • CHILE • RED

SANTA DIGNA CABERNET SAUVIGNON 1996, SOCIEDAD VINICOLA MIGUEL TORRES Curico Valley	*A powerful, herby nose based on a rich, well-balanced, yet simple wine with a good finish.*	£5.70	Widely Available	B
VIÑA CASABLANCA MERLOT WHITE LABEL 1997, VIÑA CASABLANCA Aconcagua Valley	*Minty, cassis aromas with vanilla elements lead to herbaceous blackcurrant flavours and a savoury finish.*	£5.70	JNW ODD MOR BOO	B
SANTA DIGNA CABERNET SAUVIGNON 1997, SOCIEDAD VINICOLA MIGUEL TORRES Curico Valley	*A deep, dense, tarry bouquet delivers a soft, round, fruit-driven style of wine that is well-structured.*	£5.80	Widely Available	B
MONTES CABERNET SAUVIGNON OAK AGED RESERVE 1995, DISCOVER WINES Curico Valley	*Rich, deep wonderful fruit flavours of blackcurrants and berries with notes of mint and spice.*	£5.90	Widely Available	S
ALMA TERRA MATER CABERNET SAUVIGNON 1997, TERRA MATER WINES Maipo Valley	*Jammy aromas of blackcurrants and mint carry over onto the soft palate of creamy black fruits.*	£5.90	QWW TPE SWS TOS	B
SANTA RITA MERLOT RESERVA 1996, SANTA RITA Maipo Valley	*Ripe plummy aromas with hints of white pepper lead to a soft jammy vanilla palate.*	£6.00	DIR ODD MWW VWE GRA DBY HVW	S
SANTA RITA CABERNET SAUVIGNON RESERVA 1996, SANTA RITA Maipo Valley	*Complex aromas of minty blackcurrants, liquorice and oak are followed by integrated flavours of ripe berry fruits.*	£6.00	ADN DIR MWW DBY GRA HVW ODD LCC	S
SANTA INES MALBEC RESERVA 1997, SANTA INES VINEYARD Maipo Valley	*Big, soft, jammy fruit and bags of sweet American oak with a simple, tart finish.*	£6.00	IWS THS WRC BUP	B

PIEDRAS ALTAS CABERNET SAUVIGNON 1996, FRANSISCO DE AGUIRRE Limari Valley	*Complex eucalypt and leafy fruit on the nose with strong spicy mint notes to the blackberry palate.*	£6.00	DIR AVB	B
VIÑA PORTA CABERNET SAUVIGNON 1997, VIÑA PORTA Rapel Valley	*Minty nuances to a nose and palate full of rasp- berry and loganberry fruit. A creamy finish gives elegance.*	£6.00	ODD SEA	B
SANTA INES MALBEC LEGADO DE ARMIDA RESERVE 1997, SANTA INES VINEYARD Maipo Valley	*Raspberries, herbs and spices combine on the nose and palate to form a rounded wine.*	£6.00	WRC BUP	B
ECHEVERRIA CABERNET SAUVIGNON RESERVA 1996, ECHEVERRIA Curico Valley	*Rich aromas of ripe currants with nuances of oak, mint and spicy eucalyptus. Elegant finish.*	£6.20	WES DIR HOH MIS POR VIL HVW AVB	S
CASA LAPOSTOLLE CABERNET SAUVIGNON 1996, CASA LAPOSTOLLE Rapel Valley	*Delicate aromas of red berries and smoky notes are followed by soft ripe fruit flavours.*	£6.30	Widely Available	B
SANTA CAROLINA CABERNET SAUVIGNON GRAN RESERVA 1995, VIÑA SANTA CAROLINA Central Valley Region	*Warm aromas of medicated black fruits with hints of menthol carry over onto a spicy palate with good length.*	£6.30	G&M DBY	B
LA PALMA MERLOT RESERVA 1997, VIÑA LA ROSA Rapel Valley	*Intense metholated aromas with a slightly confected cassis nose. The balanced palate has creamy hints of spicy oak.*	£6.60	HWL SVT CWS ODD JSM FUL	S

Pinpoint who sells the wine you wish to buy by turning to the stockist codes. If you know the name of the wine you want to buy, use the alphabetical index. If the price is your motivation, refer to the invaluable price guide index; red and white wines under £5, sparkling wines under £12 and Champagne under £16. Happy hunting!

VALDIVIESO CABERNET SAUVIGNON RESERVE 1996, A. VALDIVIESO Lontue Valley	*Rich aromas of fresh black fruits lead to a simple palate of juicy cassis and mint flavours.*	£6.70	NEI BUP GGW DBY BWL JSM FUL WRC	B
ECHEVERRIA MERLOT RESERVA 1995, ECHEVERRIA Curico Valley	*Ripe currants and raspberries with hints of mint and fig. A creamy balance to the finish.*	£6.70	DIR HOH NEI VIL AVB	B
VALDIVIESO RESERVE MALBEC RESERVE 1996, A. VALDIVIESO Lontue Valley	*A deep purple colour with big chunky fruit, chewy tannins and spice on the finish.*	£6.80	NEI GGW DBY BWL SAF	B
VALDIVIESO MERLOT RESERVE 1996, A. VALDIVIESO Lontue Valley	*Attractive cigar box and plum aromas precede a ripe cassis palate with a soft finish.*	£6.80	NEI GGW DBY BWL SAF WRC	B
TRIO CABERNET 1995, VIÑA CONCHA Y TORO Maipo Valley	*Luscious fruit and oak nose followed by mouth filling flavours of ripe blackcurrants and well-balanced vanilla.*	£6.80	HOU CNL DBY VLW THS WRC BUP	B
MONT GRAS CABERNET SAUVIGNON RESERVA 1995, MONT GRAS VINEYARDS Colghagua	*Ripe aromas of rich damson fruit with nuances of spice, mint and oak lead to a lingering palate.*	£7.00	JNW VIL HVW VLW NYW CHF	S
CASA LAPOSTOLLE MERLOT 1997, CASA LAPOSTOLLE Rapel Valley	*Cinnamon and mint dominate the black fruits nose of this richly concen-trated wine demonstrating well integrated tannins.*	£7.00	SHJ ODD HVW THS WRK FUL BUP RES	S
VIÑA OCHAGAVIA MERLOT RESERVADO 1997, VIÑA OCHAGAVIA Central Valley	*Intense aromas of creamy forest fruits and spicy oak and flavours of ripe juicy black fruits with vanilla.*	£7.00	VLW	S

VIU MANENT MALBEC RESRVE 1996, VIU MANENT Colchagua	*Brambly, jammy nose expands onto ripe and rounded fruit palate. Overtones of liquorice and structured tannins.*	£7.00	HWL	(S)
MONT GRAS CABERNET SAUVIGNON RESERVA 1996, MONT GRAS VINEYARDS Rapel Valley	*Medicinal, cassis and oak nose carries over to a rounded creamy blackcurrant nose.*	£7.00	JNW VIL HVW ENO CHF VLW NYW	(B)
NIEBLA MERLOT 1997, VISTAMAR WINES Maipo Valley	*Gentle aromas of damsons and plums carry over onto an approachable palate of summer fruits with a creamy finish.*	£7.00	COK VNO GLY	(B)
VIÑA OCHAGAVIA CABERNET SAUVIGNON RESERVADO 1996, VIÑA OCHAGAVIA Central Valley Region	*Sexy eucalyptus and mint nose leads onto a well-structured palate of blackcurrants and menthol.*	£7.00	VLW	(B)
UNDURRAGA CABERNET SAUVIGNON RESERVA 1997, VIÑA UNDURRAGA Rapel Valley	*Spice and mint notes on a palate full of jammy cassis and cream. A lengthy and elegant finish.*	£7.00	NEI PLB	(B)
UNDURRAGA CARMENÈRE RESERVA 1997, VIÑA UNDURRAGA Central Valley Region	*Mushroom and ripe summer fruit aromas. Stewed plums and hints of kernals on the finish.*	£7.00	TOS PLB	(B)
MONT GRAS MERLOT RESERVA 1996, MONT GRAS VINEYARDS Rapel Valley	*Complex aromas of fruits are followed by a balanced, lingering palate of jammy, plummy fruit.*	£7.10	JNW CHF ENO VIL NYW HVW QWW	(S)
CONO SUR PINOT NOIR RESERVE 1996, VIÑA CONO SUR Central Valley Region	*Light morello cherries on the nose with rich flavours of creamy strawberries with some minty notes.*	£7.20	ODD WTS	(B)

VIÑA CASABLANCA CABERNET SAUVIGNON EL BOSQUE 1996, VIÑA CASABLANCA Central Valley Region	*Menthol and cassis flavours with notes of cedar wood and oak with a clean, balanced finish.*	£7.30	JNW POR ODD MOR	B
ERRAZURIZ CABERNET SAUVIGNON RESERVA 1996, ERRAZURIZ Aconcagua Valley	*A rich nose of tobacco ripe cassis and herbs is followed by a chewy palate of ripe blackcurrants.*	£7.60	Widely Available	S
SANTA CAROLINA MERLOT GRAN RESERVA 1996, VIÑA SANTA CAROLINA Central Valley Region	*Pleasant blackcurrant and tar aromas lead to complex flavours of dried black fruits and cedarwood.*	£7.60	G&M DBY	B
CARMEN MERLOT RESERVE 1996, CARMEN Rapel Valley	*Ripe, dark fruits and oak nose with hints of spice leads onto the understated plummy palate.*	£7.70	Widely Available	S
VIÑA CASABLANCA CABERNET SAUVIGNON SANTA ISABEL 1997, VIÑA CASABLANCA Aconcagua Valley	*Creamy vanilla and spice highlights on an intense nose of forest fruits. A concentrated palate of minty berries.*	£7.80	JNW DBY MOR HVW ODD	S
VALDIVIESO PINOT NOIR RESERVE 1996, A. VALDIVIESO Lontue Valley	*Cherry fruit characters on the nose with simple slightly sweet fruit palate and balanced tannins.*	£7.80	Widely Available	B
VIÑA CASABLANCA MERLOT SANTA ISABEL 1997, VIÑA CASABLANCA Aconcagua Valley	*Intense, stewed fruits and liquorice aromas are followed by rich concentrated fruit compôte flavours.*	£7.90	JNW ODD MOR DBY HVW	S
LAURA HARTWIG CABERNET SAUVIGNON 1996, SANTA LAURA Rapel Valley	*Herbaceous, oaky aromas lead to pronounced flavours of mint, chocolate and spice on the cassis palate.*	£7.90	ENO	B

VIÑA PORTA UNFILTERED CABERNET SAUVIGNON RESERVA 1995, VIÑA PORTA Rapel Valley	*Intense aromas and flavours of soft black fruits with creamy notes of mint, cedar wood and spicy eucalypt.*	£8.00	ODD HVW SEA	B
ERRAZURIZ MERLOT RESERVA 1997, ERRAZURIZ Aconcagua Valley	*Ripe soft fruits on the nose with similar flavours and nuances of green capsicum on the palate.*	£8.00	NEI DBY ODD FRT	B
VIÑA PORTA CABERNET SAUVIGNON RESERVA 1996, VIÑA PORTA Rapel Valley	*Spicy elements of white pepper to the bramble palate with a creamy edge to the silky finish.*	£8.00	SEA	B
VIÑA GRACIA CABERNET SAUVIGNON RESERVA 1994, VIÑA GRACIA Rapel Valley	*Full aromas of ripe plums with vegetal, coffee bean notes carry over onto a rich palate.*	£8.40	COK TPE CWS TBV	S
MONTES ALPHA MERLOT RESERVA 1996, DISCOVER WINES Curico Valley	*Rich, sweet nose of ripe plummy fruit then pleasant soft fruit flavours on the simple palate.*	£8.50	HWL SVT POR VIL TPE SCK	B
VALDIVIESO CABERNET FRANC RESERVA 1996, A. VALDIVIESO Lontue Valley	*A fresh, cedary nose with blackcurrant overtones, soft tannins and a harmonious palate.*	£8.90	Widely Available	B
ERRAZURIZ PINOT NOIR RESERVA 1997, ERRAZURIZ Casablanca Valley	*Ripe berry fruit on the nose with spicy peppery characters, rich ripe fruit on the palate.*	£9.00	ODD	S

Pinpoint who sells the wine you wish to buy by turning to the stockist codes. If you know the name of the wine you want to buy, use the alphabetical index. If the price is your motivation, refer to the invaluable price guide index; red and white wines under £5, sparkling wines under £12 and Champagne under £16. Happy hunting!

VIÑA OCHAGAVIA MERLOT GRAN RESERVA 1996, VIÑA OCHAGAVIA Central Valley Region	*Rich flavours of cedar wood and pencil shavings on a plum and damson palate.*	£9.00	VLW	**S**
MONT GRAS MERLOT NINQUEN BARREL SELECT 1996, MONT GRAS VINEYARDS Rapel Valley	*Blackberry aromas with hints of pencil shavings are reflected on the light, delicate palate.*	£9.00	JNW VIL HVW ENO VLW FUL	**B**
SANTA RITA CARMENÈRE 1997, SANTA RITA Maipo Valley	*The nose has great depth with unripe, herbaceous notes. Some stewed fruits on the palate.*	£9.00	DIR GRA FRT	**B**
MONTES ALPHA CABERNET SAUVIGNON RESERVE 1995, DISCOVER WINES Curico Valley	*Leafy and oaky aromas lead to a round juicy lingering palate of currants and creamy mint.*	£9.40	Widely Available	**B**
MONT GRAS CABERNET SAUVIGNON NINQUEN 1996, MONT GRAS VINEYARDS Rapel Valley	*Smoky oak nose with violets and berries aroma followed by blackcurrant fruit palate with hints of menthol.*	£9.50	JNW VLW ENO QWW HVW NYW	**S**
CABALLO LOCO NUMERO UNO NV, A. VALDIVIESO Lontue Valley	*Aromas of currants, oak and herbs lead to a richly flavoured palate of cassis and vanilla with nuances of mint and eucalypt.*	£9.70	NEI WRC GGW VLW WTS FUL BUP	**S**
CASA LAPOSTOLLE CAB. SAUVIGNON CUVEE ALEXANDRE RESERVA 1996, CASA LAPOSTOLLE Rapel Valley	*Dried fruit aromas lead onto a minty palate with lots of ripe berry flavours and a spicy finish.*	£9.70	THS ODD WRK FUL WRC BUP	**B**

Pinpoint who sells the wine you wish to buy by turning to the stockist codes. If you know the name of the wine you want to buy, use the alphabetical index. If the price is your motivation, refer to the invaluable price guide index; red and white wines under £5, sparkling wines under £12 and Champagne under £16. Happy hunting!

ERRAZURIZ SYRAH RESERVE 1997, ERRAZURIZ Aconcagua Valley	*Fresh peppery spice and mint on the smoky nose. The full palate has rich fruit cake flavours.*	£10.20	HOU NEI UNS ODD DBY SAF TOS	(G)
NINQUÉN BARREL SELECT CABERNET SAUVIGNON MERLOT 1996, MONT GRAS VINEYARDS Rapel Valley	*Jammy red fruit aromas are followed by soft savoury plum flavours with hints of spice.*	£10.50	HVW ENO	(B)
CASA LAPOSTOLLE CUVÉE ALEXANDRE MERLOT 1996, CASA LAPOSTOLLE Rapel Valley	*Huge aromas of black-currants, mint and creamy new oak with a mouthfilling palate of berry fruit and tannins.*	£10.90	Widely Available	(G)
SANTA CAROLINA RESERVA DE FAMILIA CABERNET SAUVIGNON 1995, VIÑA SANTA CAROLINA Central Valley Region	*Classic cedary nose with pronounced black fruits aromas and flavours with nuances of sweet new oak and mint.*	£10.90	G&M	(B)
VALDIVIESO CABALLO LOCO NO 2, A. VALDIVIESO Lontue Valley	*Warm oak aromas lead to a ripe blueberry palate dominated by new oak flavours.*	£11.70	Widely Available	(B)
MANSO DE VELASCO CABERNET SAUVIGNON 1996, SOCIEDAD VINICOLA MIGUEL TORRES Curico Valley	*Pronounced minty nose with figgy plums, leading onto a palate redolent with the flavours of summer fruits pudding.*	£12.10	DIR COK JEF HOT WCS POR AMW	(S)
DON MELCHOR CABERNET SAUVIGNON 1995, VIÑA CONCHA Y TORO Maipo Valley	*Concentrated aromas and flavours of brambles and damsons with hints of oak and spice.*	£12.50	FSW SEL HOU DBY VLW	(B)

Pinpoint who sells the wine you wish to buy by turning to the stockist codes. If you know the name of the wine you want to buy, use the alphabetical index. If the price is your motivation, refer to the invaluable price guide index; red and white wines under £5, sparkling wines under £12 and Champagne under £16. Happy hunting!

MANSO DE VELASCO 1995, SOCIEDAD VINICOLA MIGUEL TORRES Curico Valley	*Complex aromas of oak, pencil shavings and herbs. Blackcurrant palate with nuances of tobacco, vanilla and mint.*	£12.60	Widely Available	G
MAGNIFICUM 1995, JOSÉ CANEPA Central Valley	*Leafy, herbal notes to the nose of this attractively flavoured wine with ripe, juicy, forest fruits palate.*	£13.40	T&T MGN SCA	B
ERRAZURIZ DON MAXIMIANO CABERNET SAUVIGNON RESERVE 1995, ERRAZURIZ Aconcagua	*Intense aromas of spicy plums and mint. Complex palate of mulberries, eucalyptus, cigar box and creamy oak.*	£13.60	HOU FUL DBY VWE ODD WRC BUP	S
SANTA RITA CASA REAL CABERNET SAUVIGNON 1995, SANTA RITA Maipo Valley	*Deep minty blackcurrant nose with a rich palate of concentrated juicy ribena and soft tannins.*	£14.20	DIR DBY ODD GRA FRT	B
CABO DE HORNOS SPECIAL RESERVE CABERNET SAUVIGNON 1994, VIÑA SAN PEDRO Curico Valley	*Smoky, tarry elements to a developed blackcurrant nose with ripe dried fruit flavours on the integrated lingering palate.*	£14.40	SEL RBS	S
ERRAZURIZ DON MAXIMIANO CABERNET SAUVIGNON RESERVE 1996, ERRAZURIZ Aconcagua Valley	*A complex wine with aromas and flavours of cassis and chocolate with hazelnut and minty notes.*	£15.00	NEI ODD VWE	B
MONTES ALPHA "M" RESERVE 1996, DISCOVER WINES Santa Cruz	*Sweet nose of soft black fruits, nuances of spice, new oak and mint. Concentrated flavours of jammy cassis.*	£18.30	WCR HWL SVT A&A VIL DBY	S

Pinpoint who sells the wine you wish to buy by turning to the stockist codes. If you know the name of the wine you want to buy, use the alphabetical index. If the price is your motivation, refer to the invaluable price guide index; red and white wines under £5, sparkling wines under £12 and Champagne under £16. Happy hunting!

CHILE • WHITE

CHILEAN DRY WHITE WINE 1997, NEVADA EXPORTS Aconcagua Valley	*A fuller vinous nose. The palate consists of delicate rose petals and light tropical fruit.*	**£3.30**	PEC	(B)
VINO DE CHILE WHITE 1997, XPOVIN LTDA Coquimbo	*Medium-bodied with with rich aromas of tropical fruits and coconuts. Balanced with good length.*	**£3.50**	WCR SMF PLB	(S)
ASDA CHILEAN SAUVIGNON BLANC 1997, VIÑA SAN PEDRO Curico Valley	*Green apples and herbs. Acidic palate with lingering, lean fruit. Great mouthfeel with very long finish.*	**£3.80**	ASD	(S)
ANTU MAPU SAUVIGNON BLANC RESERVA 1997, C.A.V. CAUQUENES BARRIA Maule Valley	*Uplifted asparagus and floral aromas. Upfront acid and broadness, showing a tropical fruit palate.*	**£4.00**	TOS	(S) WINE OF THE YEAR
CASA LEONA CHARDONNAY 1997, VIÑA PEUMO Rapel Valley	*Warm, soft flavours of bananas and pineapples appear on the nose and palate of this easily approachable wine.*	**£4.50**	HWL M&S	(B)
ANDES PEAK CHARDONNAY 1997, SANTA EMILIANA Aconcagua Valley	*Light, delicate aromas and flavours of melons and pineapples dominate this crisp young wine.*	**£4.50**	Widely Available	(B)
TIERRA DEL FUEGO CHARDONNAY 1997, TIERRA DEL FUEGO Maule Valley	*Spritzy pear drop and melon flavours dominate the palate of this attractively zingy dry wine.*	**£4.50**	GAR	(B)

Wine	Tasting Note	Price	Stockists	
PIONERO CHARDONNAY 1997, PABLO MORANDE Central Valley Region	*A mouthful of ripe bananas and cream follows an attractive nose of tinned tropical fruit cocktail.*	£4.60	LCC ASD	P
CONO SUR GEWURTZTRAMINER 1997, VIÑA CONO SUR Bio Bio	*Hints of green fruits with stalky aromas. Heavy mouthfeel and some good ripe spicy flavours.*	£4.70	ODD VWW WSO WRC BUP	B
CANEPA CHARDONNAY 1997, JOSÉ CANEPA Maipo Valley	*Hot aromas of stewed apples with tinned tropical fruits on the crisp, zingy palate.*	£4.70	MGN T&T	B
SANTA CAROLINA CHARDONNAY SEMILLON 1997, VIÑA SANTA CAROLINA Maipo Valley	*Pineapple and melon chunks carry to a rich palate with spritzy, zesty characterstics to the balanced finish.*	£4.80	HOU ODD THS WRC BUP	S
SANTA CAROLINA CHARDONNAY SEMILLON 1997, VIÑA SANTA CAROLINA Central Valley Region	*The nose on this wine is warm and slightly honeyed. Clean fruit on the palate.*	£4.90	WCR HOU THS WRC BUP	S
SOLECA SEMILLON CHARDONNAY 1997, VIÑA BISQUERTT Rapel Valley	*Fresh fragrant nose with plenty of sweet citrus fruit. Good palate weight and moderate acidity.*	£4.90	PLE PFT SAF	B
SOLECA SEMILLON 1997, VIÑA BISQUERTT Rapel Valley	*Apples and pineapple with a smoky edge. Full bodied palate, firm structure and good weight.*	£5.00	PLE THS BUP WRC	S
PALO ALTO CHARDONNAY 1997, FRANSISCO DE AGUIRRE Limari Valley	*Aromatic gooseberries and a hint of spice. This wine is subtle with crisp dry acidity.*	£5.10	QWW DIR VIL AVB WCR	B

Wine	Description	Price	Availability	
SANTA DIGNA SAUVIGNON BLANC 1997, SOCIEDAD VINICOLA MIGUEL TORRES Central Valley Region	*Clear and bright with light gooseberry aromas. A good, simple style with some residual sugar.*	£5.10	Widely Available	B
ISLA NEGRA CHARDONNAY 1996, VIÑA CONO SUR Rapel Valley	*Peaches and cream onto the ripe cantaloupe melon flavoured palate. Finish of pineapple and lychees.*	£5.30	ODD BTH FUL THS WRC BUP	S
CASILLERO DEL DIABLO CHARDONNAY 1996, VIÑA CONCHA Y TORO Aconcagua Valley	*Delicate floral characters with subtle toasty oak aromas, this is a simple lightly fragrant Chardonnay.*	£5.30	Widely Available	B
ISLA NEGRA CHARDONNAY 1997, VIÑA CONO SUR Aconcagua Valley	*Creamy, green notes to the ripe fruit on the nose and palate of this new world wine.*	£5.30	VWE BTH BUP ODD WTS FUL THS WRC	B
TRIO CHARDONNAY 1996, VIÑA CONCHA Y TORO Aconcagua Valley	*Fragrant fruit with toasty oak on the nose, tangy citrus and peach characters on the palate.*	£5.50	Widely Available	S
ROWAN BROOK CHARDONNAY RESERVE 1997, JOSÉ CANEPA Aconcagua Valley	*Restrained oranges and lemon on the nose. Dried fruit character with buttery oak on palate.*	£5.50	ASD	B
VIU MANENT SAUVIGNON BLANC 1997, VIU MANENT Colchagua Valley	*A crisp and clean austere grassy Sauvignon style. Ripe gooseberries develop later on the palate.*	£5.50	HWL	B
TRIO CHARDONNAY 1997, VIÑA CONCHA Y TORO Aconcagua Valley	*Ruby grapefruit and unwaxed lemons. Rich palate of ripe melons and pomello with honey and pineapples.*	£5.60	COK VLW WRC BUP CWA BOO HOU	S

ERRAZURIZ CHARDONNAY 1997, ERRAZURIZ Aconcagua Valley	*Scents of vanilla essence and pineapple precede a full palate of melons and apricots.*	£5.60	Widely Available	**B**
VIÑA CASABLANCA SAUVIGNON BLANC WHITE LABEL 1997, VIÑA CASABLANCA Central Valley Region	*Grassy and herbal uplifted aromas, showing acid driven apples and broad fruity structured finish.*	£5.70	Widely Available	**S**
MONT GRAS CHARDONNAY RESERVA 1997, MONT GRAS VINEYARDS Rapel Valley	*Tight elegant nose with hints of oak. Creamy soft melon characters with slightly astringent finish.*	£5.90	JNW VIL ENO	**B**
VIÑA CASABLANCA CHARDONNAY WHITE LABEL 1997, VIÑA CASABLANCA Aconcagua Valley	*Intense aromas and flavours of ripe tropical fruits and apricots with some vanilla notes.*	£5.90	Widely Available	**B**
SANTA INES CHARDONNAY RESERVA 1997, SANTA INES VINEYARD Maipo Valley	*Herbaceous aromas of lemon grass carry over onto the ripe ogen melon flavoured palate.*	£6.00	IWS SMF FUL THS WRC BUP	**S**
SANTA CAROLINA CHARDONNAY RESERVA 1997, VIÑA SANTA CAROLINA Central Valley Region	*Light lime characters with a touch of creamy vanilla oak, moderate acidity and good length.*	£6.00	JSM	**B**
VILLARD CHARDONNAY 1996, VILLARD ESTATE Aconcagua Valley	*Rich mature and hot. This sounds like your perfect partner disguised as a lovely Chardonnay.*	£6.20	Widely Available	**B**
CASA LAPOSTOLLE CHARDONNAY 1997, CASA LAPOSTOLLE Aconcagua Valley	*Creamy pear drop aromas are followed by off-dry flavours of banana and bubble gum.*	£6.50	HVW THS ODD ASD FUL	**B**

WHITE • CHILE • SOUTH AMERICA

CASTILLO DE MOLINA CHARDONNAY RESERVA 1997, VIÑA SAN PEDRO Curico	*Toasted oak overtones to a richly flavoured palate of hot pineapple chunks and crisply mouthwatering starfruit.*	£6.60	SEL	(S)
VIÑA CASABLANCA SAUVIGNON BLANC SANTA ISABEL 1997, VIÑA CASABLANCA Aconcagua Valley	*Light, uplifted tropical fruit nose with herbal nuances within the balanced, lengthy palate.*	£6.60	JNW ODD MOR NYW	(B)
VALDIVIESO CHARDONNAY RESERVE 1996, A. VALDIVIESO Lontue Valley	*Toasty oak and yeasty vegemite aromas, biscuits with a fresh lemon finish on the palate.*	£6.70	NEI GGW DBY BWL SMF FUL	(B)
VIÑA CASABLANCA GEWÜRZTRAMINER SANTA ISABEL 1997, VIÑA CASABLANCA Aconcagua Valley	*Fragrant water and spice aromas. A well defined palate with good acidity and excellent length.*	£6.80	MFS JNW POR MOR NYW ODD	(B)
SOLECA RESERVE CHARDONNAY 1997, VIÑA BISQUERTT Rapel Valley	*Soft tropical fruit flavours with vanilla and bacon characters from new oak on the nose.*	£7.00	PLE ODD	(S)
UNDURRAGA CHARDONNAY RESERVA 1997, VIÑA UNDURRAGA Maipo Valley	*Bananas and pineappple. A palate of mangoes and kiwi fruit with vanilla and lime, finishing cleanly.*	£7.00	UNS	(S)
CHATEAU LA JOYA GRAN RESERVA 1997, VIÑA BISQUERTT Rapel Valley	*Cinnamon and nutmeg, showing melon fruit with a creamy apple palate and a good clean finish.*	£7.00	PLE	(S)
VIÑA GRACIA CHARDONNAY RESERVA 1997, VIÑA GRACIA Rapel Valley	*Nose has hints of asparagus and vegetal characters. Ripe full-bodied fruit with vanilla flavours. Well-balanced.*	£7.00	UNS SOH	(S)

SANTA CAROLINA CHARDONNAY GRAN RESERVA 1996, VIÑA SANTA CAROLINA Central Valley Region	*Rich sweet buttery flavours of caramalized bananas, with nuances of melon and grapefruit. A refreshing finish.*	**£7.00**	DBY	(B)
MEDALLA REAL CHARDONNAY 1997, SANTA RITA Aconcagua Valley	*Toasty oak with herbal fragrant aromas. Palate consists of elegant banana melon and peach characters.*	**£7.00**	DIR DBY MWW GRA FRT JSM	(B)
CARMEN WINE MAKER'S RESERVE CHARDONNAY 1996, CARMEN Maipo Valley	*Fresh citrus and tropical characters on the nose. Zesty lemons and pineapple on the palate.*	**£7.20**	DIR WIN M&S	(S)
VIÑA CASABLANCA CHARDONNAY SANTA ISABEL 1997, VIÑA CASABLANCA Aconcagua Valley	*Pungent oak with hints of botrytis on the nose with peaches apricot and pineapple palate.*	**£7.60**	JNW MOR NYW ODD HVW	(B)
ERRAZURIZ CHARDONNAY RESERVA 1996, ERRAZURIZ Aconcagua Valley	*Light citrus fruit on the nose. Very fresh balanced fruit with integrated oak. Good finish.*	**£7.80**	WCR NEI DBY HVW FUL TOS	(B)
ERRAZURIZ CHARDONNAY RESERVA 1997, ERRAZURIZ Aconcagua Valley	*Creamy melon, mango and pineapple flavours with nuances of vanilla pod dominate this attractive wine.*	**£7.90**	WCR DBY HOU ODD HVW	(S)
VIÑA GRACIA CHARDONNAY RESERVA 1996, VIÑA GRACIA Rapel Valley	*Grapefruit with hints of cut grass on the nose. Fresh citrus palate, moderate acidity, good length.*	**£8.80**	TPE CWS JBR	(S)
VIÑA CASABLANCA CHARDONNAY BARREL FERMENTED 1997, VIÑA CASABLANCA Aconcagua Valley	*Ripe tropical fruit on the nose. Subtle vanilla oak characters, clean with a good finish.*	**£8.90**	JNW ODD MOR HVW	(B)

MONTES ALPHA CHARDONNAY 1997, DISCOVER WINES Curico Valley	*Pungent toasty nutty oak on the nose. Oily texture with honeyed fruit, slightly hot finish.*	£9.20	HWL SVT POR VIL TPE HAR DBY AMW	B
ERRAZURIZ WILD FERMENT CHARDONNAY 1997, ERRAZURIZ Aconcagua Valley	*Cantaloupe melon flavour with lime character dominates this creamy wine. The finish is long and sensuous.*	£9.60	NEI UNS ODD DBY THS WRC BUP	S
CASA LAPOSTOLLE CHARDONNAY CUVEE ALEXANDRE RESERVA 1996, CASA LAPOSTOLLE Aconcagua Valley	*Complex, nutty aromas, a hint of greenness. Forward fruit on palate with integrated sweet oak.*	£10.20	SEL HVW THS ODD WRK FUL RES	B
SANTA CAROLINA RESERVA DE FAMILIA CHARDONNAY 1997, VIÑA SANTA CAROLINA Central Valley Region	*Sunshine in a glass. Delicate peach fruit hints of mineral characters and integrated restrained oak.*	£10.90	G&M	B

URUGUAY • RED

DON PASCUAL TANNAT ROBLE 1996, ESTABLECIMENTO JUANICO Canelones	*An excellent balance between acids, tannins and fruit. Good, soft fruit and a long finish.*	£6.00	DIR JSM	B

SPAIN

While Spain struggles to come to terms with tired old Riojas, which continue to appear on the UK market, other more daring and modern winemakers such as Marqués de Griñon, the Lurton brothers and Hugh Ryman tour the country making fabulous modern wines. Thankfully their lead is being followed by dynamic producers such as Enate and Raimat. Jerez produced some fine wines particularly from small Bodegas de Almacenado. In the whites, modern fresh styles are to the fore especially from Albariño and Rueda. Olé

SPAIN • RED

MONASTRELL TINTO 1997, J. GARCIA CARRION Jumilla	*A supple, fruit and raisin wine that offers complexity you would not expect from this area.*	£3.00	ASD	(B)
SIERRA ALTA MERLOT 1997, SANTA RITA La Mancha	*Sweet juicy summer fruits with soft tannins leading to a delicious jammy finish.*	£3.30	SAF	(B)
CO-OP CHESTNUT GULLY 1996, BODEGAS CASTANOD Yecla	*Light, fresh fruity style with bags of cherry fruit, light acidity and low tannins.*	£3.50	CWS	(B)
VIÑA CALIZA CRIANZA 1993, BODEGAS FELIX SOLIS Valdepeñas	*Fruity with fresh raspberry, cherry fruit. Jammy texture, sweet tannins and easy finish.*	£3.50	FUL KWI	(B)
GANDIA CABERNET SAUVIGNON CRIANZA 1996, VICENTE GANDIA Utiel - Requena	*Clean, light, blackcurrant aromas are found on a palate of ripe, jammy fruits and balancing tannins.*	£3.50	CWS CRS PLB	(B)

CASA DE LA VIÑA JOVEN 1997, BODEGAS Y BEBIDAS Valdepeñas	*Fresh, lively with jammy cherry fruit, some sweet tannins and prickly, gentle acidity.*	£3.70	WCR DBY NYW	Ⓑ
AZABACHE TEMPRANILLO 1997, VIÑEDOS DE ALDEANUEVA CO-OP Rioja	*With an impressive sprinkling of spice the palate is treated to an array of hot fruit.*	£3.80	PLB	Ⓑ
CASTILLO DE LIRIA HOYA VALLEY TEMPRANILLO CRIANZA 1993, VICENTE GANDIA Utiel - Requena	*Lovely soft wines from west of Valencia. Fruity with warm flavours, light tannins and a fresh finish.*	£3.80	PLB	Ⓑ
MORALINOS TEMPRANILLO 1996, MORALES DEL TORO Toro	*Quite firm fruit with chewy tannins and a good, strong flavoured fruit driven palate.*	£3.90	JNW MOR WSO BOO	Ⓑ
VIÑA ARMANTES TEMPRANILLO 1997, CO-OP SAN GREGORIO Calatayud	*Glorious attacking intensity on the front palate. Cedar, tobacco and warm meatiness complements with sweet fruit.*	£4.00	IWS MWW	Ⓢ
CO-OP SPANISH PYRENEES TEMPRANILLO CABERNET SAUVIGNON 1996, COVISA Somontano	*Pleasing blend of two classics. Warm vanilla flavours backed by underlying blackberry and cassis notes.*	£4.00	CWS	Ⓢ
VIÑA ALBALI VALDEPEÑAS RESERVA 1991, VIÑA ALBALI Valdepeñas	*A smoky fruit nose offers a slightly chewy, cherry-like palate. Supple and light, good length.*	£4.00	BUP THS WRC	Ⓑ
VIÑA ALBALI OAK-AGED CABERNET SAUVIGNON 1993, BODEGAS FELIX SOLIS Valdepenas	*Brilliant value for this superior wine. Soft and easy drinking with low tannins and a lovely oaky feel.*	£4.00	CRS ASD	Ⓑ

SPAIN • RED

PERDIDO CABERNET SAUVIGNON CRIANZA 1995, CO-OPERATIVA MURCHANTINA Navarra	*Vibrant black cherry fruit with mint and eucalypt, the tannin is quite grippy but it finishes well.*	£4.00	TOS	B
PREFERIDO TEMPRANILLO NV, VIÑA HERMINIA Rioja	*A well endowed Rioja, yielding firm tannins and voluptuous fruit on the lengthy, ambitious finish.*	£4.00	PLB	B
GANDIA HOYA DE CADENAS RESERVA 1991, VICENTE GANDIA Utiel-Requena	*Warm damson nose followed by generous fruit on a warm palate of cherries and jam.*	£4.00	CRS PLB	B
SIERRA ALTA CABERNET SAUVIGNON 1997, SANTA RITA La Mancha	*With a vibrant purple hue, it offers much more than the region promises – surprisingly lengthy.*	£4.00	SMF	B
VIÑA ALBALI RESERVA 1991, BODEGAS FELIX SOLIS Valdepenas	*Firm fruits and hard tannins indicate its youthful nature. It has significant development potential.*	£4.10	CRS ASD FUL THS WRC BUP	B
SANTARA CABERNET SAUVIGNON MERLOT 1996, HUGH RYMAN & CONCAVINS Conca De Barbera	*Minty blackcurrant aromas are reflected on the well structured palate of this flying winemaker's wine.*	£4.20	CWS RYW FUL THS WRC BUP	B
BASO GARNACHA 1996, COMPANIA DE VINOS DE LA GRANJA Navarra	*A supple, simple wine which is ambitious enough to offer delicate raspberry fruit with firm tannins.*	£4.30	Widely Available	B
TEMPRANILLO FUENTE DEL RITMO 1996, BODEGA CENTRO ESPANOLES La Mancha	*This wine belies its La Mancha origins. Excellent quality with chewy fruit and soft vanillan tannins.*	£4.40	ASD ODD FUL THS WRC BUP	B

LAS CAMPANAS TINTO 1996, VINICOLA DE NAVARRA Navarra	*Soft on the nose but full to bursting on the palate, tasting like cherry ice cream*	£4.40	WCR DBY HVW NYW COK POR ODD	(B)
ESPIRAL TEMPRANILLO 1997, BODEGAS PIRINEOS Somontano	*Much improved wines from this area. Rich juicy fruit with well defined tannin and acidity.*	£4.50	IWS ODD ASD FUL	(B)
MARQUÉS DE MONISTROL MERLOT 1994, ARCO BODEGAS UNIDAS Penedés	*Rich mature fruit on a juicy palate of cherries with tight tannins and an elegant finish.*	£4.50	D&D CWS	(B)
BERBARANA DRAGON TEMPRANILLO 1996, ARCO BODEGAS UNIDAS Rioja	*Dried fruit flavours predominate, concentrated and sugary, almost fruit-cakey; is countered by astringent tannins.*	£4.50	CWS BWC SAF SMF FUL KWI	(B)
MORALINOS GARNACHA 1996, MORALES DE TORO Toro	*A nose of cherry and white pepper, onto a similar palate backed by strong fruit and rich tannin.*	£4.50	MOR BOO NYW	(B)
AGAPITO JUMILLA RESERVA 1994, AGAPITO RICO Jumilla	*A rich, juicy garnet colour gleams in the glass presenting soft fruit, marrying well with oak.*	£4.50	JSM	(B)
TEMPRANILLO FUENTE DEL RITMO RESERVA 1994, BODEGAS CENTRO ESPANOLES La Mancha	*Smooth and easy drinking, this has warm oak flavours on its creamy palate of rounded tannins.*	£4.60	SAF	(B)
BODEGAS PALACIO RESERVA ESPECIAL 1994, BODEGAS PALACIO Rioja	*Lively crushed fruits mingle in the mouth, vying for attention with the earthy, farm-yardiness ton the length.*	£4.70	ODF WTS THS WRC	(B)

SPAIN • RED

MARQUÉS DE GRIÑON TEMPRANILLO RIOJA 1996, MARQUÉS DE GRIÑON Rioja	*Baked slightly spiced on the palate with warm prune flavours moving towards an arid finish.*	£5.00	Widely Available	**B**
CAMPARRON TINTO 1997, BODEGAS FRANCISCO CASAS Toro	*Strong dark cassis fruit with damson and wood notes. There is pleasing tannin and good acidity too.*	£5.00	PLB	**B**
HÉCULA MONASTRELL CABERNET SAUVIGNON MERLOT 1996, BODEGAS CASTAÑO Yecla	*Impressive blend of ripe cassis and rich burnt cherry flavours on this well made wine.*	£5.00	ASD	**B**
MARQUÉS DE GRIÑON DURIUS TINTO 1996, RIBERO DEL MARQUÉS DE GRIÑON Duero	*An expansive, classy, black cherry laden liquid. Well-balanced with round juicy prune fruit, fleshy and textured.*	£5.20	WCR SEL D&D NEI BTH NYW FUL	**S**
SENORIO DE LOS LLANOS CRIANZA 1994, BODEGAS LOS LLANOS Valdepeñas	*A developed marmitey nose, almost minerally with hints of smoky vanilla and a gentle finish.*	£5.20	Widely Available	**B**
VIÑA HERMINIA CRIANZA 1995, VIÑA HERMINIA Rioja	*The deep crimson colour reflects the juicy nature of the wine within, young and fresh.*	£5.30	PLB	**B**
TORRES SANGRE DE TORO 1996, MIGUEL TORRES Penedés	*Quite lean and austere, brambley fruit. Some light tannins and a pleasant finish.*	£5.40	Widely Available	**B**
LAR DE BARROS TINTO RESERVA 1994, BODEGAS INVIOSA Ribeiro del Guadia	*With a faint whiff of rubber, tasters found that the chocolate and coffee finish bonded together well.*	£5.40	ADN DBY PFT CHF	**B**

BACH MERLOT 1996, BACH Penedés	*Minty herbaceous notes on a blackcurrant nose with smoky black fruit flavours on the palate.*	£5.50	CON SAF	B
GRAN FEUDO TINTO RESERVA 1994, BODEGAS JULIAN CHIVITE Navarra	*An interesting wild mushroom bombardment excited the tasters, although they found the finish a little short.*	£5.50	DIR COK ODD DBY THS WRC BUP	B
MURUVE CRIANZA 1994, BODEGAS FRUTOS VILLAR Toro	*An inky blackcurrant liquid oozes into flavours of spiced brambles tucked inside huge tannins.*	£5.60	Widely Available	B
DOMINIO DE MONTALVO 1995, BODEGAS Y BEBIDAS Rioja	*A soft intense red which has a significant amount of restrained dried fruit and chewy tannins.*	£5.60	Widely Available	B
PALACIO DE LA VEGA RESERVE TEMPRANILLO 1994, P R LARIOS Navarra	*An aromatic redcurrant nose shows a complex palate of charred oak and creamy vanilla.*	£5.70	DBY BAB SOH AWS	B
SENORIO DE LOS LLANOS GRAN RESERVA 1990, BODEGAS LOS LLANOS Valdepeñas	*Influenced by creamy oak this is terrific value for money with its soft rounded fruit and warm finish.*	£5.80	Widely Available	B
NAVAJAS TINTO CRIANZA 1993, BODEGAS NAVAJAS Rioja	*Warm, plump fruits with lanolin aromas. An oily, sleek palate with excellent balance of fruit and acidity.*	£5.90	JNW M&V HOU MOR BOO DBY	S
PIEDMONTE CABERNET SAUVIGNON CRIANZA 1995, BODEGAS PIEDMONTE Navarra	*Velvety tobacco and cedar edges which were mirrored in abundance on the palate alongside the delicate fine tannins.*	£6.00	ADN	S

SENOR ATARES RESERVA 1992, BODEGAS ATARES Campo de Borja	*An intense gamey perfume integrates well with the tough vanilla backbone. Drinking beautifully now.*	£6.00	UNS	B
MARQUIS DE GRIÑON CRIANZA 1996, MARQUIS DE GRIÑON Rioja	*A tangy robust red with a splattering of oak and chocolate coated plums. Drinking well now.*	£6.00	WCR BUP RBS	B
GUELBENZU CABERNET SAUVIGNON TEMPRANILLO 1995, GUELBENZU Navarra	*Warm aromas of baked blackcurrants dominate the nose and palate of this softly finishing wine.*	£6.10	Widely Available	B
MARQUÉS DE CACERES RED 1994, MARQUÉS DE CACERES Rioja	*A little coarse on the nose, it reverts to flavours of punnets of cherries and mature spices.*	£6.20	Widely Available	S
CONDE DE VALDEMAR CRIANZA 1995, BODEGAS MARTINEZ BUJANDA Rioja	*The tasters savoured the musky damson fruit which evolved into dense, tangy blackberries with belts of leathery structure.*	£6.20	Widely Available	S
EL PORTICO 1995, BODEGAS PALACIO Rioja	*A wine that certainly has its loyal following. It has bags of vanilla and leather.*	£6.50	SEL ODD HVW WSO	B
PATA NEGRA GRAN RESERVA 1991, BODEGAS LOS LLANOS Valdepeñas	*Rich smooth fruit on a mature palate, quite elegant with lifted tannins, some acidity and a creamy finish.*	£6.50	SEL DBY L&S ADW COC VLW AMW	B

Pinpoint who sells the wine you wish to buy by turning to the stockist codes. If you know the name of the wine you want to buy, use the alphabetical index. If the price is your motivation, refer to the invaluable price guide index; red and white wines under £5, sparkling wines under £12 and Champagne under £16. Happy hunting!

PRIMICIA ABADIA RETUERTA 1996, ABADIA RETUERTA Sardon Del Duero	*A broad, evolved wine which delivers a cocktail of cooked, dried fruit compote. Bitter chocolate finish.*	£6.60	DIR GGW HVW WIM CCL NYW	**B**
COSME PALACIO Y HERMANOS 1996, BODEGAS PALACIO Rioja	*Deep, dark, tight and straight down the line. A punchy, proud Rioja. Austere but approachable.*	£6.70	WCR SEL ODD HVW SAF WTS	**B**
RAIMAT CABERNET SAUVIGNON 1994, RAIMAT ESTATE Costers del Segre	*Blackberry and damson aromas lead onto a rich summer fruits palate with good length.*	£6.70	DBY CON HVW BUP THS WRC	**B**
NAVAJAS TINTO CRIANZA 1995, BODEGAS NAVAJAS Rioja	*Splendid crafted wine with a nose of damsons and soft fruit. The palate confirms this and throws in some lovely tannin too.*	£6.80	Widely Available	**G**
VIÑA HERMINIA RESERVA 1994, VIÑA HERMINIA Rioja	*Rubbery, warm nose. Big and bold with a hot finish reflecting the warm climate fruit.*	£6.80	PLB	**B**
BARON DE LEY RIOJA RESERVA 1994, BARON DE LEY Rioja	*A portly Rioja of enormous proportions, with obvious green, stalky tannins. Maurre fruit mingles with cedar and cigar aromas.*	£6.90	CWS ASD THS	**S**
FAMILIA MARTINEZ BUJANDA CRIANZA 1995, BODEGAS MARTINEZ BUJANDA Rioja	*A complex wine with elegant, juicy summer fruits all of which were wrapped up in soft, silky tannins.*	£6.90	HVW BDR	**S**
CONDE DE SIRUELA CRIANZA 1994, BODEGAS SANTA EULALIA Ribera del Duero	*Earthy nose and obviously still young. Flavours are generous, gripping tannins with intense chocolate coated spices.*	£7.00	L&S TSM SAF	**S**

SPAIN • RED

RAIMAT CABERNET SAUVIGNON 1993, RAIMAT ESTATE Costers del Segre	*An elegant wine that needs to be enjoyed now while at its peak of maturity.*	£7.00	CON BUP	B
BERBERANA RESERVA 1994, BODEGAS BERBERANA Rioja	*A good seasoning of black pepper with a twist of tangy fruit and astringent tannins.*	£7.00	D&D A&A MWW DBY BWC FUL	B
MARQUÉS DE VELILLA TINTO CRIANZA 1995, MARQUÉS DE VELILLA Ribera Del Duero	*Strong dry fruits with rich tannins. Plum and spice notes lead to a cracking finish.*	£7.30	JNW MOR BOO WRC BUP	B
VALDUERO CRIANZA 1995, BODEGAS VALDUERO Ribera del Duero	*An understated nose hides rich raisins, coffee and tobacco with glimpses of bitter chocolate. Needs time.*	£7.40	L&S BEL COC WIC TOS VLW WRC BUP	S
SIGLO RESERVA 1992, BODEGAS AGE Rioja	*The wine manages to maintain a huge amount of berry fruit, all wrapped up in a creamy palate.*	£7.50	MTL HOU DBY	S
ARTADI VIÑAS DE GAIN RIOJA CRIANZA 1995, BODEGAS ARTADI Rioja	*Wonderful cedary notes with a classic architecture which balances stewed fruits and firm tannins successfully.*	£7.60	GON CNL MWW ODD NYW GNW	B
LAR DE LARES GRAN RESERVA 1992, BODEGAS INVIOSA Almendralejo	*The tasters enjoyed the lengthy, concentrated flavours of warm black current compote and creamy, toasted oak.*	£7.70	HAS DBY PFT ADN	B
RIVOLA ABADIA RETUERTA 1996, ABADIA RETUERTA Sardon Del Duero	*Elegantly perfumed red berry fruit assail the senses. An approachable palate of plums and bitter chocolate.*	£7.80	JNW DIR GGW CCL VWE HVW WIM	S

CASTILLO LABASTIDA RIOJA CRIANZA 1995, UNION COSECHEROS DE LABASTIDA Rioja	*Vanillan oak on a plum and spice nose. This has lovely berry fruit on its enticing palate.*	£8.00	BDR	**G**
VIÑA ALCORTA RESERVA 1993, BODEGAS Y BEBIDAS Rioja	*Mature wild mushroom aromas join with the weighty palate. Stewed plums are doused with butterscotch.*	£8.00	BNK	**S**
SEÑORÍO DE LAZÁN SOMONTANO RESERVA 1993, BODEGAS PIRINEOS Somontano	*Beautifully crafted with dense plum and damson fruit all wrapped up in a parcel of sweet oak.*	£8.00	IWS	**B**
CONDE DE VALDEMAR RESERVA 1992, BODEGAS MARTINEZ BUJANDA Rioja	*A cultivated, farmyardy nose. Stewed fruits rest on the edge and will deliver for some years to come.*	£8.20	Widely Available	**S**
MARQUIS DE GRIÑON RESERVA 1993, MARQUÍS DE GRIÑON Rioja	*A Rioja in the most traditional sense; with an obvious woody edge and meaty tannins.*	£8.20	NYW WRC	**B**
VIÑA DIEZMO RIOJA RESERVA 1994, BODEGAS PRIMICIA Rioja	*Toasty damson fruit integrates well with the complex tannins. Will open up but needs time.*	£8.40	DIR BDR	**B**
MARQUÉS DE RISCAL RESERVA 1994, MARQUÉS DE RISCAL Rioja	*A soft nose leads onto a palate of soft cherry fruit with some spice and plum feel.*	£8.50	MTL GRT HOU TPE A&A UNS HOT MWW	**S**
FAMILIA MARTINEZ BUJANDA RESERVA 1993, BODEGAS MARTINEZ BUJANDA Rioja	*A lovely mature wine with ripe plum fruit, decent yet restrained tannins and just enough acidity.*	£8.60	HVW BDR	**B**

Wine	Tasting Notes	Price	Stockists	
BARON DE ONA RESERVA 1994, TORRE DE ONA Rioja	*Sweet woody notes on the damson palate with ripe vanilla overtones and succulent tannins.*	**£8.60**	FSW DBY L&S L&W LOC VLW AMW	F
MONTECILLO VIÑA MONTY GRAN RESERVA 1989, BODEGAS MONTECILLO Rioja	*Drinking now this dusty liquorice Rioja has developed a maturity difficult to find at this price.*	**£8.80**	HBJ ODD	M
SANTARA CARBONELL CABERNET SAUVIGNON 1995, HUGH RYMAN & CONCAVINS Conca De Barbera	*Aromas of forest fruits with herbal, minty chocolate notes develop on the full, lingering palate of blackcurrants and vanilla.*	**£9.00**	RYW	S
JUAN RAMON MADRID RESERVA DE LA FAMILIA RIOJA RESERVA 1994, BODEGAS PRIMICIA Rioja	*A powerful, concentrated nose. A palate of tobacco, vanilla and a substantial, harmonious acid finish.*	**£9.00**	DIR BDR	S
MARQUÉS DE GRIÑON VALDEPUSA PETIT VERDOT 1995, MARQUÉS DE GRIÑON Malppica de Tajo	*Unusual but works well with its dry fruit flavours, lively tannins and brisk acidity wrapped in smooth red fruits.*	**£9.00**	D&D	F
MARQUÉS DE GRIÑON RIOJA RESERVA 1993, MARQUÉS DE GRIÑON Rioja	*With a "fresh from the chicken house" sort of smell the tasters loved this pungent direct wine.*	**£9.00**	D&D BWC NYW WRC BUP	F
LUIS CAÑAS RIOJA RESERVA 1989, BODEGAS LUIS CAÑAS Rioja	*Tasters marked this as an approachable wine with developed spicy flavours and a surprising tart finish.*	**£9.00**	BDR	F
MARQUÉS DE MURRIETA TINTO RESERVA 1993, DOMINOS DE CREIXELL Rioja	*A superb Rioja exhibiting vegetal, heady berry vapours, but with another dimension of spiced oranges.*	**£9.20**	Widely Available	S

BERBERANA GRAN RESERVA 1988, BODEGAS BERBERANA Rioja	*Mature with drying layered tannins, the fruit just holds up – lack of acidity says drink now.*	£9.20	D&D A&A MWW DBY FUL	(B)
MARQUÉS DE GRIÑON VALDEPUSA CABERNET SAUVIGNON, MARQUÉS DE GRIÑON Malppica de Tajo	*Dark deep cassis fruit-cake aromas with vanilla elements. The palate confirms with its opulent feel.*	£9.50	D&D A&A MWW NYW FUL WRC BUP	(B)
CAMPO VIEJO TINTO GRAN RESERVA 1989, BODEGAS Y BEBIDAS Rioja	*Ever popular this is good solid stuff with its easy tannins, lifted fruits and generous vanilla palate.*	£9.70	Widely Available	(B)
ENATE CABERNET SAUVIGNON RESERVA 1994, BODEGAS ENATE Somontano	*A lovely oaky feel to this rich seductive red with its creamy oak and rich dried cassis fruit.*	£9.90	WCR DIR HOH AVB HOU ODD DBY FUL	(B)
RAIMAT ABADIA RESERVA 1989, RAIMAT ESTATE Costers del Segre	*Firmer and drier this has developed into a beauty with its soft fruits and backbone of warm tannin and low acidity.*	£10.00	CON FRT	(S)
PAGO DE CARRAOVEJAS 1994, BODEGAS OCHOA Ribera del Duero	*Characterised by a heavy, musty nose. The palate is in complete contrast, fat and rich.*	£10.00	WCR POR VWE DBY BOO THS WRC	(B)
RAIMAT CABERNET SAUVIGNON RESERVA 1987, RAIMAT ESTATE Costers del Segre	*Well integrated flavours and aromas of baked black fruits with vanilla and spice nuances.*	£10.00	CON TOS	(B)
MONTESIERRA CABERNET SAUVIGNON TEMPRANILLO CRIANZA 1995, BODEGAS PIRINEOS Somontano	*This blend works well with the blackberry cassis fruit of Cabernet matching the damsons and plums of Tempranillo.*	£10.00	IWS	(B)

SPAIN • RED

Wine	Description	Price	Availability	
MARQUÉS DE MURRIETA TINTO RESERVA ESPECIAL 1991, DOMINOS DE CREIXELL Rioja	*An impetuously natured wine with a healthy dose of stewed blackcurrant fruit and pungent vanilla.*	**£10.90**	Widely Available	**B**
CONDE DE VALDEMAR GRAN RESERVA 1991, BODEGAS MARTINEZ BUJANDA Rioja	*Still fairly young yet it has much to endear it, a leatheriness, a flash of sweetness and a refined elegance.*	**£11.10**	Widely Available	**S**
CONDE DE VALDEMAR GRAN RESERVA 1990, BODEGAS MARTINEZ BUJANDA Rioja	*Ageing indicated by the mature brown rim. Of the Rioja old school; forthright and confident in its oxidised, dried fruit style.*	**£11.20**	Widely Available	**S**
FAUSTINO I GRAN RESERVA 1991, FAUSTINO Rioja	*A cigar box treasure all the more approachable by the concentrated cassis on the mid palate. Stunning complexity.*	**£11.30**	Widely Available	**S**
EVO TINTO CRIANZA 1994, BODEGAS GUELBENZU Navarra	*Quite Bordelais in style but the use of Tempranillo gives this a lovely silky feel to its generous palate.*	**£11.30**	MOR DBY MWW BOO	**B**
VIÑA ARDANZA RESERVA 1990, LA RIOJA ALTA Rioja	*Superb wine with its smoky nose, developed rich palate of fruit cherries, plums and spice with perfect balancing tannins.*	**£11.70**	Widely Available	**G** TROPHY WINE
MURIEL RIOJA GRAN RESERVA 1985, BODEGAS MURIEL Rioja	*A vital wine which breathes fleshy ripe fruit, although fading slightly still has a lot to offer.*	**£12.60**	HOU DBY HVW	**B**
CAMPILLO TINTO GRAN RESERVA 1988, BODEGAS CAMPILLO Rioja	*A seductively smoky wine with a mellow vanilla mid palate which develops into a lingering finish.*	**£13.20**	DBY WTS PLB	**B**

JEAN LÉON CABERNET SAUVIGNON RESERVA 1991, JEAN LÉON Penedés	*Prunes and leather on the nose with warm, plummy black fruits on the integrated palate.*	£13.60	JEF GGW JCB SCA ROD (B)
MARTINEZ BUJANDA GARNACHA RESERVA 1991, BODEGAS MARTINEZ BUJANDA Rioja	*Sweet strawberry fruit bursts in the mouth, ending in a crescendo of hot, fat alcohol.*	£13.70	JNW HVW TPE VEX BDR WRC (B)
BARON DE CHIREL RESERVA 1991, MARQUÉS DE RISCAL Rioja	*Over the top ever so slightly – tasters were assailed with coconut, sweaty saddles and marmalade!*	£14.00	LPD (B)
ALVARO PALACIOS PRIORATO LES TERRASSES 1995, ALVARO PALACIOS Priorato	*A spicy aromatic nose leads to brisk tannins on a slightly cooked palate.*	£17.50	DIR BUP WRC (B)
CASTILLO YGAY TINTO GRAN RESERVA 1989, DOMINOS DE CREIXELL Rioja	*Offering plenty of morrello cherries and lean tannins this wine is formidable in its gutsy attitude.*	£17.80	Widely Available (B)
MARQUÉS DE RISCAL GRAN RESERVA 1988, MARQUÉS DE RISCAL Rioja	*A little dusty, but with a surprising amount of maturity and depth on the rich vanillan palate.*	£18.00	VLW (B)
RIOJA GRAN RESERVA 904 1989, LA RIOJA ALTA Rioja	*Firm fruit, tight tannins and balanced acidity indicate the wine's age. Exceedingly elegant and delicate.*	£18.70	Widely Available (B)
TORRES MAS LA PLANA GRAN CORONAS PAGO 1993, MIGUEL TORRES Penedés	*Plummy currants and vanilla aromas are carried over to the intense palate of minty blackcurrants.*	£19.30	Widely Available (B)

MISERERE 1995, COSTERS DEL SIURANA Priorato	*Divided opinion marked this wine; some thought it big and fruity, others found hard tannins.*	£21.60	L&S TOS VLW NYW	B
CLOS DE L'OBAC TINTO 1995, COSTERS DEL SIURANA Priorato	*A sizeable robust wine which reeks of rotting vegetation. A love it or loathe it wine.*	£28.60	SEL GON L&W DBY L&S VLW NYW	B
ALVARO PALACIOS PRIORATO FINCA DOFI 1994, ALVARO PALACIOS Priorato	*Minerally tones greeted the tasters which stood side by side with the dark damson and lush loganberry fruit.*	£47.70	DIR BUP WRC	S

SPAIN • WHITE

SANTARA CHARDONNAY 1997, HUGH RYMAN & CONCAVINS Conca De Barbera	*Ripe nose of tropical melons and mangos precede a palate of zappy citrus fruits and flint.*	£4.00	CWS ODD RYW JSM FUL THS WRC BUP	B
BASA 1997, COMPANIA DE VINOS DE LA GRANJA Rueda	*A big muscular wine with aggressive gooseberry characters and citrus fruit. Slightly disjointed middle palate.*	£4.50	Widely Available	B
TORRES VIÑA SOL 1997, MIGUEL TORRES Penedés	*Creamy buttery nose with fragrant, light citrus fruit on the palate balanced with moderate acidity.*	£4.70	Widely Available	B
CON CLASS BLANCO 1997, BODEGAS CON CLASS Rueda	*Clean melony fruit on the nose. A dry but balanced palate with a persistent finish.*	£4.70	POR MOR HVW KWI BOO	B

MARQUÉS DE GRIÑON DURIUS BLANCO 1996, ARCO BODEGAS UNIDAS Ribera del Duero	*Pungent lemon grass nose with an exotic floral complexity. Palate of citrus and grapefruit characters.*	£4.80	WCR D&D NEI BTH BWC FUL	(S)
PALACIO DE BORNOS 1997, BODEGAS DE CRIANZA DE CASTILLA LA VIEJA Rueda	*Excellent middle palate weight and a tight structure. Its only downside is a slight bitter finish.*	£5.20	COK C&D SHJ HVW	(S)
ALBACORA VERDEJO CHARDONNAY 1997, VIÑA BLANCOS DE CASTILLA Rueda	*Leesy, with a lovely toasty flavour. Greengages and pineapples lead to an intense and fabulous finish.*	£5.30	CWS ODD RYW	(S)
DOMINIO DE MONTALVO 1995, BODEGAS CAMPO VIEJO Rioja	*This sleek and glossy wine provides a subtle background of plump fruits. Finishes slightly short.*	£5.60	NRW HOU POR VWE NYW	(B)
MARQUÉS DE RISCAL SAUVIGNON BLANC 1997, MARQUÉS DE RISCAL Rueda	*Slight gooseberry aromas. Big fruit in the mouth and an oily texture with mineral characteristics.*	£5.80	SVT	(B)
MARQUÉS DE ALELLA CLASICO 1997, MARQUÉS DE ALELLA Alella	*Pale straw colour with enticing citrus nose. Palate of firm fruit, hints of aromatic spice. fine balance.*	£6.00	POR MOR DBY WSO BOO	(S)
FAMILIA MARTINEZ BUJANDA BLANCO 1996, BODEGAS MARTINEZ BUJANDA Rioja	*An elegant if oaky nose with a dry and nutty palate and a vanillan finish.*	£6.20	JNW HVW BDR	(B)
PAZO DE VILLAREI ALBARIÑO 1997, BODEGA PAZO DE VILLAREI Rias Baixas	*Bright fragrant nose with a fruit driven palate, combined with soft acidity and moderate length.*	£6.20	NRW DBY NYW	(B)

SPAIN • WHITE

CUNE BARREL FERMENTED WHITE RIOJA 1995, COMPAÑIA VINICOLA DEL NORTE DE ESPAÑA Rioja	*Touches of putty on the nose. A lean, crisp wine with a good, persistent finish.*	£6.80	WES SEL CVR CPW DBY SAF GNW	**B**
LAGAR DE CERVENA ALBARIÑO 1997, LAGAR DE FORENELOS Rias Baixas	*Delicate oak aromas integrated with peach characters on the nose and palate. Good balanced acidity.*	£7.40	Widely Available	**S**
RAIMAT CHARDONNAY SELECTION ESPECIAL 1996, RAIMAT ESTATE Costers del Segre	*Floral and fresh peach aromas, big peachy palate with pencil shaving characters on the finish.*	£9.00	CON	**B**
CONDES DE ALBAREI ALBARIÑO CARBALLO GALEGO 1996, BODEGAS SALNESUR Rias Biaxas	*Peaches, pink grapefruit and a hint of violets on the nose with a ripe fruit palate.*	£9.20	DBY VEX WBU	**B**
ENATÉ BARREL FERMENTED CHARDONNAY 1996, BODEGAS ENATÉ Somontano	*Biscuity and toasty aromas with ripe fruit characters, integrated four square oak and good length.*	£9.40	QWW DIR HOH ODD DBY AVE	**B**
TORRES FRANSOLA PAGO 1996, MIGUEL TORRES Penedés	*The palate has good, rich oak touches balanced by racy acidity and interesting soft, juicy fruit.*	£12.80	Widely Available	**S**
TORRES MILMANDA PAGO 1996, MIGUEL TORRES Penedés	*Buttery malo aromas with soft balanced fruit. Light creamy oak palate and hints of pepper.*	£15.90	Widely Available	**B**

Pinpoint who sells the wine you wish to buy by turning to the stockist codes. If you know the name of the wine you want to buy, use the alphabetical index. If the price is your motivation, refer to the invaluable price guide index; red and white wines under £5, sparkling wines under £12 and Champagne under £16. Happy hunting!

SPAIN • ROSÉ

FAMILIA MARTINEZ BUJANDA ROSADO 1997, BODEGAS MARTINEZ BUJANDA Rioja	*Delicate salmon colour with rich aromas and flavours of fresh strawberries. A clean finish.*	£5.80	BDR	B

SPAIN • SPARKLING

RAVENTOS I BLANC CAVA GRAN RESERVA 1993, JOSÉ MARIA RAVENTOS I BLANC Penedés	*Melony nose with good crisp acidity and nice yeasty tones. Clean finish and a good length.*	£10.00	WAW P&R	B
RAIMAT CAVA GRAN BRUT NV, RAIMAT ESTATE Penedés	*Fresh, biscuity nose with decent lemon palate and tones of bitter almonds. Well-balanced and good length.*	£10.00	CON	B

SPAIN • FORTIFIED

LA SACRISTÍA DE ROMATE AMONTILLADO SHERRY, SANCHEZ ROMATE Jerez	*The nose and palate are rich with hazelnut and orange peel. There is great depth.*	£6.00 (50cl)	EHL	S
LA SACRISTÍA DE ROMATE PEDRO XIMÉNEZ SHERRY, SANCHEZ ROMATE Jerez	*Full of finesse, laden with apricot and dates, which never seem to end on the continuous finish.*	£6.00 (50cl)	EHL	S

LA SACRISTÍA DE ROMATE OLOROSO SHERRY, SANCHEZ ROMATE Jerez	*A touch of caramel gives an impression of sweetness but this is definitely dry Oloroso.*	**£6.00** (50cl)	EHL	(B)
TESCO SUPERIOR MANZANILLA SHERRY, SANCHEZ ROMATE Jerez	*Clean slightly smoky aromas which persist to add complexity to the crisp, limey flavours.*	**£3.40** (37.5cl)	TOS	(B)
TESCO SUPERIOR OLOROSO SECO SHERRY, SANCHEZ ROMATE Jerez	*Caramel and coffee bean on the nose with dried figs and apricots on the palate.*	**£3.40** (37.5cl)	TOS	(G)
CO-OP AMONTILLADO SHERRY, LUIS CABALLERO Jerez	*Plenty of flavours to be found here. Layered with spicy nuts, seaweed and honeycomb.*	**£4.00**	CWS	(B)
ASDA FINO SHERRY, BODEGAS BARBADILLO Jerez	*A great Fino for those warm summer days when you're munching your way through some tapas.*	**£4.20**	ASD	(B)
SOMERFIELD MANZANILLA SHERRY, ESPINOSA DE LOS MONTEROS Jerez	*Good clean flor nose. An attractive floral, grapey palate with a long spicy finish.*	**£4.40**	SMF	(B)
SOMERFIELD AMONTILLADO SHERRY, ESPINOSA DE LOS MONTEROS Jerez	*Interesting complexity on the palate. Rich flavours of honeycomb, raisins and warm alcohol. Lingering finish.*	**£4.40**	SMF	(B)

Pinpoint who sells the wine you wish to buy by turning to the stockist codes. If you know the name of the wine you want to buy, use the alphabetical index. If the price is your motivation, refer to the invaluable price guide index; red and white wines under £5, sparkling wines under £12 and Champagne under £16. Happy hunting!

SOMERFIELD CREAM SHERRY, GONZALEZ BYASS Jerez	*Mouth filling spiced fruits offsets slightly spirity nose. Sweet but with a nice dry finish.*	£4.40	SMF	(B)
SANCHEZ ROMATE PALO CORTADO SUPERIOR SHERRY, BODEGAS SANCHEZ ROMATE Jerez	*A sherry like no other tempting you to immerse yourself in its endless sweet and savoury depths.*	£4.50 (37.5cl)	TOS	(G)
MANZANILLA "LA GOYA" SHERRY, BODEGAS DELGADO ZULETA Jerez	*All the tangy sea salt and lemon zest freshness associated with this very particular style of Fino.*	£5.40 (37.5cl)	MFS C&D	(S)
PANDO DRY FINO SHERRY, BODEGAS WILLIAMS & HUMBERT Jerez	*Nice honey and sugar almond flavours make this a richer style of Fino. A real mouth filler.*	£6.20	CFT CST	(S)
SAFEWAY'S CREAM SHERRY, BODEGAS LUIS CABALLERO Jerez	*Nice orange marmalade character, a touch of zest and good balance make this a cut above the rest.*	£6.60 (1 litre)	SAF	(S)
DOS CORTADO OLOROSO SHERRY, BODEGAS WILLIAMS & HUMBERT Jerez	*A wealth of dried orange peel, muscovado sugar and caramelised walnut flavours, to name but a few.*	£9.70	MFS SEL DBY BDR NYW GNW	(S)
DON P.X. GRAN RESERVA 1972, BODEGAS TORO ALBALA Montilla	*Wonderful textured, full-on hint of raisins makes this unmistakably Pedro Ximénez. Long, silken finish.*	£10.00	MOR	(S)
PEDRO ROMERO OLOROSO DRY SHERRY, PEDRO ROMERO Jerez	*Rich dry Oloroso with lots of vanilla and spice and a lively orange peel finish.*	£10.00	EBC	(B)

PEDRO ROMERO OLOROSO CREAM SHERRY, PEDRO ROMERO Jerez	*A sip of this nutty, raisiny and tangy beauty will send your tastebuds to nirvana.*	£10.30	EBC	**G**
MATUSALEM OLOROSO DULCE MUY VIEJO SHERRY, GONZALEZ BYASS	*Big toffee and nut flavours rounded with dried apricots and macadamias. Huge length.*	£18.00	Widely Available	**B**
OLOROSO RARE SHERRY SOLERA INDIA SHERRY, BODEGAS OSBORNE Jerez	*A very old style of sweet sherry. Rich and walnuty with a sweetness that is never cloying.*	£18.40	HBJ GON GDS DBY	**G**
APOSTOLES PALO CORTADO MUY VIEJO SHERRY, GONZALEZ BYASS Jerez	*Full of beautifully balanced flavours. Initial palate of walnuts, toffee and spice finishing with zesty fresh Fino acidity.*	£19.90	BNK MTL DBY VLW	**S**
AMONTILLADO DEL DUQUE SHERRY, GONZALEZ BYASS Jerez	*A delicately nutty, well-balanced Amontillado with a long herbacious finish.*	£20.20	ADN BNK ODD DBY VLW	**B**
PRESTIGE HIJO DE PEDRO ROMERO VILLA REAL 40 YEAR OLD PALO CORTADO, PEDRO ROMERO Jerez	*Not quite an Oloroso, not quite an Amontillado, it is packed with Christmas cake and orange curaçao.*	£29.00	EBC	**G**
PEDRO ROMERO 40 YEAR OLD PALO CORTADO SHERRY, PEDRO ROMERO Jerez	*Pale in colour with an intense nutty nose. Fresh and zesty palate even though it's over 40!*	£29.00	EBC	**S**

Pinpoint who sells the wine you wish to buy by turning to the stockist codes. If you know the name of the wine you want to buy, use the alphabetical index. If the price is your motivation, refer to the invaluable price guide index; red and white wines under £5, sparkling wines under £12 and Champagne under £16. Happy hunting!

OTHER COUNTRIES

We were disappointed to relegate English wines to this section after their excellent showing last year. Hopefully this is only due to the vagaries of the English summer and we look forward to a speedy return to the halcyon days. Greece continues its revival, producing new style wines from classical grapes and we welcome Switzerland to the fold of WINE Challenge medal winners. As this section grows it can only benefit the consumer who craves a greater choice of quality wines. Good Hunting!

ENGLAND • RED

HIDDEN SPRING DARK FIELDS 1996, HIDDEN SPRING VINEYARD Weald and Downland	*A light perfume with raspberry notes, followed by a delicate body of zippy tannins and clean fruits.*	**£6.00**	HSV F&M EWC	(B)

ENGLAND • WHITE

CHAPEL DOWN SUMMERHILL OAKED WHITE NV, CHAPEL DOWN WINES Weald and Downland	*Light, youthful and fresh with soft fruits and touches of white pepper on the finish.*	**£4.30**	CDO BNK SEL CRS TOS WTS	(B)
CHAPEL DOWN BACCHUS 1997, CHAPEL DOWN WINES Weald and Downland	*Fresh and aromatic nose with clean, grassy, asparagus flavours, balanced and refreshing.*	**£5.80**	CDO BNK SEL HOT TOS	(B)

Pinpoint who sells the wine you wish to buy by turning to the stockist codes. If you know the name of the wine you want to buy, use the alphabetical index. If the price is your motivation, refer to the invaluable price guide index; red and white wines under £5, sparkling wines under £12 and Champagne under £16. Happy hunting!

GREECE • RED

RAPSANI TSANTALI AGED WINE 1994, E. TSANTALIS Thessaly	*A plump, rich and jammy nose with a dark, chewy palate and a dusty finish.*	£6.00	DIR	(F)
BOUTARI AGIORGITIKO 1994, J. BOUTARI & SON Nemea	*A wonderfully concentrated flavour with delicious liquorice and spice hints followed by a dusty finish.*	£8.00	ODD	(F)
AMETHYSTOS CABERNET SAUVIGNON 1993, DOMAIN CONSTANTIN LAZARIDIS Drama	*Ripe flavours of blackberries with hints of cedar wood, vanilla and mint on the palate.*	£10.50	GWC	(S)
MEGAS OENOS VQPRD 1995, GEORGE SKOURAS Peloponnese	*Inky, leathery blueberry fruit. Simple, well-rounded with a youthful structure and a lingering finish.*	£10.70	ODF GWC	(S)
DOMAINE HATZIMICHALIS MERLOT 1996, DOMAINE HATZIMICHALIS Central Greece	*Soft ripe fruit aromas are followed by jammy blackcurrant flavours with herbaceous notes on the palate.*	£13.50	GWC	(F)
DOMAINE HATZIMICHALIS CAVA RED 1994, DOMAINE HATZIMICHALIS Central Greece	*The colour shows maturity with big and full fruit; chocolate hints linger in the mouth.*	£13.50	GWC	(F)
CHÂTEAU SEMILI CABERNET SAUVIGNON MERLOT VIN DE PAYS D'ATTIQUE 1995, KTIMA KOKOTOS	*Deep ruby colour and smoky aromas. Stewed ripe fruit and a nice, well-integrated palate.*	£14.00	HWL SVT	(F)

GREECE • WHITE

HATZIMICHALIS ESTATE CHARDONNAY 1997, DOMAINE HATZIMICHALIS ESTATE Central Greece	*Simple, ripe melon fruit aromas are followed by a zippy citric finish to this uncomplicated wine.*	£7.50	GWC	(B)
AMETHYSTOS FUMÉ 1996, DOMAIN CONSTANTIN LAZARIDIS Drama	*A nose of melon and toasty oak. Rich, glossy palate leading to a pithy but crisp finish.*	£9.00	GWC	(S)
CHÂTEAU JULIA SEMILLION 1996, DOMAIN CONSTANTIN LAZARIDIS Adriani	*Golden yellow coloured with a vegetal nose. Hints of smoky oak and a tart finish.*	£9.00	GWC	(B)
GENTILINI CLASSICO 1997, NICHOLAS COSMETATOS Cephalonia	*This medium-bodied wine has a floral nose with light clean fruit and crisp acidity.*	£9.00	GEN GWC	(B)
GENTILINI ROBOLA 1997, NICHOLAS COSMETATOS Cephalonia	*Ripe banana with light floral tones on the nose. Fleshy fruit palate with good acidity.*	£9.00	GEN GWC	(B)
MOSCHOFILERO WHITE 1997, J. BOUTARI & SON Mantinia	*Tropical fruit with sweet pear characters balanced by mouth watering acid and a clean long finish.*	£9.70	CNL	(B)

Pinpoint who sells the wine you wish to buy by turning to the stockist codes. If you know the name of the wine you want to buy, use the alphabetical index. If the price is your motivation, refer to the invaluable price guide index; red and white wines under £5, sparkling wines under £12 and Champagne under £16. Happy hunting!

GREECE • FORTIFIED

SAMOS GREEK VIN DOUX NV, CO-OP SAMOS Samos	*A warming wine with interesting pine kernel and honeycomb aromas. Good length and balancing acidity.*	£3.00	SMF	B
KOURTAKI MAVRODAPHNE DE PATRAS NV, KOURTAKI Patras	*Intensely sweet aromas of jammy black fruits on a warm palate which has good balancing acidity.*	£4.10	CRS BTH JSM WTS KWI	B

ISRAEL • RED

SEGAL HARVEST RED 1995, SEGAL (ASKALON) WINES Samson	*Plummy blackcurrants on the smooth palate with nuances of oak, mint and cough medicine.*	£3.90	MHV	B

LEBANON • RED

HOCHAR PERE & FILS 1994, CHÂTEAU MUSAR Bekaa Valley	*Spicy oak, herbs, thyme and rosemary balanced by soft, concentrated cherry flavours and excellent balance.*	£7.60	Widely Available	B

Pinpoint who sells the wine you wish to buy by turning to the stockist codes. If you know the name of the wine you want to buy, use the alphabetical index. If the price is your motivation, refer to the invaluable price guide index; red and white wines under £5, sparkling wines under £12 and Champagne under £16. Happy hunting!

MALTA • WHITE

ST PAULS BAY WHITE 1997, EMMANUEL DELICATA	*This well-made wine consists of pineapples, pears and honey topped off with crisp acidity.*	£4.00	CRS VER ASD	**B**

SWITZERLAND • WHITE

TREMAILLE WHITE 1996, J B & D ROUVINEZ Valais	*The palate has a complex mixture of fruit, vanilla and herbal tones. A well rounded finish.*	£4.80	WTS	**S**
DEZALEY-MARSENS DE LA TOUR GRAND CRU 1996, LES FRERES DUBOIS ET FILS Vaud	*A delicately aromatic nose with spicy, warm fruit on the refreshing palate and good balance.*	£14.80	HRV	**B**

REDS • £5 AND UNDER

Colori Primitivo 1996, *Casalbaio*	£4.40	G
Rosso Conero Riserva 1995, *Terre Cortesi Moncaro*	£5.00	G
L'Arco Friuli Grave Cabernet Franc 1996, *Cantina di Bertiolo*	£5.00	G
Iambol Bulgarian Merlot 1997, *Iambol Winery*	£3.20	S
Tesco Cape Cinsault 1996, *Vinfruco*	£3.50	S
Terra Boa 1997, *Alianca*	£3.80	S
Vina Armantes Tempranillo 1997, *San Gregorio*	£4.00	S
Co-op Spanish Pyrenees Tempranillo Cabernet 1996, *Covisa*	£4.00	S
D'Istinto Sangiovese Merlot 1997, *BRL Hardy Wine Company*	£4.10	S
Espiga 1997, *Quinta Da Boavista*	£4.50	S
Dealul Viilor Merlot Special Reserve Barrel Matured 1994, *Vinexport*	£4.50	S
Ash Ridge Merlot 1997, *Maurel Vedeau*	£4.50	S
Merlot Trentino 1995, *Concilio Vini S.P.A*	£4.50	S
Syrah Les Bateaux 1996, *Lurton*	£4.50	S
Pinotage Impala 1997, *Goue Vallei*	£4.80	S
Merlot Trentino 1997, *Concilio Vini S.P.A*	£4.90	S
Fiuza Cabernet Sauvignon 1996, *Bright Bros*	£5.00	S
Gouts et Couleurs Syrah Mourvèdre 1997, *Cazal Viel*	£5.00	S
Montepulciano d'Abruzzo Chiaro di Luna 1997, *MGM Mondo Del Vino*	£5.00	S
Balbi Cabernet Sauvignon Barrel Reserve 1997, *Bodegas Balbi*	£5.00	S
Château La Boutignane Classique 1996, *Faiure*	£5.00	S
Angove's Stoneridge Shiraz 1996, *Angove's*	£5.00	S
Asda Bulgarian Merlot 1997, *Haskovo*	£3.00	B
BVC Iambol Merlot 1997, *Iambol*	£3.00	B
Venier Montepulciano d'Abruzzo 1996, *GIV*	£3.00	B
Falua 1997, *Sociedade de Vinhos*	£3.00	B
Monastrell Tinto 1997, *Garcia Carrion*	£3.00	B
Somerfield Syrah VDP d'Oc NV, *Jeanjean*	£3.00	B
Domaine Boyar Merlot 1997, *Iambol*	£3.30	B
Domaine Boyar Cabernet Sauvignon 1997, *Iambol*	£3.30	B
Sierra Alta Merlot 1997, *Santa Rita*	£3.30	B
Asda Argentinian Bonarda 1997, *La Agricola*	£3.30	B
Co-op Chestnut Gully 1996, *Bodegas Castanod*	£3.50	B
Viña Caliza Crianza 1993, *Felix Solis*	£3.50	B
Gandia Cabernet Sauvignon Crianza 1996, *Gandia*	£3.50	B
Cheval D'Or Merlot 1997, *Sieur d'Arques*	£3.50	B
J P Tinto Barrel Selection 1992, *J P Vinhos*	£3.60	B

Co-op Dão 1996, *V.I.S.O.*	£3.70	B
Tesco Bulgarian Reserve Cabernet Sauvignon 1993, *Viniprom Haskovo*	£3.70	B
Tesco Bulgarian Reserve Merlot 1992, *Viniprom Haskovo*	£3.70	B
Maranon Malbec 1997, *Maranon*	£3.70	B
Casa de la Viña Joven 1997, *Bodegas Y Bebidas*	£3.70	B
Rafael Estate Tempranillo 1997, *Hugh Ryman*	£3.80	B
Fortant de France Grenache 1997, *Skalli*	£3.80	B
Domaine Boyar Cabernet Sauvignon Reserve 1995, *Iambol*	£3.80	B
Idlerock Merlot Reserve 1996, *Hanwood Group*	£3.80	B
Rafael Esate Tempranillo 1997, *Ryman*	£3.80	B
Azabache Tempranillo 1997, *Viñedos de Aldeanueva Co-op*	£3.80	B
Castillo de Liria Hoya Valley Tempranillo Crianza 1993, *Gandia*	£3.80	B
Jacob's Creek Rowland Flat Grenache/Shiraz 1997, *Orlando Wines*	£3.90	B
Jarrah Ridge Soft Red 1996, *Kingston Estate Winery*	£3.90	B
Moralinos Tempranillo 1996, *Morales del Toro*	£3.90	B
Segal Harvest Red 1995, *Segal (Askalon) Wines*	£3.90	B
Safeway's Mendoza Oak Aged Tempranillo 1996, *La Agricola*	£4.00	B
Safeway's Australian Shiraz Ruby Cabernet 1997, *BRL Hardy Wine Company*	£4.00	B
Nero d'Avola 1997, *Firriato*	£4.00	B
Monte Cheval Vranac 1996, *Agrikombinat July 13*	£4.00	B
Vina Albali Valdepeñas Reserva 1991, *Vina Albali*	£4.00	B
Monte Cheval Vranac Reserve 1993, *Plantaze*	£4.00	B
Vina Albali Oak-Aged 1993, *Felix Solis*	£4.00	B
Kumala Cinsault Pinotage 1997, *SONOP*	£4.00	B
Perdido Cabernet Sauvignon Crianza 1995, *Murchantina*	£4.00	B
Frederic Roger Cabernet Sauvignon Merlot 1997, *F Roger*	£4.00	B
Camas Blanc Cabernet Sauvignon 1997, *F Roger*	£4.00	B
Tesco's Côtes du Rhône Villages 1997, *Princes de France*	£4.00	B
Unwins Argentinian Sangiovese Bonarda 1997, *La Agricola*	£4.00	B
B&G Cabernet Sauvignon 1997, *Barton & Guestier*	£4.00	B
Preferido Tempranillo NV, *Viña Herminia*	£4.00	B
Gandia Hoya de Cadenas Reserva 1991, *Gandia*	£4.00	B
La Chapelle de Cray Red 1996, *Chapelle de Cray*	£4.00	B
Ermitage du Pic St. Loup 1996, *Maurel Vedeau*	£4.00	B
Sierra Alta Cabernet Sauvignon 1997, *Santa Rita*	£4.00	B
Nero di Troia Primitivo 1997, *Bright Brothers*	£4.00	B
Gypsy Hill Oaked Merlot Cabernet Sauvignon 1997, *S.E.R.V.E.*	£4.00	B
Selected Release Cabernet Sauvignon 1996, *Suhindol*	£4.00	B
Fortant de France Syrah Cabernet Sauvignon 1997, *Skalli*	£4.10	B
Vina Albali Reserva 1991, *Felix Solis*	£4.10	B
Domaine Boyar Cabernet Sauvignon Special Reserve 1990, *Iambol*	£4.20	B
Co-op Jacaranda Hill Shiraz 1997, *Angove's*	£4.20	B

Santara Cabernet Sauvignon Merlot 1996, *Ryman & Concavins*	£4.20	B
Bodega J & F Lurton Mendoza Bonarda 1997, *Lurton*	£4.20	B
Le Joanis 1997, *Jean-Louis Chancel*	£4.20	B
Fortant de France Syrah 1997, *Skalli*	£4.30	B
Asda Arius Californian Carignane 1997, *California Direct*	£4.30	B
Baso Garnacha 1996, *Compania de Vinos de la Granja*	£4.30	B
Domaine Cabrairal Organic Red 1997, *Frelin*	£4.30	B
Côtes de St. Mont Rouge 1996, *Plaimont*	£4.30	B
Malt House Vintners South African Cabernet Sauvignon 1997, *SONOP*	£4.40	B
Tempranillo Fuente del Ritmo 1996, *Bodega Centro Espanoles*	£4.40	B
Las Campanas Tinto 1996, *Vinicola de Navarra*	£4.40	B
Terrasses de Guilhem Rouge 1997, *Moulin de Gassac*	£4.40	B
Marks & Spencer Domaine Jeune Counoise 1997, *Jeune*	£4.50	B
Espiral Tempranillo 1997, *Pirineos*	£4.50	B
Isla Negra Bonarda 1997, *Vina Patagonia*	£4.50	B
Somerfield South African Pinotage 1997, *SONOP*	£4.50	B
Chianti Superiore La Cinquantina Burchino 1996, *Castellani*	£4.50	B
Marques de Monistrol Merlot 1994, *Arco Bodegas Unidas*	£4.50	B
Berbarana Dragon Tempranillo 1996, *Arco Bodegas Unidas*	£4.50	B
Marques de Griñon Tempranillo Crianza 1997, *Arco Bodegas Unidas*	£4.50	B
Oak Village Pinotage Merlot 1996, *Oak Village*	£4.50	B
Moralinos Garnacha 1996, *Moralinos de Toro*	£4.50	B
Richemont Cabernet Sauvignon 1996, *Ryman*	£4.50	B
Santa Julia Sangiovese 1997, *La Agricola*	£4.50	B
Château Valoussiere 1996, *Jeanjean*	£4.50	B
Château de Pennautier 1995, *Lorgeril*	£4.50	B
Agapito Jumilla Reserva 1994, *Agapito Rico*	£4.50	B
Tierra del Fuego Cabernet Sauvignon 1996, *Tierra del Fuego*	£4.50	B
Long Mountain Cabernet Sauvignon 1996, *Long Mountain Wines*	£4.60	B
Tempranillo Fuente del Ritmo Reserva 1994, *Bodegas Centro Espanoles*	£4.60	B
Bodegas Palacio Reserva Especial 1994, *Palacio*	£4.70	B
Château Beauvoisin 1997, *Vignerons de Cerresou*	£4.70	B
Malt House Vintners Mâcon Rouge Superieur Henri la Fontaine 1997, *Faye & Cie*	£4.80	B
Monte Velho 1997, *Herdade Do Esporao*	£4.80	B
Merlot de Jacques et François Lurton 1996, *Lurton*	£4.80	B
Cave de Valvigneres Oaked Cabernet Sauvignon 1997, *Cave de Valvigneres*	£4.80	B
Santa Julia Malbec Oak Reserve 1996, *La Agricola*	£4.80	B
Allora Primitivo 1997, *Casalbaio*	£4.90	B
Château de Campuget 1997, *Château de Campuget*	£4.90	B

Quinta das Setencostas 1996, *Quinta Da Boavista*	£4.90	B
Côtes du Rhône Carte Noir 1995, *Cellier des Dauphins*	£4.90	B
Canepa Cabernet Sauvignon 1997, *José Canepa*	£4.90	B
Mas de la Garrigue Roussillon 1996, *J P Henriques*	£4.90	B
Santa Julia Malbec 1997, *La Agricola*	£4.90	B
Tuella Douro Tinto 1996, *Cockburn Smithies*	£4.90	B
Las Lomas Merlot 1997, *Cauquenes Barria*	£5.00	B
Château Roumaniéres 1996, *Roumaniéres*	£5.00	B
Marks & Spencer La Tour du Prêvôt 1996, *Perrin*	£5.00	B
Co-op Prestige Medoc 1995, *Producta*	£5.00	B
Safeway's Australian Oaked Cabernet Sauvignon 1997, *BRL Hardy Wine Company*	£5.00	B
Château du Grison 1995, *Grison*	£5.00	B
Tramontane Reserve Oaked Cabernet Sauvignon 1996, *Maurel Vedeau*	£5.00	B
Asda Arius Californian Syrah 1997, *California Direct*	£5.00	B
Mount Disa Cape Salut 1997, *Coppoolse & Finlayson*	£5.00	B
Touraine Cabernet Franc 1995, *Domaine de la Bergerie*	£5.00	B
Barbera D'Asti Bricco Zanone 1996, *Terre da Vino*	£5.00	B
Villa Pigna Rozzano 1996, *Villa Pigna*	£5.00	B
Domaine du Jas D'Esclans Cru Classé Organic 1994, *Domaine du Jas D'Esclans*	£5.00	B
Villa Teseo 1995, *Castellani*	£5.00	B
Konyari Cabernet Sauvignon Reserve 1996, *St. Donatus Estate*	£5.00	B
Marques de Griñon Tempranillo Rioja 1996, *Marques de Griñon*	£5.00	B
Tesco Vintage Claret 1996, *Yvon Mau*	£5.00	B
Château De Paraza 1996, *Passerieux*	£5.00	B
Domaine de la Présidente Côtes du Rhône 1997, *Max Aubert*	£5.00	B
Ronchi di Villa Cabernet Sauvignon Refosco 1997, *Ronchi di Villa*	£5.00	B
Vina Carta Vieja Merlot Antigua Reserve 1996, *Vina Carta Vieja*	£5.00	B
Vina Carta Vieja Cabernet Sauvignon Antigua Reserve 1996, *Vina Carta Vieja*	£5.00	B
Camparron Tinto 1997, *Francisco Casas*	£5.00	B
Domaine De La Soleiade 1997, *SCA a Vacqueyras*	£5.00	B
Bourgogne Rouge Oak Aged 1996, *Chevallier*	£5.00	B
Vacqueyras Domaine de la Soleiade 1997, *J P Selles*	£5.00	B
Monsaraz Tinto 1997, *Reguengos de Monsaraz*	£5.00	B
Hécula Monastrell Cabernet Sauvignon Merlot 1996, *Castaño*	£5.00	B
Bright Brothers Shiraz Reserve 1997, *Bright Brothers*	£5.00	B
Château Val Joanis 1995, *Jean-Louis Chancel*	£5.00	B

WHITES • £5 AND UNDER

Rivers Meet Sauvignon Blanc Sémillion 1997, *Ginestet*	£3.90	G
Les Marionettes Marsanne 1997, *Terroir Club*	£4.00	G
Penfolds Rawsons Retreat Bin 202 Riesling 1997, *Southcorp Wines*	£4.30	G
Safeway's Woodcutter's White 1997, *Neszmely*	£3.00	S
BVC Rousse Sauvignon Blanc 1997, *Rousse*	£3.30	S
BVC Hidden Valley Chardonnay 1997, *Rousse*	£3.50	S
Vino de Chile White 1997, *Xpovin Ltda*	£3.50	S
Asda Chilean Sauvignon Blanc 1997, *San Pedro*	£3.80	S
Antu Mapu Sauvignon Blanc Reserva 1997, *Cauquenes Barria*	£4.00	S
De Bortoli Willowglen Semillon Chardonnay 1997, *De Bortoli Wines*	£4.50	S
De Bortoli Sacred Hill Oaked Semillon Chardonnay 1997, *De Bortoli Wines*	£4.80	S
Santa Carolina Chardonnay Semillon 1997, *Santa Carolina*	£4.80	S
Marques de Griñon Durius Blanco 1996, *Arco Bodegas Unidas*	£4.80	S
San Simone Sauvignon Blanc 1997, *San Simone*	£4.80	S
Tremaille White 1996, *Rouvinez*	£4.80	S
Corbans Estate Sauvignon Blanc 1997, *Corbans Wines*	£4.90	S
Verdicchio Classico 1997, *Gioacchino Garofoli*	£4.90	S
Santa Carolina Chardonnay Semillon 1997, *Santa Carolina*	£4.90	S
Kohi Point Sauvignon Semillon 1997, *Montana Wines*	£5.00	S
Cortese Alto Monferrato 1997, *Araldica*	£5.00	S
Soleca Semillon 1997, *Vina Bisquertt*	£5.00	S
Lone Gum Chardonnay 1997, *Normans Wines*	£5.00	S
Zenit Oaked 1997, *Nagyrede Winery*	£3.00	B
Tesco Niersteiner Kabinett 1997, *ZGM Zell-Mosel*	£3.20	B
Chilean Dry White Wine 1997, *Nevada Exports*	£3.30	B
Ackermann Chenin Blanc 1997, *Ackermann*	£3.50	B
Kendermann Northern Star Medium 1997, *Kendermann*	£3.50	B
Somerfield Australian Dry White NV, *Southcorp Wines*	£3.50	B
Chardonnay Garganega 1997, *Cantina di Soave*	£3.60	B
Hungaroo Pinot Gris 1996, *Interconsult*	£3.70	B
Misty Mountain Chardonnay 1996, *Syaraz Minosegi Feherbor*	£3.70	B
Porta Da Ravessa 1997, *Redondo*	£3.70	B
Safeway's Australian Oaked Colombard 1997, *BRL Hardy Wine Company*	£4.00	B
Corbans Waimanu Dry White 1997, *Corbans Wines*	£4.00	B
Merchants Bay Sauvignon Blanc Sémillon 1997, *Ginestet*	£4.00	B

Somerfield Chardonnay delle Venezie 1997, *Gruppo Italiano Vini*	£4.00	B
Co-op Own Label Spätlese 1996, *Peter Mertes*	£4.00	B
Ponte Vecchio Oaked Soave 1997, *Cantina di Soave*	£4.00	B
St Pauls Bay White 1997, *Delicata*	£4.00	B
Picajuan Peak Chardonnay NV, *La Agricola*	£4.00	B
Maurel Vedeau Grenache Viognier 1997, *Maurel Vedeau*	£4.00	B
Santara Chardonnay 1997, *Ryman & Concavins*	£4.00	B
Zeltinger Himmelreich Riesling Kabinett 1997, *Moselland Eg*	£4.00	B
Bright Bros Atlantic Vines White 1997, *J P Vinhos*	£4.00	B
Somerfield Rheinhessen Spätlese 1994, *Rheinberg Kellerei*	£4.00	B
The Bulgarian Vintners Reserve Chardonnay 1996, *Karamochev*	£4.00	B
Chapel Down Summerhill Oaked White NV, *Chapel Down Wines*	£4.30	B
Malt House Vintners Verdicchio dei Castelli di Jesi 1997, *Schenk SpA*	£4.30	B
Le Trulle Chardonnay 1997, *Cantele Le Trulle*	£4.30	B
Somerfield Frascati 1997, *Gruppo Italiano Vini*	£4.30	B
Clos des Orfeuilles 1997, *Marcel Sautejeau*	£4.30	B
Touraine Chapelle de Cray 1996, *Chapelle de Cray*	£4.30	B
McWilliam's Hawkes Run Semillon Chardonnay NV, *McWilliam's Wines*	£4.30	B
Basa Blanco 1997, *Compania de Vinos de la Granja*	£4.50	B
Les Freres Scaramouche Chardonnay 1997, *Les Vignobles La Reze*	£4.50	B
Casa Leona Chardonnay 1997, *Vina Peumo*	£4.50	B
Les Marionettes Chardonnay Rousanne 1997, *Terroir Club*	£4.50	B
Domaine de Valensac Chardonnay 1997, *Valensac*	£4.50	B
Andes Peak Chardonnay 1997, *Santa Emiliana*	£4.50	B
Tierra del Fuego Chardonnay 1997, *Tierra del Fuego*	£4.50	B
Pionero Chardonnay 1997, *Morande*	£4.60	B
Malt House Vintners New Zealand White NV, *Sacred Hill*	£4.70	B
Miranda Pioneers Raisined Muscat 1996, *Miranda Wines*	£4.70	B
Torres Vina Sol 1997, *Torres*	£4.70	B
Cono Sur Gewurztraminer 1997, *Vina Cono Sur*	£4.70	B
Con Class Blanco 1997, *Con Class*	£4.70	B
Canepa Chardonnay 1997, *José Canepa*	£4.70	B
Domaine du Tariquet Sauvignon Blanc 1997, *Grassa*	£4.70	B
La Sorte Soave Classico 1997, *Cantina Sociale Valpolicella Negrar*	£4.70	B
Cuckoo Hill Viognier 1996, *Nick Butler*	£4.70	B
Malt House Vintners Blaumeister Aüslese 1996, *ReichsgrafinVon Medem*	£4.80	B
Wyndham Estate Bin777 Hunter Valley Semillon Chardonnay 1997, *Orlando* Wines	£4.80	B
Sutter Home Chardonnay 1997, *Sutter Home Winery*	£4.80	B

Sauvignon Blanc Grave Del Friuli 1997, *Bidoli Vini*	£4.80	B
Laperouse Assemblage Blanc 1996, *Penfolds & Val d'Orbieu*	£4.80	B
Somerfield Coteaux de l'Ardeche Chardonnay, *Vignerons Ardechois*	£4.80	B
Soleca Semillon Chardonnay 1997, *Vina Bisquertt*	£4.90	B
Le Vele Verdicchio Classico 1997, *Terre Cortesi Moncaro*	£4.90	B
Hugh Ryman Roussanne 1996, *Hugh Ryman*	£4.90	B
Ernest & Julio Gallo Estate Bottled Chardonnay 1995, *Ernest & Julio Gallo Winery*	£5.00	B
Stonybrook Vineyards Chardonnay 1997, *Stonybrook Vineyards*	£5.00	B
Soave Vigneti di Sella Classico Superiore 1997, *Cav P Sartori*	£5.00	B
Primavera Spring NV, *Vinicola Cantele Lecce & Kym Milne*	£5.00	B
Wynns Coonawarra Estate Riesling 1997, *Southcorp Wines*	£5.00	B
Nottage Hill Riesling 1997, *BRL Hardy Wine Company*	£5.00	B
Laurus Côtes du Rhône Blanc 1997, *Meffre*	£5.00	B
Quinto de Azevedo 1997, *Sogrape*	£5.00	B
Château de la Tuilerie 'Carte Blanche' Blanc 1997, *Tuilerie*	£5.00	B
Cortechiara Soave Classico 1997, *Zenato*	£5.00	B
Yvon Mau Graves Blanc 1997, *Mau*	£5.00	B
Château Val Joanis 1997, *Jean-Louis Chancel*	£5.00	B

SPARKLING • £12 AND UNDER

Hunter's Miru Miru Marlborough Brut 1995, *Hunters Wine*	£9.70	G
Pierre Sparr Crémant d'Alsace Tokay Pinot Gris Mambourg Brut 1993, *Pierre Sparr*	£10.50	S
Pierre Sparr Crémant d'Alsace Mambourg Cuvée Dynastie Brut 1993 *Pierre Sparr*	£10.50	S
Green Point Brut Vintage 1994, *Domaine Chandon*	£11.80	S
Borelli Asti Spumante NV, *Martini*	£5.20	B
Douglas Green South African Sparkling NV, *Madeba Winery*	£7.00	B
Crémant de Bourgogne Brut Blanc de Blancs Paul Delane NV, *Caves De Bailly*	£7.30	B
Seaview Pinot Noir Chardonnay Brut 1995, *Southcorp Wines*	£8.50	B
Seaview Blanc de Blancs Brut 1995, *Southcorp Wines*	£9.00	B
Yalumba Cuvée Two Prestige Cabernet Sauvignon NV, *Yalumba Winery*	£9.40	B
Crémant D' Alsace Cuvée Prestige NV, *Mure*	£9.50	B
Raventos I Blanc Cava Gran Reserva 1993, *Raventos I Blanc*	£10.00	B
Raimat Cava Gran Brut NV, *Raimat Estate*	£10.00	B
Nautilus Estate Marlborough Cuvée Brut NV, *Negociants New Zealand*	£10.90	B
Deutz Marlborough Cuvée Brut N.V., *Montana Wines*	£11.00	B
Green Point Brut Vintage 1995, *Domaine Chandon*	£11.90	B
Deutz Blanc De Blancs Brut Vintage 1994, *Montana Wines*	£12.00	B
Jansz Sparkling Brut Vintage 1993, *Heemskerk Wine Company*	£12.00	B

CHAMPAGNE • £16 AND UNDER

Champagne Le Brun De Neuville Cuvée Blanc De Blancs Brut NV, *Le Brun De Neuville*	£12.80	S
Safeway Champagne Albert Etienne Brut 1990, *Lanson Pere et Fils*	£13.00	S
Champagne Le Brun De Neuville Rosé Brut NV, *Le Brun De Neuville*	£14.00	S
Champagne Drappier Demi-Sec NV, *Drappier*	£14.80	S
Champagne Devaux Grande Réserve Brut NV, *Devaux*	£15.20	S
Champagne Renaudin Brut Grande Réserve NV, *R. Renaudin*	£15.50	S
Champagne Drappier Carte d' Or Brut NV, *Drappier*	£15.50	S
Charles de Cazanove Brut Classique NV, *Charles de Cazanove*	£16.00	S
Malt House Vintners House Champagne Brut NV, *Bonnet*	£11.00	B
Champagne Le Brun De Neuville Cuvée Selection Brut NV, *Le Brun De Neuville*	£12.00	B
Champagne De Telmont Brut Grande Réserve NV, *De Telmont*	£12.50	B
Champagne Albert Etienne Brut NV, *Lanson Pere et Fils*	£13.00	B
Waitrose Champagne Brut NV, *Bonnet*	£13.00	B
Champagne Paul Langier Brut Rosé NV, *Bonnet*	£13.50	B
Champagne A R Lenoble Brut Grand Cru Blanc de Blancs NV, *A R Lenoble*	£14.00	B
Champagne De Castellane Brut NV, *De Castellane*	£15.00	B
Champagne Veuve Galien Brut NV, *Goulet*	£16.00	B

STOCKISTS

Every wine in the guide has one or more stockist codes beside its entry, identifying where the wine can be bought. The list below translates the code into the company name, with a telephone number for you to make enquiries.

Where the stockists are stated as Widely Available there are more than 10 outlets who stock this wine. In these cases you should be able to find the wine in most good wine retailers. Every effort has been made to list all the stockists with their relevant wines. Should you encounter any problems with finding a wine listed in this guide, then please write to:

The International WINE Challenge, Quest Magazines, Wilmington Publishing, 6-8 Underwood Street, London N1 7JQ

3DW	3D Wines	01205 820745	ASD	Asda Stores Ltd	0113 241 9169
A&A	A&A Wines	01483 274666	AUC	The Australian Wine Club	
A&N	Army & Navy	0171 834 1234			01753 544546
ABA	Adam Bancroft Assocs	0171 793 1902	AUS	Australian Wineries (UK) Ltd	
ABY	Anthony Byrne Wine Agencies				01780 55810
		01487 814555	AVB	Averys of Bristol	01275 811100
ACH	Andrew Chapman	01235 550707	AWB	Australian Wine Bureau	0171 887 5259
ADN	Adnams Wine Merchants		AWS	Albion Wine Shippers	0171 404 4554
		01502 727222	B&B	Bottle & Basket	0181 341 7018
ADW	Andrew Darwin	01544 230534	BAB	Bablake Wines	01203 228272
AFI	Alfie Fiandaca Ltd	0181 752 1222	BAK	Barkham Manor Vineyard	
AKT	Arriba Kettle	01386 833024			01825 722103
ALE	Alexander Wines	0141 882 0039	BAL	Ballantynes of Cowbridge	
ALI	Alivini Company Ltd	0181 880 2525			01446 774840
ALL	Alliance Wine Company Ltd		BBB	Barnsbury Bottle & Basket	
		01505 506060			0171 713 0427
ALZ	Allez Vins!	0385 264445	BBO	Barrels & Bottles	0114 276 9666
AMA	Amathus Wines Ltd	0181 886 3787	BBR	Berry Bros & Rudd	0171 396 9600
AMU	Antu Mapu U.K.	01531 670743	BBU	Bruce Burlington	01268 562224
AMW	Amey's Wines	01787 377144	BCL	Best Cellars	01364 652546
ARM	Arthur Rackham	01483 458700	BCW	Brian Coad Fine Wines	01752 896545

BDR	Bordeaux Direct	0118 903 0903
BDT	Benedict's	01983 529596
BEL	Bentalls	0181 546 1001
BEN	Bennetts	01386 840392
BFV	Baron Freidrich von Wrede Ltd	01823 451228
BFW	Bellefrance Wines Ltd	0171 706 3462
BHW	B H Wines	01228 576711
BIN	Bin 89 Wine Warehouse	0114 275 5889
BKC	Berkeley Wines (Cheshire)	01925 444555
BKT	Bucktrout	01481 724444
BLN	Belloni & Company	0171 704 8812
BLS	Balls Bros	0171 739 6466
BNK	Bottleneck (Broadstairs)	01843 861095
BOD	Bodegas Direct	01243 773474
BOO	Booths of Stockport	0161 432 3309
BOR	De Bortoli Wines UK Ltd	01725 518646
BPW	Boutinot Prince	0161 477 1171
BRF	Brown-Foreman Wines International	0171 323 9332
BRI	Bordeaux Index Ltd	0171 250 1982
BSS	Besos (UK) Ltd	01243 781617
BTH	Booths Supermarkets	01772 251701
BUD	International Brands	01892 723096
BUP	Bottoms Up	01707 328244
BUT	The Butlers Wine Cellar	01273 698724
BVC	Bulgarian Vintners	0171 278 8047
BWC	Berkmann Wine Cellars	0171 609 4711
BWL	Bibendum Wine Ltd	0171 722 5577
C&B	Corney & Barrow	0171 251 4051
C&D	C & D Wines Ltd	0181 650 9095
C&H	Cairns & Hickey	0113 267 3746
CAP	Cape Province Wines	01784 451860
CCL	Chiswick Cellars	0181 994 7989
CDE	Cote d'Or	0181 998 0144
CDL	California Direct	0171 207 1944
CDO	Chapel Down Wines	01580 763033
CDT	Cellars Direct	0191 495 5000
CEL	Cellar 5	01925 444555
CEN	Centurion Vintners	01453 763223
CER	Cellar 28	01484 717914
CES	Cellar Select Ltd/Winefinds	01722 716100
CFT	The Clifton Cellars	0117 973 0287
CGP	The Cellar Group Ltd	0181 785 7419
CHF	Chippendale Fine Wines	01943 850633
CHH	Charles Hennings	01798 872485
CLA	Classic Wines and Spirits Ltd	01244 288444
CML	Chateau Musar (UK)	0181 941 8311
CNL	Connolly's	0121 236 9269
COC	Corks of Cotham	0117 9731620
COE	Coe of Ilford	0181 551 4966
COK	Corkscrew Wines	01228 543033
CON	Codorniu	0181 410 4480
COT	Cotswold Wine Company	01242 678880
CPW	Christopher Piper Wines Ltd	01404 814139
CRS	The Cooperative Society	01706 713000
CST	The County Stores (Somerset) Ltd	01823 272235
CTH	Charterhouse Wine Co	01775 630680
CTL	Continental Wine & Food	01484 538333
CTV	Carr Taylor Vineyards	01424 752501
CVR	Celtic Vintner	01633 430055
CVW	Chiltern Valley Wines	01491 638330
CWA	Cheviot Wine Agencies	01327 860 548
CWI	A Case of Wine	01558 650671
CWL	Charles Wells	01234 272766
CWS	CWS Ltd	0800 3178270
D&D	D&D Wines Ltd	01565 650952
D&F	D & F Wine Shippers Ltd	0181 838 4399

DAV	Dartmouth Vintners	01803 832602
DBO	Domaine Boyar Ltd	0171 537 3707
DBW	David Baker Wines	01656 650732
DBY	D Byrne & Co	01200 423152
DDT	Domaine Direct	0171 837 1142
DEL	Delegat's Wine Estate (UK) Ltd	0181 246 6104
DEN	Dennhofer Wines	0191 232 3242
DIR	Direct Wine Shipments	01232 238700
DLA	Daniel Lambert Wine Agenices	01222 666128
DNL	Dunnels Ltd	01534 36418
DVD	Davisons Direct	0181 681 3222
DVP	Davenport Vineyards	01892 852380
DVY	Davy & Co Ltd	0171 407 9670
E&B	E&B Wines	01732 355988
E&J	Ernest & Julio Gallo Winery	01895 813 444
EBA	Ben Ellis Wines	01737 842160
EBC	The Exclusive Brandy Club	0169 773744
ECA	Edward Cavendish & Sons Ltd	01794 516102
EDC	Edencroft	01270 625302
EHL	Ehrmanns Ltd	0171 359 7466
ELL	Ellingham Wines Ltd	0181 892 9599
ENO	Enotria Winecellars	0181 961 4411
EOO	Everton's of Ombersley	01905 620282
EOR	Ellis of Richmond	0181 943 4033
EPO	Eldridge Pope	01305 258347
ESL	Edward Sheldon	01608 661409
ETV	Eton Vintners	01753 790188
EUR	Europa Foods Ltd	0181 845 1255
EVI	Evingtons	0116 254 2702
EWC	English Wine Centre	01323 870164
EWD	Euro World Wines	0141 649 3735
F&M	Fortnum & Mason	0171 734 8040
FAB	Fabat UK Ltd	0171 636 7640
FBG	Food Brands Group Ltd	0171 978 5300
FCA	Fraser Williamson Fine Wines	01580 200 304
FEN	Fenwick Ltd	0191 232 5100
FLC	First London Corporation	0171 436 3234
FLM	Ferrers le Mesurier	01832 732660
FNZ	Fine Wines of New Zealand	0171 482 0093
FRI	Friarwood	0171 736 2628
FRN	Frenmart	01384 892941
FRT	Matthew Clark Wholesale Ltd	01275 891400
FSA	Francis Stickney Agencies	0181 201 9090
FSW	Frank Stainton Wines	01539 731886
FTH	Forth Wines Ltd	01577 863668
FUL	Fuller Smith & Turner	0181 996 2000
FVM	FVM International Ltd	01453 860881
FWL	Fraser Williamson Fine Wines	01580 200 304
FWM	Fields Wine Merchants	0171 589 575
FWW	FWW Wines (UK) Ltd	0181 786 816
G&M	Gordon & Macphail	01343 545111
GAG	Grape & Grain	0181 426 156
GAR	Garland Wine Cellar	01372 275247
GCL	Graingers Ltd.	0114 221 088
GDS	Garrards Wine Merchants	01900 823592
GEL	Gelston Castle	01556 503012
GEN	Gentilini	0171 580 649
GFO	Gardners Folly	01453 731 50
GGW	The Great Gaddesden Wine Company	01582 840001
GHL	George Hill of Loughborough	01509 21277
GIS	Grape Ideas	01865 263303
GLO	Global Wines	0121 429 166
GLY	Gallery Wines	01504 48762
GMV	G M Vintners	01392 218166
GNW	Great Northern Wine Co	0113 246 120

GON	Gauntleys of Nottingham	0115 911 0555
GRA	Geoffrey Roberts Agencies	01275 890740
GRO	Grog Blossom	0171 794 7808
GRT	Great Western Wine Company Ltd	01225 446009
GSH	Grape Shop (London)	0171 924 3638
GWC	Greek Wine Centre Ltd	01743 364636
GYW	Guy Anderson Wines	01460 241043
H&H	Hector & Honorez	01480 411599
H&W	Hall & Woodhouse Ltd	01258 452141
HAC	Hailsham Cellars	01323 441212
HAE	Halewood International Ltd	0151 480 8800
HAG	The Hanwood Group Ltd	01455 556161
HAL	Hall & Batson	01603 415115
HAM	Hampden Wine Co	01844 201641
HAR	Harrods	0171 730 1234
HAS	Haughton Agencies	01502 727 288
HBJ	Heyman, Barwell Jones Ltd	01473 232322
HBR	BRL Hardy Wine Company Ltd	01372 738200
HBY	Hall & Bramley	0151 525 8283
HCK	Pierre Henck Wines	01902 751022
HDL	Alexander Hadleigh	01489 885959
HHC	Haynes Hanson & Clark	0171 259 0102
HHF	H&H Fine Wines	01480 411599
HOH	Hallgarten Wines Ltd	01582 722538
HOL	Holland Park Wine Co	0171 221 9614
HOT	House of Townend	01482 326891
HOU	Hoults Wine Merchants	01484 510700
HRF	Howard Ripley Fine French Wines	0181 360 8904
HRV	Harrison Vintners	0171 236 7716
HSV	Hidden Spring Vineyard	01435 812640
HVB	Harveys of Bristol	0117 927 5000
HVN	Harvey Nichols	0171 235 5000
HVW	Helen Verdcourt Wines	01628 25577
HWB	Howells of Bristol	01454 294085
HWL	Hedley Wright & Co Ltd	01279 506512
HZW	Hazeley Wines Ltd	01244 332 008
ICL	Italian Continental Food & Wine	07628 770110
IRV	Irvine Robertson	0131 553 3521
IVY	Ivy Wines	01243 377883
IWS	International Wine Services	01494 680857
J&B	Justerini & Brooks	0171 493 8721
JAR	John Armit Wines	0171 727 6846
JAV	John Arkell Vintners	0119 382 3026
JBF	Julian Baker Fine Wines	01206 262 358
JBR	J B Reynier	0171 481 0415
JBV	Julian Bidwell Vintner	0181 874 9388
JCB	J C Broadbent	01534 23356
JEF	John E Fells	01442 870900
JEH	J E Hogg	0131 556 4025
JFR	John Frazier	0121 704 3415
JHL	J H Logan	0131 667 2855
JLW	John Lay Wines	01206 713525
JNW	James Nicholson Wine Merchant	01396 830091
JOB	Jeroboams	0171 235 1612
JSM	Sainsbury Supermarkets Ltd	0171 695 6000
JSS	John Stephenson & Sons	01282 698827
KME	Kendal Milne	0161 832 3414
KWI	Kwik Save Stores Ltd	01745 887111
L&S	Laymont & Shaw Ltd	01872 270545
L&W	Lay & Wheeler Ltd	01206 764446
LAU	Lauriston Wines Ltd	01372 459270
LAW	Chalié, Richards & Co Ltd	01403 250500
LAY	Laytons Wine Merchants Ltd	0171 388 4567
LCC	Landmark Cash & Carry	0181 863 5511
LCD	Les Caves Du Cochonne	01326 340332

STOCKISTS

LEA	Lea & Sandeman	0171 376 4767		N&P	Nickolls & Perks	01384 394518
LIB	Liberty Wines	0171 720 5350		NAD	Nadder Wine Co	01722 325418
LLV	Lakeland Vintners	01539 821999		NEG	Negociants International UK Ltd	
LLY	Luciana C Lynch	01428 606619				01582 462859
LNR	Le Nez Rouge	0171 609 4711		NEI	R & I Neish Ltd	01779 472721
LOH	Larners of Holt	01263 712323		NIC	Nicolas UK Ltd	0171 436 9338
LPD	Laurent-Perrier Distribution			NOW	Nick Oakley Wines	01787 223196
		01628 475404		NRW	Noble Rot Wine Warehouses Ltd	
LUC	Luckins Wines	01371 872839				01527 575606
LVF	Les Producteurs & Vignerons de			NYE	Nyetimber Vineyard	01798 813989
	France Ltd	01273 730277		NYW	Noel Young Wines	01223 566 744
LVN	La Vigneronne	0171 589 6113		OAT	Oatley Vineyard	01278 671 340
M&S	Marks & Spencer plc	0171 268 3825		ODD	Oddbins	0181 944 4400
M&V	Morris & Verdin	0171 357 8866		ODF	Oddbins Fine Wine	0181 944 4400
MAK	Makro Self Service	0161 707 1585		ORB	Orbital Wines Ltd	01455 556161
MAR	Marco's Wines	0181 875 1900		P&R	Peckham & Rye	0141 334 4312
MCD	Marne & Champagne Ltd	01344 483200		PAG	Pagendam	01937 844711
MCO	Malcolm Cowen	0181 965 1937		PAL	Pallant Wines	01903 882288
MFS	Martinez Fine Wine	01422 320022		PAR	Partridges	0171 730 0651
MGN	Michael Morgan Wines	0171 407 3466		PAT	Patriarche Père et Fils Ltd	
MHV	Booker Belmont Wholesale Ltd					0171 381 4016
		01933 371363		PAV	The Pavilion Wine Company Ltd	
MIS	Mistral Wines	0171 262 5437				0171 628 8224
MKV	McKinley Vintners	0171 928 7300		PCC	Price Cost Co.	01708 860981
MMD	Maisons Marques et Domaines			PEA	Peake Wine Assocs	0171 733 5657
		0181 871 3955		PEC	Pechiney UK Ltd	01753 522800
MMW	Michael Menzel Wines	0114 268 3557		PFC	Percy Fox & Co	01279 626801
MON	Mondial Wine Ltd	0181 335 3455		PFT	Parfrements	01203 503646
MOR	Moreno Wine Importers	0171 723 6897		PHI	Philglas & Swiggot	0171 924 4494
MRN	Morrison Supermarkets	01924 875234		PIM	Pimlico Dozen Ltd	0171 834 3647
MTB	Martyn T Barker UK	01279 414808		PLA	Playford Ros Ltd	01845 526777
MTL	Mitchells Wine Merchants			PLB	Private Liquor Brands	01342 318282
		0114 274 0311		PLE	Peter Lehmann Wines (UK) Ltd	
MTR	Montrachet	0171 928 1990				01227 731353
MTW	Montana Wines Ltd	0181 250 1325		PMN	Phillip Morgan	01222 231570
MVG	Mille Vignes	0171 633 0278		PON	Peter Osborne	01491 612311
MWW	Majestic Wine Warehouses Ltd			POR	Portland Wine Company (Manchester)	
		01923 298200				0161 962 8752
MYL	Myliko International (Wines) Ltd			POU	Growers & Chateaux	01737 214957
		01204 392222		PRG	Paragon Vintners Ltd	0171 887 1800

PSC	Penistone Court Wine Cellars	01226 766037
PTR	Peter Green	0131 229 5925
PWI	Portland Wine Cellar (Southport)	01704 534299
QRW	Quellyn Roberts Wine Merchants	01244 310455
QWW	Quay West Wines	01392 410866
RAE	Raeburn Fine Wine & Foods	0131 343 1159
RAM	Ramsbottom Victualler	01706 825070
RAV	Ravensbourne Wine	0181 692 9655
RBS	Roberson Wine Merchants	0171 371 2121
RDS	Reid Wines	01761 452645
REM	Remy & Associates (UK) Ltd	01753 752600
REN	Renvic Wines Ltd	01763 852470
RES	La Reserve	0171 589 2020
REY	Raymond Reynolds Ltd	01663 742 230
RIC	Richard Granger	0191 281 5000
ROB	T M Robertson	0131 229 4522
ROD	Rodney Densem Wines	01270 623665
ROS	Rosemount Estate Wines	01483 211 466
ROZ	Rozès UK	0181 742 2391
RS2	Richardson & Sons	01946 65334
RSN	Richard Speirs Wines	01483 37605
RSS	Raisin Social Ltd	0181 673 3040
RSW	R S Wines	0117 963 1780
RUK	Ruinart Champagne UK Ltd	0171 416 0592
RVA	Randalls (Jersey)	01534 887788
RWD	Richards Walford	01780 460 451
RYW	Hugh Ryman	01629 640133
SAF	Safeway Stores plc	0181 848 8744
SAN	Sandiway Wine Co	01606 882101
SCA	Scatchard	0151 236 6468
SCK	Seckford Wines	01473 626681
SEA	Seagram UK Ltd	0181 250 1018
SEL	Selfridges Ltd	0171 318 3730
SGL	Stevens Garnier Ltd	01865 263300
SHB	Shaws of Beaumaris	01248 810328
SHJ	S H Jones & Company	01295 251179
SHR	Sharpham Vineyard	01803 732203
SIJ	Simpkin & James Ltd	0116 262 3132
SKW	Stokes Fine Wines Ltd	0181 944 5979
SLM	Salamis & Co Ltd	0171 609 1133
SMF	Somerfield Stores Ltd	0117 935 9359
SOH	Soho Wine Supply	0171 436 9736
SOM	Sommelier Wine Co	01481 721677
SPR	Spar Landmark	0181 863 5511
SSV	St. Sampson Vineyard	01726 833707
STB	Stokes Brothers (UK) Ltd	01303 252178
STE	Stephane Auriol Wines	01252 843190
STG	Tony Stebbings	01372 468571
STH	Styria Wine Hamer	0181 296 0770
STT	Santat Wines	01483 450494
SVT	Smedley Vintners	01462 768214
SWB	Satchells	01328 738272
SWI	Sherston Wine Co (St Albans)	01727 858841
SWN	S Wines	0171 351 1990
SWS	Stratfords Wine Shippers & Merchants Ltd	01628 810606
T&T	Thierry's Wine Services	01794 507100
T&W	T&W Wines	01842 765646
TAN	Tanners Wines Ltd	01743 232400
TBV	The Bulgarian Vintners Co Ltd	0171 278 8047
TBW	T B Watson (Dumfries)	01387 720505
TCV	Three Choirs Vineyards Ltd	01531 890555
THC	Haselmere Cellar	01428 645081
THR	Throwley Vineyard	01795 890276
THS	Thresher	01707 328244
TOS	Tesco Stores Ltd	01992 632222
TPA	Thomas Panton	01666 503088
TPE	Terry Platt Wines	01492 592971

TPW	Topsham Wines	01392 874501
TRO	Trout Wines	01264 781472
TWB	The Wine Bank	01892 514343
UNC	Uncorked	0171 638 5998
UNS	Unwins Ltd	01322 272711
UWM	United Wine Merchants	01232 231231
V&C	Valvona & Crolla	0131 556 6066
VAU	Vaux Breweries	0191 567 6277
VDO	Val D'Orbieu Wines Ltd	0171 736 3350
VDV	Vin du Van Wine Merchants	
		01233 758727
VER	Vinceremos Wines	0113 257 7545
VEX	Vinexports Ltd	01584 811333
VIC	Vica Wines Ltd	01273 477132
VIL	Village Wines	01322 558772
VIW	Vintage Wines	0115 947 6565
VLW	Villeneuve Wines	01721 722500
VNO	Vinoceros Imports Ltd	01209 314711
VWC	Victoria Wine Cellars	01483 715066
VWE	Victoria Wine	01483 715066
WAC	Waters of Coventry Ltd	01926 888889
WAV	Waverley Vintners Ltd	01738 629621
WAW	Waterloo Wine Co	0171 403 7967
WBU	Wine Bureau	01403 256446
WCR	Greenalls Wine Cellars Ltd	
		01925 444555
WCS	The Wine Cellar (Sanderstead)	
		0181 657 6936
WEP	Welshpool Wine Company	
		01938 553243
WES	Wessex Wines	01308 427177
WFB	Mildara Blass (UK) Ltd	0181 947 4312
WFD	Wine Finds	01584 875582
WFL	Winefare Ltd	01483 458700
WHS	Wine House	0181 669 6661

WIC	Jolly's Drinks	01237 473292
WIL	Willoughby's of Manchester	
		0161 834 6850
WIM	Wimbledon Wine Cellar	
		0181 540 9979
WIN	The Winery	0171 286 6475
WKM	Wickham Vineyard	01329 834042
WMK	Winemark	01232 746274
WNS	Winos	0161 652 9396
WOC	Whitesides of Clitheroe	
		01200 422 281
WOI	Wines of Interest Ltd	01473 215752
WON	Weavers of Nottingham	0115 958 0922
WOO	Wooldings Vineyard & Winery	
		01256 895200
WOW	Wines of Westhorpe	01283 820285
WRC	Wine Rack	01707 328244
WRI	Wrightson Wines	01325 374134
WRK	Wine Raks	01224 311460
WRO	Wroxeter Roman Vineyard	
		01743 761888
WRT	Winerite Ltd	0113 283 7654
WRW	The Wright Wine Co	01756 700886
WSA	Wineshare Ltd	01306 742164
WSG	Walter S Siegel Ltd	01256 701101
WSO	The Wine Society Ltd	01438 741177
WSP	Wine Schoppen Ltd	0114 255 3301
WST	Western Wines Ltd	01746 789411
WTD	Waitrose Direct	01344 824694
WTP	W T Palmer	01865 263303
WTS	Waitrose Ltd	01344 824694
WWI	Woodhouse Wines	01258 452141
WWT	Whitebridge Wines	01785 817229
YVM	Yvon Mau	01372 468571
YWL	Yates Brothers Ltd	01204 391777

INDEX

INDEX

INDEX

INDEX

INDEX

INDEX

INDEX

INDEX

INDEX

INDEX

INDEX

INDEX

INDEX

INDEX

ACKNOWLEDGMENTS

Compiling this book has at times felt like searching for a pot of gold at the end of the rainbow. In this case the rainbow was the International WINE Challenge – the world's largest wine tasting and it led to quite a lot of gold. Over 7,500 wines were tasted, generating over 55,000 hand-written tasting notes. For this formidable task of compilation we would like to thank:

- **the International WINE Challenge team** – for their dedication and good humour and for performing so well under pressure, especially the computer boffins and the hand–writing decipherers. We hope your full recovery and integration back into society is both speedy and painless. Thanks, also, to all the tasters who gave their time and expertise to help us, Screwpull for their help in opening the bottles and Carrs Water Biscuits for keeping the tasters' mouths fresh.
- **from WINE magazine** – Robert Joseph, Charles Metcalfe, Kirsty Bridge, Alan Scott and Georgina Severs.
- **for subbing and database management** – the editorial team of Tom Forrest, Dominic Kelly and Nathan Burley.
- **for design and layout** – Philip Davis

Finally, thanks go to **publishing editor** Chris Mitchell and **editor** James Gabbani for dealing with the temperamental database and taking us all to the pub!

HOW YOU CAN HELP US

If you have any ideas about how we can improve the format of the **WINE Magazine Pocket Wine Buyer's Guide** then please write to:
James Gabbani, WINE PWBG, Wilmington Publishing, 6-8 Underwood Street, London N1 7JQ

The type of subjects we would particularly like to hear about are:
- **Do you prefer to have countries sub-divided by region or grape variety?**
- **Do you find the £5 and Under guides useful?**
- **Would food and wine pairing suggestions be useful?**
- **How else might you like to see the wines sorted or divided?**
- **What other information regarding wines and stockists would be of interest?**
- **Would you prefer the Guide to be ring-bound or loose leafed?**